ANTON BRUCKNER–
A DOCUMENTARY BIOGRAPHY

ANTON BRUCKNER–
A DOCUMENTARY BIOGRAPHY
Volume 1

From Ansfelden to Vienna

Crawford Howie

Studies in the History and Interpretation of Music
Volume 83a

The Edwin Mellen Press
Lewiston•Queenston•Lampeter

Library of Congress Cataloging-in-Publication Data

Howie, Crawford, 1942-
    Anton Bruckner : a documentary biography: from Ansfelden to Vienna / Crawford Howie.
        p. cm. -- [Studies in the history and interpretation of music ; v. 83a]
    Includes bibliographical references (p.) and index.
    ISBN 0-7734-7300-9
    1. Bruckner, Anton, 1824-1896. 2. Composers--Austria--Biography. I. Title.

ML410.B88 H69 2002
780'.92--dc21
[B]
                                                                    2001042755

This is volume 83a in the continuing series
Studies in the History and Interpretation Music
Volume 83a ISBN 0-7734-7300-9
SHIM Series ISBN 0-88946-426-X

A CIP catalog record for this book is available from the British Library.

The Edwin Mellen Press
Box 450
Lewiston, New York
USA 14092-0450

The Edwin Mellen Press
Box 67
Queenston, Ontario
CANADA L0S 1L0

The Edwin Mellen Press, Ltd.
Lampeter, Ceredigion, Wales
UNITED KINGDOM SA48 8LT

Printed in the United States of America

To my parents who set me on the path of Bruckner discovery

Volume 1: Table of Contents

Volume 2: Table of Contents

List of Plates

1 'Ausarbeitungen von nakten Satzen' (May - end of June, 1838), 1st page.
Reproduced by kind permission of the *Wiener Stadt- und Landesbibliothek*
(*Handschriftensammlung* I.N. 36.793)

2 Letter from Bruckner to Julius Gartner, Vienna, 31 December 1874.
Reproduced by kind permission of the *Oberösterreichische Landesbibliothek*,
Linz (*Handschriftensammlung* 958)

3 Letter from Bruckner to Moritz von Mayfeld, Vienna, 13 February 1875.
Reproduced by kind permission of the *Österreichische Nationalbibliothek*,
Musiksammlung, Vienna (*Handschriftensammlung* Autogr. 126 / 58-24)

4 Letter from Bruckner to Theodor Helm, Vienna, 19 June 1885.
Reproduced by kind permission of the *Wiener Stadt- und Landesbibliothek*,
(*Handschriftensammlung* I.N. 34.355)

5 Letter from Bruckner to Hermann Levi, Vienna, 24 July 1892.
Reproduced by kind permission of the *Gesellschaft der Musikfreunde*,
Handschriftensammlung, Vienna

List of Abbreviations

ABB   Auer, Max, ed. *Anton Bruckner. Gesammelte Briefe. Neue Folge.* Regensburg, 1924

ABDS   Grasberger, Franz, Othmar Wessely et al., eds. *Anton Bruckner Dokumente und Studien.* Graz and Vienna, from 1979

ABSW   Nowak, Leopold et al., eds. *Anton Bruckner Sämtliche Werke. Kritische Gesamtausgabe.* Vienna, 1951-

BJ   Grasberger, Franz, Othmar Wessely et al., eds. *Bruckner Jahrbuch.* Linz and Vienna, from 1980

BSL   Grasberger, Franz, Othmar Wessely et al., eds. *Bruckner Symposion Linz Bericht.* Linz, from 1980

FSBB   Schalk, Lili. *Franz Schalk. Briefe und Betrachtungen.* Vienna/Leipzig, 1935

G-A   Göllerich, August and Max Auer. *Anton Bruckner. Ein Lebens- und Schaffensbild.* 4 volumes in 9. Regensburg, 1922-37

GrBB   Gräflinger, Franz, ed. *Anton Bruckner. Gesammelte Briefe.* Regensburg, 1924

GrBL   Gräflinger, Franz. *Anton Bruckner. Bausteine zu seiner Lebensgeschichte.* Munich, 1911

GrBLS   Gräflinger, Franz. *Anton Bruckner. Leben und Schaffen.* Berlin, 1927

iv

HMSAB	Hawkshaw, Paul. *The Manuscript Sources for Anton Bruckner's Linz Works.* Ann Arbor, 1984
HSABB	Harrandt, Andrea and Otto Schneider, eds. *Anton Bruckner Briefe 1852-1886.* Vienna, 1998
IBG	Internationale Bruckner-Gesellschaft
LBSAB	Leibnitz, Thomas. *Die Brüder Schalk und Anton Bruckner.* Tutzing, 1988
ÖNB	Österreichisches Nationalbibliothek, Vienna
SchABCR	Scheder, Franz. *Anton Bruckner Chronologie 1824-1896. Band II: Registerband.* Tutzing, 1996
SchABCT	*Band I: Textband.* Tutzing, 1996
WAB	Grasberger, Renate. *Werkverzeichnis Anton Bruckner.* Tutzing, 1977

Foreword

Although Vienna, Linz and St. Florian will always be the main centres of Bruckner research, the most striking feature of recent Bruckner scholarship has been the increasing recognition of the composer's importance outside central Europe and the efforts made by English-speaking scholars to subject him to the same close scrutiny that other composers have enjoyed in the past few years. The centenary of Bruckner's death in 1996 prompted several articles and publications in English, and the main purpose of this book is to help maintain the momentum of this scholarly interest and provide a biography of the composer which is based primarily on the available documents, in particular the letters and the critical reviews of his works during his lifetime. Bruckner's works will be mentioned in context but, as this is not a 'life and works' study, discussion of the music has been focussed on essential details of sources and editions; analytical comment has been kept to a minimum.

While several of the letters are of only marginal interest, many throw important light on aspects of his personality and the revision of his works. Letters of a more personal nature to his friend Rudolf Weinwurm during the late 1850s and 1860s provide us with a glimpse of Bruckner the man, often racked by loneliness and self-doubt. The twelve months between his breakdown in 1867 and his move to Vienna in 1868 are particularly well-documented and reveal Bruckner going through a crisis of self-confidence finally allayed by the repeated reassurances of Johann Herbeck, the court music director and the man largely responsible for encouraging Bruckner to take the 'leap of faith' from a provincial capital to a city which was recognized as one of the most important cultural centres in the world. His letters to Wilhelm

Tappert, a Berlin music journalist he met at Bayreuth in 1876, make particularly interesting reading, not least for the references to work on the revision of his Fourth Symphony and information about the Third Symphony, the second version of which had its disastrous first performance in Vienna in December 1877. Ten years later, as we read his correspondence with the German conductor Hermann Levi, one of the first committed champions of his music, we see an apologetic Bruckner, undertaking to revise his Eighth Symphony the Finale of which had caused Levi serious problems.

My task has been made easier by three publications, one in the late 1980s and the other two more recent. In his *Die Brüder Schalk und Anton Bruckner* (Tutzing, 1988), Thomas Leibnitz makes extensive use of the Schalk correspondence in the Austrian National Library and reveals how the two brothers, in their praiseworthy desire to champion the composer and facilitate the dissemination of his music, often transgressed the bounds of 'artistic licence' in revising his works. The first volume of the projected two-volume *Bruckner Briefe* (*Anton Bruckner Gesamtausgabe* XXIV/1), edited by Andrea Harrandt and the late Otto Schneider (Vienna, 1998), includes many letters which have come to light since the 1920s when Max Auer and Franz Gräflinger were responsible for the first printed collections of Bruckner's correspondence. Finally, Franz Scheder's two-volume *Anton Bruckner Chronologie* (Tutzing, 1996) is undoubtedly one of the most important books on Bruckner to have been written since the first major biography by Göllerich and Auer in the 1920s and 30s which, although a storehouse of invaluable information, is riddled with inaccuracies, unsubstantiated statements and anecdotes of questionable authenticity.

Like Scheder, I have been fortunate to have access to a considerable amount of new material which has been put at the disposal of Bruckner scholars by the *Anton Bruckner Institut Linz*. Bruckner's calendar-diaries, located in the Austrian National Library, have also been an important source of information, not least because they provide a faithful record of his personal religious devotions during the last twenty years of his life.

Unless otherwise stated, the translations of extracts from letters and reviews are my own.

Preface

Biography has not been kind to Bruckner. Beyond the principal chronological facts of his life, which are well-documented and indisputable, partial-truths and misunderstandings abound. Analyses of his enigmatic personality have been highly speculative, in many cases supported as much by wishful thinking as anything else. An incredible, often contradictory, and undoubtedly distorted picture has emerged. Depending upon whom one reads, Bruckner was an impoverished, misunderstood victim of Viennese society; an uneducated country bumpkin; a mystic simpleton victimized by his students; a slavish devotee of Wagner; a profound individual thinker confident in his convictions; a devout Roman Catholic; a great organist; a great German composer; a great Austrian composer; etc.; with peculiar personality traits including a death fetish, a number psychosis and an inexhaustible, if unsatisfied, predilection for young women. Some of the particulars, of course, have achieved a considerable degree of notoriety; all have some basis in fact. At one time or another, they have all been taken out of context or exaggerated, by admirers and detractors alike, in the service of the various aesthetic, political and personal agendas that have infused our current understanding of the Bruckner persona.

Until recently, the principal source for biographical information on the composer has been the exhaustive, frustrating, yet indispensable *Anton Bruckner: ein Lebens- und Schaffensbild* begun by the composer's pupil, August Göllerich, in 1924 and finally completed by the indefatigable Max Auer in 1937. Göllerich, who was in direct contact with countless acquaintances of the composer, accumulated his information through personal interviews and reams of correspondence. Auer had previously edited the incomplete volume of Bruckner letters that served for most of the twentieth century. The two generations of

x

scholars who followed Göllerich and Auer added little by way of original biographical research, preferring to comb materials accumulated by the earlier authors, often with a view to finding personal or psychological explanations for the extraordinary editorial issues posed by Bruckner's music.

Only toward the end of the twentieth century have scholars - Theophil Antonicek, Renate Grasberger, Andrea Harrandt, Elisabeth Maier and Manfred Wagner, to name but a few - begun once again to systematically search out, catalogue and publish the composer's letters, calendars, anecdotes, and archival and iconographic documents. They have forced a reassessment of many aspects of Bruckner's life and personality. The picture (the provenance of which can be traced to Bruckner himself) of an impoverished victim of Viennese society, for example, is changing to one of a composer who was in fact financially quite comfortable by the end of his life. He was well aware of his position in the forefront of the avant-garde and highly respected, especially among the younger denizens of the city.

Crawford Howie's biography presents the documents of the composer's life - many of them translated into English for the first time - in a fresh context. In the process of collating and assessing these materials as he does, detached from specific agendas, stereotypes fade and layers of special interest disappear. A new and more interesting history of the life of this enigmatic personality emerges: one of an extraordinary artist and teacher who lived in a fascinating place at a fascinating time.

Paul Hawkshaw
Yale School of Music

December 2000

Acknowledgements

With grateful thanks and appreciation especially to the following:
Dr. Paul Hawkshaw, University of Yale, for his encouragement and close reading of several chapters.
Dr. Tim Jackson, University of North Texas, and Dr. Benjamin Korstvedt, University of St. Thomas, Minnesota for their constructive comments.
Dr. Christian Enichlmayr, Director, *Oberösterreichische Landesbibliothek*, Linz, Dr. Walter Obermaier, Director, *Wiener Stadt- und Landesbibliothek*, Vienna, HR Univ.-Professor Dr. Ernst Gamillscheg, Director and Dr. Thomas Leibnitz, *Österreichische Nationalbibliothek*, Vienna, and Prof. Dr. Otto Biba, *Gesellschaft der Musikfreunde*, Vienna - for supplying photocopies of letters and documents.
Dr. Andrea Harrandt, *Anton Bruckner Institut Linz*, for her constant and uncomplaining supply of invaluable information about the locations of several of Bruckner's letters.
David Cheepen and the Portal Gallery, London, for kind permission to make use of his painting 'Anton Bruckner at the Age of Seventy, Fondly Remembering his Symphony no. 2 in C minor' for the cover of the book.
Michael Pollard and his colleagues in the Photographic Department, University of Manchester for their preparation of photographs.
My colleagues in the Department of Music, University of Manchester, for their support.
And last, but by no means least, my long-suffering wife Liz, daughter Gillian and sons Jonathan and Andrew for their patience, tolerance and understanding during the several years' preparation of this book!

CHAPTER 1

The Early Years (1824-1845)

Joseph Anton Bruckner, born in Ansfelden near Linz on 4 September 1824, came from a typical rural working-class background. The Bruckner family had lived in Ansfelden, in the Traun district of Upper Austria, since 1776, and young Bruckner's initial aspiration was to follow in the footsteps of both his father and grandfather and become a village schoolmaster.[1] He may have remained in this respectable but

---

1 Further information about Bruckner's forebears and the four younger brothers and sisters (from a total of eleven) who survived early infancy can be found in Göllerich-Auer, *Anton Bruckner: ein Lebens- und Schaffensbild* I (Regensburg: Bosse, 1922) [hereafter *G-A*], 49-75, and Heinz Schöny, 'Anton Bruckner zum 100. Todestag. Seine Ahnenliste als Geschichte seiner Vorfahren' in *Mitteilungsblatt der Internationalen Bruckner-Gesellschaft* 48 (Vienna, June 1997), 10-24. There are useful English summaries of the former in Hans-Hubert Schönzeler, *Bruckner* (London: Calder and Boyars, 1970) and Derek Watson, *Bruckner* [in *The Master Musicians* series] (Oxford: OUP, 2/1996). Facsimiles of the Ansfelden baptismal roll and Bruckner's baptismal certificate can be found between pages 64 and 65 of *G-A* I. *G-A* IV/4 (1937) includes, as a supplement, Ernst Schwanzara's *Stamm- u. Ahnentafel des Tondichters Anton Bruckner* in which the composer's family tree is traced back as far as Jörg Pruckner (c.1400). More up-to-date information about the family background of Bruckner's mother Therese (née Helm), father Anton and the latter's earlier proposal of marriage to Julie Hartung can be found in Franz Zamazal's article 'Ein Beitrag zur Familiengeschichte', *Bruckner Jahrbuch* [hereafter *BJ*] *1982/83* (Linz, 1984), 117-28. Zamazal has also written an extensive article about the education system in Austria and the teaching activities of three generations of the Bruckner family: 'Familie Bruckner - Drei Generationen Lehrer. Schulverhältnisse - Ausbildung - Lebenslauf' in *Anton Bruckner Dokumente & Studien* [hereafter

2

relatively unrewarding occupation for the rest of his life had not circumstances and his own indomitable will led him to embark eventually on an exclusively musical career. While always retaining strong connections with his roots, he progressed inexorably from unexceptional beginnings to a position of some eminence in Vienna by the end of his life.

The Industrial Revolution had not yet gathered momentum in Austria in the 1820s and the population of Austria and the Habsburg monarchy was still mainly rural and predominantly agricultural. Even by 1840, when industrialization was gradually increasing, '80 per cent of the total were still living in villages or scattered farms and 73-4 per cent still derived their livelihoods from agriculture, forestry or fisheries'.[2] Although conditions on the land were much better in Upper Austria than in many other parts of the Monarchy, smallholders had invariably to work very long hours to maintain a reasonable standard of living. Bad harvests or natural disasters like flooding could have a catastrophic effect on whole communities. Harsh though a rural life could be, it was no doubt preferable to conditions in the new factories being built in parts of Lower Austria where the average working day was anything from twelve to sixteen hours and the wages were minimal.

While the Catholic Church was still a force to be reckoned with particularly in rural communities, church music had not yet fully recovered from the restrictions imposed by Emperor Joseph II in the 1780s and only partially repealed by his successor, Leopold II. The spirit of the Enlightenment and the general religious indifference had also taken their toll. There was a gradual change in the relationship between state and church. 'Other patrons', remarks G.R. Scragg, 'competed for the service of the arts; often they offered greater latitude and seemingly more exciting

ABDS] 10: *Staat - Kirche - Schule in Oberösterreich* (Vienna: Musikwissenschaftlicher Verlag, 1994), 97-251.

2 C.A. Macartney, *The House of Austria* (Edinburgh: Edinburgh UP, 1978), 64.

opportunities. Those who now composed religious music regarded it as one interest among many others, and the contagion of the secular spirit increasingly affected what they wrote'.[3] The large cathedrals lacked the means of maintaining choirs and, because they were unable to employ as many professional singers and instrumentalists as before, had to fill the gaps with amateurs. In Salzburg, for instance, the cathedral music differed little from village chapel music until 1841 when, largely through the initiative of the Prince Archbishop, Friedrich von Schwarzenberg, the *Dommusikverein und Mozarteum* was founded with the dual purpose of resuscitating church music and reviving Mozart's music. In Vienna and other large towns like Graz, Klagenfurt and Linz, middle-class Music Societies and Church Music Societies were formed with the purpose of promoting and teaching serious music. These societies helped in the re-organization of church choirs, but the process took decades to accomplish.

Music continued to be cultivated, however, in the many abbeys and monasteries throughout Austria and Germany, and the enormous amount of manuscript material dating from the late eighteenth and early nineteenth centuries to be found in church music archives bears eloquent witness to great industry and remarkable endeavour.[4]

In fact, sheer delight in music-making provided the town and country church

---

3 G.R. Scragg, *The Pelican History of the Church* IV (London, 1962), 278.

4 The most important of these abbeys and monasteries, many of which contain manuscripts of sacred works by the Haydn brothers, Mozart and Schubert, are St. Florian, Gmunden, Göttweig, Herzogenburg, Klosterneuburg, Kremsmünster, Lambach, Melk, St. Peter's (Salzburg) and Seitenstetten. For further information about the impact made by the Josephine reforms on Upper Austrian monasteries in particular, see 'Musiktraditionen in den oberösterreichischen Klöstern' in *Bruckner-Symposion Linz* [hereafter *BSL*] *1990: Musikstadt Linz - Musikland Oberösterreich* (Linz, 1993), 179-209. The effect of these reforms on religious life in Linz is discussed in detail by Rudolf Zinnhobler in his article 'Das Bistum Linz zwischen Spätjosephinismus und Liberalismus', *ABDS* 10 (Vienna, 1994), 33-58.

4

choirs with much resilience, and orchestrally-accompanied music was performed even in small villages where the Josephine restrictions were no longer in force. On the other hand, the standard of performance was determined by amateurs and was often abysmally low; nor was the music provided usually of any lasting artistic value. Often it was nothing more than sacred salon music of a very facile kind. Kocher, a contemporary, provides revealing information about the level of musical performance in German village churches, drawing particular attention to the extremely bad instrumental playing 'which often tortures both one's musical feelings and one's ears to such an extent that one has to stop listening and watching'.[5] In Austria a comparable situation was viewed with alarm by the F.X. Glöggl, a conductor and the choirmaster of Linz Cathedral, who, in an unfinished book, presented proposals for the improvement of the musical part of worship in churches. His work was continued by his son who stressed the importance of the organist in congregational singing and considered it essential that he should possess 'intelligence, discernment and self-respect', be able to 'push the singing forward when it lags behind, without causing confusion' and always choose a registration 'in accordance with the number of people present, so that the singing will not be drowned by the organ, except when the congregation have made a mistake [!]'[6]

---

5 From L. Kocher, *Die Tonkunst in der Kirche* (Stuttgart, 1823); quoted in H. Allekotte, *C.M. von Webers Messen* (Bonn, 1913), 25f.

6 F.X. Glöggl, *Erklärendes Handbuch des musikalischen Gottesdienstes* (Vienna, 1828); quoted in Robert Haas, *Anton Bruckner* (Potsdam, 1934), 29ff. For further information about Franz Xaver Glöggl, who played an extremely active part in both the secular and sacred musical life of Linz in the late 18th and early 19th centuries, see Elisabeth Maier, '"Kirchenmusik auf schiefen Bahnen". Zur Situation in Linz von 1850 bis 1900', Franz Zamazal, 'Johann Baptist Schiedermayr. Ein Vorgänger Bruckners als Linzer Dom- und Stadtpfarrorganist', and Anton Voigt, 'Mozart und Linz' in *BSL 1990* (Linz, 1993), 109f., 124ff., and 214f.

Glöggl's statement that conditions in country churches were most often inadequate when the musical direction was entrusted to the village schoolmaster is corroborated   by Johann Herbeck whose illustrious career as a conductor and composer developed, like Bruckner's, from humble beginnings. Drawing on his early experience as a teacher in the village of Münchendorf in Lower Austria, he provides a damning account of the position of rural church music in Austria. Viennese popular tunes were set to the Latin text and there was a general atmosphere of utter profanity. Even the schoolmaster who supervised the musical proceedings was normally 'a man... personifying narrow-mindedness and laziness, full of arrogance and self-importance and, to crown it all, usually drunk'.[7]

Judging from Vincent Novello's observations during a European journey in 1829, the standard of performance at many of the larger churches and cathedrals was also very low.[8] Only sixty years or so before this, Charles Burney, during his musical tour of Europe, had commented very favourably on church music in the Austrian capital and had come to the conclusion that the 'excellent performances that are every day heard for nothing in the churches by the common people more contribute to refine and fix the national taste for good music than any other thing that I can at present suggest'.[9]   While Novello was quite impressed by some of the church music he heard in Vienna, he was clearly disappointed by a Mass   which he

7 Johann Herbeck, 'Gedanken über den Zustand der Kirchenmusik auf dem Lande' (1848), in Ludwig Herbeck, *Johann Herbeck. Ein Lebensbild von seinem Sohne Ludwig* (Vienna: Gutmann, 1885), Appendix, 106f.

8 The Novellos travelled to Vienna by way of Antwerp, Cologne, Mannheim, Heidelberg, Munich, Salzburg and Linz, and attended Mass and often Vespers at each place. See N. Medici di Marignano, ed. Rosemary Hughes, *A Mozart Pilgrimage, being the Travel Diaries of Vincent and Mary Novello in the Year 1829* (London, 1955), 254-322.

9 Percy A. Scholes, ed., *Dr. Burney's Musical Tours in Europe*, II: *An Eighteenth-Century Musical Tour in Central Europe and the Netherlands* (London, 1959), 75ff.

6

heard at St. Stephen's which was 'in a poor commonplace old style like what might have been written by Hasse or Vinci - all the movements were short and unsatisfactory'; furthermore, the orchestral players - 'about half a dozen violins, viola, 'cello, double bass and trombones' - were 'of the mediocre kind'. And yet, with talent, imagination and youthful vigour, and no doubt encouraged by his former teacher Michael Holzer, choir director, and his brother Ferdinand, unpaid organist, it was still possible for Franz Schubert to write enterprising church music (including four early Mass settings) for his local parish church at Lichtenthal in the Vienna suburbs. According to the church archives, there was a larger than usual body of singers and instrumentalists available, particularly for festival performances.[10]

It was in such an environment that Anton Bruckner grew up and gained his first experiences of church music. As a young lad he accompanied his parents to Sunday services in Ansfelden where his father played the organ and his mother sang in the choir. The orchestra at the church was a very modest one, consisting usually of two violins, bass, clarinet and horn. Occasionally, on special feast days such as *Corpus Christi*, this meagre force would be augmented by two trumpeters and a timpani player brought from Linz. As the village schoolmaster, Bruckner's father was not only responsible for the education of the children but had to be a musician of sorts, particularly a church musician. He had to acquire as part of his training the basic technical and theoretical knowledge of music insofar as it was required in organ playing, be it the realization of a figured bass or the improvisation of a short

---

10 From the autumn of 1813 for about three years, Schubert lived at the family home. For the first ten months of this period (until August 1814) he studied successfully at the Imperial Teachers' Training College to be an assistant elementary schoolteacher. For the remainder of the time he was employed as one of his father's assistants at the school in the Säulengasse. See Walther Dürr, 'Schubert in seiner Welt' and Manuela Jahrmärker, 'Von der liturgischen Funktion zum persönlichen Bekenntnis: Die Kirchenmusik' in Walther Dürr and Andreas Krause, eds., *Schubert Handbuch* (Kassel: Bärenreiter, 1997), 50-54 and 346-77.

prelude. A schoolmaster's family understandably formed an essential part of the church choir, providing music completely by itself if necessary. In most villages, schoolchildren and, perhaps, some adults were trained for participation in the musical part of the church service, both as singers and instrumentalists. And so the typical village schoolhouse would often take on the appearance of a small Conservatory.[11] Young Bruckner received his basic instrumental tuition - in violin, piano and organ - from his father and soon began to show signs of musical talent. As a ten-year-old he was proficient enough to play the organ at Sunday services.

Occasional visits to the magnificent abbey at St. Florian, where he would have heard the fine three-manual Chrismann organ, were undoubtedly inspirational. In 1835 and 1836 young Bruckner spent eighteen months at the home of his 21-year-old cousin, Johann Baptist Weiß (1813-50), who was schoolmaster and organist at Hörsching, a small town nearby. The Weiß family was gifted musically. Anton Weiß, Johann's uncle, was organist at Wilhering abbey and well-known as far as Vienna where he had played on several occasions. Johann had the reputation of being one of the best Upper Austrian musicians of his generation. He was a fine organist and gave Bruckner further organ lessons. He also taught him harmony and counterpoint, using as models works by Bach, Handel, Joseph and Michael Haydn, Mozart and Albrechtsberger.[12] Weiß's own Requiem in E flat was one of young Bruckner's favourite works. Its scoring suggests that Hörsching was able to boast

---

11 The situation did not change appreciably later in the century. See Rolf Keller, 'Anton Bruckner und die Familie Albrecht' in *BJ 1984/85/86* (Linz, 1988), 53-56.

12 Weiß was Bruckner's 'godparent' when he was confirmed in Linz by Bishop Gregorius Ziegler on 1 June 1833. There is a facsimile of the confirmation form in Leopold Nowak, *Anton Bruckner. Musik und Leben* (Linz, 1973), 20; the original is in the ÖNB. In 1836-35 Weiß introduced his young cousin to Joseph Haydn's *The Creation, The Seasons* and *The Seven Last Words,* and gave him a copy of the first edition of the F minor Variations for piano as a present. See Leopold Nowak, op.cit., 21 for a facsimile of the title page of the latter with Weiß's and Bruckner's signatures.

a slightly larger orchestra than Ansfelden.[13] Bruckner also had a high opinion of another Weiß work, a Mozartian Mass in G major.[14] One of his own first surviving compositions, a *Pange lingua* WAB 31, was possibly written during his stay in Hörsching. Indeed he thought highly enough of this early piece of sacred music to revise it more than 50 years later.[15] It is also possible that five short organ preludes, WAB 127 and 128, were written at this time, but doubts have been cast on their authenticity.[16]

At the end of 1836 young Bruckner had to return home to Ansfelden to assist his ailing father in his duties as schoolmaster, church organist, verger and fiddler for village dances. Overwork, nervous exhaustion and heavy drinking were contributory

---

13 Weiß's Requiem is scored for first and second violins, bass, two clarinets, oboe (ad lib.), two horns, two trumpets, organ continuo and voices; it was later published privately (1904) by Ernest Lanninger, parish priest of Hörsching.

14 Bruckner also possessed a copy of Weiß's gradual *Ecce sacerdos magnus*, dated 17 January 1836.

15 It may have been written slightly later, during his period as a choirboy at St. Florian, but it certainly pre-dates his teacher training year in Linz. It was printed for the first time in *G-A* II/1 (1928), 228; see also Leopold Nowak, ed., *Anton Bruckner Sämtliche Werke* [hereafter *ABSW*] XXI/1 (Vienna, 1984), 3 and commentary in *ABSW* XXI/2, 3f. The revised version (April 1891) was also printed for the first time - in a facsimile of the autograph, Mus. Hs. 3184 in the *Österreichische Nationalbibliothek, Musikabteilung* [hereafter *ÖNB*] - in *G-A* II/1, 230; see also *ABSW* XXI/1, 158 and commentary in *ABSW* XXI/2, 145ff.

16 The Prelude in E flat WAB 127 was printed for the first time in Max Auer, *Anton Bruckner* (Vienna, 2/1934) and the Four Preludes WAB 128 were printed for the first time in *G-A* II/1, 97-102. Othmar Wessely, in his article 'Der junge Bruckner und sein Orgelspiel', *ABDS 10* (Vienna, 1994), 62ff., draws attention to the rudimentary pedal technique required, describes the pieces as typical products of a style of organ playing common in 'rural cultural backwaters' at the time, and adds that it is entirely possible that Weiß was the composer and Bruckner merely copied them. Another organ prelude in B flat major is mentioned in *G-A* IV/4 (supplementary volume, Regensburg, 1974), 319.

factors to his father's death of consumption on 7 June 1837 at the early age of 46. Franz Perfahl, his father's assistant, and Joseph Peither, newly appointed as an additional assistant in May 1837, would almost certainly have undertaken the bulk of the teaching duties. Perfahl was another of Bruckner's music teachers, giving him lessons in violin 'and other musical subjects' probably during the period between his first return from Hörsching and his second visit in June / July 1837 when he was sent there to recover from the shock of his father's death and to enable his mother to give some attention to the other four younger children.[17]

Joseph Bruckner's successor as schoolmaster, Joseph Hametner, took up his position in Ansfelden in July and Bruckner's mother was forced to take the sacrificial step of moving away from the village to lodgings in Ebelsberg, a small village in the vicinity of St. Florian where, no doubt due to the intervention of the abbot, Michael Arneth, Bruckner was admitted as a chorister at the end of August.[18] He entered the third class of the village school at St. Florian and boarded with the school director, Michael Bogner.[19] Bogner also acted 'in loco parentis' for two other choirboys, Karl Seiberl and Anton Haus, and one of his responsibilities was to coach

---

17   See G-A IV/3 (1936), 62. Bruckner must have got on well with Perfahl. There are reports of his visiting him in Bad Goisern later. Perfahl (b. 1813) received his teaching certificate in 1835, moved from Ansfelden to Neuhofen in 1838 and was a teaching assistant is Ischl in 1843. See the *Verzeichnis des Personal-Standes der deutschen Schulen in der Diöcese Linz, Ordinariatsarchiv,* Linz.

18   Joseph Seebacher (1767-1848), the parish priest of Ansfelden, had written to Arneth about the death of Anton Bruckner sen. and the unsympathetic attitude of his parishioners who expected the problem of having a teacher's widow with five children on their hands to be resolved in the traditional way, viz. that a suitable school assistant should marry her! See Karl Rehberger, 'St. Florian und Anton Bruckner bis 1855. Einige neue Aspekte' in *BSL 1994* (Linx, 1997), 32.

19   Michael Bogner (1802-1879) was trained as a teacher in Linz. He taught at Ansfelden, Peilstein, Urfahr and Ried before moving to St. Florian where he was principal teacher at the school from 1834 until his retirement in 1875. He died in St. Florian in 1879.

them in the voice parts of those pieces which the St. Florian choir director, Eduard Kurz, brought to the school every Monday.[20]

Instrumental teachers at St. Florian included Franz Raab who taught violin and was highly thought of as a church composer and a bass singer in the abbey choir, and Franz Gruber who was on the administrative staff of the abbey but also taught violin.[21] But the musician who made the greatest impression on Bruckner was undoubtedly the cathedral organist, Anton Kattinger.[22] Bruckner stayed at St. Florian for three years and received both general and musical education, showing early signs of above-average talent as an organist as a result of excellent tuition from Kattinger.[23] His involvement in the performance of a great variety of church music, ranging in style from Renaissance polyphony to Classical and early Romantic homophony, left a deep impression and bore rich fruit later in his own sacred music.[24]

---

20 Eduard Kurz had been a pupil of the theorist and composer, Johann Georg Albrechtsberger, in Vienna. He was choir director at St. Florian (with interruptions) from 1810 to 1841, as well as being on the clerical staff there from 1813 to 1845. He was often unwell and was replaced by Franz Xaver Schäfler who was later a member of the male-voice quartet founded by Bruckner.

21 Gruber had been taught in Vienna by the noted violinist, Ignaz Schuppanzigh, and had studied at the Conservatory possibly with Joseph Böhm or Georg Hellmesberger.

22 Anton Kattinger (1798-1852) was employed as an organist at St. Florian from 1816 onwards and as a clerk of the court from 1819. After the death of his wife in December 1849 he moved to Kremsmünster where he married again in 1851. He died on 17 June 1852 after a number of strokes.

23 See *G-A* I (1922), 129-32 for details of Bruckner's exercises in grammar - *Ausarbeitungen von nacten Sätzen* - and arithmetic - *Rechnen-Aufgabenheft*, including a facsimile of a page from the latter on page 133. See **Plate 1** for a facsimile of the first page of the *Ausarbeitungen*, the original of which is in the *Wiener Stadt - und Landesbibliothek.* The original of a 'model letter' to his mother from a school exercise book can be found in the *ÖNB*; there are facsimiles of other 'model letters' in Bruckner's birth house in Ansfelden.

24 Walter Pass, in his article 'Studie über Bruckners ersten St. Florianer Aufenthalt', *Bruckner-Studien 1824-1974* (Vienna, 1975), 11-51, presents in full the *Verzeichnis aller aufgeführten*

Although Bruckner's voice broke in 1839 he was able to remain at the abbey for another year as a violinist and occasional organist. Having decided to become a schoolteacher, he was coached for the entrance examination to the *Präparandenkurs* (Teacher Training Course) at the Linz *Normalhauptschule* by the St. Florian school assistant, Georg Steinmeyer, and acquitted himself very creditably.

There is no real parallel between the *Normalhauptschule* and today's 'secondary school', 'high school' or college, nor does the term *normal* signify normal or usual. It was, rather, 'the most important, standard-setting educational establishment in Upper Austria and, consequently, it held teacher-training courses'.[25] Bruckner remained in frequent contact with his young friend and 'house mate', Karl Seiberl until his death, and Seiberl later reminisced on those early years.[26] Karl's brother Joseph was on the same teacher-training course as Bruckner and, from 1843 to 1847, was Weiß's assistant in Hörsching. Karl remembered young Bruckner's very proficient accompaniment of a Preindl Mass from a figured bass part at his parents' house in Marienkirchen in 1839 and observed that his improvisatory skills were in evidence at this early age. The two brothers were able to observe Bruckner's progress as an organist and to recognize the important part played by Kattinger and Weiß as his early mentors:

Kirchenmusikstücke in St. Florian from November 1838 to September 1841 (it actually continues until the end of 1841) and shows that there was a highly organized church music life in the abbey at this time. See also Joachim Angerer, 'Bruckner und die klösterlichen Lebensformen seiner Zeit' in *BSL 1985: Anton Bruckner und die Kirchenmusik* (Linz, 1988), 41-49.

25   For more information about the teacher-training course at Linz and the higher standards set by Johann Nepomuk Pauspertl von Drachental, who was director from 1835 to 1843, see Othmar Wessely, 'Anton Bruckners Präparandenzeit' in *BSL 1988* (Linz, 1992), 21-25.

26   Karl Seiberl (1830 - 1918) later became a distinguished lawyer.

12

He [Weiß] was a superb improviser on the organ and displayed his skills in St. Florian abbey when he gave a concert there' with Kattinger, the abbey organist, and Bruckner. The three organists, Kattinger - a masterly organ player for whom Bruckner had the greatest respect - on the main organ, Bruckner and Weiß on the two side organs, improvised on a theme provided by Kattinger. I myself did not witness this encounter of the three best organists in the district and beyond, and their improvisation which was a veritable musical event, but my brother Joseph was present and told me that most of the audience, who listened intently to the improvisations, considered schoolmaster Weiß to be the best... I can say that Bruckner, by virtue of his great talent, the tireless industry which he brought to his theoretical training, his opportunities of hearing the quite excellent abbey organist Kattinger, and the Classical church and chamber music cultivated at the abbey at that time, was able to build on the foundation of Weiß's instruction and to become the organist who then did not rest until, developing year by year, he reached the heights which invited our admiration.
... Bruckner often visited Weiß during the period when my brother was his school assistant in Hörsching. On the occasion of one such visit when Bruckner no doubt demonstrated his skill again, Weiß said to my brother, 'Watch out, he will make his mark'. Weiß died young and did not live to see the fulfilment of his prophecy. It is a great pity, as the same might have been said of him had his talent been able to flourish along the right lines.[27]

After successfully negotiating the entrance examination to the *Hauptschule*,

---

27   From Franz Gräflinger, *Anton Bruckner. Bausteine zu seiner Lebensgeschichte* [hereafter *GrBL*] (Munich: Piper, 1911), 102f. Seiberl does not give a date for the 'organ contest' but it probably took place between 1845 and 1850 by which time there would have been a significant improvement in Bruckner's finger- and pedal-technique. The 'Weiß' who took part in the contest was probably Anton Weiß from Wilhering, Johann's uncle. In 1850 Johann Weiß took his own life after innocently accepting responsibility for a church fund from which, unknown to him, a considerable sum of money had been embezzled. From them until his own death in 1896 Bruckner wrote many requests to the church authorities at Hörsching for a mass to be said for the repose of Weiß's soul. He even tried to persuade the authorities to entrust Weiß's skull to him - an act of genuine affection rather than necrolatry.

Bruckner embarked on the teacher-training course in Linz which began on 15 October 1840 and ended on 18 August 1841. As well as mastering the 'three Rs', a trainee teacher was required to take courses in religious instruction and music. The curriculum followed by Bruckner was in accordance with the *Politische Verfassung der deutschen Schulen in den k.k. Erblanden* (1840 revision). Bruckner's music teacher in Linz was a remarkable musician called August Dürrnberger who had provided music tuition free of charge at the college since 1832.[28] The scope of his activities at the *Hauptschule* is made clear in a letter sent by the college to the episcopal consistory in Linz in March 1846 recommending that he be awarded a civil service gold medal in recognition of his selfless contribution. As well as providing unpaid instruction in harmony, counterpoint, organ playing and plainchant singing, he had provided his trainee teachers with an understanding of and performing experience of 'genuine church music' and had not only devoted all his spare time to the college but had also 'rendered the state a great service by taking care of the purchase and repair of instruments and by buying musical material'.[29] Dürrnberger's multifarious activities in the town included the direction of performances of Classical works with full choir and orchestra, involving the participation of a number of students, in the *Minoritenkirche*, the instruction of college students in organ playing and plainchant singing, the regular participation every Sunday and feast-day for ten years in services at an approved school - the *Provinzial-Zwangarbeits- und Besserungsanstalt* - the composition of church songs, and the direction of the Linz town band.

Dürrnberger taught at the *Normalhauptschule* from 1832 to 1861 and made use

---

28 J.A. Dürrnberger (1800-1880) was in turn a law student in Jena and a trainee book-keeper in Linz before studying music in Vienna. Like his famous pupil after him he accumulated a number of certificates testifying to his musical abilities.

29 This letter of recommendation can be found in the *Ordinariatsarchiv*, Linz.

14

of his own *Choral-Gesangslehre in einfacher Darstellung und Ordnung der Grundregeln* and *Elementar-Lehrbuch der Harmonie- und Generalbaßlehre* as well as Marpurg's *Handbuch bei dem Generalbaße und der Composition*. He gave Bruckner a copy of the latter to take with him to his first teaching position in Windhaag.[30] Elisabeth Maier sums up Dürrnberger's importance as follows:

> It is to Dürrnberger's lasting credit that he provided the beginnings of that solid theoretical foundation without which Bruckner's later mastery would not have been possible. In addition, no doubt as a result of his year-long involvement with young people, he developed a keen eye for true talent. He provided Bruckner with strong support as long as it was in his power to do so, and he was able to exert a positive influence on the future of his brilliant student until he obtained the post of Linz cathedral and parish church organist.[31]

While we have some idea of the music instruction which Bruckner received at the *Normalhauptschule*, we have very little knowledge of the precise content of the rest of the syllabus. The music examinations were held in July and those in the other disciplines in August each year. Apart from Bruckner there were 40 other trainee teachers during the 1840/41 session.. Only 22 went forward to the examination and, of these, two graduated as secondary school teachers and fourteen as primary school teachers.[32]

In the certificate he received covering primary school subjects Bruckner obtained

---

30 In Bruckner's copy there are annotations like 'klingt schlecht' ('sounds bad') and 'unkirchlich' ('secular'). The original of Bruckner's copy is in the *ÖNB*; there is a photograph of the title-page in Leopold Nowak, *Anton Bruckner. Musik und Leben* (Linz, 1973), 40.

31 Elisabeth Maier, 'Bruckners oberösterreichische Lehrer' in *BSL 1988* (Linz, 1992), 42.

32 A copy of Pauspertl v. Drachenthal's report for the year, dated Linz, 15 November 1841, can be found in Franz Zamazal's article, 'Familie Bruckner - Drei Generationen Lehrer' in *ABDS* 10 (Vienna, 1994), 219ff.

nine 'very good' marks and fourteen 'good' marks. Each subject was given two marks, one assessing the candidate's knowledge of the subject, the other his ability to teach the subject. The evaluation of Bruckner's teaching skill was significantly higher than that of his subject knowledge. He received six 'very good' marks for the former and three for the latter, namely in religion, arithmetic and German language - an assessment that runs counter to the belief that Bruckner possessed very little teaching ability.[33]

Although he was not allowed to frequent the theatre during his stay in Linz, Bruckner would almost certainly have availed himself of opportunities to attend concerts. The Linz *Gesellschaft der Musikfreunde*, founded by Anton Mayer (1780-1854) in 1821, put on an average of four 'regular' concerts each year but also sponsored 'extraordinary' events, for instance concerts for charity and student concerts. The *Tonkünstler* society arranged regular performances of oratorios by Handel, Haydn (*The Creation* and *The Seasons*) and Beethoven (*Mount of Olives*). A typical concert programme of the time would have been a mixture of overtures (for example, Weber's *Der Freischütz* or *Euryanthe*), movements from symphonies, concertos, virtuoso pieces (variations, potpourris, polonaises), arias, choral items and operatic ensembles. In addition Bruckner would have been encouraged to listen to church music in the three main churches - the Cathedral, the Parish Church and the Minorite church - and would have been required to sing in the latter on

---

33 The originals of Dürrnberger's catalogue and list of pupils on the teacher training course in 1840-41 and the certificate for the conclusion of the course (signed J.P.von Drachenthal and dated 16 August 1841) are in the *ÖNB*; there are facsimiles in Leopold Nowak, op.cit., 42 and 45. The original of Dürrnberger's own classification and account of progress made by students in harmony and figured bass during 1840-41 (signed by both Dürrnberger and Drachtenthal and dated 30 July 1841) is in St. Florian.

Sundays.[34]

Bruckner's musical training in Linz also included piano lessons. His instruction manual was the *Kleine theoretisch-praktische Klavier-Schule*, published by Haslinger in 1825, which contained pieces from Pleyel's, Dussek's and Cramer's piano tutors. He possessed handwritten copies of piano sonatas and variation works by Haydn which he had received from Weiß, and made his own copy of Bach's *Art of Fugue*.

Having obtained excellent results in his final examinations, Bruckner duly qualified as an 'assistant teacher for primary schools'. He was disappointed to obtain only 'good' rather than 'very good' marks in organ playing and rectified this anomaly four years later in the organ recital which he gave as part of the final examination for prospective high school teachers. Dürrnberger was more generous in his appraisal and awarded Bruckner a 'very good' commendation.[35] After leaving Linz Bruckner remained in touch with his former teacher. In 1855 Dürrnberger was particularly helpful in encouraging Bruckner to apply for the vacant position of cathedral organist in Linz. Eleven years later, in 1866, Dürrnberger spent some time in Grünburg near Steyr, possibly to recuperate from an illness. A letter which Bruckner sent him on his name-day is sufficient evidence of the high esteem in

---

34 For further information about musical life in Linz during this period, see the following articles by Othmar Wessely: 'Das Linzer Musikleben in der ersten Hälfte des 19 Jahrhunderts' in *Jahrbuch der Stadt Linz 1953* (Linz, 1954), 283; 'Anton Bruckner und Linz' in *Jahrbuch der Stadt Linz 1954* (Linz, 1955), 201; 'Linz' in *MGG* 8 (Cassel, 1960), cols. 914-23; 'Von Mozart bis Bruckner. Wandlungen des Linzer Musiklebens 1770 bis 1870' in *Österreichische Musikzeitschrift* 25 (1970), 151; 'Linz' in *The New Grove* 9 (1980), 12f. See also R. Flotzinger and G. Gruber, eds., *Musikgeschichte Österreichs II. Vom Barock zur Gegenwart* (Graz, 1979), 221ff. and 349ff., and H. Zappe, 'Anton Bruckner, die Familie Zappe und die Musik. Zur Musikgeschichte des Landes Oberösterreich 1812-1963 bzw. 1982' in *BJ 1982/83* (Linz, 1984), 129-61.

35 The original of this certificate, signed by Franz Rieder, Franz Schierfeneder and Dürrnberger and dated 24 June 1845, is in St. Florian.

which he still held him:

> ... It is an expression of gratitude for the trouble which you took with me when you were once my teacher. It also comes from my deep respect for your almost unparalleled fair-mindedness and the energy which you expended in pursuing what was obviously right. It is further an expression of love - in response to the love which particularly touched me through your goodwill and benevolence of which I was often the recipient. Under such circumstances, who would not avail himself of an opportunity of giving expression to his feelings?... May God keep you in health for many, many years, bless you and amply reward you! So many of your pupils will echo that today! I join my voice to theirs and have every reason to do it in a strong 'forte'...[36]

Bruckner's scrupulousness in financial matters can already be seen at this early age - he took out a personal insurance policy for pension purposes just as he was embarking on a teaching career. It is possible, of course, that he was strongly advised to do so.[37]

In October 1841 Bruckner took up his first teaching appointment as assistant schoolmaster at a *Trivialschule* (elementary or primary school) in the small village of Windhaag situated near the border with Bohemia in the northern extremity Upper Austria. It was very difficult to reach and conditions were fairly primitive. To make matters worse, Bruckner's superior, Franz Fuchs, was not an easy man to get on with. As an assistant teacher, Bruckner was on the lowest band of the teaching scale and his wages, 40 florins per annum, were extremely modest in relation to the average for the time, but he received free board and lodging (a small room in a

---

36 See Andrea Harrandt and Otto Schneider, eds., *Briefe 1852-1886, ABSW* 21/1 [hereafter *HSABB* 1], 57 for this letter, dated Linz, 16 May 1866. The original has been lost; it was first printed in *G-A* 1, 149f.

37 See *G-A* 1, 154 for details of this policy with the *Pensionsinstitut für Schullehrers-Witwen und -Waisen*.

relatively safe part of the old school building which had been 'condemned' in 1822).[38]   In June 1841, four months before Bruckner took up his appointment, a fire destroyed nine houses and the roof of the village church, severely damaging the bell and the clock.   The new church tower and bell were consecrated in October 1842.

Apart from teaching, however, Bruckner was expected to undertake a variety of duties which included ringing the church bell in the morning (4 a.m. in the summer, 5 a.m. in the winter) and evening, cutting the grass in the schoolmaster's property, helping the parish priest to put on his vestments for each service, and playing the organ during the service or acting as server if the principal schoolmaster played.   In the afternoons there were a number of other duties which changed from season to season - haymaking, threshing, digging potatoes, tilling and sowing.   Bruckner also had to tidy the sacristy, help in administering the sacraments, and act as scribe for the church choir.   Fuchs appeared to resent Bruckner's easy way with the children and his superior musical ability, and frequently deprived him of his free periods by requiring him to cut quills into pens for the children.   He also gave him only limited access to his spinet, but Bruckner was able to make frequent use of the organ in the village church.   He made further studies of Bach's *Art of Fugue* which he had already copied in Linz and Albrechtsberger's *Preludes and Fugues*.   He also worked his way through the various lecture notes he had taken in Linz and compiled a 218-page manuscript of Drachenthal's *Allgemeine Methodik*.[39]

---

38   Work on the new school building was begun in June 1842 and progressed well enough for the schoolmaster to be able to move in on 31 October 1843; the building was dedicated on 13 November. But there were all sorts of delays, and the final building certificate was not issued until February 1849. 27 years had elapsed since the original recommendation for a new building!   Franz Zamazal provides a vivid description of a nineteenth-century teacher's living and working conditions in rural areas in 'Bruckner als Volksschullehrer', *BSL 1988* (Linz, 1992), 27-34.

39   There is a facsimile of the title-page of Bruckner's manuscript in Elisabeth Maier, *Bruckners oberösterreichische Lehrer*, *BSL 1988*, 43. The original can be found in the Linz *Stadtarchiv*.

19

Like his father before him Bruckner supplemented his income by playing the
fiddle at local dances, an obvious drain on his energy as it often kept him up until
the early hours of the morning.[40] But there were some compensations, not least
the friendship of Johann Sücka, a weaver by trade, and his family. Bruckner gave
music lessons to his three children, Maria, Rosalia and Franz, and prepared Franz for
the teacher-training course in Linz. By way of recompense Bruckner enjoyed a
regular hearty breakfast at the Sücka household and Mrs. Sücka did his laundry.
Johann played both clarinet and trumpet and would join his son (first violin) and
Bruckner (second violin) in some domestic music-making. Bruckner was delighted
when Sücka purchased a spinet as he was able to practise on it to his heart's content!

It had been obvious for some time that Bruckner and Fuchs did not get on well.
There were complaints that Bruckner was spending too much of his time composing.
Nevertheless, he received a very good report during the school inspection carried out
by Josef Leuthäuser in June 1842.[41] Matters came to a head when Bruckner one day
failed to carry out one of his obligatory non-teaching duties - bringing manure to the
fields - and was reported to the abbot, Michael Arneth. The latter was astute enough
to recognize the potential in young Bruckner and, far from punishing him, arranged
for him to spend some time as a school assistant in the more pleasant village
of Kronstorf until such time as a place could be found for him in the village

---

40   See Helga Thiel, Gerda Lechleitner and Walter Deutsch, 'Anton Bruckner - sein
soziokulturelles Umfeld, seine musikalische Umwelt' in *BSL 1987* (Linz, 1989), 111-19 for a
discussion of Joseph Jobst's fair copy (in 1872) of the Ländler he had played in Windhaag with
Bruckner, Sücka, Toni and Johann Mauer. See also Walter Deutsch, 'Eine Ländlersammlung von
Windhaag', idem, 124-49, for the facsimile of Jobst's copy. There were two main types of Bavarian
/Austrian folk dance - the Ländler in three time and the 'Hopser' in four time. Bruckner also
possessed two sheets of dance music; these are in the *ÖNB*.

41 The supervision of schools was the responsibility of the church. Josef Leuthäuser was dean of
the Freistadt district.

school at St. Florian.[42] In spite of their differences, Bruckner and Fuchs seem to have parted on reasonably good terms. Fuchs's reference, corroborated by a reference from the parish priest, Franz von Schwinghaimb, made favourable mention of Bruckner's 'tireless energy' as a teacher and his scrupulous fulfilment of other duties.[43]

During his sixteen months in Windhaag Bruckner wrote a Mass in C, WAB 23, for the best singer in the church choir, an alto called Anna Jobst, two horns and organ. It is unpretentious, obviously circumscribed by the limited musical forces available in a village church, and therefore typical of the many *Landmessen* or 'country Masses' written during the first half of the nineteenth century. The designation *Choralmesse* does not refer to any particular association with a pre-existing Gregorian plainchant but suggests that it was written specifically for one of

---

42   In a conversation with Theodor Altwirth in Vienna in July 1895, Bruckner remarked that he had been transferred not for disciplinary reasons but because he was unhappy in Windhaag and had asked Michael Arneth to be moved to a better situation; see Altwirth, 'Bei Anton Bruckner' in the *Linzer Montagspost*, 29 July 1895, 1.

43   See *G-A* I, 207f. and Manfred Wagner, *Bruckner* (Mainz, 1983), 233f. for the texts of these references, both dated 19 January 1843. There is a facsimile of Fuchs's reference in Nowak, *Anton Bruckner. Musik und Leben*, 52. Franz Seraph Amerer von Schwinghaimb (1790-1850) was parish priest at Windhaag from November 1831 to January 1843. Some manuscripts in St. Florian and one or two printed booklets reveal him to be a zealous supporter of the anti-Josephine viewpoint. He was a learned man and a skilled theologian - a cut above the average parish priest. That Bruckner was not completely aware of this and no doubt partly misunderstood Schwinghaimb was one of the factors which contributed to his move away from Windhaag in 1843. For more recent information about Franz Fuchs (1787-1860), Franz von Schwinghaimb, Windhaag and Bruckner's Windhaag experience, see Othmar Wessely, 'Zu Bruckners Windhaager Jahren' and Franz Zamazal, 'Neues zu Bruckners Aufenthalt in Windhaag', *BSL 1992* (Linz, 1995), 49-56 and 57-72. Both articles draw on documentary material in the Freistadt and Windhaag parish archives, in particular the school inspection of 1842.

the more penitential periods of the church year, Advent of Lent.[44]

Bruckner was school assistant in Kronstorf from 23 January 1843 until 23 September 1845. He was much nearer the more pleasant surroundings of St. Florian, about ten miles away, and Enns and Steyr, both about six miles away. The village was half the size of Windhaag, with a little over 100 inhabitants, and Bruckner's duties as schoolmaster, sexton and part-time 'community worker' were similar to those at Windhaag, although there is no specific mention of agricultural activities in the contract.[45] His starting salary was the same as at Windhaag but was soon increased, and he was therefore able to send some of it to help his mother and siblings. The inhabitants of the village were friendlier and, more important, he formed a good working relationship with his superior, Franz Lehofer, and got on well with the parish priest, Alois Knauer. He quickly made friends with a keen amateur musician, Joseph Födermayer, who lent him his old piano so that he could practise on it in the schoolroom whenever it was convenient. In 1865 Mathias Leutgäb was school assistant in Kronstorf. He later described the schoolhouse there as follows:

> ... [The] cowshed is the nicest part of the house. There was still an open stove in the kitchen and the pots had to be placed on top of it. Walls and window were completely black. At my request, however,

---

44 The work was first printed in *G-A* I (1922), 173-89. For a modern edition and commentary, see *ABSW* XXI/1, 4-11 and 183-87 and *ABSW* XXI/2, 4-9. There is a facsimile of a page from the autograph of the organ part (end of *Gloria*, beginning of *Credo*) in *ABSW* XXI/1, XIV. The original is in the Wels *Stadtmuseum* (no. 2692). For a recent discussion of the *Landmesse*, see Rudolf Flotzinger, 'Versuch einer Geschichte der Landmesse' in *BSL 1985: Anton Bruckner und die Kirchenmusik* (Linz, 1988), 59-69.

45 See *G-A* I, 211f. for the text of the contract, which is dated 23 January 1843.

I received a transportable stove with two copper containers [for heating water][46]

Bruckner's room, about 18' x 18', was on the first floor of the building next to the classroom and can still be seen today.

With seemingly boundless youthful energy Bruckner pursued lessons in organ, piano and music theory with Leopold von Zenetti, organist and director of the church choir in Enns. As Zenetti was a regular guest at St. Florian, Bruckner had probably got to know him when he was a choirboy there in the late 1830s. Three times a week Bruckner made the journey on foot to Enns and back (a round trip of twelve miles), and it was not unknown for him to have a lesson with Zenetti on a Sunday morning, walk back to Kronstorf, complete an assignment, and return to Enns for another lesson in the evening! Like many church organists at the time, Zenetti wrote music of his own to supplement the repertoire.[47] Zenetti was not only a musician of some distinction - in Enns he also directed the Music Society and a male-voice choir as well as organizing concerts - but was an extremely well-read man. He possessed a fine library of musical scores (mainly the Viennese Classics), books on music and on literature, history and geography.[48] Bruckner paid tribute to Zenetti's understanding of music theory on several occasions later in his life. When he moved to St. Florian in 1845 he continued to travel to Enns for lessons with Zenetti, and it was as a result of his encouragement (as well as that of Dürrnberger) that the somewhat hesitant young man applied for the vacant post of cathedral

---

46 From Leutgäb's unpublished autobiography, as quoted by Zamazal, *BSL 1988*, 31.

47 There is a list of works, some definitely by Zenetti (1805-1892), others probably by him, in Elisabeth Maier and Franz Zamazal, 'Anton Bruckner und Leopold Zenetti', *ABDS 3* (Graz, 1980), 119.

48 See Maier and Zamazal, ibid., 116f. and, in particular, 201-39 for a list of music in Zenetti's library.

23

organist in Linz in 1855. By this time the teacher-pupil relationship had developed into a firm friendship. After Bruckner moved to Vienna in 1868 he often spent part of his summer vacation in St. Florian and frequently took the opportunity of visiting his old teacher on these occasions. The two main textbooks which Zenetti used were D.G. Türk's *Von der wichtigsten Pflichten eines Organisten* (1787) and *Kurze Anweisung zum Generalbaßspiel* (1791), but Bruckner would also have had access to tutors like J.B. Vanhal's *Anfangsgründe des Generalbaßes* (Vienna, 1817), Ambros Rieder's *Anleitung zur richtigen Begleitung der vorgeschriebenen Kirchengesänge wie auch zum Generalbaß* (1830) and Simon Sechter's *Praktische Generalbaß-Schule* op. 49 (1830).[49] The emphasis in Zenetti's teaching was clearly on the practical outworking of what was learned theoretically. He also introduced Bruckner to Bach's *Wohltemperirte Klavier* and chorale harmonizations.

Among the acquaintances Bruckner made in Enns was the parish priest Joseph von Peßler (1803-1877) for whose birthday in 1843 the fledgling composer wrote an *a cappella* male-voice chorus, *An dem Feste* WAB 59, to words by the Kronstorf priest, Alois Knauer. It was first performed in Enns Parish Church on 19 September 1843 and is of particular interest because, fifty years later, Bruckner made some corrections to it, added dynamic markings, and had new words provided by Karl Ptak. With its new title *Tafel-Lied* (WAB 86), it was performed by the *Wiener Akademischer Gesangverein* on 11 March 1893 and was reviewed favourably in two Viennese papers, the *Deutsche Zeitung* and the *Deutsches Volksblatt*. In the former, Theodor Helm, a friend and admirer of Bruckner, drew attention to the 'unpretentious but successful choral writing of the nineteen- year- old Upper Austrian school assistant who at that time had certainly no inkling that he

---

49 Bruckner's handwritten *Kurze Generalbaß-Regeln*, wrongly attributed by Göllerich to an earlier date, viz. the period of study with his cousin Weiß in Hörsching, undoubtedly belong to his period and were his essentially his attempts to codify Zenetti's teaching. See *G-A* I, 90 for a facsimile of a page.

would become one of the greatest masters of the symphony and of church music'.[50]

Bruckner paid frequent visits to Steyr, a town of some 10,500 inhabitants with a large parish church in the Gothic style and, as far as he was concerned, the no less impressive Chrismann organ to which he was granted access by the accommodating parish priest, Joseph Plersch. According to Göllerich, another incentive was the opportunity to play Schubert's piano works for four hands with Karoline Eberstaller who had played these works with Schubert himself when he spent some time in Steyr in the 1820s.[51] In later years Bruckner was a welcome guest of the parish priests, Georg Arminger and Josef Aichinger. When he spent part of his summer vacations in Steyr he particularly enjoyed the company of three music-loving businessmen, Carl Almeroth, Isidor Dierkes and Karl Reder who, in the 1880s, indulged the composer in two of his favourite pursuits - coach riding and Pilsner beer drinking - and were involved in a short-lived scheme to provide him with some financial help. Franz Bayer, director of the parish church choir from the late 1880s,

---

50 See *G-A* I, 229-35 for the words of the original and revised versions and the music of the original version, and 237ff. for extracts from the two reviews.

51 See *G-A* I, 228. There is no first-hand evidence for this supposed Schubert-Bruckner link via Karoline Eberstaller (1812-1902), however. It is possible that what was either entirely fictitious or, at best, partly true eventually became 'fact' through the writings of Gregor Goldbacher, a local Steyr historian, who wrote several books and various articles in Upper Austrian papers, including 'Karoline Eberstaller, die letzte Freundin Franz Schuberts' in the *Linz Tagespost*, 20 February 1927, and 'Von Franz Schubert bis Anton Bruckner. Die hervorragendsten Meister zweier weit auseinanderliegenden Musikepochen persönlich gekannt - Was wir von der Steyrerin Karoline Eberstaller wissen' in *Oberdonau Zeitung*, 25 March 1944. My thanks to Janet Wasserman, New York, for supplying this information. In a recent article, 'Oberösterreich als Schubert-Quelle: Was kannte Bruckner von Schubert" in *BSL 1997* (Linz, 1999), Franz Zamazal writes that there is no evidence either to support or to disprove the possibility of a meeting between Bruckner and Eberstaller; even 'the information passed on by word of mouth is contradictory' (p. 142); Bruckner could have met her either during the Kronstorf years or much later, in the 1890s, during one of his holiday visits to the town.

was an enthusiastic advocate of Bruckner's music and was responsible for several performances of Bruckner's sacred works. On one such occasion - a performance of his D minor Mass in Steyr Parish Church on 2 April 1893 - Bruckner played the organ part; at a special reception afterwards the delighted composer paid tribute to conductor and performers for their exemplary preparation of the work.[52]

St. Florian held fond memories for Bruckner and he was now able to resume his strong connections with the town and abbey. He was introduced to the distinctive sound of the male-voice quartet by Hans Schläger.[53] Bruckner formed his own male-voice quartet in Kronstorf and sang first bass.

It was common practice for school assistants to sit an examination after at least three years' experience so that they could qualify for a more senior post. Supplied with two very favourable testimonials from his superior, Franz Lehofer, and the parish priest, Alois Knauer, both of whom had nothing but praise for his teaching and musical skills, Bruckner successfully completed the examination in Linz in May

---

52 Bruckner repeated his praise in a letter to Bayer written from Vienna on 22 April 1893. See Max Auer, *Anton Bruckner; gesammelte Briefe* [hereafter *ABB*] (Regensburg, 1924), 271f. for the text of this letter and Franz Gräflinger, *Anton Bruckner. Bausteine zu seiner Lebensgeschichte* (Munich, 1911), 58f. for a facsimile. For further information about Bruckner's connections with Steyr, see J. Bayer, *Anton Bruckner in Steyr* (Steyr: Vereinsdruckerei, 1956), Erich W. Partsch, 'Zum Musikleben Steyrs' in *BSL 1990* (Linz, 1993), 267-72, idem, *Anton Bruckner in Steyr: 'Wo ich alljährlich so gern weile' - eine Ausstellung im Stadtpfarrhof 15. Juni - 28. Juli and 15. September - 27. Oktober 1996* (Steyr: Stadtpfarramt Steyr, 1996), and idem, '"Unser berühmter Landsmann". Zur Bruckner-Berichterstattung in der Steyrer Presse bis 1896' in *BJ 1994/95/96* (Linz 1997), 289-94.

53 Hans Schläger (1820-1885), who was a choirboy at St. Florian from 1832, took the teacher training course in Linz from 1836 to 1838 and preceded Bruckner as assistant teacher at St. Florian, wrote many pieces for the medium. He studied under Gottfried Preyer at the Vienna Conservatory from 1845 to 1847 and was later appointed conductor of the *Wiener Männergesangverein* (1854-1861) and director of music at Salzburg Cathedral and Mozarteum (1861-67).

1845 and made a particularly favourable impression on his former teacher, Dürrnberger, who had no hesitation in awarding him a distinction in theoretical and practical music. His lessons with Zenetti had not been in vain![54] Three months later, in September, Bruckner was officially appointed to a new position in St. Florian. Although he was still only an assistant teacher, his salary was duly increased.[55]

The compositions written during the Kronstorf period reflect the limited resources available to Bruckner, but provide evidence of a clearer grasp of traditional styles and an improved technical facility for which Zenetti should no doubt take much of the credit. Most of the works are occasional pieces for mixed voices, with or without organ accompaniment, written for church services. Some works have been lost, including a setting of *Salve Maria* WAB 134 and a *Requiem* WAB 133 for male voices and organ which was written in memory of his friend Johann Nepomuk Deschl, schoolmaster in Kirchberg bei Eferding, and first performed in March 1845, with Bruckner playing the organ. Of the works still extant the most interesting stylistically - insofar as they illustrate features which the composer was to employ with much greater originality in later compositions - are the two settings of *Asperges me* WAB 4 for mixed voices and organ, the *Maundy Thursday Mass* (*Messe für den Gründonnerstag* WAB 9, including a setting of the

---

54 See *G-A* 1, 277ff. for the texts of Lehofer's and Knauer's testimonials, dated 12 May 1845. The originals are in St. Florian. See earlier and footnote 35 for further information about Dürrnberger's certificate, dated 24 June 1845. Also see Franz Zamazal, *ABDS 10*, 188f. and 227ff. for further information about the nature of the examination and additions made in 14 July and 19 August to Bruckner's original teaching certificate.

55 See *G-A* 1, 315-19 for the contract and two further testimonials from Lehofer (23 September 1845) and Knauer (25 September 1845). The originals are in St. Florian. Also see Zamazal, ibid., 228f., footnotes, concerning mistakes made in the transcription of Lehofer's two and Knauer's two testimonials in *G-A* I.

gradual, *Christus factus est*, and the *Messe ohne Gloria und Credo* WAB 146.[56] Apart from *An dem Feste*, the only other secular work to survive from the Kronstorf period is a cantata which exists in three versions, all dating from 1845 and scored for eight-part mixed-voice choir, four soloists and piano accompaniment. The three versions are identical, apart from some slight changes in the accompaniment figuration introduced in the second version and retained in the third. The first version was described by Bruckner on the manuscript title-page as a *Musikalischer Versuch nach dem Kammer-Styl über ein kurzes Gedicht* and, as it also has the annotation 'Cand.', we can assume that it was written before his music examination in Linz which was held on 29 May. The second version has a similar title but has an added dedication to Alois Knauer, the parish priest.[57] The third version, entitled *Vergissmeinnicht* (WAB 93), was dedicated to Friedrich Mayr, prebendary of St. Florian abbey at the time and later to succeed Michael Arneth as abbot.[58]

When Bruckner moved to St. Florian in September 1845, he was about to commence the important second stage in his musical career. Ansfelden, Windhaag, Kronstorf, three 'stations' in the first stage of his musical pilgrimage, were by no means forgotten by the composer. Before his move to Vienna in 1868 he paid an annual visit to his father's grave in Ansfelden. After 1868 he continued these visits,

56 For the music of these works and critical commentary, see *G-A* I (1922), 243ff., *G-A* II/2 (1928), 67-76, *ABSW* XXI/1 (1984), 12-33 and 167-71, and *ABSW* XXI/2, 10-31.

57 This 'attempted musical setting of a short poem in the chamber style' was a name-day gift (21 June 1845).

58 There is a facsimile of the autograph of the third version in *G-A* 1, 283-300; a modern edition of all three versions can be found in Leopold Nowak and R. Führer, eds., *ABSW* XXII/1-5: *Namenstag-Kantaten 1845-1857* (Vienna, 1987, 2/1999), 1-13 (first version), 14-27(second version) and 28-41(third version). See also Leopold Nowak, 'Die Kantate "Vergißmeinnicht von Anton Bruckner' in *Über Anton Bruckner. Gesammelte Aufsätze* (Vienna, 1985), 249-53.

28

albeit less frequently. In 1870 he was granted honorary citizenship of the village and in 1895 the *Frohsinn* choir in Linz, with which he was closely associated in the years 1865-68, unveiled a memorial plaque on the house where he was born. Bruckner was too ill to attend - his place was taken by his brother Ignaz - but sent a letter of thanks.[59] Bruckner also maintained his connections with Windhaag until the late 1870s. On 4 July 1897 a memorial plaque was unveiled at the new schoolhouse there. Connections with Kronstorf continued much longer - until 1894 - and he remained on friendly terms with the Lehofer family until his death. A memorial plaque was unveiled at the old schoolhouse there on 14 June 1913.

---

59   See *G-A* 1, 325 and Franz Gräflinger, *Anton Bruckner. Gesammelte Briefe* [hereafter *GrBB*], 32 for the text of this letter, dated Vienna, 19 May 1895.

CHAPTER 2

Bruckner at St. Florian: Apprentice Years (1845-1855)

2.1 Bruckner and St. Florian

The Augustinian monastery at St. Florian, founded about 1071, has a rich musical tradition, a splendid Chrismann organ and a large library containing both manuscripts and printed volumes.[1] When Bruckner returned to what was to prove to be his spiritual home for the rest of his life, he was undoubtedly more able to appreciate and to avail himself of the resources at his disposal.[2] The music which

---

1 The organ, now known as the 'Bruckner organ', had three manuals, 59 registers and 5230 pipes during Bruckner's time at St. Florian. It was overhauled by Matthäus Mauracher in 1873-75 and modernized in the 1920s. It now has four manuals, 103 registers and 7343 pipes. Although much material in the abbey library was lost through rebuilding in the 18th century and maladministration in the mid-19th century, it is well-stocked, containing about 121,000 printed volumes and 800 manuscripts. See E. Kirchner-Doberer, *Stift St. Florian* (Vienna, 1948); L. Hager, *Die Brucknerorgel im Stifte St. Florian* (Linz, 1951); Othmar Wessely, *Musik in Oberösterreich* (Linz, 1951), Altman Kellner, 'St. Florian', *Musik in Geschichte und Gegenwart* 4 (1955), cols. 423-29; O. Wutzel, *Das Chorherrenstift St. Florian* (Linz, 1971); Altman Kellner, 'St. Florian', *The New Grove* 16 (1980), 387f.; Joachim Angerer et al., 'Musiktraditionen in den oberösterreichischen Klöstern', *BSL 1990* (Linz, 1993), 179-209.

2 For Bruckner's connections with St. Florian, see I. Hollensteiner, *Das Stift St. Florian und Anton Bruckner* (Leipzig, 1940); W. Schulten, *Anton Bruckners künstlerische Entwicklung in der St. Florianer Zeit* (typewritten dissertation, Soest/Westf., 1956); idem, 'Über die Bedeutung der St.

30

he copied for study purposes included some of Bach's keyboard works and Mozart's piano-duet works as well as passages from larger sacred works, for instance Mendelssohn's *St. Paul*, Eybler's *Mass in D*, Preindl's *Mass in B flat*, and Haydn's *St. Nicholas Mass*.[3] Two composers in particular exerted a considerable influence on the budding composer - Joseph Haydn in his sacred works and Franz Schubert in his secular instrumental and vocal pieces. Writing to his parents from Steyr in July 1825, Schubert had expressed his pleasure in finding so many of his works available in Upper Austria, 'particularly in St. Florian and Kremsmünster monasteries'.[4] The St. Florian abbey library possesses a large number of early editions of many of Schubert's works. Young Bruckner seized on these avidly, accompanying the tenor Ludwig Ehrenecker in Schubert lieder and forming a male-voice quartet with Ehrenecker, Johann Hueber (his future brother- in- law) and Franz Schäfler to sing works like Schubert's *Das Dörfchen* D. 598, *Die Nachtigall* D. 724, *Geist der Liebe*

Florianer-Jahre Anton Bruckners', *Beiträge zur Anton Bruckner Forschung der Sektion der Internationalen Bruckner-Gesellschaft* I (Aachen, 1960); Walter Pass, *Bruckner-Studien 1824-1974*, 11-51; Karl Rehberger, 'St. Florian und Anton Bruckner bis 1855. Einige neue Aspekte', *BSL 1994* (Linz, 1997), 31-36.

3 Facsimiles of Bruckner's copies of the 'cum sancto Spiritu' fugue from the *Credo* of Eybler's Mass can be found in *G-A* II/1, 34; facsimiles of copies of extracts from a Cherubini Mass and a piano sonata can be found in Robert Haas, *Anton Bruckner*, 34 and 50. On 1 November 1848 Bruckner used Mendelssohn's *St. Paul* as the basis for some contrapuntal studies. See Leopold Nowak, 'Mendelssohns "Paulus" und Anton Bruckner' in *Über Anton Bruckner. Gesammelte Aufsätze* (Vienna, 1985), 194; there is a facsimile of an extract from these studies in *ibid.*, 191.

4 Otto Erich Deutsch, ed., *Franz Schubert Briefe und Schriften* (Vienna, 1954), 116ff. For further information about musical life in Steyr, see the sources listed in Chapter 1, footnote 52. For supplementary information about musical life in Upper Austria in general, see the sources listed in Chapter 1, footnote 34 as well as Rudolf Flotzinger, 'Oberösterreich in der Musikgeschichte' and Georg Heilingsetzer, 'Die Trägerschichten der Musikkultur in Oberösterreich vom 16. bis zum 19. Jahrhundert' in *BSL 1990* (Linz, 1993), 15-21 and 23-29.

D.747 and *Der Gondelfahrer* D.840.[5] As well as being intimately involved with music-making in St. Florian, Bruckner travelled occasionally to Linz to attend organ recitals at the Cathedral and choral and orchestral concerts organized by the *Musikverein*. It is possible that he was at one of the two performances of Mendelssohn's oratorio *St. Paul* in December 1847 and January 1848. Although Mendelssohn was not represented by the same quantity of works as Schubert in the St. Florian library, his influence on Bruckner was by no means inconsiderable.[6]

Bruckner's duties at the village school in St. Florian included four hours' teaching each day (8-10, 12-2) in the two most junior classes, teaching in the Sunday school, giving piano and violin lessons to four of the choirboys and private tuition to two young aristocrats. He received organ lessons from Anton Kattinger, the abbey organist, continued travelling to Enns for a year or so for theoretical studies with Zenetti, and worked his way through the syllabus of the *Oberrealgymnasium* (upper secondary school) with one of the novices at the abbey, Josef Rom. He stayed at the home of his former teacher, the headmaster Michael Bogner with whom he was on

---

5 Schubert's influence on Bruckner is discussed by Max Auer in 'Anton Bruckners Beziehungen zu Franz Schubert. Zum Beginn des Schubert-Jahres', *Organon* 5 (1928), 1-4, and 'Anton Bruckner und Franz Schubert', *Linz Tagespost* (17 June 1928); also by Eugen Schmitz, *Schuberts Auswirkung auf die deutsche Musik bis zu Hugo Wolf und Bruckner* (Leipzig, 1954). The Schubert-Bruckner connection is also explored in three more recent articles in *BSL 1997* (Linz, 1999), viz. Erich W. Partsch, 'Bruckner und Schubert. Zu Interpretation und Kritik einer vielbehaupteten Beziehung', 79-97; Hans-Joachim Hinrichsen, '"*Himmlische Länge*" und "*symphonischer Strom*". Bruckner, Schubert und das Problem der "Form"', 99-116; and Franz Zamazal, 'Oberösterreich als Schubert-Quelle: Was kannte Bruckner von Schubert?', 117-76.

6 Mendelssohn's influence on Bruckner is discussed by Othmar Wessely in 'Bruckners Mendelssohn-Kenntnis', *Bruckner-Studien 1824-1974* (Vienna, 1975), 81-112, and by Michael Märker in 'Hat Bruckner das Adagio der Zweiten im "Mendelssohnschen Stil mit Honigsüße" komponiert? Über die Mendelssohn-Rezeption Anton Bruckners', *BSL 1997* (Linz, 1999), 177-86.

good terms and with whose daughter Aloisia he was on even better terms, judging from some pieces specifically dedicated to her![7] During his time at St. Florian Bruckner took on more piano pupils and was sufficiently motivated by his teaching to compose a few pieces for piano duet.[8]

One of Bruckner's closest friends during these early St. Florian years was Franz Sailer (1803-1848), a judicial actuary and the godfather of Bruckner's younger brother, Ignaz. He was a keen music lover, an admirer of Bruckner's improvisational skills and the possessor of a new Bösendorfer grand piano upon which Bruckner was able to practise. When Sailer died suddenly of a heart attack in mid-September 1848, Bruckner inherited the piano which remained with him until the end of his life and became the 'sounding board' for all his compositions. He certainly practised long and hard on it in these early days as well as spending many hours on the so-called 'workday organ' in the abbey. In memory of Sailer Bruckner wrote his first important major work - the *Requiem* in D minor WAB 39, completed in 1849 and first performed on 15 September - the first anniversary of Sailer's death - in St. Florian. According to a diary entry by Father Beda Piringer, another performance of the work three months later, on 11 December, in Kremsmünster abbey was well received:

> A Requiem by the St. Florian school assistant Bruckner was performed. It made a very good impression. The young man is an organ virtuoso. He performed after Vespers. He and his companion

---

7 These are a *Lancier-Quadrille* WAB 120 for piano (c. 1850), a *Steiermärker* WAB 122 for piano (c. 1850) and a *Frühlingslied* WAB 68 for voice and piano (1851). See later in the chapter, p. 60.

8 These include a *Quadrille* WAB 121 (1854), dedicated to Georg Ruckensteiner whose daughter Marie was one of his pupils, and *Drei kleine Vortragsstücke* WAB 124 (1852-54), written for the children of the St. Florian notary, Josef Marböck. See later in the chapter, pp. 60-61 and note 71.

were invited to dine with us.[9]

Bruckner was comparatively untouched by the revolutionary happenings of 1848, although he enrolled in the National Guard and took part in some military exercises.[10] Of greater consequence for his musical development and his future career was his appointment as provisional organist at St. Florian on 28 February 1850. Kattinger had been promoted to a position as tax inspector at Kremsmünster and Bruckner, who had often acted as Kattinger's deputy since 1845, now had the responsibility of taking a more prominent part in the performance of church music in the abbey. Earlier, in 1848, he had received a fine testimonial from Kattinger who complimented him on his figured bass playing - 'the fruit of conscientious theoretical study' - and his improvisational abilities, and was confident that he would acquit himself with distinction in an open examination.[11] It was probably at about this time that Bruckner was able to test himself against Kattinger and Anton Weiß from Wilhering abbey in an organ improvisation contest at St. Florian. According to Joseph Seiberl,

---

9 See G-A II/1 (1928), 69. See also Altman Kellner, *Musikgeschichte des Stiftes Kremsmünster* (Kassel, 1956), 673ff. where the diarist is given as Theodor Hagn.

10 There is a facsimile of a double page of the register of members of the St. Florian branch of the National Guard, signed by the commandant, Georg Ruckensteiner, and dated 7 February 1849, in Erich W. Partsch, 'Unbekannte Bruckner -Dokumente zum Revolutionsjahr 1848' in *IBG Mitteilungsblatt* 44 (Vienna, June 1995), 24f. The original is in the *Oberösterreichisches Landesarchiv*, Linz.

11 The full text of the testimonial, dated St. Florian, 2 March 1848, can be found in G-A II/1, 95f. and Leopold Nowak, *Anton Bruckner. Musik und Leben* (Linz, 1973), 311. There is also a facsmile of the testimonial in the latter, p. 69; the original is in St. Florian. Kattinger's testimonial cannot be considered as a recommendation for Bruckner to succeed him as abbey organist (as stated in G-A II/1, 95), but should simply be viewed in the same light as another testimonial from Joseph Pfeiffer in 1848; see footnote 13. Nor is there any evidence to suggest that Bruckner was appointed provisional organist as early as 1848. It seems that Kattinger did not leave St. Florian until late 1849, after the death of his wife.

Bruckner's playing at this time did not have the contrapuntal mastery, not to say the rich inventiveness, evident in later performances.[12] Nevertheless, he was a good enough player to impress Josef Pfeiffer, a well-known provincial composer and the organist of Seitenstetten abbey, who furnished Bruckner with a glowing testimonial and predicted a very bright future for the young musician both as an organist and, on the strength of some compositions he had seen, as a composer.[13]

As the provisional organist Bruckner received an annual salary of 80 florins. This, together with the income he received as a schoolteacher and private teacher, made him feel 'like a prince', as he recalled later in life. He was certainly not attracted to a piano teaching position at as school in Kremsmünster which was offered to him in 1848. Bruckner's growing mastery of the organ and his sensitivity to the splendid surroundings were, as Göllerich points out, to exert an influence on his later symphonic compositions:

> ... Bruckner's later stature as a symphonist can only be properly understood when it is traced back to his time of growing and maturing at the great organ of St. Florian. His unbounded youthful enthusiasm and keen imagination were overwhelmed by the total art work of the Catholic religion with its colossal architecture, magnificent paintings, splendid vestments, narcotic clouds of incense, majestic singing and the sound of the full organ.[14]

---

12 See also Chapter 1, footnote 27. For further remarks about Bruckner's organ playing in his early years, see Othmar Wessely, 'Der junge Bruckner und sein Orgelspiel' in *ABDS* 10 (1994), 62ff., and Erwin Horn, 'Zwischen Interpretation und Improvisation. Anton Bruckner als Organist' in *BSL 1995* (Linz, 1997), 111-39.

13 See *G-A* II/1, 97f. and Othmar Wessely, *ABDS* 10, 94 for the text of this testimonial, dated Seitenstetten, 1 July 1848; the original is in St. Florian. Josef Anton Pfeiffer (1776-1859) was also a school director in Seitenstetten. One of his pupils was Josef Seiberl, later organist of St. Florian abbey [not to be confused with the other Josef Seiberl who attended the teacher-training course in Linz at the same time as Bruckner! - see also footnote 17].

14 *G-A* II/1, 99.

Although music was beginning to occupy more and more of Bruckner's energy and attention, he by no means neglected his schoolmaster duties. A new improved two-year course to prepare candidates for high school teaching had been introduced in Linz, and Bruckner entered the course as an external candidate in 1850, receiving help from Johann Paulitsch and Ferdinand Aigner, two of the St. Florian priests. Between May 1850 and October 1851 Bruckner sat four sets of examinations, passing most of them with distinction. References which he received from Michael Arneth, abbot of St. Florian, and Jodok Stülz, the parish priest, have been interpreted as a kind of corrective to criticism he may have received from some townspeople concerning the possible neglect of his teaching duties. Franz Zamazal, however, is inclined to the view that it was 'the assurance of a service contract with St. Florian abbey for an indefinite period, with the qualification that it would last as long as Bruckner fulfilled his duties to the satisfaction of his superiors'.[15] Both Arneth and Stülz were entirely satisfied with his conduct and conscientious application. Indeed, Stülz was at pains to point out that Bruckner had:

> ... gained the respect and love of all the parishioners not only because of his devotion to teaching and friendly and benevolent treatment of the schoolchildren but also as a result of his indefatigable efforts to develop his skills as a teacher and musician and his general behaviour which was entirely respectable and beyond reproach.[16]

---

15 Franz Zamazal, 'Bruckner als Volksschullehrer', *BSL 1988* (Linz, 1992), 33; cf. *G-A* II/1, 110f. See also idem, *ABDS* 10, 231 and 237ff. for details of the examination certificates Bruckner received; the originals are in St. Florian.

16 The texts of Stülz's and Arneth's testimonials, dated 6 and 13 September 1851 respectively, can be found in *G-A* II/1, 111f. There is a facsimile of the former in Hans Conrad Fischer, *Anton Bruckner. Sein Leben. Eine Dokumentation* (Salzburg, 1974), 69; the originals of both are in St. Florian. Jodok Stülz (1799-1872) was a noted theologian and historian. He became parish priest of St. Florian in 1853, dean of the abbey in October 1854, and succeeded Friedrich Mayr (1793-1858) as abbot in 1859. For further information about both Stülz and Mayr, see Karl Rehberger, 'St.

Life at St. Florian was by no means idyllic. By 1852 Bruckner was clearly unsettled and was feeling more and more isolated. Perhaps he was niggled by the fact that his provisional appointment as organist had not been made definitive.[17] His desire to get married remained unfulfilled, and there was yet another unrequited love affair - this time involving a girl called Antonie Werner, daughter of the local tax inspector. In March Bruckner wrote to his friend Josef Seiberl, now a teacher in St. Marienkirchen, informing him of some of the changes that had taken place at St. Florian and enclosing the manuscript copy of *Die Geburt* WAB 69, a piece for male-voice choir dedicated to Seiberl and written specially for his name-day. Bruckner was quite clearly at a low ebb emotionally:

> ... I have very few friends that I can really call friends, and when one of them asks for something, it will certainly not be forgotten - particularly when that one is you! Ehrenecker is in Enns. His successor, Ebner from Dietach, has had to return home again to visit his ailing father. Schäfler has died of a nervous disease; my Requiem was performed at his funeral on 11 March. You can see what terrible changes there have been. I sit all alone in my little room, forsaken and very sad. Let me hear from you soon...[18]

Florian und Anton Bruckner bis 1855. Einige neue Aspekte' in *BSL 1994* (Linz, 1997), 33-36.

17 It is possible, of course, that there was a 'gentlemen's agreement' about this (perhaps later?) In the reference which Ignaz Traumihler supplied for Bruckner in December 1855 when he was applying for the post of organist at Linz Cathedral, there is a clear suggestion that Bruckner was by that time officially recognized as principal organist.

18 See Andrea Harrandt and Otto Schneider, eds., *Bruckner Briefe 1 (1852-1886)* [hereafter *HSABB* 1], *ABSW* 24/1(Vienna: Musikwissenschaftlicher Verlag, 1998), 1, for this letter, the first of his to be preserved, from Bruckner to Seiberl, dated St. Florian, 19 March 1852. Josef Seiberl (1824-1908) was school assistant in Hörsching and Eferding in the years 1843-47 and head teacher in St. Marienkirchen bei Eferding from 1856. Anton Ehrenecker (b. 1826) was another school assistant and tenor singer at St. Florian before his move to Enns. Ebner (from Dietach, a village between Enns and Steyr) was Ehrenecker's successor for a short time, and Franz X. Schäfler had

Bruckner turned his attention once again to studying for another examination - the *Hauptlehrer-Prüfung* - in Linz with a view to gaining additional qualifications as a teacher. He applied on 3 April 1852 to sit the examination on 22 and 23 June but did not include all the necessary certification. Permission was eventually granted on 12 June, but, by that time, Bruckner seems to have had second thoughts about taking the examination. It was not until January 1855 that he secured this qualification. Franz Scheder suggests that the death of Anton Kattinger in Kremsmünster on 17 June 1852 may have caused Bruckner to postpone the examination temporarily.[19] But Bruckner was also setting his sights beyond St. Florian and Linz to Vienna. In 1851, Ignaz Aßmayr, the principal director of music at the Viennese court, met Bruckner for the first time when he visited St. Florian.[20]

At the beginning of 1852 Bruckner travelled to Vienna to visit Aßmayr, taking with him a copy of his *Requiem*. In the course of the year Bruckner was particularly active as a composer, writing settings of *Psalm 22* WAB 34, the *Magnificat* WAB 24, and *Psalm 114* WAB 36. He dedicated the latter to Aßmayr and sent it to him on July for his name-day. The accompanying letter is full of gratitude for Aßmayr's advice and encouragement to 'continue composing diligently', but also contains further evidence of Bruckner's increasing sense of isolation at St. Florian. It was generally recognized that priests in the Augustinian order maintained a rather cool

---

been on the administrative staff of the abbey as well conducting the choir from 1841 to 1852. His funeral was on 11March 1852.

19 See Franz Scheder, *Anton Bruckner Chronologie. Textband* [hereafter *SchABCT*] (Tutzing: Schneider, 1996), 61. See *HSABB* 1, 1f. for Bruckner's letter of application to the Episcopal Consistory, Linz, dated St. Florian, 3 April 1852; also Franz Zamazal, *BSL 1988*, 33 and *ABDS* 10, 231f. and 239ff. for further details of the application procedure in 1852; the original documents are located in the *Ordinariatsarchiv*, Linz.

20 Ignaz Aßmayr (1790-1862) was a prominent figure in Viennese musical life. Formerly a pupil of Michael Haydn and a friend of Schubert he had now attained one of the most prestigious posts in Vienna and was a respected composer of church music.

and distant relationship with those who were employed by them but not officially part of them:

> ... There is hardly anyone here to whom I can open my heart and I am frequently misunderstood - I often find that very difficult to bear. Our monastery treats music and consequently musicians as well with complete indifference. If only I could speak to you again very soon! I know your excellent heart - what a consolation! I can never be happy here, and dare not reveal any plans I might have...[21]

When Bruckner complained in his letter about the abbey's poor treatment of musicians, he possibly had in mind the fact that Kattinger's emolument had been supplemented by a much larger salary from his secular occupation. In recalling later that he felt 'like a prince', he obviously forgot his disenchantment with conditions at St. Florian while he stayed there. Bruckner even took on the unpaid job of a civil servant in the town from 1851 to 1853, no doubt an attempt to gain the necessary experience so that he could eventually aspire to the same kind of salary as Kattinger. There was also an element of uncertainty about where his future lay. By now an inveterate collector of testimonials, he procured one from Johann Mauser, the district judge, on 20 July 1853 and used it in applying unsuccessfully for a vacant full-time post in the civil service.[22] Göllerich is no doubt right in suggesting that the successful legal career being pursued by his former schoolboy friend Karl Seiberl,

---

21 See *HSABB* 1, 2f. for this letter, dated St. Florian, 30 July 1852; the original is owned privately.

22 Bruckner sent a letter, dated St. Florian, 25 July 1853, to the *Organisierungs-Kommission*, Linz. He enclosed various documents, including a baptismal certificate, a medical certificate and teaching certificates; the original of this letter is in St. Florian. See *HSABB* 1, 3f. for this letter and for the eventual reply (9 October 1854) [!] There is a facsimile of a portion of this letter in Franz Grasberger, *Anton Bruckner zum 150. Geburtstag. Eine Ausstellung im Prunksaal der Österreichischen Nationalbibliothek* [*ABA* hereafter] (Vienna, 1974), 10; there is also a facsmile of Mauser's testimonial in Hans C. Fischer, op.cit., 68.

now a student in Vienna, as well as the attraction of the city itself were further contributory factors to Bruckner's unease at the time.[23] Two months later, in September 1853, Bruckner received some timely advice and direction from Franz Scharschmid. Scharschmid advised him against embarking upon a career, namely the legal profession, to which he was not suited by nature, criticised him for his one-sided leaning on Mendelssohn as a model and held up Bach as *the* example to be followed. He advised him further to stay in his present job because it would possibly lead to another in which he would be able to devote himself exclusively to music. 'The path of the true artist' was 'strewn with thorns', but it was those who were able 'to summon up the moral strength within them' and were not afraid to 'struggle against these external difficulties' who 'achieved recognition, fame and heavenly blessing'.[24]

In 1854 Bruckner's compositional activities increased, largely as the result of an event which caused him great personal sadness, the death of Michael Arneth who had been a sort of father-figure to him since the death of his own father in 1837. For Arneth's funeral ceremony on 28 March he wrote *Vor Arneths Grabe* WAB 53 for male voices with trombone accompaniment, and a *Libera me* in F minor WAB 22 for five-part mixed voice choir, trombones, cello, bass and organ.[25] For the inauguration of Arneth's successor, Friedrich Mayr, on 14 September Bruckner wrote his most ambitious work to date, a *Missa solemnis* in B flat minor WAB 29

---

23 See *G-A* II/1, 145 and *GrBL*, 102f. After completing his studies, Seiberl came to St. Florian in 1855 as a probationary lawyer. Even at this time Bruckner was still contemplating a legal career and was pursuing further Latin studies to this end.

24 See *HSABB* 1, 4f. for Scharschmid's letter to Bruckner, dated Dresden, 20 September 1853; the original is in the *ÖNB*. This is Scharschmid's reply to a letter from Bruckner which has been lost. Bruckner had evidently written or spoken to Scharschmid, Baron of Adlertreu (1800-77), an appeal judge and president of the district court in Salzburg and Vienna, and asked him for career advice.

25 Bruckner's *Requiem* was performed at the exequies a week later.

40

40

for four-part mixed voice choir, soloists, orchestra and organ. Having worked furiously to prepare the Mass for the first performance, Bruckner was deeply hurt when he was not invited to dine with the guests at the banquet after the ceremony. Göllerich records that he booked a table for himself at one of the local inns and ordered a five-course meal and three different types of wine because, as he quaintly put it, 'the Mass deserved it'.[26] The following month Bruckner asked Aßmayr to examine his organ playing, including the improvisation of a double fugue. The examination took place in Vienna in October and Aßmayr was duly impressed, noting that Bruckner had shown himself to be a 'skilful organist with a sound technique'.[27]

Bruckner's studies for the *Hauptlehrer-Prüfung* in Linz reached a successful conclusion in January 1855 when he received 'very good' results.[28] There is no indication that he made immediate use of his new certificate to apply for a better teaching position. In any case, Bruckner's career was gradually beginning to take a different direction. A visit to St. Florian by the celebrated organ virtuoso from Prague, Robert Führer, prompted Bruckner to show him his recently completed B flat minor Mass and to improvise on the organ. Führer not only provided him with

---

26 *G-A* II/1, 176. Mayr, who had been director of the abbey chancellery from 1825 to 1848, was well-disposed towards music and musicians, however. During his brief spell as abbot (he died in Rome in 1858), he made it his concern to improve the standard of plainchant singing which appears to have gone into decline.

27 See *G-A* II/1, 148f. and Othmar Wessely, *ABDS* 10, 94 for further details, including the text of Aßmayr's testimonial, dated Vienna, 9 October 1854. The original of the testimonial is in St. Florian; there is a facsimile in Alfred Orel, *Anton Bruckner. Sein Leben in Bildern* (Leipzig, 1936), no. 12.

28 The examination was spread over two days, 25 and 26 January. See *G-A* II/1, 177f. for the text of the certificate Bruckner received, dated Linz, 28 January 1855. The original of the certificate is in St. Florian; there is a facsimile in Leopold Nowak, *Anton Bruckner. Musik und Leben* (Linz, 1973), 72.

an extremely complimentary testimonial, praising his theoretical and compositional skills and describing him as 'one of the most talented and skilful organists of our time', but advised him to continue his theoretical studies with Simon Sechter in Vienna.[29] As Friedrich Mayr had given him similar advice after hearing the Mass, Bruckner took this as confirmation that he should take the necessary steps to contact Sechter.[30] In July 1855 he visited Sechter in Vienna, showed him his recent Mass and was accepted as his pupil. Schubert had one counterpoint lesson from Sechter shortly before his death in 1828. Now, 27 years later, Bruckner was about to embark on a marathon course of harmony and counterpoint studies which was to last for six years. Much of it was carried out by correspondence, but a considerable amount was achieved during visits to Vienna - normally twice a year, at Advent or Lent or during the summer vacations - when the eager student would often spend entire days with his teacher working through exercises, almost certainly using Sechter's recently published *Die Grundsätze der musikalischen Kompositionslehre* as his main text book.[31]

Sechter's perception that Bruckner's musical development would not gain

29 See *G-A* II/1, 185 for the details of Führer's testimonial, dated St. Florian, 27 April 1855. The original is in the *ÖNB*; there is a facsimile in Franz Grasberger, *Anton Bruckner zwischen Wagnis und Sicherheit. Ausstellung im Rahmen des Internationalen Brucknerfestes* (Linz, 1977), 29.

30 Simon Sechter (1788-1867) was born in Friedberg, Bohemia and moved to Vienna in 1804. He established an international reputation as a composer, organist and, not least, theoretician. He was court organist in Vienna from 1824 to 1863, professor of Harmony and Counterpoint at the Vienna Conservatory from 1851 to 1866, and an honorary member of the Salzburg *Mozarteum* and the Vienna *Gesellschaft der Musikfreunde*.

31 Bruckner wrote copious notes in the margins of his copies of the three volumes of *Die Grundsätze* (Leipzig, 1853/54). These are now in the *ÖNB*. See *G-A* III/1 (1932), 72 and *ABA*, 68 for facsimiles of pages from these volumes. See also Ernst Tittel, 'Bruckners musikalischer Ausbildungsgang' in *Bruckner-Studien* (Vienna, 1964), 105-11.

further momentum if he remained at St. Florian accentuated his feelings of discontent and led him to apply for the vacant position of cathedral organist at Olmütz during the summer of 1855, an unsuccessful venture which, furthermore, earned him the stern rebuke of Mayr. On 13 November Alfred Just, an organ tuner from Linz, visited St. Florian abbey to tune the organ, expecting Bruckner to be at Linz participating in the contest to decide who should succeed Wenzel Pranghofer as cathedral organist.[32] He was amazed that Bruckner had not formally applied for the post and persuaded him to go to Linz. Bruckner first called on his former teacher, August Dürrnberger, and then accompanied him to the parish church to listen to the other two applicants, Engelbert Lanz, a schoolteacher and composer from Linz, and Raimund Hain, also a schoolteacher from Linz. It was with some reluctance that Bruckner finally entered the competition and improvised on a theme submitted by Dürrnberger himself. There was no doubt that he was by far the most accomplished organist and, although he was not the unanimous choice, he was appointed to the post, albeit on a provisional 'caretaker' basis.[33] On 14 November Bruckner received a letter from the administrative office of the cathedral, signed by Schiedermayr, Dierzer von Traunthal and Franz Guggeneder. This was both an official confirmation of his appointment and an indication of what would be expected of him:

---

32   Wenzel Pranghofer (c. 1805-1855) had held the post on a provisional basis from 1 February 1840 and on a permanent basis from 13 June 1843. He died on 9 November 1855.

33   The members of the listening panel were the cathedral canon, Johann Baptist Schiedermayr, and curate, Georg Arminger, Vinzenz Fink, assistant mayor of Linz, Anton M. Storch, choirmaster of the Linz choir, *Frohsinn*, Karl Zappe, orchestral director at the Landständisches Theater in Linz, and August Dürrnberger. Further details of the contest and the adjudicators' reactions can be found in *G-A* II/1, 191ff., Othmar Wessely, 'Anton Bruckner und Linz' in *Jahrbuch der Stadt Linz 1954* (Linz, 1955), 211ff. and Elisabeth Maier, '"Kirchenmusik auf schiefen Bahnen". Zur Situation in Linz von 1850 bis 1900' in *BSL 1990* (Linz, 1993), 112f. The original documents are located in the *Stadtpfarrarchiv*, Linz

... You are expected to take up this position immediately and are required to discharge your duties in public worship with propriety at all times and in such a manner as to edify the congregation. You must not be dilatory in your duties, you should strive to form good relationships with the musical director and with the other musicians, and you should do your utmost to maintain the good reputation which you have acquired...[34]

On 15 November the following report of the contest appeared in the *Linzer Zeitung*:

... The contest for the provisional post of cathedral organist in Linz, held on the 13th, was of particular interest. The adjudicators consisted of Dr. Schiedermayr, canon of the cathedral; Arminger, the curate; Vinzenz Fink, representative of the town council; Professor Dürrnberger and A.M. Storch, the music director. A considerable number of music lovers and connoisseurs were also present. The candidates were set the task of developing a theme, provided by Professor Dürrnberger and written down immediately before the performance, into a complete fugue according to the rules of strict counterpoint. This task was performed by the candidates with much skill for the most part but, according to the unanimous decision of the jury and the connoisseurs, was undertaken with distinction by Mr. Anton Bruckner from St. Florian, with the result that, as announced yesterday, the position of cathedral organist in Linz was offered to him on a provisional basis.[35]

A contest for the definitive, permanent appointment was arranged for 25 January 1856. By mid-December, however, Bruckner had not put his name forward as an

---

34 See *G-A* II/1, 191f. Bruckner's provisional appointment was reported in the *Linzer Zeitung* 271 (14 November 1855) and the *Linzer Abendbote* (also 14 November 1855).

35 See Franz Gräflinger, *Anton Bruckner. Bausteine zu seiner Lebensgeschichte* (Munich, 1911), 18f., Elisabeth Maier, *BSL 1990*, 112 and Othmar Wessely, *ABDS* 10, 95 for the text of this article which appeared in the *Linzer Zeitung* 272 (15 November 1855), 1131. There is a facsimile of the article in *ABA*, 12. The report is not completely accurate. Zappe, one of the adjudicators, is not mentioned, and Bruckner won a majority, but not a unanimous decision.

44

official competitor, although he had played at the Cathedral for the first time in his capacity as provisional organist on 8 December.[36] His seeming reluctance and dilatoriness came to the attention of two well-wishers, Georg Ruckensteiner and Joseph Weichardt, who recognized his worth and advised him to be more careful about his personal appearance while 'on duty' and to make a greater effort to cultivate friends in high places, including Schiedermayr and Josef Dierzer von Traunthal, president of the chamber of commerce and a town councillor![37] Bruckner's reluctance to put himself forward was almost certainly due to misgivings about taking such a major step and leaving the comparative security of St. Florian for the unknown and faster-paced town life of the provincial capital. Having received Mayr's blessing together with his assurance that the organist post at St. Florian would be kept free for two years in the event of his not staying at Linz, Bruckner finally made an official application on 18 December. At the same time he obtained two testimonials - a character reference from his parish priest, Jodok Stülz, and a reference giving particular prominence to his musical abilities from Ignaz Traumihler, choir director at St. Florian.[38] On 25 December he wrote to the parish

---

36 See G-A II/1, 193 and Altman Kellner, op.cit., 213.

37 See HSABB 1, 5f. for the texts of these letters, the first from Georg Ruckensteiner (see footnote 8), a judge at St. Florian and district councillor in Linz (dated Linz, 17 December 1855), the second from Joseph Weichhart, a church administrator in Linz (dated 18 December 1855); the originals of both are in St. Florian. The second survived in spite of Weichardt's request that Bruckner destroy it immediately. The particular official occasion to which they were referring was probably the 'oath of service' ceremony on 26 November.

38 See HSABB 1, 6f. for the text of Bruckner's application in a letter to the Linz parish council, dated St. Florian, 18 December 1855. The original is in the Archiv der Stadt Linz; there is a facsimile of part of it in ABA, 13. See G-A II/1, 208ff. for the texts of Stülz's testimonial, dated 15 December 1855, and Traumihler's testimonial (countersigned by Mayr), dated 19 December 1855. The originals are in St. Florian.

office in Linz, expressing concern about the condition of the new organ (built by Ludwig Mooser in 1852) in the parish church. Manuals and pedals were in need of mechanical repair and a better windflow was required for the sake of good intonation. Bruckner was clearly taking his position, albeit still provisional at this stage, very seriously![39]

Although the Linz district council gave its official recognition to Bruckner as the most suitable candidate for the permanent postion of cathedral organist, Schiedermayr insisted that a second competition be held. On 21 January 1856 Bruckner was sent official notice of his participation in the competition.[40] Four days later he was to prove once again that he was the best man for the job. His fellow competitors were Georg Müller, a music teacher from Linz, Ludwig Paupié, parish organist from Wels, and Raimund Hain. Engelbert Lanz, who had participated with Hain and Bruckner in the earlier contest, had obviously lost interest. The adjudicators included Joseph Storch, a priest, Vinzenz Fink, Franz Guggeneder, a diocesan commissioner in Linz, August Dürrnberger, Georg Arminger and Anton Storch. According to the official diocesan report of the proceedings, Bruckner was the clear winner, and only one of his rivals, Raimund Hain, came anywhere near his level of competence. He evidently acquitted himself with distinction in the two tests - improvisation of a fugue on a

---

39 See *HSABB*, 8 for the text of this letter. The original is in the *Archiv der Stadt Linz*. Also see Elisabeth Maier, *BSL 1990*, 111 and 114 for further references to the state of the organ in letters from Hofstedter to Mooser (3 January 1856) and from Mooser to the Linz district council (15 February 1856).

40 See *G-A* II/1, 196 for the text of this letter, signed by Dierzer von Traunthal. Also see Othmar Wessely, *Anton Bruckner und Linz*, 216f. for the council's original recommendation (dated 11 January 1856) and Schiedermayr's counter-recommendation (c. 18 January 1856) that another contest be held. The relevant documents, including further correspondence between the 'sacred' and 'secular' departments of the administration after the contest, can be found in the *Stadtpfarrarchiv*, Linz.

given theme, and plainsong accompaniment - and reference was also made to the mastery he had already shown in his 'well-known and very well-written church music compositions'.[41] Another report, signed by Dierzer Ritter von Traunthal who had been present at both contests, was unequivocal in its assessment of Bruckner's merits:

> ... I believe that I should recommend Anton Bruckner as the most suitable and deserving for the following reasons, viz.
> 1. Because he had already shown that he was the most able candidate at the provisional contest and was appointed provisionally in the expectation that he would be offered the position permanently, since a provisional appointment normally becomes a permanent one;
> 2. Anton Bruckner has already justified the confidence placed in him to the fullest extent during the period of his provisional appointment, and we have good reason to expect that with his artistic tastes and particular love of music, especially church music, he will continue to justify this confidence in the future;
> 3. He has been educated in an extremely prestigious abbey where he has had more opportunity than any of the other candidates to develop his skill in plainsong accompaniment which is particularly necessary for a cathedral;
> 4. In order to pursue his musical career he has given up his position as organist and school assistant at St. Florian and, if one of the other candidates were preferred to him, would consequently be unemployed as he pursued his honourable vocation - an outcome all the more unjust in view of the fact that each of the other candidates still has a position or at least a means of livelihood in which to further his career.[42] Moreover, according to the report of the

---

41 See *G-A* II/1, 197-201 and *GrBL*, 21-24 for the text of this report which was written on the same day as the competition; the original is in the *Stadtpfarrarchiv*, Linz. Dates are given in *GrBL* for notes confirming the appointment sent by the bishop's office to the provincial and church administration offices in Linz (11 April 1856) and the reply from the district council (20 May 1856); the original of the former is in the *Oberösterreichisches Landesarchiv*, and that of the latter is in St. Florian.

42 Bruckner had indeed 'burned his boats' in the expectation of securing the appointment. He received his final payments as school assistant and organist just before Christmas 1855 and moved

examination held on 25 January this year, Anton Bruckner clearly distinguished himself above the other candidates. In these circumstances the esteemed church administrators (according to the note attached) are in complete agreement with these recommendations. In conclusion, I believe that I should also mention the fact that Anton Bruckner has a poor, ageing mother for whose sake he has given up his former posts so that he can be more readily in a position to support her in her old age. His moral integrity is beyond doubt, according to the most reliable sources, and is certainly not exceeded by any of the other candidates. For all these reasons I take this liberty of requesting that Anton Bruckner's appointment as cathedral and parish church organist be given favourable consideration and that these recommendations be implemented.[43]

On 25 April a formal contract was sent to Bruckner. He was officially appointed cathedral and parish church organist with an annual salary of 448 florins. He was also eligible for certain additional fees and could stay rent-free in one of the church houses - the 'Meßnerhäusel' on the Pfarrplatz.[44] Bruckner took his oath of office on 14 May.[45] But he was certainly acting in some kind of official capacity as early as March. On 30 March, he played the organ at a special service in the cathedral to celebrate the anniversary of the founding of *Frohsinn*, the choral society which he had already joined as a second tenor. There were favourable comments on his organ

---

temporarily to the Florianerhaus, Landstraße 22 in Linz.

43 See *GrBL*, 19ff. for this letter, dated Linz, 5 March 1856; the original is in the *Oberösterreichisches Landesarchiv*, Linz.

44 See *G-A* II/1, 203f. and Manfred Wagner, *Bruckner* (Mainz, 1983), 58ff. for the full text of the contract; the original is in St. Florian. The fact that there was no pension with the job was later to assume some importance when Bruckner was in two minds whether to move to Vienna in 1868. The actual date of his move from temporary to permanent accommodation in Linz is not certain. There are conflicting views in the Bruckner literature.

45 See Wessely, *Anton Bruckner und Linz*, 219f. for the text of this oath of office; the original can be found in the *Stadtpfarrarchiv*, Linz.

playing in the *Linzer Abendbote* the following day.[46]

Although the important physical break with St. Florian had now been made, giving Bruckner the opportunity to spread his wings and continue his development as a composer in a more favourable environment, he maintained close links with the abbey. In the Vienna years in particular, it became a spiritual sanctuary for him, a place to which he could escape from the pressures of teaching and composing and in which he could both relax and work in a more restful atmosphere. As a keen swimmer he made use of the facilities of the abbey's private swimming pool. He was also able to spend some time with his brother Ignaz who was employed at the abbey first as a gardener, then as a general handyman. His visits to St. Florian in the years 1881-86 are particularly well documented in the correspondence between two admirers of his compositional and organ-playing skills, Simon Ledermüller, a priest at St. Florian, and Oddo Loidol, a priest at Kremsmünster and former pupil of his at the Vienna Conservatory.[47] Bruckner was on good terms with the musical staff at St. Florian. When his successor as organist, Josef Seiberl, died in 1877 Bruckner recommended Hans Rott, one of his pupils at the Vienna Conservatory, for the post. But when the post was eventually filled in 1878, it went to Josef Gruber. In July 1879 Bruckner composed the gradual *Os justi* WAB 30 and dedicated it to Ignaz Traumihler, choir director at the abbey. Traumihler was seriously ill when Bruckner visited St. Florian in the summer of 1884. He died in October and Bruckner played the organ at his funeral. After a performance of Mozart's *Requiem*, Bruckner improvised on the themes of the double fugue from the end of the *Agnus Dei*.[48]

---

46 See Wessely, op.cit., 223f. for an extract from this review; there is also a facsimile of the review in the *Stadtarchiv*, Linz.

47 Extracts from this correspondence can be found in *G-A* II/1, 273ff.

48 Ignaz Traumihler (1815-1884) came to St. Florian in 1835 and was ordained as a priest in 1840. He was choir director at the abbey from 1852 until his death and a firm supporter of the Caecilian church music reform movement. Bruckner dedicated his *Magnificat* WAB 24 (1852), *Ave Maria*

Traumihler's successor, Bernhard Deubler, corresponded regularly with Bruckner and was responsible for several performances of the composer's works in the abbey, including two performances of his *Requiem* in November 1887 and November 1888 and the first performance of the motet *Vexilla regis* WAB 51 on 15 April 1892. Karl Aigner, choirboy at the abbey and, from 1881, music teacher of the choirboys, became a close friend of Bruckner in the later 1880s and was often asked to give his opinion of the composer's latest revisions of his symphonies, some of which were undertaken during his St. Florian vacations. Aigner has left the following account of his cordial relationship with Bruckner:

> ... Musically his formative influence was of great value to me. He often asked me to be with him when he was working, and if I ventured my opinion his response was really like that of a happy child. When Bruckner played on the large organ I was regularly called upon to change the registration. I was able to identify with his playing in such a way that I had an extremely free hand in combining the different stops without any indication from him; indeed he was so accustomed to my help that he would not play if I was not there.
> Above all, I will never forget his incomparable, masterly organ organ performances. On another occasion he listened, without my being aware of it, to my violin playing; he often asked me to play one or another passage from his splendid Adagios to him.[49]

Bruckner for his part referred in glowing terms to Aigner's virtuoso violin playing and excellence as a pianist and organist in a testimonial he provided for his young

---

WAB 5 (1856) and two organ works, *Vorspiel* WAB 130 (c.1852) and *Nachspiel* WAB 126 (c.1852) to him.

49 Karl Aigner (1863-1935) was a bank clerk by profession. He possessed a few original manuscripts and several copies of Bruckner's works which were later procured by the *ÖNB*. See *G-A* II/1, 261f. for Aigner's account.

50

friend in April 1894.[50] He had just returned to Vienna after spending Holy Week at St. Florian and participating in some of the services. On Easter Sunday he had played the abbey organ for the last time, a free improvisation on the fugal theme from his setting of *Psalm 150* WAB 38.

Two and a half years later, on 15 October 1896, Bruckner's coffin was brought into the abbey, accompanied by reminiscences from Wagner's *Parsifal*. His own setting of *Libera me* WAB 22, which had been sung for the first time at Michael Arneth's funeral 42 years earlier, was then performed. In accordance with his wishes his coffin was placed below the organ and a marble plaque now marks the spot below which it rests. The following day another Bruckner work closely associated with the abbey - the *Requiem* - was performed at a memorial service, a fitting tribute to a composer whose links with St. Florian spanned a period of nearly 60 years.

2.2 The Music

Bruckner's St. Florian works show a gradual development in technical expertise but, with one or two exceptions, rarely rise above the average level of contemporary sacred and secular music. At the age of 31 Mozart, Schubert and Mendelssohn had all written the bulk of their finest work and Beethoven was embarking upon the 'second period' of his creative life. At the same age Bruckner was on his way from St. Florian to Linz having composed nothing as yet which gave any indication of the stature of the works to come. The reasons are not difficult to find. First of all, he had very little opportunity to hear and participate in contemporary music. His duties

---

50   See *G-A* II/1, 262f. for the text of this reference, which is dated Vienna, 4 April 1894 here but 14 April by Elisabeth Maier in '"Es wird schon einmahl eine Zeit kommen, wo es einen Wert haben wird..." Bruckneriana in Vöcklabruck', *Studien zur Musikwissenschaft* 42 (Tutzing, 1993), 297, note 27. The original of the reference is in the *ÖNB*.

as an organist prevented him from regularly attending concerts in Linz, and the music to which he had access at the monastery consisted mainly of Baroque and Classical works. Second, just as he was in awe of his superiors at St. Florian so he was afraid of going beyond the strict rules of music theory in his compositions. Indeed, this almost slavish observance of rules was to become even more marked during his period of study with Sechter. He was to remain 'imprisoned' within the Classical period until the early 1860s when, freed at last from the constraints of theoretical instruction, he began to write music of striking originality. All in all, in the areas of harmony, melody, rhythm and orchestration, these St. Florian works are predictable and, for the most part, unadventurous.

2.2.1 Secular and semi-sacred choral works

The most interesting of these works are *Der Lehrerstand* WAB 77 (c.1847) for *a cappella* male voices, dedicated to Michael Bogner, Bruckner's superior, and possibly performed by the St. Florian *Liedertafel* in the late 1840s; *Sternschnuppen* WAB 85 (1848) for *a cappella* male-voice quartet, written for Bruckner's own quartet and displaying strong Mendelssohnian influence; *Entsagen* WAB 14 (c. 1851) for soprano (or tenor) soloist, mixed voice choir, organ or piano, a 'spiritual song' in three sections, the outer sections in the form of a Protestant chorale and the middle section, a solo for soprano or tenor, rather repetitious and unappealing in its arid three-part semi-contrapuntal style; *Ständchen* WAB 84 (early 1850s) for *a cappella* male-voice quartet, essentially a tenor solo with a three-part 'humming' accompaniment which later has words added, and dedicated to Mrs. Schlager, the wife of the mayor of St. Florian from 1850 to 1862; *Die Geburt* WAB 69 (1852) for *a cappella* male-voice choir, an appealing work betraying a fondness for Schubertian mediant relationships; and *Vor Arneths Grabe* WAB 53 (1854) for male voices and three trombones, written specifically for the burial ceremony of Michael Arneth.[51]

On a larger scale are three occasional compositions: *Heil, Vater! Dir zum hohen Feste* WAB 61 (1852), a cantata for six-part mixed-voice choir, three horns, two trumpets and a trombone, written to a text by Ernst von Marinelli for the name-day of Michael Arneth and performed at the abbey on 28 or 29 September; *Auf, Brüder! auf, und die Saiten zur Hand* WAB 60 (1855), a cantata for male-voice quartet, male-voice choir, mixed-voice choir and a wind band consisting of two oboes, two bassoons, solo horns, two horns, two trumpets and three trombones, written on 17 July for the name-day of Friedrich Mayr; and *Sankt Jodok spross aus edlem Stamm* WAB 15 (1855), a cantata for soloists, mixed-voice choir and piano, completed on 6 December for the name-day of Jodok Stülz, the parish priest and perhaps intended

---

51 *Der Lehrerstand* is discussed in *G-A* II/1, 35ff. and its music is printed in *G-A* II/2, 16-22; the dedication reads:'gewidmet dem hochverehrten Herrn Michael Bogner, Schullehrer in St. Florian'. *Sternschnuppen* is discussed in *G-A* II/1, 65f. and its music is printed in *G-A* II/2, 94ff.; the text was provided by Ernst von Marinelli (1824-1887) who came to St. Florian as a novitiate priest in 1845, was curate there from 1850 to 1854, and was later active in Vienna as professor at the *Technische Militärakademie*. The text of the cantata *Entsagen*, dedicated to Michael Arneth on his name-day, is taken from Oskar von Redwitz's poem, *Amaranth*; it is discussed in *G-A* II/1, 44ff., there is a facsimile of the autograph in *G-A* II/2, 47-58, and there is a modern edition in *ABSW* XXII/1(Vienna, 1987), 49-56. *Ständchen* is discussed in *G-A* II/1, 47-51where there is also a facsimile of the sketch of the work; there is a facsimile of the fair copy in *G-A* II/2, 61-64; it was also printed by Robitschek in 1954 (A.R. 7178). *Die Geburt* is discussed in *G-A* II/1, 132ff. and its music is printed in *G-A* II/2, 147-50; Bruckner sent this work to his friend Josef Seiberl with an accompanying letter on 19 March 1852 - see page 39 and footnote 18. *Vor Arneths Grab* is discussed in *G-A* II/1, 152f. and its music is printed in *G-A* II/2, 184-88. See also Christoph Meran and Elisabeth Maier, 'Anton Bruckner und Charles O'Hegerty. Zur Geschichte eines lange verschollenen Bruckner-Autographs', *BJ 1994/95/96* (Linz, 1997), 195-210, concerning the five-part male-voice chorus *Des Dankes Wort sei mir vergönnt* WAB 62 (text by Marinelli) which Bruckner composed c. 1851 for Charles O'Hegerty whose daughters were piano pupils of Bruckner.

as a parting musical gift.[52] Another cantata - *Laßt Jubeltöne laut erklingen* WAB 76, scored for male-voice choir, two horns, two trumpets and four trombones - is undated but was possibly written for the *Frohsinn* choir to be performed at the reception in Linz of Princess Elisabeth on 22 April 1854.[53]

2.2.2 Sacred works

As one would expect from a young composer involved with music at St. Florian, there are several short sacred works. Most of them are no more than competent, but

---

52 The title-page of the autograph of *Heil, Vater!* contains a note to the effect that the work was performed again with an altered text five years later on the evening of 17 July 1857, the day before Friedrich Mayr's name-day. Bruckner used another Marinelli poem, omitted one of the solo quartet movements and made some slight alterations in the voice parts. The same music was used again - to a text by Beda Piringer: *Heil Dir zum schönen Erstlingsfeste* - for a performance in Kremsmünster. The cantata is discussed in *G-A* II/1, 112-30 (including a facsimile of the autograph of the second version). The music of the first version is printed in *ABSW* XXII/1, 57-75, and the music of the second version is printed in *G-A* II/2, 131-40 and *ABSW* XXII/1, 77-95. For a very full discussion of the different versions, see Paul Hawkshaw, *The Manuscript Sources for Anton Bruckner's Linz Works* (Ann Arbor, 1987), 214-21. *Auf, Brüder!*, *auf* is discussed in *G-A* II/1, 179-83; its music is printed in *G-A* II/2, 229-39 and *ABSW* XXII/1, 98-126. *Sankt Jodok spross* is discussed in *G-A* II/1, 205-08; there is a facsimile of the original manuscript, in which the piano part is incomplete, in *G-A* II/2, 241-54. See *ABSW* XXII/1, 127-45 for a modern edition of the work with a completed piano part.

53 The piece is discussed in *G-A* III/1 (1932), 536f., and the music is printed in *G-A* III/2, 162-79. The original text was by A. Weiß but a new text, *Dir holde Heimat soll erklingen*, was provided by A.A. Naaff in 1898. As there is no mention of a performance in the *Singakademie* [*Frohsinn*]archives (*Stadtarchiv*, Linz), contemporary newspaper reports and commemorative publications, it is probable that this chorus was not performed on 22 April but was replaced by another piece. For further information about this chorus and later pieces for male-voice choir, see Andrea Harrandt, 'Bruckner und das bürgerliche Musiziergut seiner Jugendzeit' in *BSL 1987* (Linz, 1989), 93-103; idem, 'Bruckner und die Chormusik seiner Zeit', in *Oberösterreichische Heimatblätter* 51 (1997), 184-95, and Angela Pachovsky, 'Bruckners weltliche Chorwerke', in *Bruckner-Vorträge. Bruckner-Tagung Wien 1999 Bericht* (Vienna, 2000), 35-46.

Bruckner had a high enough opinion of five of them - *Vier Tantum ergo* WAB 41 (1846) for mixed-voice choir and organ ad lib., and another setting of the same text, a *Tantum ergo* in D major WAB 42 (1846) for five-part mixed-voice choir and organ - to revise them in 1888.[54] Yet another setting of the text - a *Tantum ergo* in B flat major WAB 44 (1854 or 1855), scored for mixed-voice choir, two trumpets, violins and organ - has a typically 'busy' string accompaniment but is more adventurous melodically and harmonically.[55] As well as providing a secular piece, *Die Geburt*, in 1852 for his friend Josef Seiberl in Marienkirchen, Bruckner also sent him two *Totenlieder* WAB 47 and 48 for *a cappella* mixed-voice choir.[56] In similar vein, but for the mellow combination of three trombones, are the two *Aequale* WAB 114 and

---

54 The order of the first four settings of this *Corpus Christi* hymn according to the autograph parts in St. Florian and in Bruckner's 1888 revision is No. 1 in B flat major, No. 2 in A flat major, No. 3 in E flat major and No. 4 in C major. When Groß of Innsbruck published the pieces in 1893, the order was changed to E flat, C, B flat, A flat, and no organ part was provided. The fifth setting was also published by Groß in 1893. On the autograph parts there are some dates of performances at St. Florian, namely 20 January, 7 April and 4 August 1853, and 19 January 1854. The five pieces are discussed in *G-A* II/1, 52-58, *ABSW* XXI/1, 184 and *ABSW* XXI/2, 35-41 and 139-45. There are modern editions of the original versions in *ABSW* XXI/1, 41-51, and of the revised versions in *ABSW* XXI/1, 150-57.

55 This setting of the *Tantum ergo* is discussed in *G-A* II/1, 212f. and *ABSW* XXI/2, 55f. The music is printed in *G-A* II/2, 255-58 and *ABSW* XXI/1, 68-74.

56 These two short funeral pieces are discussed in *G-A* II/1, 131f. and *ABSW* XXI/2, 47-50; the music is printed in *G-A* II/2, 141-44 and *ABSW* XXI/1, 56f.

57 They are discussed in *G-A* II/1, 63 and *ABSW* XXI/2, 42ff. The first piece is printed in *G-A* II/2, 83; both pieces are printed in *ABSW* XXI/1, 52f., with the missing bass part of the second provided by Hans Bauernfeind.

115, written in January 1847 possibly in memory of his aunt, Rosalia Mayrhofer.[57] The longest and most impressive of these short sacred works is undoubtedly the *Libera me* in F minor WAB 22, written in March 1854 for Michael Arneth's funeral service and performed during the benediction after the Requiem Mass. As in the contemporary *Missa solemnis* in B flat minor, the influence of Haydn and Mozart is very much in evidence.[58]

On a much more substantial scale are five larger sacred works, the *Requiem* in D minor WAB 39 (1848-49), settings of the *Magnificat* WAB 24 (1852), *Psalm 22* WAB 34 (1852), *Psalm 114* WAB 36 (1852) and the *Missa solemnis* in B flat minor WAB 29 (1854).

The *Requiem*, Bruckner's first composition of any length, was written in memory of his friend Franz Sailer and was first performed at the abbey on 15 September 1849, the first anniversary of Sailer's death. It is scored for four soloists, mixed-voice choir, strings, three trombones and organ continuo.[59] Bruckner's knowledge of the *Requiem* literature in 1848 was almost certainly confined to a few settings of his Austrian predecessors, particularly those of Mozart and Weiß, whose Requiem in E flat had been a favourite of his since his year's stay at Hörsching in the mid-1830s, and probably did not include Cherubini's two settings in C minor (1815-16)

58 The *Libera me* is discussed in *G-A* II/1, 153ff. and *ABSW* XXI/2, 51-55. It was published for the first time by Universal Edition (U.E. 4976) in 1922. There is a modern edition in *ABSW* XXI/1, 58-67.

59 The first detailed discussion of the work can be found in *G-A* II/1, 68-92. The autograph full score (Mus. Hs. 2125 in the *ÖNB*) was completed on 14 March 1849. Various later annotations in the manuscript indicate that Bruckner revised the work during the summer of 1892. In its revised version it was dedicated to Franz Bayer, director of the parish church choir in Steyr who performed it there on 2 December 1895. The *Requiem* was first published by Benno Filser Verlag, Augsburg in 1930. See Leopold Nowak's comments regarding the layout of the score in the foreword to *ABSW* XIV (Vienna, 1966).

and D minor (1836) or Berlioz's highly individual and colourful setting (1837). Bruckner's particular debt to Mozart in points of style and structure and in a number of other details becomes evident in any detailed comparison between their works.

Bruckner's setting of the *Magnificat*, scored for soloists, chorus and an orchestra consisting of strings (without violas), two trumpets, timpani and organ continuo, was composed in August 1852 and dedicated to Ignaz Traumihler.[60] The Magnificat, part of the text of the Vespers, has its own traditional plainsong with which Bruckner would undoubtedly have been familiar. We do not know which earlier settings of the text - either as part of the sung Evening Service or as an independent work - Bruckner would have heard or studied, but we can surmise that he had some knowledge of works by Michael Haydn, Mozart and Schubert as well as those of lesser-known provincial composers. As in the *Requiem*, so in this work Mozart - the Mozart of the Litanies and Vespers - is the main influence.

The texts of Bruckner's five psalm settings are all in the German vernacular. His first two settings in particular - *Psalm 22* and *Psalm 114* - are more in the tradition of the Protestant psalm motets of Mendelssohn than the Catholic psalm motets and psalm cantatas (settings of the Vespers) of eighteenth- and early nineteenth-century composers. Having already studied Bach's chorale harmonizations, Bruckner was aware of the musical value of the Protestant chorale. In the mid-1840s he copied out Josef Preindl's collection of German church songs 'together with new cadences and introductions, which will be sung by the congregation with organ accompaniment throughout the year at St. Stephen's

---

60 The *Magnificat* is discussed in *G-A* II/1, 100-03 and by Paul Hawkshaw in the foreword to his edition of the full score, *ABSW* XX/3 (Vienna, 1996). There is also a short score of the work in *G-A* II/2, 99-110. The St. Florian abbey library contains an unsigned and undated set of parts, some written by Bruckner himself, some by an unknown copyist. The dedication date is 15 August 1852.

Cathedral in Vienna'.[61] Both *In jener letzten der Nächte* WAB 17 (c.1848) and *Dir, Herr, dir will ich mich ergeben* WAB 12 (c.1845) for *a cappella* mixed-voice choir are chorale harmonizations, probably the result of his studies with Zenetti.[62] When Bruckner moved to Linz in 1856 he retained his interest in Protestant church music. This is borne out by a letter which Gräflinger received from Iosef Hoffmann, choir director of the Lutheran church in Linz:

... Bruckner was very interested in the chorale 'O Haupt voll Blut und Wunden', well-known and sung often in all Lutheran congregations. On one occasion when I was with him in the organ loft (of the old cathedral) during a service, I had to sing very quietly and in an undertone the first line of this chorale, although it was very well known to him, whereupon he proceeded to make use of these seven notes as the theme of a masterly free fugue which he played as a postlude at the close [of the service].
So that he might hear this chorale sung by the congregation, he asked me once to inform him as soon as I knew that it would be sung in the Lutheran church in Linz. It was not long before I was able to comply with this request and I had hardly finished the opening voluntary on the day in question (it was during Lent) when he came with head bowed - probably so as to draw less attention to himself - through the choir entrance, sat down quite near the organ bench, and listened with the greatest devotion and attention to the congregational singing. He declined with thanks my invitation to him to accompany the singing. After he had heard four verses of the chorale he expressed his satisfaction with it in the words 'Ah, that is

---

61 Josef Preindl (1756-1823) was associate music director at St. Stephen's, Vienna from the early 1790s until his death.

62 *In jener letzten der Nächte* is a Maundy Thursday setting. It is discussed in *G-A* II/1, 94 and *ABSW* XXI/2, 44-47; the piece is printed in *G-A* II/2, 97f. and *ABSW* XXI/1, 54f. The autograph of *Dir, Herr, dir will ich mich ergeben* contains corrections made by Josef Pfeiffer, the organist of Seitenstetten abbey who provided Bruckner with a testimonial in 1848; see page 36 and footnote 13. The piece is discussed in *G-A* II/1, 110, *ABSW* XXI/1, 184 and *ABSW* XXI/2, 31f.; it is printed in *G-A* II/2, 114f. and *ABSW* XXI/1, 37.

58

beautiful' and left the church just as discreetly and imperceptibly as he had entered it'.[63]

There is a direct quotation from 'O Haupt voll Blut und Wunden' in the semi-sacred cantata *Entsagen* WAB 14 (c.1851).[64]

Bruckner's setting of *Psalm 22* WAB 34 is scored for four-part mixed-voice choir and piano and was composed presumably for private performance at St. Florian. It is quite clear that Bruckner was acquainted with the fine setting of the same text (Psalm 23 in the Lutheran translation and the Authorized Version of the bible) by Schubert, *Gott ist mein Hirt* D.706 (1820) for female voices and piano. There are several similarities in the piano writing.[65] The contemporary *Psalm 114* WAB 36, scored for five-part mixed-voice choir (SAATB) and three trombones, was dedicated to Ignaz Aßmayr and sent to him with an accompanying letter. The text is equivalent to verses 1-9 of Psalm 116 in the Lutheran translation and Authorized Version. One can discern Mendelssohnian influences in several places, but Bruckner was being unduly modest when he described the work as a 'weak attempt' in his dedication to Aßmayr.[66]

---

63   *GrBL*, 96.

64   See earlier and footnote 51.

65   Bruckner's setting of this Psalm remained unknown until 1921 when it was 'discovered' in St. Florian by Franz Müller. Its first 'modern' performance took place at the abbey on 11 October 1921, the 25th anniversary of Bruckner's death. Bruckner used the German translation by Allioli in the third edition of his 'The Scriptures according to the Old and New Testaments' (Landshut, 1838); there is a copy in the St. Florian library. For further discussion, see *G-A* II/1, 106ff. and Paul Hawkshaw's foreword to his edition of the work, *ABSW* XX/2 (Vienna, 1997); there is a facsimile of the original autograph in *G-A* II/2, 119-30.

66   See earlier and footnote 21 for details of Bruckner's letter to Aßmayr. The first performance of this Psalm was a private one, in the music room of the abbey, probably in July 1852. Göllerich

The *Missa solemnis* in B flat minor WAB 29, scored for soloists, mixed-voice choir and an orchestra consisting of two oboes, two bassoons, two horns, two trumpets, three trombones, timpani, strings and organ continuo, is the crowning achievement of Bruckner's years at St. Florian and, in Leopold Nowak's words, a 'summa musices' of the first thirty years of his life.[67] Sketches of two *Kyrie* movements, a *Kyrie* in G minor WAB 140 and a *Kyrie* in E flat major WAB 139, both undated but probably written in the mid- to late-1840s, reveal that Bruckner had already been contemplating a larger-scale setting of the Mass. The latter, a 58-bar fragment scored for mixed-voice choir, two oboes, three trombones, strings and organ continuo, is fairly ambitious in scope but can hardly be regarded as a preparation for the *Missa solemnis*.[68]

---

conducted the first public performance of the work in Linz in April 1906. The autograph score is in St. Florian, and the dedication copy sent to Aßmayr, which was not found until 1921, is privately owned. For further discussion, see *G-A* II/1, 136-42 and Paul Hawkshaw's foreword to his edition of the score, *ABSW* XX/1 (Vienna, 1997); there is a facsimile of the autograph in *G-A* II/2, 152-77. See also Paul Hawkshaw, 'Bruckners Psalmen' in *Bruckner-Vorträge, Bruckner-Tagung Wien 1999 Bericht* (Vienna, 2000), 7-19, for further information about Bruckner's psalm settings.

67 From the foreword to Nowak's edition of the full score, *ABSW* XV (Vienna, 1975). According to Bruckner's own insertion at the end of the dedication score for Mayr, the work was completed on 8 August 1854 'at midnight'. The parts for the first performance were copied between 24 August and 4 September by Franz Schimatschek from Linz whom Bruckner used frequently in later years to copy scores and parts. For further discussion, see *G-A* II/1, 155-77, Nowak's foreword and the *Revisionsbericht* of *ABSW* XV (Vienna, 1977) in which Robert Haas's earlier revision report of the Mass in the old Complete Edition (Vienna, 1930) is updated, corrected and amplified by Nowak. There is a facsimile of the original dedication score in *G-A* II/2, 189-228.

68 The *Kyrie* in G minor is discussed in *G-A* II/1, 63, *ABSW* XXI/1, 186, and *ABSW* XXI/2, 163. There is a facsimile of the original manuscript in *G-A* II/2, 84f. and a realization in *ABSW* XXI/1, 172. The *Kyrie* in E flat major is discussed in *G-A* II/1, 63f., *ABSW* XXI/1, 186, and *ABSW* XXI/2, 164-67. There is a facsimile of the original manuscript in *G-A* II/2, 86-93 and a realization in *ABSW* XXI/1, 173-78.

2.2.3 Songs and instrumental pieces

Of the secular songs of the period only one has survived in complete form. The voice part of *Mild wie Bäche* WAB 138 (c.1845) is complete but the piano part is sketched in only a few places. In *Wie des Bächleins Silberquelle (Duetto)* WAB 137 (c.1845) for two sopranos and piano, the voice parts are again complete but there is no piano accompaniment apart from a few bass notes. The Mendelssohnian *Frühlingslied* WAB 68 (1851) was dedicated to Aloisia, Michael Bogner's daughter, described by Bruckner as a 'blossoming spring rose'.[69]

The two solo piano pieces also dedicated to Aloisia are a *Lancier-Quadrille* WAB 120 (c.1850) and a *Steiermärker* WAB 122 (c.1850). The former is in four movements and Bruckner makes use of themes from Lortzing's opera *Der Wildschütz*

---

69   Bruckner probably intended to dedicate both *Mild wie Bäche* and *Wie des Bächleins Silberquelle* to Michael Arneth who was no doubt the 'Vater' mentioned in the text of the former. The text of the latter is the same as that of *Ständchen* WAB 84 for male-voice quartet. The author of the poems is unknown but was possibly Ernst Marinelli. The autograph sketch material is in St. Florian and the *Stadtmuseum*, Wels. *Mild wie Bäche* and *Wie des Bächleins Silberquelle* are discussed in *G-A* II/1, 46f. and 51 and by Angela Pachovsky in her edition of the *Lieder für Gesang und Klavier, ABSW* XXIII/1 (Vienna, 1997), foreword and *Revisionsbericht*. There are facsimiles of the sketches of both pieces in *G-A* II/2, 59f. and 65f. and transcriptions of the music in *ABSW* XXIII/1, 30ff. *Frühlingslied*, written for Aloisia Bogner (1836-92), is a setting of a poem by Heinrich Heine. The autograph fair copy can be found in the library of the *Oberösterreichisches Landesmuseum*, Linz. For further information, see *G-A* II/1, 41ff. (including a facsimile of the original manuscript) and *ABSW* XXIII/1, foreword and *Revisionsbericht*, 33; the music is printed in *G-A* II/2, 44ff. and *ABSW* XXIII/1, 1f.

70   These two pieces are discussed in *G-A* II/1, 39-42 and by Walburga Litschauer in *Anton Bruckner. Werke für Klavier zu zwei Händen, ABSW* XII/2 (Vienna, 1988/2000), foreword and *Revisionsbericht*, 36f., and her article 'Bruckner und das romantische Klavierstück', *BSL 1987* (Linz, 1989), 105-110. They are printed in *ABSW* XII/2, 1-11.

and *Zar und Zimmermann* which were performed in Linz several times during the 1840s. The *Steiermärker* is a kind of stylized Ländler in A-B-C-A form.[70] The *Drei kleine Vortragsstücke* for piano duet (the 'Primo' part at least) are slightly more demanding technically.[71]

Although he was a very proficient organist, Bruckner left very few compositions for the instrument. Three works survive from the St. Florian period, a *Vorspiel und Fuge* in C minor WAB 131 (1847) which has annotations on the original manuscript suggesting that it was undertaken as a compositional or theoretical exercise, and a *Nachspiel* in D minor (c.1846) and *Andante (Vorspiel)* in D minor (c.1846).[72]

---

71 See earlier and footnote 8. There is a facsimile of the autograph of the *Quadrille* WAB 121 in *G-A* II/2, 24-42. There are two sources of the piece (an incomplete Bruckner autograph and a copy with autograph entries) in the music archives of Kremsmünster abbey. The autograph of the *Drei kleine Stücke* WAB 124 written for the Marböck children can be found in the *ÖNB*; there is a facsimile of this autograph in *G-A* II/2, 178-83. Further information can be found in Walburga Litschauer, ed., *Werke für Klavier zu vier Händen*, *ABSW* XII/3 (Vienna, 1994), foreword and *Revisionsbericht*, 25ff. See also Frida Reingrüber, '"Randbemerkungen" zu Anton Bruckners Klavierstücken für vier Händen', *BJ 1987/88* (Linz, 1990), 79f. for additional background information about the *Drei kleine Vortragsstücke*. The music of the *Quadrille* and the *Drei kleine Stücke* is printed in *ABSW* XII/3, 4-7 and 8-23.

72 The *Vorspiel und Fuge* is dated 15 January 1847 at the beginning and the end of the autograph which is located in Seitenstetten abbey. A note in the upper margin of the first page - 'NB. Versuchen versch[iedener] Contr[apunkte]' - indicates that Bruckner was experimenting with different contrapuntal techniques, for instance stretto and organ point which appear towards the end of the fugue. The work is discussed in *G-A* II/1, 60ff. (including the facsimile of a page from the original manuscript) and in the foreword to Erwin Horn, ed., *Werke für Orgel, ABSW* XII/6 (Vienna, 1999), vi and xii; the music is printed in *G-A* II/2, 78-82, Franz Philipp, ed., *Vorspiel und Fuge C-moll für Orgel von Anton Bruckner* (Augsburg, 1929) and *ABSW* XII/6, 5-8. The precise dates of the *Nachspiel* and *Andante* are not known. The fair copy of both is on a single sheet of manuscript, unsigned and undated. A comment in the margin (not in Bruckner's handwriting) indicates that

However, it is in the *Missa solemnis* - in spite of the unevenness of inspiration and often uneasy juxtaposition of different styles - that we have a foretaste of the future, in particular the strikingly original Mass in D minor which was to herald the arrival of the mature Bruckner ten years later. In between lay a long period of rigorous and methodical application to various musical disciplines which provided a solid foundation and launching-pad for the great sacred works and symphonies. It is to this period that we must now turn.

---

they were given to (dedicated to?) Ignaz Traumihler. He was appointed choirmaster at St. Florian in 1852, but stylistically the two pieces belong to the beginning of the St. Florian years. They were first published by Anton Böhm Verlag (Augsburg, 1927). See *ABSW* XII/6, v-vi and xi-xii for Erwin Horn's comments and 1-4 for the music. See also Erwin Horn, 'Zwischen Interpretation und Improvisation. Anton Bruckner als Organist', *BSL 1995* (Linz, 1997), 111-39; idem, 'Die Orgelstücke Bruckners' in *Bruckner-Vorträge, Bruckner-Tagung Wien 1999* (Vienna, 2000), 21-34 which also includes facsimiles of these and other organ pieces.

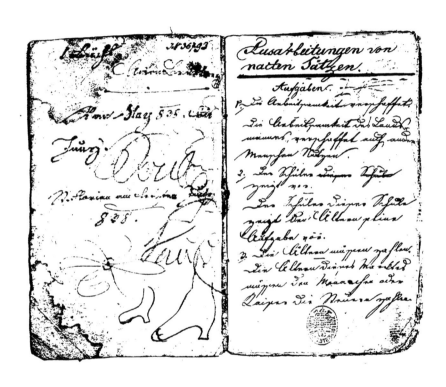

Plate 1. 'Ausarbeitungen von nakten Satzen'(May - end of June, 1838),1st page.
Reproduced by kind permission of the *Wiener Stadt- und Landesbibliothek*
(*Handschriftensammlung* I.N. 36793)

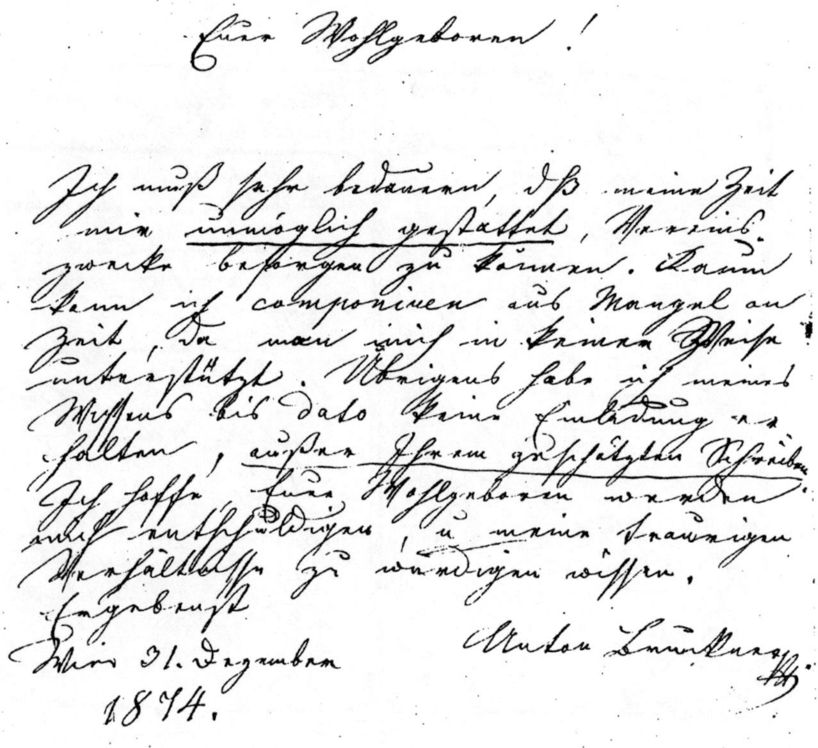
Euer Wohlgeboren!

Ich muß sehr bedauern, daß meine Zeit mir unmöglich gestattet, Vereinszwecke befördern zu können. Kaum kann ich componiren aus Mangel an Zeit, da man mich in keiner Weise unterstützt. Übrigens habe ich meines Wissens bis dato keine Einladung erhalten, außer Ihrem geschätzten Schreiben. Ich hoffe Euer Wohlgeboren werden mich entschuldigen u meine traurigen Verhältnisse zu würdigen wissen.

Ergebenst

Anton Bruckner m.p.

Wien 31. Dezember 1874.

Plate 2. Letter from Bruckner to Julius Gartner, Vienna, 31 December 1874. Reproduced by kind permission of the *Oberosterreichisches Landesbibliothek, Linz.* (*Handschriftensammlung* 958)

Plate 3, i. Letter from Bruckner to Moritz von Mayfeld, Vienna, 13 February 1875
Reproduced by kind permission of the *Osterreichische Nationalbibliothek,
Musik-Sammlung, Vienna.* (*Handschriftensammlung* Autogr. 126 / 58-24)

Plate 3, ii. Letter from Bruckner to Moritz von Mayfeld, Vienna, 13 February 1875 Reproduced by kind permission of the *Osterreichische Nationalbibliothek, Musik-Sammlung, Vienna.* (*Handschriftensammlung* Autogr. 126 / 58-24)

Plate 3, iii. Letter from Bruckner to Moritz von Mayfeld, Vienna, 13 February 1875 Reproduced by kind permission of the *Osterreichische Nationalbibliothek, Musik-Sammlung, Vienna.* (*Handschriftensammlung* Autogr. 126 / 58-24)

Plate 3, iv. Letter from Bruckner to Moritz von Mayfeld, Vienna, 13 February 1875
Reproduced by kind permission of the *Osterreichische Nationalbibliothek,
Musik-Sammlung, Vienna. (Handschriftensammlung* Autogr. 126 / 58-24)

Plate 4, i. Letter from Bruckner to Theodor Helm, Vienna, 19 June 1885
Reproduced by kind permission of the *Wiener Stadt- und Landesbibliothek*
(*Handschriftensammlung* I.N. 34.355)

Plate 4, ii. Letter from Bruckner to Theodor Helm, Vienna, 19 June 1885
Reproduced by kind permission of the *Wiener Stadt- und Landesbibliothek*
(*Handschriftensammlung* I.N. 34.355)

Hochwohlgeborner Herr
'General = Musikdirektor!'

Heute erfuhr ich zu meiner größ-
ten Freude, daß mein hochedler
Gönner sich bedeutend wohler be-
finde. Gott sei gedankt! und
gratulire ich herzlichst aus
vollstem Herzen!

Ich bin leider leidend an den
Leben, die drückt auf den
Magen und auf die Venen;
daher schwacher Magen u. geschwol-
lene Füße! Gebrauche aber
die Carlsbader = Cur.
Post molestam senectutem —

Plate 5, i. Letter from Bruckner to Hermann Levi, Vienna, 24 July 1892.
Reproduced by kind permission of the *Gesellschaft der Musikfreunde,
Handschriftensammlung, Vienna.*

Plate 5, ii. Letter from Bruckner to Hermann Levi, Vienna, 24 July 1892. Reproduced by kind permission of the *Gesellschaft der Musikfreunde, Handschriftensammlung, Vienna.*

CHAPTER 3

Bruckner in Linz: Growing Maturity (1856-1868)

3.1. Linz

By the mid-1850s Linz had grown in importance as an industrial centre.[1] As elsewhere in Europe, the influential middle class sought edification and recreation in music and the growth of choral societies and expansion of concert activities helped to cater for this. Concerts in Linz were provided by the *Gesellschaft der Musikfreunde* (later *Musikverein*), a mixture of professional and amateur singers and instrumentalists. According to its statutes, it had to give two oratorio performances and four 'society concerts' every year. While Bruckner was in Linz the musical directors of the *Gesellschaft* were Anton Michael Storch, Engelbert Lanz and Eduard Hauptmann, and the works performed included Haydn's *The Creation* and *The Seasons*, Mendelssohn's *St Paul* and *Elijah*, and orchestral works by Haydn, Mozart, Beethoven, Mendelssohn and Schumann.[2] The *Gesellschaft* also had its own music

---

1 For further historical information about Upper Austria during the period 1815-1870, see Harry Slapnicka, 'Oberösterreich zwischen Wiener Kongreß und den Anfängen der politischen Parteien (1815-1870), *ABDS* 10 (Vienna, 1994), 9-32.

2 Anton Michael Storch (1813-1877) was a fine choir trainer who during his career also conducted the *Wiener Männergesangverein* and the *Niederösterreichisches Sängerbund* and later became a theatre music director in Vienna; he composed several pieces for male-voice choir. Engelbert Lanz (1820-1904), one of Bruckner's rivals for the cathedral post, was active in Linz as a teacher at the

academy which provided instruction in a limited number of instruments. It later became known as the *Bruckner Konservatorium*. Choral music was originally the exclusive responsibility of the *Gesellschaft* but, in 1845, several of the members of the society formed themselves into a male-voice choir. In 1849 this became a separate association called *Liedertafel 'Frohsinn'* (later *Linzer Singakademie*). Bruckner was a member of this choral society for some time and became its director for two short periods in 1860-61 and 1868. Other directors during the 1856-68 period included the *Gesellschaft* directors Storch (1855-60), Lanz (1861-65) and Hauptmann (1865-68). Occasionally this male-voice choir combined with the *Frohsinn* ladies' choir (founded 1854). As well as giving its own concerts, which included such significant events as the Linz premieres of Schumann's *Der Rose Pilgerfahrt* (April 1860), Wagner's *Liebesmahl der Apostel* (March 1866) and, under Bruckner's baton, the final scene of Wagner's *Die Meistersinger* (April 1868), it participated in *Gesellschaft* concerts and solo recitals and performed with success in choral festivals in Germany and Austria.[3] In 1857 Bruckner's friend, Alois Weinwurm, founded a choir called *Sängerbund* which Bruckner occasionally conducted. There were also several wind and military bands in Linz and they frequently combined with *Frohsinn* to give concerts.

Präparandie (Teacher-Training Institute) and as a composer; earlier he had worked first as an assistant then as a principal teacher in Kremsmünster. Eduard Hauptmann was a retired lottery official and keen musical amateur.

3 The *Linzer Singakademie* has several of Bruckner's choral works in its library, including the autograph scores of *Trauungschor* WAB 49 (1865) and *Inveni David* WAB 19 (1868) and a copy score, with some autograph insertions, of *Herbstlied* WAB 73 (1864). Bruckner's activities as conductor of the choir are recorded in the *Chronik der Liedertafel 'Frohsinn' in Linz umfassend den Zeitraum vom 17. März 1845 bis Ende März 1870* (Linz, 1870), and in Karl Kerschbaum, ed., *Chronik der Liedertafel 'Frohsinn' in Linz über den 50 jährigen Bestand vom 17. März 1845 bis anfangs März 1895* (Linz, 1895).

One of the most active figures in Linz musical life at the time was Karl Zappe who held posts as orchestral director at the *Landständische Theater*, violin teacher in the *Musikverein* and musical director of the cathedral and parish church.[4] He was also the leader of a string quartet which gave regular concerts of the standard chamber music repertoire in Linz. It included another professional musician, Otto Kitzler, as cellist, but two amateurs, Josef Schmierer, an engraver by profession, as second violinist, and Franz Gamon, a draughtsman, as viola player. In 1842 Zappe was confirmed as successor to Johann Baptist Schiedermayr as musical director of the two largest churches in town.[5] When he began his duties, the personnel for whom he was directly responsible included the organist, two sopranos, one alto, one tenor and one bass. He was also expected to engage other musicians and his duties were specifically to 'ensure a well-maintained vocal and instrumental music for the cathedral and parish church, the regular stringing of instruments, not only for the normal services but also for the extra unscheduled services which could be held in the churches'.[6] There was no pension attached either to his post or to that of the cathedral and parish church organist, but he was allowed free lodgings in one of the parish houses, the *Stadtpfarrmesnerhaus*, until 1868.[7] Zappe supplemented the church choir with enthusiastic musical amateurs and drew mainly on the members of the theatre orchestra for his instrumentalists. The records of the old cathedral

---

4 Karl Zappe (1812-1871) was born in Prague where he received his early education. He settled in Linz in 1834 after spells as a theatre musician in Graz and Vienna.

5 Johann Baptist Schiedermayr sen. (1779-1840) had earlier been active as cathedral and parish church organist, theatre conductor and composer.

6 From the *Dienstvertrag der geistlichen und weltlichen Vogtei der Dom- und Stadtpfarrkirche*, a type of job description (Linz, 14 April 1843).

7 Zappe, Bruckner and Wenzel Lambel, a cathedral singer, lived in this house which was nicknamed the *Musikantenstöckl* or *Mesnerhäusl* and was situated near the parish church (Pfarrplatz 5 today). Bruckner occupied three rooms on the second floor.

66

show that the Masses with orchestral accompaniment performed in the 1850s and 1860s included works by Cherubini, Danzi, Diabelli, Eberlin, Führer, Gänsbacher, Habert, Joseph and Michael Haydn, Labler, Mozart, Preindl, Schiedermayr, Seyfried, Stadler, Süssmayr, Tuczek and Vitásek.[8] Zappe was a member of the panel which listened to and assessed the competitors for the provisional post of cathedral and parish church organist in December 1855, but was not directly involved in the competition for the permanent appointment. Under his overall direction Bruckner occupied the position of organist at both churches from 1856 to 1868. The relationship between music director and organist seems to have been cordial and respectful.[9]

The sacred and secular musical diet in Linz was fairly conservative but, during Eduard Kriebig's and Carl Pichler-Bodog's periods of artistic directorship (1860-65 and 1865-68 respectively) at the Linz Theatre, the predominance of Italian opera was mitigated by the production of three Wagner operas, *Tannhäuser* (February 1863), *Der fliegende Holländer* (October 1865) and *Lohengrin* (February 1866).[10] The conductor was the forward-looking Otto Kitzler, a colleague of Zappe's and Bruckner's erstwhile teacher and friend.

---

8 The records of the old cathedral are preserved in the *Oberösterreichisches Landesmuseum*, Linz.

9 For further information about Karl Zappe, see the article by his great-grandson Hermann Zappe, 'Anton Bruckner, die Familie Zappe und die Musik. Zur Musikgeschichte des Landes Oberösterreich 1812-1963 bzw. 1982', *BJ 1982/83* (Linz, 1984), 129-61.

10 See Franz Zamazal, 'Das Linzer Landestheater zur Zeit Bruckners' in *IBG Mitteilungsblatt* 52 (June 1999), 7-13, for some details of the organization of the theatre, including vocal and orchestral forces. Of particular interest is the reproduction of an article which first appeared in the *Linzer Zeitung*, 12 November 1862.

3.2 Bruckner and Linz

During his twelve years in Linz Bruckner laid the foundations of his career as a symphonist and respected teacher in Vienna. They were arduous years, the first half being spent completing a prolonged 'distance learning' harmony and counterpoint course with Sechter and with very little to show in the way of original composition, the second half beginning with lessons in analysis and orchestration from Kitzler and leading to a veritable explosion of original works. But all this took its toll and Bruckner had a nervous breakdown in 1867 which required sanatorium treatment and period of recuperation. On his recovery Bruckner was faced with a major decision, and much of the earlier part of 1868 was spent weighing up the pros and cons of a possible move to Vienna. It is easy to forget that Bruckner's main occupation during these years was that of church organist. As his reputation grew, his advice was sought concerning the construction of several organs in a number of Austrian churches. In 1871, reconstruction work was begun on the St. Florian abbey organ, largely at Bruckner's instigation. The organ with which he was particularly identified and in the reconstruction of which he played an important role was the organ in the so-called old cathedral in Linz. When he was appointed early in 1856, the organ at his disposal was a three-manual Chrismann. In October 1856 he provided, at Bishop Rudigier's request, information about the condition of the organ with a view to its eventual repair.[11] By the beginning of 1857, however, a decision had been made to rebuild the organ. Bruckner referred to this in a letter to the bishop's office and stressed the need for the provision of two or three more eight-

---

11   See Hans Winterberger, 'Die Hauptorgel der Ignatiuskirche ("Alter Dom") in Linz', *Historisches Jahrbuch der Stadt Linz, 1971* (Linz, 1972), 125.

68

foot and sixteen-foot stops as well as an immediate tuning of the instrument.[12] It took eleven years for the rebuilding work to be completed , and the organ builder responsible was Josef Breinbauer. Bruckner's successor at Linz, Karl Waldeck, requested a slight change in the stop disposition in 1892, and it is more than likely that he consulted Bruckner in advance. The alteration work was carried out by Josef Breinbauer's son, Leopold.[13]

---

12 See *HSABB* 1, 9 for the text of this letter, dated Linz, 14 January 1857; the original can be found in the *Ordinariatsarchiv*, Linz. See also Rupert Gottfried Frieberger, 'Die Bruckner-Orgel im alten Dom von Linz' in *In Ehrfurcht vor den Manen eines Großen. Zum 75. Todestag Anton Bruckners* (Linz, 1971), 47 for the text of a letter from Josef Breinbauer (14 April 1857)to the bishop's office concerning the planned rebuilding of the organ; the original is in the *Diözesanarchiv*, Linz.

13 Josef Breinbauer (1807-1882) and Leopold Breinbauer (1859-1920) had an organ-building business in Ottensheim, near Linz. In 1979-80 a modern restoration of the organ was carried out by the firm Rieger-Orgelbau, Schwarzach (Voralberg). Further details of the organ, including Bruckner's connection with it, are provided by Otto Biba, 'Die Orgel im Alten Dom zu Linz - ein Dokument zu Bruckners Orgelpraxis' in *BJ 1982/83* (Linz, 1984), 75-79. Bruckner's activities as an organist and organ consultant are discussed in the following books and articles: (a) 'Die Linzer Dom-Orgel', *Linzer Zeitung* (19 September 1867), 909; (b) Leopold Hager, *Die Bruckner-Orgel im Stifte St. Florian* (St. Florian, 1951); (c) Altman Kellner, 'Der Organist Bruckner', in *Bruckner-Studien* (Vienna, 1964), 61-65; (d) Rudolf Quoika, *Die Orgelwelt um Anton Bruckner. Blicke in die Orgelgeschichte Alt-Österreichs* (Ludwigsburg, 1966); (e) Hermann Busch, 'Anton Bruckners Tätigkeit als Orgelsachverständiger' in *Ars Organa* 39 (1971), 1585-93; (f) Rupert Frieberger, 'Die Bruckner-Orgel in der Ignatiuskirche in Linz - ein historisches Instrument' in *Singende Kirche* 18 (1971), 151-54;

(g) Otto Biba, 'Anton Bruckner und die Orgelbauerfamilie Mauracher' in *Bruckner-Studien* (Vienna, 1975), 143-62; (h) Gerald Mitterschiffthaler, 'Die Beziehungen Anton Bruckners zum Stift Wilhering', *ibid*, 113-41; (i) Karl Schnürl, 'Drei niederösterreichische Bruckner-Orgeln. Tulln - Langenlois - Krems, *ibid*, 163-69; (j) Jiri Sehnal, 'Ein Brief A. Bruckners an den mährischen Orgelbauer Franz Ritter von Pistrich' in *BJ 1980* (Linz, 1980), 129-32; (k) Otto Biba, 'Anton Bruckners Orgel im Alten Dom zu Linz restauriert' in *Singende Kirche* 28 (1981), 120ff.; (l) Otto

One man who had a very high opinion of Bruckner's organ playing was Franz Josef Rudigier who, after spending two years as prebendary of Brixen Cathedral, was appointed diocesan bishop on Linz in 1852. Bishop Rudigier would often slip into the cathedral to listen to Bruckner practising and is known to have derived great spiritual comfort from his improvisations. One of Rudigier's grandest designs was to have a new cathedral built in a neo-Gothic style, and the renowned church architect, Vincenz Statz, was commissioned to accomplish this task. Bruckner was asked to write a festival cantata, *Preiset den Herrn* WAB 16, for the foundation stone laying ceremony on 1 May 1862. The entire construction work took sixty years and only the votive chapel was completed during Rudigier's lifetime. On the occasion of the dedication of this chapel in the autumn of 1869, Bruckner conducted the first performance of his own *Mass in E minor* WAB 27 in the cathedral square in Linz. Rudigier, the dedicatee, was sufficiently impressed to send the composer, now resident in Vienna, an honorarium of 200 florins, and Bruckner expressed his astonishment and gratitude in a letter to the bishop.[14] Rudigier's great esteem for Bruckner's musical abilities was mingled with a caring pastoral concern for the composer. When Bruckner spent three months in Bad Kreuzen in 1867 recovering from a nervous breakdown, he had a priest in regular attendance. Bruckner maintained strong connections with Linz after taking up appointments in Vienna in 1868. Rudigier kept his Linz post provisionally open for him until 1870 by which time Bruckner felt reasonably secure in the Austrian capital. Nevertheless, Bruckner continued to make 'guest appearances' as organist at the cathedral. In 1877, he wrote one of his finest miniatures, the motet *Tota pulchra es* WAB 46, for the 25th anniversary of Rudigier's enthronement as bishop and dedicated it to him. He played

---

Biba, 'Die Orgel im Alten Dom zu Linz (Oberösterreich)' in *Ars Organa* 30 (1982), 30-36; (m) Erwin Horn, 'Zwischen Interpretation und Improvisation. Anton Bruckner als Organist' in *BSL 1995* (Linz, 1997), 111-39.

14 See *HSABB* 1, 113 for the text of this letter, dated Vienna, 19 October 1869; the original of this letter is not extant.

the organ at Rudigier's funeral service in December 1884. The clearest documentary evidence of Bishop Rudigier's high regard for Bruckner is a letter which he wrote to the composer in October 1874. In it he expressed his disappointment that Bruckner had lost one of his part-time appointments in Vienna but recalled with pleasure his accomplishment as a cathedral organist in Linz and commented on his growing reputation as a composer and his already established reputation as an organist - 'perhaps the foremost player in Europe'.[15]

Bruckner's reputation as an organist was beginning to spread beyond provincial bounds already in 1856. At the beginning of September the *Frohsinn* choir, of which Bruckner was a member, travelled to Salzburg to take part in the *Mozart-Fest*. While he was there Bruckner played on the cathedral organ; and it is reported that his playing was criticised by Robert Führer - who had provided him with a testimonial only eighteen months earlier! This led to a kind of 'organists' duel' - a contest between the two men on the Salzburg cathedral organ.[16] Two newspaper reviews of Bruckner's organ playing in 1858 attest to a growing appreciation of his skills. His playing at the Easter Sunday morning service in Linz Cathedral made a particularly favourable impression on the *Linzer Zeitung* correspondent:

> ... The cathedral organist, Mr. Bruckner, also provided eloquent proof of his skill at the close of the church service [Haydn's *Nelson Mass* was performed]. The partly free, partly contrapuntal development of

---

15 See *HSABB* 1, 152 for the text of this letter, dated Linz, 7 October 1874; the original is in St. Florian. For further information about Rudigier (1811-1884), see Konrad Meindl, *Leben und Wirken des Bischofs Franz Josef Rudigier von Linz*, 2 vols. (Linz, 1891/92); Harry Slapnicka, 'Bischof Rudigier und die Kunst', *BSL 1985* (Linz, 1988), 23-31; Rudolf Zinnhobler, 'Das Bistum Linz zwischen Spätjosephinismus und Liberalismus', *ABDS* 10 (Vienna, 1994), 33-58, partic. 53ff.

16 This contest was reported in the *Monatsschrift für Theater und Musik* 2 (1856), 544. See Gerhard Walterskirchen, 'Bruckner in Salzburg - Bruckner Erstaufführungen in Salzburg' in *IBG Mitteilungsblatt* 16 (December 1979), 14-20, which includes some extracts from the article.

the principal theme in the Easter song, combined with a majestic chorale which ended with a free fantasia, was truly uplifting. Only a very few cathedrals can possess an organist of the calibre of Mr. Bruckner...[17]

In July 1858 Bruckner brought the first part of his theoretical course with Sechter to a splendid conclusion by improvising on the *Piaristenkirche* organ in Vienna before an invited audience which included Ludwig Speidel, the music critic of the *Wiener Zeitung*. In his later review Speidel mentioned the background to the recital, including 'glowing testimonials' from Sechter, and reported that Bruckner's playing had brought him 'uncommon pleasure'.[18] His musical understanding was obviously not confined to harmony exercises:

> ... He stated a theme and developed it with a more than respectable display of imagination and musical ability. He showed how proficient he was in both free fantasia and strict contrapuntal playing. With his great skill, enthusiasm and ambition, and given the serious lack of good organists at present, a fine future is assured him.[19]

---

17 See *GrBL*, 29, *G-A* III/1, 50 and Othmar Wessely, 'Anton Bruckner in Linz' in *Jahrbuch der Stadt Linz 1954* (Linz, 1955), 225 for extracts from this review in the *Linzer Zeitung* 78 (7 April 1858); there was also a report of the service in the *Linzer Abendbote* (6 April 1858). See also Susanna Taub, *Zeitgenössische Bruckner-Rezeption in den Linzer Printmedien (1855-1869)* [Music Education thesis, Salzburg 1987] for facsimiles of other articles in which Bruckner's organ playing during church services is mentioned, e.g. reports in the *Linzer Zeitung,* 24 November and 29 December 1857.

18 See *G-A* III/1, 48f. for Sechter's 'testimonials' which refer to Bruckner's organ playing (12 July 1858) and the successful completion of his harmony course (10 July 1858); the original of Sechter's report is in St. Florian.

19 This report appeared in the evening edition of the paper, Saturday 24 July 1858. See *G-A* III/1, 48f. for the complete review and *HSABB* 1, 10ff. for Bruckner's letter to Rudolf Weinwurm (Linz, 1 August 1858), in which he enthuses over the review and thanks Weinwurm for his help; the

One of Bruckner's musical contemporaries in Linz was Josef Hoffmann, choir director of the Lutheran church. His later recollection of Bruckner's impressive improvisation of a fugue on a chorale theme and a 'clandestine' visit of the composer to the church has already been mentioned.[20]

In September 1858 - at a time when he was still studying intensively with Sechter - Bruckner attempted to reduce the pressure of his work-load by requesting that the organist posts at the cathedral and parish church become two separate appointments. In an official letter to the bishop's office he pointed out that the present salary for the cathedral appointment, 300 florins, was not large enough for anyone to be able to subsist on it without extra earnings, namely from parish church duties. On the other hand, combined duties at the cathedral and parish church could not always be fulfilled by one person as they involved attendance not only every Sunday and feast day but also frequently on ordinary working days. The result was that the help of a deputy had to be sought. Unfortunately, the present deputy was old and unreliable. Bruckner suggested that the two posts be separated and an income of 600 florins be made available for the cathedral post. The official reply was that this request was premature but could be reviewed when the oversight of the parish of St. Joseph was transferred to the cathedral.[21]

Bruckner supplemented the regular income from his official post with some private piano, singing and harmony teaching. Most of his free time, however, was spent in a relentless pursuit of theoretical knowledge. His studies with Simon Sechter, Otto Kitzler and Ignaz Dorn prepared the way for a series of compositions,

---

original of the letter is owned privately.

20 See Chapter 2, page 61 and footnote 63. For another account of Bruckner's playing, also his tendency to try the patience of the ministrant priest by indulging in over-long interludes during a service, see Hans Soukup's recollection of Bruckner at Wilhering abbey in Mitterschiffthaler's article in *Bruckner-Studien* (1975) [see footnote 13 (h)]

21 See *HSABB* 1, 12f. for Bruckner's letter, dated Linz, 14 September 1858, and the reply, dated Linz, 27 October 1858; the originals of both letters are in the *Ordinariatsarchiv*, Linz.

beginning with the *Mass in D minor* WAB 26 (1864) in which Bruckner threw off his earlier restraints and spoke with a voice of bold originality.

Bruckner's long harmony and counterpoint course with Sechter had already begun before his definite move to Linz. It now continued unremittingly until 1861, culminating in a final theory examination at the Vienna Conservatory and an organ examination in the *Piaristenkirche*, three and a half years after the successful completion of the first stage of the course in July 1858.[22] In between came the second ('simple counterpoint'), third ('double, triple and quadruple counterpoint') and fourth ('canon and fugue') stages. Bruckner regularly spent some time in Lent and Advent each year with Sechter. He also used a large part of his summer vacation to complete the second stage of the course in Vienna in 1859. On 3 June he wrote to Sechter to confirm that he would be spending six weeks in Vienna and on 6 June he informed Rudolf Weinwurm that he would be travelling from Linz to Vienna by Danube steamer on the 30th of the month and asked him to reserve a room for him in a suitable hotel near Sechter's house - 'as quiet and cool as possible and ideally looking on to a garden'.[23] The fruit of Bruckner's intensive studies in the summer heat of Vienna was a certificate from Sechter.[24] Six months later Sechter informed his industrious pupil that he was more than satisfied with his progress and counselled him not to over-stretch himself:

---

22 More than 600 pages of Bruckner's harmony and couterpoint exercises for Sechter are preserved in two sources in the *ÖNB* - Mus. Hs. 34.925 (128 folios) and Mus. Hs. 24.260 (192 folios). See *ABA*, 69 for the facsimile of a page.

23 See *HSABB* 1, 15 for the texts of Sechter's reply to Bruckner's letter, dated Vienna, 5 June 1859, and Bruckner's letter to Weinwurm. The original of the former is in the *ÖNB* and the original of the latter is privately owned. The original of Bruckner's letter to Sechter (3 June) is not extant.

24 The original of this certificate, which is dated 12 August 1859 and officially signed by Sechter as 'principal imperial court organist and professor of harmony at the Conservatory of Music', is in St. Florian.

... I have read through your 17 work books of double counterpoint exercises and am amazed by your industry and the progress you have made... So that you are in good health when you come to Vienna I entreat you to take more care of yourself and give yourself the necessary rest. In any case I have absolutely no doubt about your industry and eagerness and would not want you to damage your health by over-stretching yourself intellectually. I feel constrained to tell you that I have never had any student as industrious as you...[25]

On 3 April 1860 Sechter was able to provide his pupil with a certificate marking the successful completion of the third stage of the course.[26] In order to prepare for the examination Bruckner had stayed for a few weeks in a hotel on the Mariahilferstraße. When he wrote to Weinwurm at the beginning of the following year, asking him once again to find suitable accommodation from the middle of February to the end of March, he stated his preference for private lodgings:

... there is no peace day or night in a hotel. In the 'Kreuz' in Mariahilf last year I could never get to sleep before 3 or 4 in the morning because of unruly neighbours. I cannot and will not put up with that again unless absolutely necessary...[27]

---

25 See *HSABB* 1, 17 for the text of Sechter's letter, dated Vienna, 13 January 1860; there is a facsimile of this letter in Leopold Nowak, *Anton Bruckner. Musik und Leben* (Linz, 1973), 89. Also see *HSABB* 1, 16 for the text of another letter from Sechter to Bruckner, dated Vienna, 3 November 1859, in which the theorist answers a particular technical question from Bruckner; there is a facsimile of this letter in *G-A* III/1, 64f. The originals of these letters are in the *ÖNB*.

26 See *G-A* III/1, 63f. There is a facsimile of this certificate in Leopold Nowak, op.cit., 90; the original is in St. Florian.

27 Extract from letter, dated Linz, 10 February 1861. Bruckner had already written to Weinwurm on 30 January, stressing the desirability of peacefulness, good heating and a toilet. See *HSABB* 1, 21 for texts of both letters.; the original of the earlier letter is privately owned, the original of the second is not extant.

Yet another certificate from Sechter confirmed Bruckner's successful completion of the fourth and penultimate stage of the course.[28] All that remained was for Bruckner to obtain official recognition of his achievements. In the meantime Sechter, by now just as much a friend as a teacher, spent a few days with him in Linz at the beginning of September and, on the 5th, presented him with a fugue on the motto 'An Gottes Segen ist alles gelegen' as a sort of official record of the formal completion of the course.[29]

In October, Bruckner sent a formal letter to the directorate of the Vienna Conservatory, enclosing Sechter's certificates and requesting an examination with a view to receiving a diploma and permission to use the title 'Professor of Harmony and Counterpoint'. Bruckner's first request was granted but he was informed that the *Gesellschaft der Musikfreunde* did not possess the authority to bestow the title of professor.[30] In a second letter to the directorate Bruckner mentioned that there were one or two precedents, viz. people who had been granted the title in the past, but affirmed that he would be satisfied with an acknowledgment in his diploma that he was qualified to teach in a conservatory. The official reply fixed the date of his

---

28 See *G-A* III/1, 96. The original of this certificate, dated 26 March 1861, is in St. Florian.

29 There is a facsimile of this fugue in *G-A* III/1, 108; the original is in the *ÖNB*. See *HSABB* 1, 25 for Sechter's letter to Bruckner, dated 31 August 1861, confirming his visit and his time of arrival at Linz station; the original of this letter is in the *ÖNB*. Also in the *ÖNB* is Bruckner's copy of Sechter's *Grundsätze* in which he wrote 'Sechter selbst in Linz anno 1861 3. Sept' (on page 41 of the second section).

30 Bruckner's letter is dated Linz, 20 October 1861 and the reply, signed by the registrar, Moritz Anton Ritter von Becker, is dated Vienna, 25 October 1861. See *HSABB* 1, 26f. for the texts of both letters. The originals (the second letter is in draft form) are in the *Gesellschaft der Musikfreunde* library; there is a facsimile of Bruckner's letter in Hans Conrad Fischer, *Anton Bruckner. Sein Leben. Eine Dokumentation* (Salzburg, 1974), 111.

76

examination as Tuesday 19 November, and Bruckner was asked to forward some examples of his counterpoint exercises and free composition.[31] In complying with this request Bruckner drew attention to the fact that his theoretical studies since 1855 had effectively prevented him from composing any substantial original works:

> ... The candidate has not had the necessary time for free composition during his period of study (since 1855); he has written only a few songs and some choral pieces for the choral society of which he was the choirmaster, and these, the *Ave Maria* in particular, have been exceptionally well received both in Salzburg and in Linz. He will devote himself to free composition immediately after the examination. The candidate has tried to prevent his inspiration from running dry by improvising extensively on the organ and by listening to a considerable amount of excellent music in Vienna.[32]

The examining board on the evening of 19 November consisted of Josef Hellmesberger, director of the Conservatory, Johann Herbeck, director of the *Gesellschaft der Musikfreunde*, Otto Dessoff, conductor of the court opera orchestra, and Moritz Becker, the registrar of the Conservatory. According to Bruckner's own account of the proceedings, the examiners, presented with clear evidence of his theoretical aptitude, were uncertain as to what should happen next until Herbeck finally suggested that they re-convene two days later in the *Piaristenkirche* and listen to Bruckner improvise a fugue on a given theme. Accordingly, on Thursday 21

---

31 Bruckner's second letter is dated Linz, 29 October 1861, and the reply, signed by Becker, is dated Vienna, 8 November. See *HSABB*, 28f. for the texts of both letters. The original of the former is in the *Gesellschaft der Musikfreunde* library, the original of the latter is in St. Florian.

32 Extract from letter, dated Linz, 10 November 1861, enclosing some of the contrapuntal exercises requested, the others to be brought with him when he attended the examination on 19 November. See *HSABB* 1, 29; the original is in the *Gesellschaft der Musikfreunde* library.

November, Sechter was asked to provide a four-bar theme which Herbeck immediately extended to eight bars. Bruckner, by now a seasoned organist, had no difficulty in developing it into a large-scale introduction and fugue which astonished the examiners and drew from Herbeck the response, 'He should have been examining us!'[33] The official diploma, signed by each member of the examining board, drew attention to Bruckner's contrapuntal fluency and outstanding skills as an organist and confirmed that he was now well qualified to teach at a music conservatory.[34] Press reports of Bruckner's success appeared in both Linz and Vienna. The *Linzer Zeitung* of 3 December contained the information that Hellmesberger had been so impressed that he had asked Bruckner to write a string quartet.[35] Of greater importance for the composer's future was the report in the *Wiener Zeiung* which brought him to the notice of a wider public:

> Anton Bruckner, organist of Linz Cathedral, who drained the brimful cup of Simon Sechter's theoretical learning to the dregs over a number of years, has been in Vienna recently to take a music examination at the Conservatory. The certificate, signed by Hellmesberger, Herbeck, Dessoff and Sechter, is of such merit that Bruckner can regard it as a veritable testimonial of excellence. According to this certificate, 'the submitted pieces of work provide evidence of the most comprehensive studies in counterpoint and a thorough knowledge of the strict style in its different forms. As an organist, Mr. Bruckner proved to have considerable gifts and a precise knowledge of the instrument, and demonstrated that he was equally skilled in performing the compositions of others as in

---

33 Bruckner's full account, as related to Göllerich, can be found in *G-A* III/1, 114-17.

34 See *G-A* III/1, 117f. and Hans C. Fischer, op.cit., 100 for the wording of this certificate; a facsimile can be found in the latter, 112 and in Leopold Nowak, *Anton Bruckner. Musik und Leben*, 97; the original is in St. Florian.

35 There is a facsimile of this article, which is essentially a reprint of the article which appeared in the *Wiener Zeitung* on 1 December, is Susanna Taub, op.cit., 12.

improvising on his own and on given themes'... Mr. Bruckner is also highly recommended as a potential music teacher in conservatories.. May the composer, who is as modest as he is proficient, be fortunate enough to find a position commensurate with his ability in Vienna.[36]

The occasional phrase in letters to his friend Weinwurm during this period suggest that Bruckner was beginning to find the provincial Linz atmosphere somewhat stifling and was setting his sights on a more prestigious position. His success in Vienna came as a welcome boost after the disappointing outcome of his attempt to secure the vacant position of director of the Salzburg *Dom-Musikverein* and *Mozarteum* which involved travelling to Salzburg on 19 September and conducting the cathedral choir on the following two days. According to Bruckner, Franz von Hilleprandt, the founder and secretary of the *Dom-Musikverein*, was not well-disposed towards him, and so it came as no surprise that a former St. Florian colleague, Hans Schläger, was appointed.[37]

Bruckner had also recently severed connections with *Frohsinn*. He had joined the choir in 1856 as a second tenor and had been its assistant librarian for a short time (1856-57). Its conductor from 1855 to 1860 was Anton Michael Storch. Bruckner succeeded Storch as conductor at the end of 1860, and one of his first appearances with the choir in February 1861 inspired the following favourable review in the *Linzer Abendbote*:

... May the choral society form a close relationship with their well-trained, accomplished conductor, Mr. Bruckner; we recognize in him

---

36 Quoted in *GrBL*, 31 and *G-A* III/1, 119 (abridged).

37 Bruckner gave a full account of the whole episode in a letter to Rudolf Weinwurm, dated Linz, 3 October 1861. See *HSABB*, 25f. for the text of this letter; the original is privately owned.

the man who can lead them to fame and honour.[38]

Bruckner achieved some notable successes with *Frohsinn* at two large choir festivals in Krems (29-30 June) and Nuremberg (19-24 July). In the official report of the former, the choir was commended for its precision, assurance and delicate nuances in its singing of Storch's *Waldeinsamkeit* and Valentin Becker's *Jägers Aufenthalt*.[39] After the Nuremberg success, however, Bruckner took umbrage at a practical joke played on him by the choir. It involved a restaurant waitress called Olga who had caught the composer's eye. She was encouraged by the choir to dress seductively and visit the unsuspecting Bruckner in his room. Shocked and distressed, Bruckner left the room in great haste and later resigned his conducting post.[40]

Before taking up the position of choral conductor in 1860, Bruckner had tried to increase his involvement in the musical life of Linz by collaborating with Engelbert Lanz in proposing the institution of a Singing Academy in the town. The Lanz-

38 See *GrBL* for this extract from this review in the *Linzer Abendbote*, 11 February 1861; see Susanna Taub, 20f. for the complete review and a facsimile.

39 See *G-A* III/1, 101f., Gräflinger, *Anton Bruckner. Leben und Schaffen* (revised and enlarged *Bausteine*, Berlin, 1927) [hereafter *GrBLS*], 67f. and Othmar Wessely, *Anton Bruckner und Linz*, 254f.
for extracts from the report of the Krems festival and for further details of the Nuremberg festival. See also Andrea Harrandt, 'Aus dem Archiv der Liedertafel "Frohsinn". Zum Chorwesen im 19. Jahrhundert' in *BSL 1990* (Linz, 1993), 59ff. for 'Erinnerungen an das Sängerfest Nürnberg' in the *Frohsinn* archives., and 62 for a facsimile of the list of Linz participants. Herbeck and the *Wiener Männergesangverein* also participated in both festivals and Bruckner would almost certainly have met Herbeck.

40 This is one of several 'reminiscences' and anecdotes printed in *G-A* III/1, 102-05. Bruckner alluded to his resignation at the end of his letter to Weinwurm, 3 October 1861; see footnote 37.

80

Bruckner project would certainly have been perfectly respectable on artistic grounds. Engelbert Lanz, four years older than Bruckner, had the same educational background. As well as being a talented singer, he was a proficient organist.[41] Bruckner for his part was an accomplished accompanist, a practised theoretician and a good teacher. Between them they would have made a success of a venture of this kind. But nothing came of the proposals and Lanz and Bruckner formally withdrew their request in February 1859.[42] It is possible that Bishop Rudigier, who knew of the project from the beginning, advised Bruckner to abandon the idea.

A contributory factor to Bruckner's growing feeling of unease was the conviction that all his attempts at self-improvement as a musician were largely misunderstood. His normally cordial relationship with Storch became somewhat strained in May 1860 after a series of articles about Schumann's *Der Rose Pilgerfahrt* written by Storch appeared in the *Linzer Zeitung*. In the final article on 26 May, Storch made the following observation:

> ... Schumann was never one of those sad figures (composers) who slink around with heads bowed, believing that they have done enough for art when they approach their task from the formal side only, when they manipulate counterpoint very efficiently to dreary abstraction and when they rummage around in arid scholarship.[43]

Although Storch was almost certainly criticising the advocates of the Caecilian

---

41   See pages 63-64 and footnote 2 for further information about Lanz.

42   For further information, see Elisabeth Maier, 'Anton Bruckners Gesangsakademie' in *BJ 1982-83* (Linz, 1984), 89-94

43   Storch conducted *Frohsinn* in a performance of Schumann's work in Linz on 15 April 1860. He resigned from his position the following day. His six articles appeared in the *Linzer Zeitung* on 3, 4, 8, 17, 23 and 26 May.

reform movement here and perhaps also countering a recent reviewer's argument that Schumann's music lacked melodic distinction, the over-sensitive Bruckner took it as a personal slight, remarking in a letter to Weinwurm that he was 'the only person who studied counterpoint in Linz' but certainly did not go around with his head bowed or believe that when he finished his contrapuntal studies he would have 'done enough for art'.[44] Any feelings of animosity towards Storch seem to have been short-lived, however. In December 1866, Bruckner responded to Storch's request for a male-voice piece for the *Niederösterreichisches Sängerbund* by writing him a friendly letter in which he enclosed three pieces, one of which - *Vaterlandslied* (*O könnt' ich dich beglücken*) WAB 92 - was specifically dedicated to the *Sängerbund*. Bruckner was so grateful that there was a prospect of one of his works being performed in Vienna that he was quite prepared to forego a fee![45]

No sooner had Bruckner completed his theoretical studies and received his certificate from the Vienna Conservatory than he embarked on another 'self-improvement' venture - a course of form and orchestration with Otto Kitzler. Kitzler had joined the Linz theatre orchestra as a cellist in 1858 and was appointed principal conductor in 1861. As a quartet player and cellist in the orchestra which participated in the performances of larger sacred works in the cathedral he was already well known to Bruckner. Between 1861 and 1863 when he moved to Brno

---

44 See *HSABB* 1, 18f. for this letter to Rudolf Weinwurm, dated Linz, 7 June 1860; the original of the letter is in the *ÖNB*. Bruckner mentioned that Weinwurm's brother, Alois, would have written a reply to Storch's implied criticism of conntraputal church music had not an excellent counter-article by Karl Santner, secretary of the Salzburg *Mozarteum* appeared in the Linzer Abendbnote.

45 See *HSABB* 1, 64 for Bruckner's letter, dated Linz, 11 December 1866; the original is in the library of the *Gesellschaft der Musikfreunde*. The other two pieces which Bruckner enclosed were the second setting of *Der Abendhimmel* WAB 56 and *Vaterländisches Weinlied* WAB 91. Bruckner also mentioned Storch's request in a letter to Rudolf Weinwurm. See *HSABB* 1, 63 for this letter, dated Linz, 2 December 1866; the original is the *Wiener Stadt- und Landesbibliothek*.

to take up the post of theatre orchestra conductor he was largely responsible for introducing Bruckner to a considerable amount of modern music, unbinding him from the self-imposed restrictions of six years of harmony and counterpoint exercises, and encouraging him to find his own original voice.[46] Most of the exercises which Bruckner undertook for Kitzler are contained in one volume, a manuscript of 163 folios of different sizes arranged in chronological order from December 1861 to July 1863.[47] The American scholar, Paul Hawkshaw, has provided the following description of the manuscript to which he has given the name *Kitzler Studienbuch*:

> The volume contains autograph sketches, verbal annotations, as well as complete and incomplete compositions, all testifying to the rigorous training Bruckner undertook and illustrating the systematic process with which he polished his technique.

There are only a few annotations by Kitzler himself and it would seem that he

> chose the course of studies and then served in an advisory capacity - leaving Bruckner to work out the details of the exercises for himself, rather than correcting every exercise as a harmony teacher might for a young student.[48]

---

46   Otto Kitzler (1834-1915) had an interesting early career. In 1846 he sang in Dresden in a performance of Beethoven's Ninth Symphony conducted by Wagner. In 1847 he sang in the first performance of Schumann's *Das Paradies und die Peri* in Dresden. Before moving to Linz he worked for periods in Königsberg, Strasbourg and Lyon where he formed a German male-voice choral society. Later in Brno he became director of the Music Society and choirmaster of the Male-Voice Society.

47   The manuscript is owned privately.

48   Paul Hawkshaw, *The Manuscript Sources for Anton Bruckner's Linz Works: A Study of his Working Methods from 1856 to 1868* [hereafter *HMSAB*] (Ann Arbor: UMI, 1984), 85 and footnote 4. Hawkshaw's research into the Linz period works has also resulted in several important articles,

83

Kitzler's main influence, apart from introducing Bruckner to modern music, particularly the music of Wagner, was in the areas of full score layout and formal structure. The exercises ranged from cadence structure and modulations to closely related keys through two- and three-part song form and instrumental forms such as the waltz, the mazurka and the minuet and trio to the more advanced sonata form. The culmination of this was the String Quartet in C minor WAB 111 which was completed on 15 August 1862. After a few exercises in orchestration, including scoring the opening movement of Beethoven's *Pathétique* sonata, Bruckner wrote the March in D minor WAB 96 (October 1862), the Three Orchestral Pieces WAB 97 (November 1862), the Overture in G minor WAB 98 (November / December 1862), the Symphony in F minor WAB 99 (January - April 1863) and, finally, Psalm 112 WAB 35 (completed 10 July 1863). During his period of study with Kitzler, Bruckner's three main textbooks were Ernst Friedrich Richter's *Die Grundzüge der musikalischen Formen und ihre Analyse* (Leipzig, 1852), Kitzler's own copy of Adolf Bernhard Marx's *Die Lehre von der musikalischen Komposition, praktisch-theoretisch* (Leipzig, 1837) and Johann Christian Lobe's *Lehrbuch der musikalischen Komposition* (Leipzig, 1850). As he grew more confident in putting his own ideas down on paper, he began to develop a working procedure which was retained by and large when he moved to Vienna in 1868. The composition of smaller works was usually worked out in a composition score starting from an initial

---

including 'The Date of Bruckner's "Nullified" Symphony in D minor', *19th-Century Music* vi/3 (Spring 1983), 252-63; 'From Zigeunerwald to Valhalla in Common Time. The Genesis of Anton Bruckner's Germanenzug', *BJ 1987-88* (Linz, 1990), 21-30; 'Weiteres über die Arbeitsweise Bruckners während seiner Linzer Jahre: Der Inhalt von Kremsmünster C56.2', *BSL 1992* (Linz, 1995), 143-52; 'Das Kitzler-Studienbuch: ein unschätzbares Dokument zu Bruckners Arbeitsweise', *BSL 1995* (Linz, 1997), 95-109; 'A composer learns his craft: lessons in form and orchestration, [1861-63]', *The Musical Quarterly* 82/2 (Summer 1998), 336-61 and *Perspectives on Anton Bruckner* (Aldershot: Ashgate, 2001), in preparation.

melody-bass skeleton, and then a fair copy was made either by Bruckner himself or by one of his copyists. In composing his larger works he began with a melody/bass continuity draft which encompassed either a complete movement or an extended section of a movement and included a working-out of the important structural details (outline of harmonic progressions, occasional contrapuntal passages, a few indications of orchestration and, in the case of choral works, precise textual underlay). This was written either on two / three staves for instrumental works or three / four staves for combined choral and instrumental works. The next steps in the process were first, the transfer of the sketch to full-score paper; second, the orchestration of the score which was accomplished in two or more stages, normally strings first then wind, except in combined choral and orchestral works where the voice parts were completed first; third, final corrections and the addition of detailed performance markings (dynamics, rehearsal letters etc.).[49]

After Bruckner's death, Otto Kitzler provided Franz Gräflinger with a detailed account of Bruckner's studies with him:

> ... I had already made Bruckner's acquaintance during the first years (Autumn 1858 - 1860) of my stay in Linz. We had got to know each other as a result of my involvement with the church choir when I voluntarily played the cello in performances of the larger Masses. From the autumn of 1861, Bruckner had regular lessons in orchestration from me. Before commencing the orchestration course, I gave him some instruction in musical form with the assistance of a by now completely out-of-print book by Richter, and took him through all the important structural schemes from eight-bar period to sonata form. Beethoven's sonatas formed the comparative basis of our exercises, and Bruckner was always particularly happy when he came across a musical procedure or feature which ran counter to his earlier studies with Sechter. Given his great talent and indefatigable industry, he made very speedy progress. In instrumentation we made

---

49   See *HMSAB*, 105-210 for a thorough examination of Bruckner's compositional procedures during the second half of the Linz period.

use at first of Marx's book which, however, does not go any further than Meyerbeer in its examples. At that time there were no teaching manuals which included details of Wagnerian and Lisztian instrumentation techniques. Wagner's operas had not yet been performed in Linz. To my knowledge, Bruckner had not yet heard any of Wagner's operas, because, during the time that he was having lessons from Sechter in his short breaks in Vienna, he was so preoccupied with his studies that he would have had hardly any time to visit the *Hofoper* to see a work by a composer whose style would then have been quite foreign to him. And so he was quite astonished when I told him that I was going to perform *Tannhäuser*, and he became more surprised when I brought him the score and drew his attention to the beauties of the work and the originality of the instrumentation. That was in December 1862. Consequently it is wrong to assume that Bruckner did not know any of Wagner's music before composing his Mass in D minor and his First Symphony in C minor and that his orchestration was not influenced in any way by Wagner. On the contrary, Bruckner studied the score of *Tannhäuser* thoroughly both before and after the performances. Shortly before this, and so not yet under the influence of this work, Bruckner had completed what was actually his first symphony - the Symphony in F minor - while studying with me. This was more of a student work and, because it was not particularly inspired, I could find nothing special to praise in it. He appeared to be upset by my guarded attitude - and this surprised me, because he was extremely modest. Many years later, he conceded, laughingly, that I had been absolutely right... Shortly afterwards he began a new symphony. I can no longer remember today, forty years later, if it was the First Symphony in C minor...

As our lessons had come to an end and the period of my Linz contract was also drawing to a close, he asked me one day, 'When am I going to be released?' When I replied that it could happen at any time as he had already overtaken his teacher who had nothing more to teach him, he refused such an easy way out and invited my wife and me on a coach excursion which took us to the charming hunting lodge of Kürnberg situated in the woods. There, during a happy meal, the desired 'release'[from 'apprenticeship'] took place. We had an uninterrupted friendship until his death. Whenever I came to Vienna, I visited my friend. I had an opportunity of becoming acquainted with his somewhat primitive domestic life, and on one occasion, in view of the state of rather easy-going disorder which prevailed in his house, I ventured to ask why he did not marry so as to enjoy a more settled domestic life. Almost shocked by this suggestion, he retorted, 'Dear friend, I don't really have the time - I have my Fourth Symphony to write at the moment'! I saw him for the last time two months before his death and, in spite of my request that he should not rise from his sick bed, he was determined to get up to greet me.[50]

That the relationship between the two men remained a cordial one long after Kitzler had left Linz is supported by several letters which passed between them. In June 1875, Bruckner informed Kitzler that he was in the process of writing his Fifth Symphony and that both Wagner and Liszt had described his Third Symphony as a 'very significant work'. He suggested that Kitzler perform his Second Symphony and signed the letter affectionately 'Your pupil A. Bruckner'.[51] Writing from St. Florian seventeen years later, Bruckner sent Kitzler warm greetings for the New Year and thanked him for his offer to conduct the Fourth Symphony. Because of his declining health, however, it was unlikely that he would be able to come to the performance. Once again he referred to himself as 'your former pupil'.[52] A few months later Bruckner supplied Kitzler with further information about his ill health. He mentioned that he had retired from both the *Hofkapelle* and the Conservatory and was no longer allowed to play the organ. As he had to avoid situations which might cause stress there was a great deal of uncertainty about his travelling to Brno to attend Kitzler's projected performances of the Fourth Symphony and *Te Deum* with the *Musikverein* choir and orchestra. Bruckner was also unable to attend a performance of his Second Symphony by Kitzler and the Brno *Musikverein* orchestra on 25 March

---

50 Translated from *GrBL*, 25ff.

51 See *HSABB* 1, 155 for this letter, dated Vienna, 1 June 1875; the original is owned privately.

52 See *ABB*, 266 for the text of this letter, dated St. Florian, 27 December 1892.

1896 but sent a letter of thanks.[53]

Shortly after Kitzler had left for Brno a young Viennese musician called Ignaz Dorn came to Linz to play violin in the *Landständisches Theater* orchestra.[54] He was an accomplished instrumentalist and composer and was soon appointed Kitzler's assistant at the theatre. As a modern music enthusiast Dorn continued Kitzler's work of extending Bruckner's horizons. He studied Wagner's *Der fliegende Holländer* and *Lohengrin* with Bruckner and introduced him to Berlioz's and Liszt's works, in particular the *Symphonie Fantastique* and the *Faust Symphony*. He made a present of the score of the latter to Bruckner with the handwritten dedication, 'as a souvenir from your sincere friend Ig. Dorn'.[55] Like Kitzler before him he encouraged Bruckner to develop his own compositional skills, which resulted in the Mass in D minor WAB 26 and the Symphony no. 1 in C minor WAB 101. In the spring of 1866 Dorn left Linz to become Kitzler's assistant in Brno. Writing to Bruckner from Brno in May 1866 he said how much he would like to hear this new C minor symphony and asked him to postpone any planned performance of it until August when he would be on his honeymoon.[56] Dorn's story has a tragic ending. The wedding plans - he hoped to marry Karl Zappe's daughter, Maria - did not materialize. An increasingly serious drinking problem led to dismissal from his post in Brno in 1871. He managed to find another position in Vienna as a conductor at the *Neue Welt* concert hall in the

53 Bruckner's letters to Kitzler are dated Vienna, 14 March 1893 and Vienna, 27 March 1896 respectively. The texts can be found in *ABB*, 269f. and *GrBB*, 56f. For the text of Kitzler's letter to Bruckner inviting him to the 1896 performance (dated Brno, 20 March 1896), see *ABB*, 312f.

54 Ignaz Dorn (1830-72) played second violin in the Vienna Court Opera Orchestra before coming to Linz.

55 'Andenken von seinem aufrichtigen Freund Ig. Dorn'. According to Göllerich (*G-A* III/1, 246), Bruckner lent this score to Otto Kitzler.

56 This letter, dated Brno, 7 May 1866, was in reply to one sent by Bruckner. See *HSABB* 1, 56 for the text of Dorn's letter. The originals of both letters are not extant.

Hietzing suburbs, a hall in which Eduard and Josef Strauss gave concerts and the Vienna *Männergesangverein* performed regularly during the summer months. There was a final reunion of the three friends - Bruckner, Kitzler and Dorn - after the famous Wagner concert in Vienna on 12 May 1872 when Wagner conducted Beethoven's *Eroica* symphony and excerpts from *the Ring*. Dorn was admitted to a lunatic asylum in Vienna soon afterwards and died there of delirium tremens. An obituary notice written by Eduard Kremser appeared in a later edition of *Das Vaterland*. Bruckner wrote to Kremser, thanking him for the obituary and saying how moved he was by the fact that Kremser's review of the first performance of his own F minor Mass had appeared in the same edition.[57]

One of Bruckner's closest friends during the Linz years was Alois Weinwurm, singing teacher at the secondary school in the town and founder of the *Sängerbund*

---

57 Kremser's obituary notice and review of Bruckner's Mass in F minor were published on 20 June 1872. See *HSABB* 1, 135 for Bruckner's letter to Kremser, the original of which is owned privately. For further information about Dorn, see Hermann Zappe, 'Anton Bruckner, die Familie Zappe und die Musik' in *BJ 1982-83* (Linz, 1984), 140f.; Elisabeth Maier, 'Brahms und Bruckner. Ihr Ausbildungsgang' in *BSL 1983* (Linz, 1985), 69f.; idem, 'Ignaz Dorns Charakteristische Symphonie "Labyrinth-Bilder"' in *BSL 1987* (Linz, 1989), 69-78. This third article includes a reprint of Selmar Bagge's review in the *Deutsche Musik-Zeitung* 2 (1861), 44f. of a concert in the *Musikvereinsaal*, Vienna on 2 February 1861 in which four of Dorn's works, including his symphony, were performed.

58 Alois Weinwurm (1824-79) was educated in Zwettl and Vienna. From 1844 until his move to Linz in the 1850s he was a piano and singing teacher in Vienna.

59 Rudolf Weinwurm (1835-1911) was also educated in Zwettl and Vienna where he founded the *Akademischer Gesangverein* in 1858 and held appointments as singing teacher at the University, conductor of the *Singakademie* (1865-78), and conductor of the *Männergesangverein* (1866-80). He was the composer of several choral pieces and the author of some vocal teaching manuals.

choir in 1857.[58] There appears to have been a temporary breach in the relationship in 1865/66 but it was soon patched up. Alois's younger brother, Rudolf, first made Bruckner's acquaintance in Linz in the early autumn of 1856 and maintained a regular correspondence with him from Vienna where he was permanently based.[59] Rudolf Weinwurm kept Bruckner in touch with what was happening in Vienna and, along with Johann Herbeck, was instrumental in persuading him to move there in 1868. Bruckner's letters are often purely factual, dwelling on events in Linz and, in the 1860s, the progress of his compositions, but his deeper feelings and internal struggles occasionally come to the surface. The earliest recorded letter to Weinwurm dates from November 1856, and it was evidently a long-delayed reply to an earlier letter from his new friend. Bruckner recalled with pleasure Weinwurm's visit to Linz in September, in particular a joint outing with some friends to St. Florian and Steyregg, and asked his friend to send him a copy of a recent journal which had contained a reference to his organ playing in Salzburg Cathedral at the beginning of September.[60] The conclusion to the letter is more personal:

... My longing to see you and my confidence in you increase day by day. Write to me soon... Please remember me; I would never forget it. With deepest affection, and with greetings from your brother as

---

60 See earlier for Bruckner's visit to Salzburg (6 - 9 September) and his participation in an organ contest with Robert Führer. Anton Scheele was the editor of a monthly music journal for which Rudolf Weinwurm provided an article on Bruckner's playing in Salzburg. There was also a report in the *Österreichische Bürgerblatt* (edition of 14 September 1856), 864 which was published before Weinwurm's return to Vienna (on 20 or 21 September). See footnote 16 for the reference to the *Monatsschrift für Theater und Musik* 2 (1856) which is presumably the 'berühmte Monatblatt' which Bruckner asked Weinwurm to purchase for him and send to him.

well...[61]

Bruckner's letters to Weinwurm and Sechter's letters to Bruckner during the period 1857-1861 reveal that Weinwurm often acted as a go-between, collecting exercises from Sechter to send to Bruckner. Bruckner evidently required some medical treatment during August 1857, possibly from a doctor recommended by Weinwurm. Writing to Rudolf at the beginning of September, he enclosed some money and asked his friend to pay the doctor's bill. He reminded Weinwurm that he had not yet sent his brother Alois some choruses he had promised. Finally, he mentioned that Sechter had written to him, and asked Weinwurm to collect some exercises from his teacher. 'Don't be annoyed, and write to me soon', he wrote in conclusion.[62] During Bruckner's study visit to Vienna in July 1858, Rudolf Weinwurm introduced him to some of Schumann's songs and dedicated an organ prelude (op. 5 in F major) to him.[63] This visit culminated in an organ recital in the *Piaristenkirche* which was something of a personal triumph. A week later, he wrote to Weinwurm thanking him for his letter and expressing his deep gratitude for all that he had done on his behalf. He asked his friend to send him some copies of

---

61 See *HSABB* 1, 8 for the complete text of this letter, dated Linz, 30 November 1856. The original of this letter is in the Pierpont Morgan Library, New York. The originals of the majority of Bruckner's letters to Weinwurm, however, are to be found in the *ÖNB* and the *Wiener Stadt- und Landesbibliothek* (shelf nos. I.N. 35309-332). For further information about Weinwurm, see Leopold Nowak's article, 'Rudolf Weinwurm - Zum 150. Geburtstag' in *IBG Mitteilungsblatt* 26 (October 1985), 26; for further information about the Bruckner - Weinwurm relationship, see Andrea Harrandt, '"... den ich als einzigen wahren Freund erkenne...". Anton Bruckner und Rudolf Weinwurm', *BSL 1994* (Linz, 1997), 37-48.

62 See *HSABB* 1, 10 for the text of this letter, dated Linz, 1 September 1857. The original is owned privately; there is a facsimile of the letter in Bassenge's *Auktionskatalog* 57 (Berlin, May 1991), 191.

63 The organ prelude has not survived, but one of Bruckner's workbooks from this period (harmony and counterpoint exercises, 128 pages) can be found in the *ÖNB* (Mus. Hs. 24.260).

Ludwig Speidel's favourable review in the evening edition of the *Wiener Zeitung* (24 July) and to ascertain Speidel's address so that he could write him a letter of thanks.[64] Weinwurm collected some more counterpoint exercises from Sechter in September but appears to have delayed in sending them to Bruckner.[65] At the end of October, Bruckner wrote to Weinwurm in good spirits, congratulating his friend on his recent appointment as choirmaster of the *Akademisches Gesangverein* and giving him the good news that Alois had formed a new choir in Linz called *Sängerbund* for which he had great plans:

> ... I too have a lot to do. I am very well and once again a little in love. Alois must now take your place at my side (in Linz, of course), and he does it very well. Write again soon...[66]

Before spending six weeks (end of June - middle of August) in Vienna during the summer of 1859, Bruckner confirmed with Sechter that he would be able to teach him, and then wrote to Weinwurm to ask him to find suitable lodgings. He longed

---

64 See *HSABB* 1, 10f. for the text of this letter, dated Linz, 1 August 1858; see earlier and footnote 19.

65 In his letter to Bruckner, dated Vienna, 26 September 1858, Sechter refers to Bruckner's letter of 22 September (which has been lost); this had contained a copy of one of Bruckner's works, *Litanei* WAB 132, but, to Sechter's surprise, there had been no mention of the receipt of the exercises. A month before this, on 26 August 1858, Sechter had also written to Bruckner, enquiring with some concern why Bruckner had not contacted him and fearing that he might have caught a chill on his return to Linz during a spell of very bad weather. See *HSABB* 1, 11 and 13f. for the texts of these letters; the original of the August letter is in the *ÖNB*; the original of the September letter, which was first published in *ABB*, 350f., is not extant.

66 See *HSABB* 1, 14 for the full text of this letter, dated Linz, 30 October 1858; the original is in the *ÖNB*.

to see him again as he did not have 'a friend like him' in Linz.[67]

Bruckner's next study visit to Vienna was towards the end of February or the beginning of March 1860. He had to change his original plan of arriving in Vienna on 22 February because he had not yet received any reply to two letters he had sent to Sechter and suspected that his teacher, who had recently suffered one or two bouts of ill health, might be indisposed. He asked Weinwurm to visit Sechter and ask him if it was convenient to come.[68] Another letter sent to Weinwurm about six weeks later indicates that Bruckner had been in Vienna in the meantime. He had been loath to leave his friend and hoped that Weinwurm would be able to visit Linz during the summer. He had obviously made the acquaintane of a certain 'Frl. Pepi' - probably Rudolf's sister Josepha - during his visit and asked to be remembered to her.[69]

How much importance he attached to his friendship with Rudolf Weinwurm is revealed in his next letter to him. Bruckner described Weinwurm as his 'one true friend'. He treasured all the letters sent from Vienna, and had been particularly delighted to receive a portrait of Rudolf which would now have a place of honour in his apartment. The possibility of a visit from his friend later in the summer also

---

67 Bruckner's letter to Sechter (dated Linz, 3 June 1859) is not extant. See *HSABB* 1, 15 for Sechter's reply to Bruckner's letter, dated Vienna, 5 June 1859, and Bruckner's letter to Weinwurm, dated Linz, 6 June 1859. The original of the former is in the *ÖNB* and the original of the latter is privately owned. See also page 73 and footnote 23.

68 See *HSABB* 1, 17 for the text of this letter, dated Linz, 25 February 1860; the original is owned privately. Sechter's most recent communication with Bruckner had been on 13 January - see page 74 and footnote 25.

69 See *HSABB* 1, 18 for the text of this letter, dated Linz, 6 April 1860; the original is owned privately.

filled him with joy.[70] The possibility became an actuality. Weinwurm stayed with Bruckner as his guest in the *Stadtpfarrmesnerhaus* from 23 August until 10 September 1860.

Three months later Bruckner was in a difficult financial position and asked Weinwurm to contact a certain Mr. Kaan who was now in Vienna and remind him that he had promised to send the sum of 45 florins which he owed.[71] Bruckner would almost certainly have had to pay the funeral expenses of his mother who had died in Ebelsberg on 11 November and obviously required immediate payment of the debt.[72] Bruckner's financial problem appears to have been resolved satisfactorily. The following month he wrote again to Weinwurm, mentioning that he was hoping to spend the entire Lenten season (from Ash Wednesday, 13 February onwards) in Vienna, and asking his friend to find him some quiet, well-heated lodgings preferably in the inner city.[73] When Weinwurm replied, giving him the address of a hotel, Bruckner recalled his unhappy experience of the previous year when he had stayed at the *Kreuz* hotel in the Mariahilf area and had not been able to get to sleep until three or four in the morning. He said he would much prefer to stay with a 'nice solid family'. He gave Weinwurm the time of his expected arrival in Vienna, said that he had much to tell him and looked forward to 'put Linz behind me for

---

70 See *HSABB*, 18f. for the text of this letter, dated Linz, 7 June 1860. It was in the second part of this letter, referred to earlier, that Bruckner complained of Storch's description of 'sad figures who slink around with heads bowed'. See page 81, footnote 44.

71 See *HSABB* 1, 20 for the text of this letter, dated Linz, 9 December 1860; the original is owned privately.

72 See *HSABB* 1, 19 for Bruckner's letter to his sister, Rosalie Hueber, about their mother's death. It is dated Ebelsberg, 11 November 1860, and the original is in private possession in Vöcklabruck.

73 See *HSABB*, 21 for the text of this letter, dated Linz, 30 January 1861; the original is owned privately. See also earlier and footnote 27.

94

a while.[74]

While he was in Vienna, Bruckner made an official request to the committee of the *Wiener Männergesangverein* to borrow a number of choral pieces for *Frohsinn* in Linz.[75] Bruckner, Alois and Rudolf Weinwurm were all involved with their respective choirs in Krems at the end of June 1861. Just before this, Bruckenr wrote to Rudolf to thank him and the *Männergesangverein* on his own behalf and on behalf of *Frohsinn* for sending the music he had requested. He had recommended fairly simple pieces for his choir in order to avoid 'too severe criticism'. 'If only the rehearsals were better attended', he complained.[76] In this letter Bruckner also referred to the post of director of the *Dommusikverein* and *Mozarteum* in Salzburg which had become vacant as a consequence of Alois Taux's death in April. He had heard that there was a possible candidate for the post from Innsbruck and asked Weinwurm if he himself was interested. Bruckner's own interest in the position seems to have declined when he discovered that Hans Schläger, a former colleague in St. Florian, was the front runner, and yet he regarded it as a matter of honour to undergo the ordeal of travelling to Salzburg in September and conducting the *Singakademie* choir.[77] The whole story was graphically related by Bruckner in another letter to Weinwurm. At the end of the letter, he referred to his intention to be formally examined in Vienna in November:

---

74 See *HSABB*, 21 for the text of this letter, dated Linz 10 February 1861; the original has been lost. See also earlier and footnote 27.

75 See *HSABB* 1, 22 for the text of this letter, dated Vienna, 23 March 1861; the original is in the choir archives.

76 See *HSABB* 1, 22f. for the text of this letter, dated Linz, 21 June 1861; the original is owned privately.

77 See *HSABB* 1, 23f. for the text of Bruckner's official application for the post, dated Linz, 22 June 1861. It included a curriculum vitae and several certificates which attested to his qualifications for the post; the original of the letter is in the archives of the Salzburg *Dommusikverein*.

... Schläger is dictator under Hilleprandt in Salzburg. I could say a lot about this but will confine myself to the following. I received letter after letter, i.e. written invitations to travel to Salzburg to take rehearsals. This was after I had already heard from Schläger, who was with me, that he was the favourite. And so I did not go. When I eventually received an urgent letter, however, and realised that it was now a question of salvaging my reputation, I decided to travel to Salzburg on the night of Thursday 19ᵗʰ last month. I conducted there on the Friday and Saturday and returned here on Saturday night. Hilleprandt had spoken to some people about my ability in insulting, even contemptuous terms. I will never forget the struggles I had on the Friday evening. You can well imagine the situation. The ladies of the *Singakademie*, stirred up by the Hilleprandt faction, were all against me - it was shocking. But I did not give up and, in the end, my choral piece (7-part *Ave Maria*) was very well received and applauded twice. At the end Hilleprandt was *very frank*, indeed *too frank*, with me. But I will tell you all about it in November. It is reported that Schläger was appointed at a reduced salary of 600 florins. All the best to him!

The newspapers already knew about the situation before there was a meeting in Salzburg. I made enquiries on your behalf. We will have a good laugh about it here in Linz. A novel could be, indeed ought to be, written about the filling of this 600-florin post.

In September I resigned from the choir as a result of gross insults. Sechter stayed with me for a few days. I am thinking of travelling to Vienna in the second half of November. Could you please be available and, perhaps, make a few preparations. In any case I would like to invite Randhartinger, the court music director, and Gottfried Preyer to be members of the examining committee. Write to me soon. Sechter will be in charge of the examination.[78]

---

78 See *HSABB*, 25f. for the text of this letter, dated Linz, 3 October 1861; the original is owned privately. Franz von Hilleprandt (1796-1871), a Salzburg lawyer, was largely responsible for the foundation of the *Dommusikverein* and the *Mozarteum* in 1841 as an artistic institution for 'the promotion of all branches of music, especially choral music'. He was its administrative director for thirty years. Its first music director was Alois Taux (1817-61). Benedikt Randhartinger (1802-93) became assistant court music director in Vienna in 1844 and succeeded Ignaz Aßmayr as principal music director in 1862. He retired four years later, in 1866. Gottfried Preyer (1807 - 1901) was director of music at St. Stephen's, Vienna and became Randhartinger's assistant in 1862.

In the summer of 1862 Bruckner took the first steps to secure a post at the Court Chapel in Vienna. Ignaz Aßmayr died at the end of August and was replaced as chief music director by Benedikt Randhartinger. Gottfried Preyer became assistant director, and Sechter and Ludwig Rotter were the two paid organists. Sechter visited Bruckner on his way back to Vienna from Friedberg and promised that he would recommend him to Randhartinger as a supernumerary organist-designate. Joseph von Arneth, a government official and the brother of the abbot of St. Florian, heard Bruckner play the organ at the St. Augustine's day service in St. Florian on 28 August and was so impressed that he was willing to use his influence, and Count O'Hegerty, a former student of Bruckner's from the St. Florian days, undertook to speak on his behalf to Prince Karl Liechtenstein, the Lord Chamberlain. Bruckner also had another friend in high places, a certain Count Johann Karl Huyn, an officer in the Austrian army, who had heard his organ playing and was convinced that his future lay in a move to Vienna. On 4 September Weinwurm wrote to Bruckner about the vacancy in the music staff of the Court Chapel and gave him some good advice about the various diplomatic steps he should take, including the submission of original compositions, in order to muster support for a possible application.[79] In his reply Bruckner assured Weinwurm that he had already taken certain steps, including a letter to Randhartinger to express interest in a possible post. Unfortunately, because of his extended period of study with Sechter, he had very few original compositions to his name. Enclosing a copy of his seven-part *Ave Maria*, he asked Weinwurm to try to persuade Ferdinand Stegmayer, professor of choral singing at the Conservatory, to perform it. If there was a performance, he would try to approach all the music critics, for instance Selmar Bagge, from whom he could expect favourable reviews. In the meantime, if Weinwurm had an opportunity to speak to Randhartinger

---

79 See *HSABB* 1, 30f. for the text of this letter; the original is in St. Florian.

on his behalf, he would be most grateful.[80] All Bruckner's efforts were in vain. At first he was informed by Randhartinger that there would be a competition for the vacancy in due course and that he would certainly be apprised of any developments. At the same time he heard a conflicting report from another person (unnamed) in Vienna that Pius Richter was being considered for the post.[81] At the end of September or beginning of October both Sechter and Arneth wrote to Bruckner to confirm that no supernumerary organist would be appointed in the meantime. In any case, since such a post would be an unpaid one, the successful candidate would have to reside in Vienna. Because of the uncertainty of any other prospects for Bruckner in Vienna at this stage in his career, he decided not to pursue his application.[82] Six months later Bruckner heard from Sechter that he had been forced by ill health to give up his position at the Court Chapel (for which he had received the imperial 'long service' medal) and that his duties were now confined to teaching at the Conservatory. Pius Richter, known to both Randhartinger and the Lord Chamberlain, had been appointed first organist-designate and Rudolf Bibl second organist-designate.[83]

80 See *HSABB* 1, 31f. for the text of this letter, dated Linz, 7 September 1862; the original is in the *Sängermuseum des Fränkischen Sängerbundes DSM 18553*, Feuchtwangen.

81 Bruckner conveyed this information to Weinwurm in a letter, dated Linz, 23 September 1862. See *HSABB* 1, 33 for the text of this letter; the original is owned privately.

82 See *HSABB* 1, 34 for Bruckner's letter to Weinwurm, dated Linz, 20 October 1862; the original is in the *ÖNB*. Bruckner was also able to congratulate his friend, who had been experiencing severe financial difficulties, on his appointment as singing teacher at Vienna University. The letters from Sechter and Arneth have been lost.

83 See *HSABB* 1, 34f. for Sechter's letter to Bruckner, dated Vienna, 27 March 1863; the original is in the *ÖNB*. Pius Richter (1818-1893) was a piano tutor at the court from 1857. He became a paid organist at the court in 1868 and was appointed assistant music director in September 1893, three months before his death. Rudolf Bibl (1832-1902), a pupil of Sechter, was appointed organist

Bruckner spent the summer of 1863 putting the finishing touches to his Symphony in F minor WAB 99 and Psalm 112 WAB 35. He referred to both these works and to another composition he was preparing for the *Oberösterreichisches Sängerbundesfest (Festival of Upper Austrian Choral Societies)* in 1865 - *Germanenzug* WAB 70 - in a letter written to Weinwurm at the beginning of September. He was intending to go to a music festival in Munich at the end of the month and hoped to see Weinwurm there.[84] But his friend was unable to attend and Bruckner had to be satisfied with a letter to which he replied shortly after his return from Munich early in October. While in Munich he had met the renowned critic Hanslick who had mentioned Weinwurm several times. Otherwise, he had not had the opportunity of 'making the acquaintance of important men, far less playing to them'. However, he had introduced himself to Franz Lachner:

> ... I eventually introduced myself to Lachner and asked him to have a quick look at my compositions. After two days he said, 'My congratulations, your works are distinguished by a good flow of ideas and awareness of structure and a fine sense of direction. I am not averse to performing your symphony sometime in the future. I have already selected Herbeck's for this winter season'.
> These were his words, more or less. He then told me how both he and Schubert had been rejected by the court chapel in Vienna. He became very friendly after I related my own story to him...
> I have started making preparations for a tour next year - it is my intention to give organ concerts...[85]

---

at St. Stephen's in 1859. He eventually became court music director in 1897.

84 See *HSABB* 1, 37 for this letter, dated Linz, 1 September 1863; the original is owned privately.

85 Extract from Bruckner's letter to Weinwurm, dated Linz, 8 October 1863. See *HSABB* 1, 37f. for complete text; the original is owned privately. Franz Lachner (1803-1890) studied with Sechter in Vienna in the 1820s and made the acquaintance of both Beethoven and Schubert. From 1836 until his retirement in 1868 he played a prominent part in the musical life of Munich as director of the court opera, conductor of choral and orchestral concerts, and director of music festivals in 1855

Bruckner again mooted the possibility of giving organ concerts in Germany when he wrote to Weinwurm in February 1864. After providing his friend with information about his *Germanenzug* and asking him if he could recommend a Viennese harpist who would be able to play the harp part in the solo quartet and be prepared to travel to Linz the following year when the work was to be formed during the Choral Festival in the town, he added:

> ... Could I ask you either to write yourself or arrange for a letter to be sent to Dresden and Leipzig to determine whether it would be possible to give concerts or whether I should play, unpaid, only free fantasias? The audiences should include many influential invited guests. Bagge etc. would certainly make the best recommendations. Please, this is a matter of urgency because of the preparations I will have to make...[86]

Writing to Weinwurm again at the beginning of the following month, Bruckner passed on some advice from Alois concerning the instrumentation of the piece he (Rudolf) was writing for the Choral Festival - he should keep it as simple as possible. Bruckner again broached the subject of a concert tour:

> ... In connection with the tour, I have to tell you that, unfortunately, I do not have any repertoire, although I have played Bach and Mendelssohn. I have neither the time nor the volition to be particularly concerned about this, as it serves no purpose. Organists are always badly paid, and, in my opinion, if concerts cannot be arranged to run at a profit, the best solution is to perform without a fee and to improvise fantasias etc. without music. I believe that there are any number of competent players around who can perform the works of other composers well. Do you not agree? I prefer not to waste time wondering whether I can give concerts. Please don't

---

and 1863.

86 Extract from letter, dated Linz, 25 February 1864. See *HSABB* 1, 40f. for the complete text; the original is not extant. It was first published in *ABB*, 54f.

forget to write to Dresden and Leipzig...

At the end of the letter he confessed to feelings of depression and disenchantment, referred to recent changes in the administration of the Linz *Musikverein* and alluded to forthcoming concerts in Vienna which he might attend.[87] The proposed concert tour did not materialize.

In referring to changes in the *Musikverein* Bruckner was no doubt recalling his own involvement a few months earlier. At the end of October 1863, the committee of the *Musikverein* asked Bruckner to succeed Engelbert Lanz as artistic director, take charge of the next concert and perform one of his own compositions. In his reply Bruckner gave clear indication of how concerned he was that the Society should have a much more secure financial and artistic standing:

> ... Honoured as I am by the invitation of your esteemed committee to assume the artistic direction of the *Musikverein*, may I be permitted to point out that this direction would be contingent upon the following conditions:
> The Society can only fulfil its duties if it is furnished with the necessary means, viz. active and supporting members.
> What is particularly necessary is a recruiting drive both within the Society and the numerous musical bodies outside the Society so that its artistic strength can be gauged. There should be an accurate register of those ladies who are not pupils of the Society as well as pupils of the Society who can sing soprano and alto, of those men who can sing tenor and bass, and of those who are string players, wind players etc.
> This urgent appeal to participate as active members should be made not only to the fairly large number of current musical friends

---

87 See *HSABB* 1, 41f. for the complete text of this letter, dated Linz, 1 March 1864; the original is in the University library, Leipzig. On 22 March, the Tuesday of Holy Week, Bruckner heard a performance of Bach's *St. John Passion* in Vienna, conducted by Johann Herbeck. As Weinwurm stayed with Bruckner in Linz from 26 March until 7 April it is possible that Bruckner stayed in Vienna until the end of the week and returned to Linz with his friend.

but also to those who have an enthusiasm for beautiful art, one condition being that they promise to attend a weekly practice regularly.

The supporting members should be levied to supply the material resources.

Although an increase in the number of supporting members can be accomplished especially by the good performance of first-rate works, it would be extremely important, immediately after determining who the active members were, to produce a circular letter in which the entire situation, viz. the need for financial support, was brought to the attention of the religious and civic dignitaries and the townspeople and a voluntary annual subscription was sought. Men like the mayor will certainly be able to commit themselves to more than two florins annually, even if they are members already.

NB. As His Majesty the Emperor already releases large sums of money to the music societies not only in Vienna but in the provinces as well, a petition to the Emperor should have the greatest effect of all.

In this way the material standing of the Society could be improved. As far as raising the artistic standing is concerned, I will gladly devote all my energy, knowledge and ability to accomplish this, if it is facilitated by the preparation and organization outlined above. I am obliged to make a sincere request for an annual salary commensurate with the great effort and responsibility attached to the artistic direction of the Society, a salary which cannot possibly be considered unreasonable by those gentlemen who have some conception of thorough musical training in relation to the expenditure and enormous effort involved, who understand what it means to raise the musical standards of a Society, and who are also aware of my own circumstances.[88]

Bruckner's ideas were premature. Engelbert Lanz had not received any financial remuneration for his efforts and, as there was very little money available, Bruckner's

---

88 See *HSABB* 1, 39 for the complete text of this letter, dated Linz, 6 November 1863, which was in reply to the request made on 22 October; the original is in the Linz *Singakademie* archives.

suggestions were declined.[89]

Bruckner spent the summer of 1864 working on his D minor Mass. His original intention was to have it ready for performance at the Emperor's summer residence in Bad Ischl, but he was not able to meet this self-imposed deadline. In his next letter to Weinwurm, written in October, he apologized for not writing earlier. He had been expecting to see Weinwurm again in Linz in August, but, when the visit did not go ahead, had decided to postpone writing until he could share the news that his Mass was finished. He was hoping for a performance on St. Caecilia's day. In the meantime, he had played the organ at Bad Ischl for the Emperor's name-day on 4 October.[90] In his reply two days later, Weinwurm informed Bruckner that there was a proposal to begin an organ class in the Conservatory, and registered his surprise that Sechter had not mentioned this in recent letters to Bruckner. As the lecturer appointed would also share in harmony teaching, Weinwurm thought that his friend would be ideally suited to the post. Even though the pay would be fairly low, at least it would provide a basis for other activities in Vienna.[91] Perhaps because Weinwurm also mentioned that a certain Hermann Köhler had been named as a candidate for the position, Bruckner did not make any reference to the possibility of

---

89   According to some commentators, including Auer, *ABB*, 53 footnote and Nowak, *Anton Bruckner und Linz. Katalog zur Ausstellung 1964* (Linz, 1964), 70, Lanz resumed his unpaid position. According to the report of the Linz *Musikverein* published in 1871 to commemorate its 50th birthday, however, Karl Weilnböck succeeded Lanz.

90   See *HSABB* 1, 44 for the text of this letter, dated Linz, 10 October 1864. The original is owned privately; there is a facsimile of the first page in J.A. Stargardt, *Versteigerungskatalog* 630 (Marburg, 1983), 251.

91   See *HSABB* 1, 45f. for the text of this letter, dated Vienna, 12 October 1864. Weinwurm also provided news of his own activities and other musical happenings in Vienna, lamenting the dearth of performances of modern music. The original of this letter has been lost; it was first published in *ABB*, 373-76.

moving to Vienna in his next letter to his friend. Instead, in a fit of melancholy, he complained about the lack of harmony and piano pupils as a result of fee undercutting in Linz, and said that he would be prepared to go abroad - to Russia, even Mexico! - if he did not obtain any recognition in Linz.[92] Two months later, however, his mood had changed. Two performances of his new Mass in D minor WAB 26 in Linz, the first in the cathedral on 20 November, the second in the *Redoutensaal* on 18 December, had pleased Bruckner immensely. After congratulating Weinwurm on his own recent conducting successes in Vienna, he mentioned the two Linz performances of the Mass and enclosed copies of the favourable reviews in the *Linzer Zeitung* and the *Abendbote*. He continued:

> ...Archduke Josef also attended my concert... I am having a fair copy of the full score made at present. Do you think that I should send it later through you to Hanslick and Herbeck? It requires too many rehearsals for a church performance (even when the singers and instrumentalists involved are the most capable court musicians). And what choir director would be pleased with that state of affairs? My own feeling is that the best solution would be if Herbeck found it good enough to perform as part of a *Musikverein* concert. (Or Dessoff, if that was not appropriate) - or Krenn? - but who would hear it there? What do you think? I hope to speak to you soon, as I intend travelling over for the Ninth Symphony and for the Philharmonic concert. I don't know when it will be. Please write to me...[93]

---

92   See *HSABB*, 46f. for the text of this letter, dated Linz, 18 October 1864; the original is owned privately. Bruckner also referred to Mexico in another letter to an unknown recipient - dated Linz, 10 October 1864; see *HSABB* 1, 44 for the text of this letter, the original of which is in the library of the University of Basel. Apparently both Weinwurm and Bruckner had been approached about a position in the court of Archduke Maximilian, the younger brother of Franz Josef and Emperor of Mexico.

93   See *HSABB* 1, 47f. for the complete text of this letter, dated Linz, 26 December 1864; the original is owned privately; there is a facsimile of the first page in Stargardt, *Versteigerungskatalog*

104

Weinwurm did write to him, and communicated the excellent news that he would be prepared to conduct a performance of the Mass during the University of Vienna's 500th birthday celebrations in 1865. Not only Bruckner but 'almost the whole of Linz' was delighted by this honour:

> ... As soon as a fair copy of the score has been made, you will receive it together with all the individual parts. From now on the Mass should not be performed anywhere else before the University jubilee. Above all I must tell you that it is very difficult to perform. Even with the best Viennese forces at your disposal, you will require very thorough study of the chorus parts and many rehearsals because the intonation is difficult. Several orchestral rehearsals will be necessary on account of the very precise nuances. And then, finally, a couple of dress rehearsals. It goes without saying that I will place all the means that I possess at your disposal. (Perhaps you could also use this opportunity to perform my 7-part *Ave Maria*.) I beg you to remain firm and not to accept any other Mass. (You will probably be harassed on all sides.) When is the jubilee this year? In July? I will come in any case, as will Alois and several others from Linz. Alois sends you his greetings. He is going to write to you today. I now feel very happy. To have such a friend as you is a great blessing. Perhaps I will come to see you during Lent...[94]

Later in the month Bruckner sent Weinwurm the score and parts of the Mass, emphasised once again the need for the chorus parts to be rehearsed thoroughly, and asked his friend to let Hanslick and other potential reviewers see the score. He also added as a postscript the request that Weinwurm return the score of his symphony -

---

628 (Marburg, 1983), 245. Franz Krenn (1816-97) was music director of a church in the Mariahilf district of Vienna. He later became one of Bruckner's teaching colleagues at the Vienna Conservatory. The performance of Beethoven's Ninth was given by the Vienna Philharmonic on 26 December, the date of this letter!

94 See *HSABB* 1, 48f. for the complete text of this letter, dated Linz, 3 January 1865; the original is in the *Wiener Stadt- und Landesbibliothek*. Weinwurm's letter to Bruckner has not been traced. Perhaps he wrote to his brother Alois, and Alois passed on the good news to Bruckner?

presumably the F minor symphony - as soon as he had perused it.[95] In his reply Weinwurm mentioned how helpful it would be to have a piano score of the Mass for rehearsal purposes. Bruckner, writing again a few days later, said that he did not have any time at present to prepare a piano score. He recommended Dorn, who was in Vienna at the time, as a suitable accompanist, and added that it would not be difficult to construct a piano part from the vocal parts. He hoped to be able to send Weinwurm 100 florins for the Vienna performance and suggested that some of the money be used to prepare a proper piano score. In the meantime he was busy working on his C minor symphony and now had more private pupils to teach. But he was in low spirits - a recent proposal of marriage to the adopted daughter of a respectable family had been declined - and wished that he lived nearer Rudolf.[96]

There is a gap of almost twelve months before Bruckner's next letter to Rudolf Weinwurm. That Weinwurm was not able to perform Bruckner's Mass as promised is a possible explanation. Events at the *Upper Austrian Choral Festival* in Linz in June 1865 no doubt put a further strain on the friendship. Before the festival Bruckner, accompanied by Carl Pichler-Bodog, director of the Linz theatre, and Franz Schober, one of his harmony students, travelled to Munich to be present at the first performance of Wagner's *Tristan und Isolde* on 15 May. He met Wagner, who gave him a signed photograph, Hans von Bülow and Anton Rubinstein and showed von Bülow and Rubinstein the completed sections of his C minor Symphony. According to Bruckner, they had a few reservations but were enthusiastic on the whole.[97] Because of the indisposition of Mrs. Schnorr-Carolsfeld, the first Isolde,

---

95   See *HSABB* 1, 49 for the text of this letter, dated Linz, 21 January 1865; the original is in the *Wiener Stadt- und Landesbibliothek*.

96   See *HSABB* 1, 50f. for the text of this letter, dated Linz, 29 January 1865; the original is owned privately.

97   See *G-A* III./1, 315f. for Bruckner's account. Reports of Bruckner's visit to Munich in the *Linzer Zeitung* 111 (14 May 1865) and the *Neue Freie Presse* 257(18 May 1865) are cited in

the first three performances of the opera had to be postponed. Bruckner had to return to Linz to conduct his *Germanenzug* at the Choral Festival (4 - 6 June) and, as a result, did not see *Tristan und Isolde* until its third performance on Monday 19 June.[98] Between his visits to Munich he won second prize at the Festival. Rudolf Weinwurm's *Germania* won first prize - but Bruckner did not accept this decision with good grace, believing that his composition was superior to that of his friend! He was also suspicious that Alois Weinwurm, who was one of the adjudicators, had influenced the other members of the adjudicating committee in favour of his brother.[99] The immediate result was a temporary breach in the relationship until the beginning of 1866. In the meantime Bruckner was sufficiently heartened by Hanslick's encouragement to continue setting his sights on Vienna. Hanslick was present at the Festival, and, at the end of the year, recalled his visit with pleasure by sending Bruckner a signed copy of Schumann's Mass op. 147.[100]

Leopold Nowak, op.cit., 144f. See also Othmar Wessely, 'Anton Bruckner und Linz', *Jahrbuch der Stadt Linz 1954* (Linz, 1955), 262 for the text of Ludwig Speidel's report in *Fremdenblatt* of the postponement of the premiere of *Tristan und Isolde* in which he mentions Bruckner's difficulties at the Austrian / Bavarian border because he did not have the proper travelling documents with him. Evidently Herbeck came to his rescue!

98   According to Bruckner's own account (*G-A* III/1, 317), he returned to Munich immediately after the end of the festival. See *GrBL*, 39 for a reference to a report in the *Linzer Zeitung* 129 (7 June 1865) of Bruckner's intended return visit to Munich. According to Uwe Harten, however, Bruckner was in Munich from 13 to 20 July. See Uwe Harten, 'Zu Anton Bruckners vorletzten Münchener Aufenthalt' in *Studien sur Musikwissenschaft* 42 (Tutzing, 1993), 324.

99   See later in the chapter for further information about *Germanenzug* and its reception.

100   Othmar Wessely, op.cit., 261 cites a report in the *Linzer Zeitung* 130 (8 June 1865) that Hanslick had asked Bruckner for a copy of the score of *Germanenzug*. Hanslick's gift to Bruckner is mentioned in *G-A* III/1, 321, Wessely, op.cit., 229, and Manfred Wagner, 'Bruckner in Wien', *ABDS* 2 (Graz, 1980), 50. The dedication is 'Herrn Anton Bruckner zur freundschaftlichen Erinnerung an Eduard Hanslick Wien im Dezember 1865'. This dedication score is not extant - it

Bruckner's next letter to Rudolf Weinwurm at the beginning of 1866 suggests that the breach in the relationship had been essentially between Bruckner and Alois Weinwurm. Some words which Bruckner had uttered somewhat rashly to Franz Melichar, a member of *Frohsinn*, had been reported to Alois who had taken offence and had written in very cool terms to Bruckner, withdrawing the hand of friendship. But Alois had been ill, Bruckner had visited him several times, and their friendship had been restored, albeit without the same cordiality as hitherto. Bruckner was now working on the Adagio of his symphony. The other movements, including a new Scherzo, had been written, and he looked forward to showing them to Weinwurm.[101] The cooler tone of Weinwurm's reply took Bruckner aback, and he was eager to repair any damage that had been caused unwittingly and to reassure Weinwurm of his affection and high regard for him. He also mentioned that Alois was still not well, and that Hanslick had been in Linz again and had suggested that Bruckner give an organ recital in Vienna in the autumn.[102] When he wrote to Weinwurm again the following month, Bruckner congratulated him on his recent appointment as conductor of the *Wiener Männergesangverein* and reiterated his expressions of esteem and friendship in spite of recent events. Alois was still having trouble with his eyes. Rehearsals of his First Symphony were about to begin but there were doubts about an early performance on account of the impending war.[103] Nevertheless, the suggestion was made to Bruckner that he arrange a performance of the symphony

---

is in neither the *ÖNB* nor the *Gesellschaft der Musikfreunde* libraries.

101 See *HSABB* 1, 52 for the text of this letter, dated Linz, 27 January 1866; the original is in the *Wiener Stadt- und Landesbibliothek*.

102 See *HSABB* 1, 52f. for the text of this letter, dated Linz, 25 March 1866; the original is in the *Wiener Stadt- und Landesbibliothek*. Weinwurm's letter to Bruckner is not extant.

103 See *HSABB* 1, 54 for the text of this letter, dated Linz, 14 April 1866; the original is in the *Wiener Stadt- und Landesbibliothek*. The war referred to was the war against Prussia which resulted, after two initial successes, in a crushing defeat at Königgrätz on 3 July.

108

for patriotic purposes. But Alois, who was of the opinion that all the music associations should respond to requests of this nature by singing only a few patriotic songs, advised him against it and, in any case, an undertaking of this nature would inevitably require a considerable amount of expenditure (rehearsals, writing out of parts) which would cause financial difficulties. Indeed, the rehearsals held so far had been very poorly attended.[104]

Bruckner in the meantime had been renewing his attempts to secure some kind of position in Vienna. In April 1866 Benedikt Randhartinger retired from his position as chief musical director at the Court and his place was taken by Johann Herbeck. The new Lord Chamberlain, Prince Constantin von Hohenlohe-Schillingsfürst, had also initiated some much-needed reforms in the Court Chapel, and Bruckner clearly felt that the time was ripe for a positive approach. In a congratulatory letter to Herbeck, Bruckner reminded him of his encouraging words five years earlier and said that his future now lay in Herbeck's hands. Feeling more and more restricted by the lack of opportunity in Linz he made a heartfelt plea for help and ended with the rather dramatic words - 'otherwise I am lost'.[105] It was not long before Herbeck was in a position to give Bruckner the help he needed.

Bruckner's next letter to Weinwurm touches on a subject that was of great importance to the composer at this particular point in his life. His many brief 'affairs of the heart' throughout his life point to a desire for female companionship. He was obviously attracted to the fair sex and made many proposals of marriage, all of them

104 See *HSABB* 1, 57f. for Bruckner's letter to Weinwurm, dated Linz, 8 June 1866; the original is in the *Wiener Stadt- und Landesbibliothek*.

105 See *HSABB* 1, 55 for the text of this letter, dated Linz, 30 April 1866. The original is in the *ÖNB*; there is a facsimile of the final page in Schneider. Musikantiquariat, *Katalog 316* (Tutzing, 1990), 17. Bruckner also thanked Herbeck for lending him the score of Schumann's *Scenes from Faust* (which he had just returned to him at his Conservatory address) and mentioned that he had been working on a symphony which he hoped to bring to Vienna.

rejected. His mother's death in 1860 had been a severe blow, particularly as he had often encouraged her to come to stay with him in Linz. His sister, Maria Anna, came to live with him in 1866 and moved with him to Vienna in 1868 but here untimely death in 1870 deprived him of another source of female companionship. According to Gräflinger,

> It would be wrong to interpret Bruckner's relationship to women other than it actually was - a harmless weakness of the composer. His life was not transfigured by a woman as, for instance, Robert Schumann's was by Clara Wieck or Richard Wagner's by Mathilde Wesendonck. He did not worship an 'immortal beloved' as Beethoven did.[106]

Most of Bruckner's attempts to form deeper relationships with women were short-lived. Although he had a healthy appreciation of physical beauty, his strict moral and religious code would have prevented him from indulging in any improprieties. Thus his often irrational pursuit of a young lady who had attracted him would invariably lead to a marriage proposal which would inevitably be declined. There were a very few exceptions to these brief, platonic 'love affairs' and one example was a more serious relationship (on Bruckner's part) concerning Josefine Lang, the comely daughter of a Linz butcher. He had first made her acquaintance at the end of the 1850s when he was employed for a short time as a supply teacher at the local school and she was one of his pupils. He had then invited her to join the church choir, had made friends with her brother Anton, and eventually, in August 1866, plucked up the courage to write to her, making a formal proposal of marriage. He urged her to be completely honest and to give a definite yes or

---

106 Franz Gräflinger, *Liebes und Heiteres um Anton Bruckner* (Vienna: Wiener Verlag, 1948), 84.

no![107] She declined, saying that, as a seventeen-year-old, she was really too young, and she returned his presents - a prayer-book and a gold watch. Although initially disappointed, Bruckner harboured no ill feelings. Indeed, 24 years later, he decided to visit Josefine, now Josefine Weilnböck, at her home in Neufelden and was surprised and delighted to meet her fourteen-year-old daughter, Caroline who reminded him so much of her mother in younger days.[108]

At the beginning of the year Bruckner had informed Weinwurm of several improvements which had been made to his flat - at a cost of 300 florins which he had to borrow from his insurance society.[109] Was he thinking seriously about marriage and 'putting his house in order', as it were, for such an eventuality? After the disappointment of Josefine Lang's rejection of his suit, he immediately turned his attention to another young lady, the eighteen-year-old Henriette Reiter, who lived with her mother, the owner of a flower shop in the Josefstadt area of Vienna. Having made further enquiries about her through a friend in Steyr, he had been informed that her dowry would probably be 3000 florins. As he calculated that this sum, combined with his present level of income, would not be sufficient to provide her with the standard of living to which she was accustomed, he asked Weinwurm to find out more about her but, under no circumstances, to divulge his age. He considered

---

107 See *HSABB* 1, 58f. for the text of this letter, dated Linz, 16 August 1866. The original is in the *Oberösterreichisches Landesmuseum*, Linz; there is a facsimile in Nowak, *Anton Bruckner. Musik und Leben* (Linz, 1973), 113-16.

108 Josefine Lang (1844-1930) married Josef Weilnböck, a merchant, in 1870. On 21 April 1891, Bruckner wrote to Caroline, recalling the pleasant day he had spent. See *ABB*, 244 for the text of this letter. See also Bruckner's letter to Karl Waldeck, dated Vienna, 20 November 1891, in which 'Fräulein C' is probably a reference to Caroline. Further information of Bruckner's visit to Neufelden in September 1890 is provided in Chapter 6, page 593 and footnote 101.

109 See letter dated Linz, 27 January 1866 (footnote 101).

that he looked younger than his 42 years![110] Bruckner also passed on a request from a Steyr choirmaster for further information about a choral piece which had been sung recently by the *Wiener Männergesangverein* at the Dresden Song Festival. Weinwurm replied by return of post, enclosing the necessary information, and Bruckner wrote again, mentioning both the Viennese girl and a girl from Salzburg whose name he would like Weinwurm to send. He added, on a more serious note, that he had sent the score of his First Symphony to Dessoff and was awaiting his reaction.[111] Writing to Weinwurm again a fortnight later, he felt constrained to warn him that he had heard in confidence about a group opposed to him within the *Männergesangverein*. He hoped that there was no foundation to this rumour but had every confidence that Weinwurm would know what to do if there was a potentially difficult situation.[112]

At the end of October Bruckner heard from Sechter, now 78 years of age, that persistent illness was confining him to his house, with the result that his Conservatory pupils had now to come to him for their lessons. Sechter hoped that Bruckner would pay him a visit the next time he was in Vienna and show him some of his recent compositions.[113] A few days later, Bruckner, concerned about Sechter's health, asked Weinwurm if he could obtain further information about his former teacher's domestic situation and, if possible, arrange for some other medical assistance to be made

---

110 See *HSABB* 1, 59f. for the text of this letter, dated Linz, 30 August 1866; the original is in the *Wiener Stadt- und Landesbibliothek*.

111 See *HSABB* 1, 60f. for the text of this letter, dated Linz, 2 September 1866; the original is in the *Wiener Stadt- und Landesbibliothek*.

112 See *HSABB* 1, 61 for the text of this letter, dated Linz, 18 September 1866; the original is in the *Wiener Stadt- und Landesbibliothek*. The opposing faction apparently preferred Adolf Lorenz, a member of the choir from 1846 until 1900.

113 See *HSABB* 1, 62 for the text of this letter, dated Vienna, 31 October 1866; the original is in the *ÖNB*. Sechter was suffering from what he described as 'chronic diorrhea'.

available. He himself was recovering from a bout of flu but hoped to have the time and energy to attend a forthcoming performance of Beethoven's Ninth in Vienna. He expressed his concern about Weinwurm in view of an outbreak of cholera in the city.[114] Early in December he wrote again to Weinwurm, asking him to obtain two tickets - for Alois and himself - for the Berlioz concert, and adding that he also wanted to hear Beethoven's Ninth even if it meant travelling to Vienna again on another occasion. He also mentioned that he had completed his E minor Mass, written specifically for the dedication of the Votive Chapel of the new cathedral in Linz, and a piece for male-voice choir.[115]

The first signs of a severe depression which led to a nervous breakdown during the spring of 1867 are alluded to in Bruckner's next letter to Weinwurm. In enclosing ten florins, presumably the cost of the December concert tickets, he apologized for the delay and hinted at some kind of exhaustion which prevented him from writing sooner. He was pleased to report that his friendship with Alois had returned to its earlier cordiality, and passed on a request from *Frohsinn* for the name of a chorus by Schumann which Weinwurm had conducted several years previously. He was intending to travel to Vienna for Herbeck's performance of his D minor Mass in the Court Chapel on 10 February and asked for Weinwurm's advice about when he

---

114 See *HSABB* 1, 62f. for the text of this letter, dated Linz, 4 November 1866; the original is in the *Wiener Stadt- und Landesbibliothek*. There was a cholera epidemic in Vienna in August 1866 which claimed the lives of about 5,000 people.

115 See *HSABB* 1, 63 for the text of this letter, dated Linz, 2 December 1866; the original is in the *Wiener Stadt- und Landesbibliothek*. Berlioz himself conducted his *Damnation of Faust* in the large *Redoutensaal* in Vienna on 16 December 1866. The performance of Beethoven's Ninth did not take place until 24 February 1867. The male-voice piece mentioned by Bruckner is *O könnt' ich dich beglücken* WAB 92, written for the *Niederösterreichische Sängerbund*, conducted by Storch.

should come and what he should do.[116]

The day before his letter to Weinwurm Bruckner wrote to Herbeck, thanking him for his willingness to perform the D minor Mass and asking him if his *Afferentur* WAB 1 and *Ave Maria* WAB 6 could be used as the Gradual and Offertory respectively. He hoped to be in Vienna on the 8th or 9th of February.[117] Ludwig Speidel, who had written a complimentary report of Bruckner's organ playing in the *Piaristenkirche* nine years earlier, had the distinction of providing the first review of the performance of a Bruckner work in Vienna. Writing about the performance of the D minor Mass in the *Hofburgkapelle*, with Herbeck conducting and Bruckner playing the organ, he pointed out that Bruckner had nothing to be modest about, in view of his 'great theoretical knowledge' and his 'truly outstanding organ playing'[118]

Bruckner's next three letters to Weinwurm were written from Bad Kreuzen where he spent a three-month period of convalescence - from 8 May until 8 August - after his nervous breakdown in the spring of 1867. Some indication of the nature of the illness is given in the first letter:

> ... You have heard nothing more from me since my journey back from Vienna. You also did not attempt to find out how I was getting on. As I presume that you still want to hear from me and as other reasons also make it necessary, I am taking this opportunity of writing to you and, above all, of apologizing for not yet being able to grant your wish. In case you are thinking or have thought - or have heard anything at all! - it was not laziness! It was much, much

---

116 See *HSABB* 1, 65f. for the text of this letter, dated Linz, 18 January 1867; the original is in the *Wiener Stadt- und Landesbibliothek*. The Schumann chorus was his *Ritornelle in canonischen Weisen* for male-voice choir which Weinwurm performed on 24 January 1861.

117 See *HSABB* 1, 65 for the text of this letter, dated Linz, 17 January 1867; the original is in The Music Division of the New York Public Library.

118 From Speidel's review in the *Fremdenblatt* 41 (11 February 1867). This review was reprinted in the *Linzer Abendbote* on 13 February; see Susanna Taub, op.cit., 66 for facsimile.

114

more!!! It was total collapse and desolation, complete overstress and nervous breakdown! I was in the most shocking state. I am confessing it to you alone - don't breathe a word. A little longer and I would have been finished, totally lost. Dr. Fadinger in Linz has already informed me that madness would have been a possible outcome. God be praised! He has saved me from that. I have been in Bad Kreuzen near Grein since 8 May. I have felt a little better over the last few weeks. But I am not allowed to play, study or work. Can you imagine such ill fortune! I am a poor fellow! Herbeck sent me the scores of my Mass [in E minor] and Symphony [no. 1 in C minor] without writing a word. Is everything quite so bad, then? Please find out, dear friend and write to me here, wretched and forsaken in my exile. If you had come to Linz at Easter, you would have been shocked by my condition.[119]

Bruckner was overjoyed to receive a letter from Weinwurm but did not reply immediately because of a temporary setback in his recovery. As he put it rather quaintly in his next letter, he delayed writing until he could relate 'only good things'. He also provided Weinwurm with a brief timetable of his daily activities at the sanatorium. Perhaps outside visitors were discouraged, but Bruckner's poignant 'no one from Linz has ever visited me here' makes particularly sad reading.[120]

In response to Weinwurm's request for a more detailed description of what was involved in the cure - one of Weinwurm's friends had evidently been making enquiries - Bruckner wrote that it was a 'cold water establishment, with very good air and springs but not particularly good drinking water'. The treatment consisted of a mixture of baths - foot baths, 'sitting baths', 'wave baths' - and sessions during

119 See *HSABB* 1, 66 for the text of this letter, dated Bad Kreuzen, 19 June 1867. The original is in the *Wiener Stadt- und Landesbibliothek*; there is a facsimile of the second page in Leopold Nowak, op.cit., 127.

120 See *HSABB* 1, 68 for the text of this letter, dated Bad Kreuzen, 15 July 1867. The original is in the *Wiener Stadt- und Landesbibliothek*; the facsimile of part of the first page was reproduced in the brochure for *BSL 1994*. Weinwurm's letter to Bruckner is not extant.

which the patient had to sit swathed in wet linen cloths. He had to drink frequently from the springs. Apart from a three-course midday meal, the diet included only milk ('cold, sour, and hot') and fruit. The treatment was geared to the needs of the individual patient and was determined on a daily basis by the doctor. It was a long day, beginning at about 4 a.m. and finishing at about 9 p.m. There were about 100 patients, and social activities were organized regularly. Bruckner, however, preferred to be on his own. The cost differed from patient to patient. Bruckner's monthly outgoings amounted to about 80 florins. The normal length of stay was six weeks, but some conditions required three-month or even six-month treatment.[121]

The loan of 250 florins from his Insurance Society which Bruckner had arranged at the beginning of his three-month cure covered the total cost of approximately 226 florins. About a month after leaving Bad Kreuzen Bruckner wrote to the episcopal office in Linz requesting some financial help in view of the amount of money he had

---

121   See *HSABB* 1, 69 for the text of this letter, dated Bad Kreuzen, 21 July 1867; the original is in the *Wiener Stadt- und Landesbibliothek*. Bruckner also recommended that Weinwurm's friend contact Dr. Keyhl for further information. Dr. Maximilian Florian Keyhl (d. 31 May 1870) established the 'cold water sanatorium' in Bad Kreuzen in 1846. There is a list of those who took the cure (which was printed in 1874) in the library of the *Oberösterreichisches Landesmuseum*; see Rupert Gottfried Frieberger, 'Beiträge zur Musikgeschichte und Musikpflege im Mühlviertel' in *BSL 1990* (Linz, 1993), 263 for a facsimile of the title page and one page from this list. Although Bruckner did not receive any visits from acquaintances in Linz, two letters from Alois Brutscher, a tradesman from Krems who had apparently been at Bad Kreuzen for treatment and had befriended the composer while he was there, are extant. They show a touching concern for Bruckner's health and well-being. Brutscher asks to be remembered to Dr. Keyhl, J.B. Schiedermayr, dean of Linz Cathedral, and Simon Kremshuber, a priest from Linz (probably the priest sent by Bishop Rudigier to provide Bruckner with spiritual help), all of whom he had presumably met at Bad Kreuzen. So Bruckner was certainly not forgotten by the church at least! See *HSABB* 1, 67 and 70 for these two letters, dated Krems, 5 July and 10 August 1867 respectively; the originals are in St. Florian. Bruckner's reply to Brutscher's first letter (alluded to at the beginning of Brutscher's second letter) is not extant.

116

to spend on his treatment. He received 60 florins.[122]

Towards the end of November Weinwurm was informed that Bruckner's D minor Mass was to be performed in Linz at the beginning of January 1868. As the score of the Mass had been lent to Count Laurencin d'Armond in Vienna and Bruckner now required it for rehearsal purposes, he asked his friend to recover it as quickly as possible and send it immediately to Linz.[123]

Bruckner had occasion to write to Weinwurm several times in 1868 when a move to Vienna was no longer a possibility but was becoming a very strong probability. After 1868 there was no longer the need for such regular epistolary contact, and what letters are available were written to mark such significant events as Weinwurm's 50th birthday, the first performance of Bruckner's *Te Deum*, the award of the Franz Josef Order to Bruckner, and Bruckner's 70th birthday.[124]

Two of Bruckner's most understanding friends during his Linz years were the district commissioner, Moritz von Mayfeld, and his wife Betty.[125] They gave him immense encouragement when his first truly original compositions began to appear

---

122 See *HSABB* 1, 71 for the text of Bruckner's letter, dated 3 September 1867. The original of the letter, the text of which was first published in *GrBL* (1911), 44 is not extant. Bruckner's request was granted on 6 October. See Elisabeth Maier, '"Kirchenmusik auf schiefen Bahnen". Zur Situation in Linz von 1850 bis 1900' in *BSL 1990* (Linz, 1993), 113; the originals of the relevant documents are in the *Ordinariatsarchiv*, Linz.

123 See *HSABB* 1, 74 for the text of this letter, dated Linz, 27 November 1867; the original is in the *Wiener Stadt- und Landesbibliothek*. Count Ferdinand Peter Laurencin d'Armond (1819-1890) was a music critic and keen supporter of Liszt and Wagner.

124 See *HSABB* 1, 253 (17 April 1885), 283f. (13 January 1886), 307 (9 July 1886) and *ABB*, 377f. (3 September 1894) for the texts of these letters.

125 Moritz von Mayfeld (1817-1904) was a keen art- and music-lover. He dedicated one of his two *Tristan* transcriptions to Bruckner. Betty von Mayfeld (1831-1908) was an accomplished amateur pianist. Bruckner derived great pleasure from listening to them playing the Beethoven symphonies in piano-duet versions.

in the 1860s. After his move to Vienna they saw him frequently because they had an apartment in the city where they lived during the winter months. In later years Bruckner visited his two friends in their country house at Schwanenstadt. Their concern for Bruckner and desire that he should make his way socially in the Austrian capital occasionally led to some expressions of dismay at his sartorial habits! But even such pointed remarks as 'did you make these clothes yourself or did you have them cut by a joiner?' made no impression on the stubborn Bruckner whose Upper Austrian dress sense was a source of much amusement. In matters musical, however, Bruckner was clearly indebted to Mayfeld who, in his capacity as music critic of the *Linzer Zeitung*, was one of the first to recognize and draw attention to the composer's creative gifts.

Another of Bruckner's acquaintances in Linz was Karl Waldeck. Waldeck first came to Linz as a student teacher in 1856/57 when he had organ lessons from Bruckner and deputized for him at the early morning Mass.[126] From 1858 to 1861 he was employed as an assistant teacher outside Linz but returned in 1861 to take up a teaching position in the town and to be organist at the Capuchin church. On renewing his acquaintance with Bruckner he was the witness of many of the latter's hasty 'affairs of the heart'. He often accompanied the composer on Sunday afternoon walks or, if the weather was poor, would spend time with him in his rooms listening to excerpts from his latest compositions:

> ... As a result of showing great interest in Bruckner's playing and of taking the opportunity of recommending him as a piano teacher, I came into favour again. I attended the cathedral services to hear him play and usually went walking with him after Vespers. If the weather was bad, he would play me sketches from his compositions of which only the outer parts were generally available as outlines. After he

126   As a trainee teacher, Karl Waldeck (1841-1905) also received musical instruction from Dürrnberger and Lanz.

had played me the sketch of the *Credo* from his F minor Mass one day, he asked for my opinion. I said that the 'Et incarnatus est' seemed to me not to be on the same high level as the other parts of the *Credo*. After reflecting for a short time Bruckner said, 'How would this be?', whereupon he improvised a theme for solo tenor with quaver accompaniment in a high register. This struck me as being much better, and Bruckner immediately wrote it down and retained it. Whenever Bruckner improvised on the piano, the light had to be put out. I had to play my own attempts at composition to him and I was always praised. When the conversation turned on one occasion to the subject of how much effort was involved in being able to play thematically, contrapuntally, and extempore, Bruckner said, 'When you come to write my biography, you can say that in St. Florian I practised the piano for ten hours and the large organ for three hours almost every day, as well as spending many hours at night studying music.[127]

Waldeck also had some first-hand experience of Bruckner's fixations and tendency to numeromania which was one of the symptoms of the illness leading to his breakdown in 1867:

... In spite of his strong constitution and healthy appetite, such over-exertion [viz. hours spent in instrumental practice and in completing Sechter's theory course] had its consequences. Bruckner suffered a great deal from mental disturbances, depressions, fixations, etc. For instance, during a walk he would stand next to a tree in order to count its leaves. On one occasion he came into my house without knocking at the door or introducing himself, sat down at the piano, and played for a while. When I asked him what he was playing, he said 'The Kyrie of my new [F minor] Mass'. Most people were amused by his behaviour, but I took the unfortunate man under my wing and provided him with as much company as I could. When I wished to leave him late at night, he begged me to stay with him because, left on his own, he would be troubled by his fixations. As can be seen from his letters, Bruckner to his dying day was grateful to me for supporting him during the saddest period of his life. He also

127   From Waldeck's account, as related to Franz Gräflinger, *GrBL*, 114f.

promised me that, when he became court music director - which was nothing less than he deserved - he would bring me to Vienna as court organist.[128]

When Bruckner moved from Linz to Vienna in 1868, Bishop Rudigier agreed to keep the position of cathedral organist open for two years in the event of a decision on Bruckner's part to return to Linz. Waldeck became provisional cathedral organist, and then, on Bruckner's recommendation, was appointed to the post on a permanent basis when Bruckner finally resigned in July 1870.[129]

During his years in Vienna Bruckner kept in touch with Waldeck, writing to him on his name-day and occasionally meeting him. In October 1871, for instance, when Bruckner was in very low spirits because of the threat of disciplinary action being taken against him following an alleged 'pass' at a female student, he thanked Waldeck for his support during 'days of severe trial' and assured him that he would not be trying to get his old job back in Linz![130] In 1891, Bruckner spent Easter as usual at St. Florian. He was to play the organ at Linz Cathedral on Easter Sunday, 29 March, however, and, in a letter to Waldeck, confirmed that he would arrive in Linz in good time for the service.[131] Waldeck was present at the Vienna performance of the F minor Mass conducted by Gericke on 4 November 1894. He also accompanied Bruckner to a performance of Mozart's *Requiem* in the *Hofkapelle*

---

128   *GrBL*, 115f.

129   See *HSABB* 1, 119 for the text of Bruckner's letter to the episcopal office, dated Vienna, 18 July 1870. The original is not extant - the letter was first published in *ABB*, 113.

130   See *HSABB* 1, 127ff. for the texts of two letters from Bruckner to Waldeck, dated Vienna, 21 and 28 October 1871 respectively. The original of the former (first published in the *Neue musikalische Presse* 14 [1905]) is not extant, but the original of the latter is in the *ÖNB*.

131   See *ABB*, 242 for the text of this letter, dated St. Florian, 27 March 1891; the original is not extant.

two days earlier and attended the final rehearsal of the Mass. It was the last time the two old friends met. In a University lecture he gave on 5 November 1894, Bruckner referred to the performance of the Mass and recalled how Waldeck had been primarily responsible for the 'Et incarnatus est' section as it now stood, having compared the original setting unfavourably with the parallel passage in the D minor Mass.[132] Eight years after Bruckner's death, Waldeck was present at a Festival Concert given in Linz on Palm Sunday, 27 March 1904, at which Göllerich conducted Bruckner's Symphony no. 6 and the F minor Mass. He was deeply moved particularly by the performance of the Mass as it brought back memories of the days of its conception. In a letter to Gräflinger, Waldeck recalled the time when Bruckner 'played parts of his Mass which had been composed during a time of the most painful feelings and mental torments'.[133]

Shortly after Bruckner's return from his three-month cure at Bad Kreuzen, Simon Sechter died. More eager than ever to move to Vienna, he made some preliminary attempts to accomplish this. First, he wrote a *Promemoria* to the Lord Chamberlain, Prince Hohenlohe-Schillingsfürst, enclosing a *curriculum vitae* which drew attention to his long period of theoretical training, his activities as a teacher, organist, conductor and composer, and ended with a request for an appointment as 'court organist or supernumerary unpaid assistant director'. At the same time he sent Herbeck documents in support of his application.[134] Second, he wrote to

---

132 See *G-A* IV/3 (1936), 444f. for an account of this lecture.

133 Part of this is quoted in *GrBL*, 118. Waldeck also wrote a letter to Göllerich on the day after the performance. This is quoted in *G-A* III/1, 624. Further information about Waldeck can be gleaned from Franz Gräflinger, *Karl Waldeck* (Linz, 1905), Franz Gräflinger, *Karl Waldeck. Kirchenmusikalische Streifleichter* (Linz, 1911) and *SchABCR*, 365f.

134 See *HSABB* 1, 71f. for the complete text of the *Promemoria*, dated Linz, 14 October 1867; see also Franz Grasberger, 'Anton Bruckner und die Wiener Hofmusikkapelle', *ABDS* 1 (Graz, 1979), 31 - 43 for the text with annotations. The original is in the Vienna *Staatsarchiv*; there is a facsimile

Ottokar Lorenz, Dean of the Faculty of Philosophy at Vienna University, requesting the creation of a teaching post in 'musical composition (in particular, harmony and counterpoint)' at the University and the appointment of himself as teacher. At a faculty meeting held on 16 November 1867 Bruckner's request was considered but refused. As Professor of Music History and Aesthetics at the University, Eduard Hanslick was responsible for an official response. He mentioned a similar request made previously by Rudolf Weinwurm and the Faculty's decision at that time that the proper place for the teaching of composition was not a University but a Conservatory. Furthermore, in view of his position as director of the University choir, Weinwurm had a stronger claim than a third party (viz. Bruckner) who had no connections with the University. Lorenz informed Bruckner of the Faculty's decision a few days later.[135]

At the end of 1867, Bruckner's prospects of moving to Vienna appeared to be no brighter. To make matters worse, he was finding his organist's duties more demanding now that composition was assuming a much more important role in his life. As there had been no increase in remuneration since 1856, he made an official request to the bishop's office for a 'salary increase or additional annual allowance'. Bruckner was informed that he should direct his request to the appropriate

---

in Hans C. Fischer, *Anton Bruckner. Sein Leben. Eine Dokumentation* (Salzburg, 1974), 120. See *HSABB* 1, 72 for the text of Bruckner's letter to Herbeck, dated Linz, 15 October 1867; the original is in the *ÖNB*. Constantin Prinz zu Hohenlohe-Schillingsfürst (1828-1896) succeeded Prince Karl Liechtenstein as Lord Chamberlain in July 1866. As an enthusiastic patron of music and the arts he instituted fairly sweeping reforms in the Court Chapel.

135 See *HSABB* 1, 73f. for Bruckner's letter, dated Linz, 2 November 1867, and for Lorenz's reply, dated Vienna, 20 November 1867. The original of the former is in the University library, Vienna, but the original of the latter is not extant. *G-A* III/1, 414-19 also contains Hanslick's official response. For fuller details, see Robert Lach, *Die Bruckner-Akten des Wiener Universitätsarchives* (Vienna, 1926), 25-28. Ottokar Lorenz (1832-1904) was Professor of Philology and History at the University of Vienna. He was appointed Rector in 1880.

government department, but there is no indication that he did this.[136]

The main musical event in Bruckner's life at the beginning of 1868 was a performance of his D minor Mass in Linz Cathedral on 6 January. Writing to Anton Imhof von Geißlinghof, a councillor in the court chancellery, and Johann Herbeck to convey his good wishes for the New Year, he mentioned that he had experienced a considerable amount of trouble training a large choir for the performance.[137] But the performance was a success and, in a letter to Rudolf Weinwurm the day afterwards, he provided further information and outlined future plans. The postscript suggests that Weinwurm had asked him for a choral piece.

> Dear friend,
>
> I have just completed a major undertaking. The performance was yesterday, the 6th, and it went very well, far better than three years ago. The church was packed full and there was unprecedented interest and involvement in the proceedings. I had at my disposal a very large choir and very good orchestra which consisted mainly of players from the military band. Alois produced excellent results. Three cheers for him! I am deeply grateful to you for your devoted efforts on my behalf at this point in time. They have taken me completely by surprise. Unfortunately, I have no further information for you. As there are so many good violinists at the theatre here, it has been suggested that I have my symphony performed during Lent; I will perhaps arrange for it to be played in a Philharmonic concert. I do not want any financial reward, and the performers should share the proceeds among themselves. At least in this way I will be able to hear it.

---

136 See *HSABB* 1, 74f. for the text of Bruckner's letter to the bishop's office, dated Linz, 2 December 1867; the original is not extant.

137 See *HSABB* 1, 75f. for the texts of these letters, both dated Linz, 30 December 1867; the original of the former is in the *ÖNB*, the original of the latter is in the Music Division of New York Public Library. Imhof was the dedicatee of the F minor Mass and, in both letters, Bruckner refers to ongoing work on it - the *Credo* was virtually complete, and the *Kyrie* and *Gloria* had been sketched.

The Credo of the new Mass will soon be finished. Unfortunately, the first two movements have only been sketched. I am rather tense again - probably the result of recent exertions.

I wish you a really good New Year and appeal for your life-long affection and friendship. If only I could spend the rest of my days near you!

With a thousand affectionate greetings,

Your friend,

A. Bruckner

N.B. Unfortunately I have no composition for you. What do you require and for what forces - male voices or mixed, with or without accompaniment? Many thanks for your gracious invitation.[138]

Moritz von Mayfeld's review of the performance was somewhat guarded in tone:

... Yesterday's performance surpassed the first in precision and assurance, with the result that the work was more readily understood. While it cannot be regarded as a standard work in the old church style, it is nevertheless an important sacred composition. When Mr. Bruckner succeeds in refining or, rather, curbing his imagination, in avoiding over-violent cadences and strident dissonances and, on the other hand, in allowing his themes to flow more freely and with more harmonic interest, we are convinced that he will not surprise and astonish his listeners again in a second work of this kind but will truly uplift and edify them.[139]

---

138 See *HSABB* 1, 77f. for the text of this letter, dated Linz, 7 January 1868; the original is in the *Wiener Stadt- und Landesbibliothek*. Alois Weinwurm was responsible for training the choir. The symphony referred to is the Symphony no. 1 in C minor, completed in 1866.

139 From the review which appeared in the *Linzer Zeitung*, 9 January 1868; see *G-A* III/1, 420f. There is a facsimile of this review in Susanna Taub, op.cit., 67f. The first performance of the Mass was in Linz on 20 November 1864 and there was a second performance on 18 December.

Having inadvertently distressed Bruckner with this review, Mayfeld attempted to put matters right in a subsequent article in which he clarified some of his earlier statements and stressed that he had no doubts whatsoever that Bruckner was richly talented and more than able to write original compositions.[140]

Another review of the performance drew attention to the problems of setting traditional liturgical words in a modern musical idiom:

> ... On the 5th [sic] of this month the already known Mass in D by our cathedral organist, Anton Bruckner, was performed once again after an interval of about three years. Following the first performance there was a thorough and very appreciative review of this extremely effective and original composition in a local paper. We came to know Bruckner in this significant work as an adherent of the so-called Wagnerian movement, approaching his task with great seriousness of purpose. Although it is open to question whether the new musical style with its complicated apparatus can be accommodated within the church as easily as the simple classical style of older composers, Bruckner has certainly proved that an unusual effect can be obtained with the dramatic handling of the religious text. The performance was very precise and energetic and deserves all the more praise because this composition for voices and orchestra presents extraordinary difficulties.[141]

---

140   See *G-A* III/1, 421f. for extracts from this article in the *Linzer Zeitung*, 12 January 1868; there is a facsimile in Susanna Taub, op.cit., 69.

141   From review in the *Linzer Tagespost* 6, 9 January 1868. See *G-A* III/1, 422f.; there is a facsimile of the review in Susanna Taub, op.cit., 68. The earlier 'thorough and very appreciative review' was by Franz Gamon and appeared in the *Linzer Zeitung* on 20 and 29 December 1864 as the final two parts of a weekly series (commencing 30 November) on the development of the Mass from the end of the fifteenth century until Bruckner's time. See later in this chapter, when the D minor Mass will be discussed in further detail. There was also a report of the January 1868 performance in the *Linzer Neueste Nachrichten*; see Susanna Taub, op.cit., 67 for a facsimile. And it was mentioned in the *Neue Freie Presse* 1211, Vienna, on 14 January.

Members of the *Frohsinn* choral society in Linz had taken part in the performance of the Mass and, in a letter to the choir committee, Bruckner officially thanked them for allowing them to use their premises for rehearsal purposes. He also paid tribute to the members of the choir for their excellent contribution to the performance as well as their efforts in the strenuous rehearsals, and said that he would be only too pleased to be of service to the committee in the future.[142] A week later Dr. Matthias Weißmann, the secretary of *Frohsinn*, contacted Bruckner and offered him the position of conductor![143]

On 16 January Bruckner wrote a curious and rather morbid letter to his friend Weinwurm in Vienna. Both he and Weinwurm had been invited to go to Mexico as court organists of Emperor Maximilian, the younger brother of Emperor Franz Josef of Austria. Bruckner had been considering the possibility when the news of Maximilian's death reached him. Maximilian's body had evidently been brought back to Vienna, and Bruckner asked Weinwurm to enquire on his behalf at the Lord Chamberlain's office if the body was likely to be on view (either open in a coffin or visible in a glass frame!) or if only the closed coffin would be visible. He requested a quick reply by telegram for which he would defray the expenses.[144]

---

142 See *HSABB* 1, 77 for this letter, dated Linz, 10 January 1868; the original is in the 'Frohsinn-Archiv' of the *Linzer Singakademie*.

143 See *HSABB* 1, 79 for the text of this letter, dated Linz, 17 January 1868. The original is in the archives of the *Linzer Singakademie*; there is a facsimile in the possession of Dr. Franz Scheder. Bruckner had been a second tenor in the choir from 1856 to 1858 and had already been its conductor for a short period (from the end of 1860 to the autumn of 1861).

144 See *HSABB* 1, 78 for the text of this letter, the original of which is in the *Wiener Stadt- und Landesbibliothek*. There is an English translation of part of this letter in Hans F. Redlich, *Bruckner and Mahler* (London: Dent, 2/1963), 30. Ferdinand-Josef Maximilian (1832-1867) became Emperor of Mexico in 1863. He was soon embroiled in a civil war, was captured while defending Querétaro in May 1867, and was executed on 19 June.

On the same day, Bruckner received a letter from Dr. Maximilian Keyhl, one of the doctors who had treated him at Bad Kreuzen the previous year. Keyhl was pleased to hear that Bruckner was on the way to a full recovery, but suggested that he continue the recommended treatment and diet.[145]

In January Richard Wagner was elected an honorary member of *Frohsinn*. Bruckner also wrote to him to request either an existing choral piece or a new composition which would be performed at the choir's anniversary concert in April. In his friendly reply to Bruckner, Wagner both graciously acknowledged honorary membership and suggested that the choir sing the closing scene (beginning with Sachs's words 'Verachtet mir die Meister nicht') from his new opera *Die Meistersinger*. He advised Bruckner to contact the publisher (Schott) for a specimen copy of the vocal score.[146] At the anniversary concert on 4 April Bruckner and the choir had the distinction of giving the first performance of this extract from the opera. The concert also included performances of the 'Chorus of Nobles and Ladies' from Act 2 of Wagner's *Tannhäuser* and Bruckner's own choral piece, *O könnt' ich dich beglücken*, WAB 92 (1866), and was enthusiastically reviewed in the *Linzer Zeitung*.[147] Later in the same month, on 21 April, Bruckner composed one of his finest smaller sacred works - *Inveni David* WAB 19, for male-voice choir and four trombones - to be sung as the offertory in a special service held to commemorate the founding of *Frohsinn* on 10 May. The sung Mass was by Antonio

---

145 See *HSABB* 1, 78f. for this letter, dated Bad Kreuzen, 16 January 1868; the original is in St. Florian.

146 See *HSABB* 1, 79f. for this letter, dated Munich, 31 January 1868; the original is in the *Bayerische Staatsbibliothek*, Munich.

147 See *G-A* III/1, 432f. for an extract from this review which appeared in the *Linzer Zeitung* 81 on 7 April 1868; there is a facsimile of the review in Susanna Taub, op.cit., 35. The concert was also reviewed in the *Linzer Abendbote* on 7 April and the *Linzer Tagespost* 82 on 8 April; there is a facsimile of the latter review in Susanna Taub, op. cit., 37.

Lotti and the gradual was Bruckner's own setting of *Ave Maria* WAB 6 (1861) for unaccompanied seven-part chorus.

Early in 1868 Weinwurm asked Bruckner if he would be prepared to play the organ at a concert to be given by the *Akademischer Gesangverein* in Vienna on the Thursday of Holy Week (9 April). In his first reply Bruckner made detailed enquiries about the organ on which he would be expected to play - its size (he preferred the effect of a larger organ to which his own style of playing was more suited) and type of pedal-board (the position of the pedals was different in some of the newer makes of organ, and he was not prepared to play on one of those). As he no longer had the time to learn new organ pieces, he would rather improvise fantasias and fugues on given themes; in any case there were plenty of good organists in Vienna capable of playing the standard repertoire. He would prefer the recital to take place at a time other than Holy Week as he had his own official organ duties to fulfil in Linz during that week and would have to obtain permission from the Bishop to be exempted from them. In a second letter, written a few days later, Bruckner informed his friend that he would not be granted exemption from his duties during Holy Week, and asked him not to divulge this information to anyone else as he did not want his superiors to be criticised in the press! He felt, in any case, that a public organ recital would be too much of an emotional strain in the present circumstances.[148]

Although he had set his sights on a position in Vienna, Bruckner was sufficiently attracted by the vacant position of Director of Music of the *Dommusikverein und Mozarteum* in Salzburg to make an official application at the end of March 1868. He was clearly not daunted by his lack of success seven years earlier when he applied for the same post in the summer of 1861. No doubt his achievements in the

---

148 See *HSABB* 1, 80ff. for the texts of both letters, dated Linz, 8 and 16 March respectively; the originals are in the *Wiener Stadt- und Landesbibliothek*.

intervening years had given him the confidence to try again.[149] In a separate letter to the *Mozarteum* a few days later, Bruckner enclosed his D minor Mass and mentioned that he was working on a new Mass for the court chapel in Vienna. A week later, the secretary of the *Dommusikverein und Mozarteum* wrote to Bruckner to acknowledge receipt of the Mass and to assure him that it would be rehearsed and performed in the cathedral at the earliest opportunity.[150]   At the same time, Franz von Hilleprandt, the President of the *Mozarteum*, wrote to Dr. Ferdinand Krakowizer who had recently moved from Salzburg to Linz and had recommended Bruckner for the vacant position. Although he outlined some of the prerequisites for the position, he gave no indication as to who was likely to be successful. However, he mentioned the possibility of a performance of Bruckner's D minor Mass in May.[151]   On 11 May Bruckner received official notification that the position had been offered to Dr. Otto Bach, but that he (Bruckner) had been granted honorary membership of the *Dommusikverein* in recognition of his submission of the Mass.[152]

---

149   See *HSABB* 1, 82f. for Bruckner's letter of application, dated Linz, 29 March 1868. The original is in the *Konsistorialarchiv*, Salzburg, and there is facsimile of the first three pages in Ernst Hintermaier, 'Anton Bruckner und der "Dommusikverein und Mozarteum" in Salzburg', *IBG Mitteilungsblatt* 16 (1979), 11-13. See pages 94-95 and footnotes 77-78 for further details of Bruckner's application in 1861.

150   See *HSABB* 1, 83f. for the texts of these two letters, dated Linz, 4 April 1868, and Salzburg, 10 April 1868 respectively. The original of the former and a draft of the latter can be found in the *Stiftung Mozarteum*, Salzburg.

151   See *HSABB* 1, 84 for the text of this letter, dated Salzburg, 10 April 1868. The location of the original is unknown; it was first printed in *G-A* III/1, 426f. Bruckner's D minor Mass was not performed in Salzburg (at the cathedral) until September 1870.

152   See *HSABB* 1, 85 for this letter, a draft of which can be found in the *Konsistorialarchiv*, Salzburg. On 4 June Bruckner wrote a short letter of acknowledgment in which he mentioned that he had been offered the post of Professor of Harmony and Counterpoint at the Vienna Conservatory; see also *HSABB* 1, 88. The original of this letter is also in the *Konsistorialarchiv*, Salzburg; it is

In Linz Bruckner was able to draw some encouragement from the successful first perfomance of his Symphony no. 1 in C minor in the *Redoutensaal* on 9 May. The usual orchestra was augmented by band members of the two regiments garrisoned in Linz. There were various difficulties in rehearsal - the quintuplet figures for strings in the slow movement seem to have caused the most trouble - but Bruckner adamantly refused to comply with suggestions that he simplify some passages.[153] As the concert was held at an unusual time of day (5 p.m.) and as there was more public interest in the recent collapse of the Danube bridge (on 5 May), the audience was a fairly select one, consisting mainly of members of the aristocracy and clergy. Writing to Weinwurm to congratulate him on his receipt of a 'high honour', Bruckner expressed his satisfaction with the performance of the symphony although the concert was anything but a financial success.[154] Reviews in the *Linzer Zeitung* and the *Linzer Tagespost* were favourable.[155] But it is Hanslick's report of the concert in the *Neue Freie Presse* that is the most interesting, because it provides a convenient link to the main event of the year - Bruckner's move to Vienna - which, as we shall see, was only finalized after a considerable amount of heart-searching and indecision.

> ... A new symphony by Anton Bruckner was performed in Linz recently and enjoyed an extremely favourable reception from a large,

---

printed in *HSABB* 1, 88.

153 According to Franz Schober, a member of the Linz *Musikverein* and a cellist in the orchestra. See *G-A* III/1, 434.

154 See *HSABB* 1, 85 for this letter, dated Linz, 11 May 1868; the original is in the *Wiener Stadt- und Landesbibliothek*.

155 See *G-A* III/1, 436ff. for Moritz von Mayfeld's review in the *Linzer Zeitung* 111, 13 May 1868, and 438ff. for the report in the *Linzer Tagespost* 110, 12 May 1868. Facsimiles of both reviews can be found in Susanna Taub, op.cit., 75ff.

very select audience and from the critics. The composer was called back to the rostrum several times. When news of Bruckner's forthcoming appointment at the Vienna Conservatory is confirmed, we can only congratulate this education establishment.[156]

Herbeck had already set wheels in motion for Bruckner to come to Vienna. He had arranged for him to play the organ to the Lord Chamberlain in the Vienna Hofburg chapel in the autumn of 1867, and was surprised when he learned from Eduard Hauptmann, the director of the Linz *Musikverein*, in April 1868 that Bruckner had not yet made an official application to the Conservatory for the position of Harmony and Counterpoint lecturer made vacant by the death of his former teacher, Sechter, in the summer of 1867. Herbeck went out of his way to spend some time with Bruckner on 24 May. According to Bruckner's own account of events on that day, they travelled together from Linz to St. Florian where Bruckner played the organ. During the journey Herbeck talked to Bruckner about the position in Vienna and intimated that he was the obvious choice. It would clearly be better if an Austrian was appointed, and, if Bruckner did not accept, it would have to be offered to a German musician. If Bruckner became a teacher at the Conservatory, he would almost certainly be able to secure an appointment as organist-designate at the Court Chapel.[157]

But Bruckner had 'reservations' and it becomes clear from subsequent correspondence that these reservations were mainly of a financial nature. Writing to Herbeck only two days after their meeting, he mentioned that some well-meaning friends of his had already approached his present employer and asked about pension

156 See *G-A* III/1, 440 and Elisabeth Maier, *ABDS* 2, 178 for this report, dated 19 May 1868. It is not absolutely certain, although most likely, that Hanslick was the writer of this review - and it may have been 'second hand'.

157 See *G-A* III/1, 443f. for Bruckner's account.

facilities:

Most highly esteemed Court Director,

I sincerely hope, Sir, that you returned safely to the welcoming arms of your loving family. If I had known the exact time of your return journey, I would gladly have greeted you, my second father, at the station!

The more that time goes by and the more I recover from the enormous surprise, the more prestigious this calling seems to be and the more indescribable your gracious and noble efforts on my behalf. When I first heard the news, I was so dumbfounded and had no idea of its import - my nerves were so on edge! Now I am more aware of the significance of this honour and anticipate it more and more keenly. I will come to Vienna myself if you should so wish, Sir (that is, after the customary exchange of letters, as you intimated to me).

I have faith in God and entrust to my noble patrons that unshakeable hope for the future which will not allow me to falter.

As far as the Bach fugues are concerned, I owe it to myself to inform you that I have played some, including those with an independent pedal part. I found them in my possession, but could not recall them immediately; it is some time since I played them, however.

Unknown to me, and without my consent, a deputation from the choral society went recently to His Grace the Bishop and asked for his assistance etc. He is reported to have said that he will not leave me in the lurch and will secure a pension for me.

As a result of this, I went not to him but to the appropriate government department, as I knew that the Bishop is not in a position to do this. I learned that, if there should be a particular need for such a pension and I petitioned the Emperor, I could possibly be granted one as a special dispensation. The other possibility of obtaining a pension could only be effected through the Ministry; again there would have to be a special need and I myself would have to make some financial contribution. All this as a result of your request!

I await with longing and keen anticipation a comforting and encouraging letter from you. I beg you to remain favourably disposed towards me. I will certainly make every effort to show you how grateful I am for the double honour that has been bestowed upon me. My respects to your gracious wife and your sons.

Your most grateful servant,

Anton Bruckner[158]

The next day, Bruckner wrote to Weinwurm, providing him with details of the positions offered and asking for advice:

Dear friend,

My apologies for not providing you with information before now. I was also taken aback by the article in the [Neue] Freie Presse, but, as I knew nothing about it myself at the time, was not able to write to Dr. Hanslick. Shortly after receiving your delightful letter, however, I was visited by Court Director Herbeck who told me that I could become Sechter's successor at the Conservatory with an annual income of 600 florins. My weekly duties would be 9 hours - 6 hours of Counterpoint and 3 of Organ. He said that I would receive written confirmation and then I would have to decide. Although, under normal circumstances, I can never receive payment for being an organist at the Court Chapel - and that is very unfortunate - it is an extremely favourable offer. What is your opinion? Write to me soon! I also have no claims on a pension in Linz - except in the case of need and by petition to the Emperor. Please give me the benefit of your wise, helpful advice!

Counsel me, dear friend. Most of my acquaintances, including Alois, think I should move, no matter what. The choral society and some of the clergy are not in favour. But you know the situation and can certainly give me your honest opinion. Please write soon.

It is unbearably hot here! How are things with you in Vienna? Will 600 florins be enough for me to live on in the event of difficult circumstances?

Many greetings from Ozelsberger (sic) who is back in Linz after his business trip and will remain here. Alois and other of your acquaintances send greetings.

Your old friend,

---

158   See *HSABB* 1, 86 for this letter, dated Linz, 26 May 1868; the original is owned privately.

Anton Bruckner[159]

Bruckner must have communicated his vacillating feelings to other friends.
Ludwig Ehrenecker, an old acquaintance from St. Florian days, wrote to him from
Steyr, reminding him that he was also in two minds at the time of the Linz
appointment twelve years earlier and advising him to go to Vienna.[160] Herbeck,
aware of Bruckner's hesitancy and reluctance to move because there was no
guarantee of absolute financial security, provided an extremely honest appraisal of the
whole situation in this letter to Bruckner:

Dear Sir,

Immediately on my return [to Vienna] I spoke on your behalf to
Mr. Imhof, the privy councillor, and ascertained what I had already
predicted in Linz, viz. that nothing can be done under the existing
circumstances, although Mr. Imhof himself has every sympathy with
your request for some kind of guarantee (assistance in the possible
event of indisposition).

No one knows better than you how eager I have been and still am
to bring you to Vienna, and it is for precisely this reason that I must
be frank with you and say to you once again that I cannot
categorically advise you to take up a position in Vienna, which is
prestigious but by no means financially watertight, and to give up your
present position which, of course, is also prestigious, more
remunerative, and provides financial security in the event of
indisposition. Local enquiries have also revealed that there has never
been a case of a cathedral employee who has given outstanding
service being left destitute.

Should you, nevertheless, decide on your own initiative to come

159 See *HSABB* 1, 87 for this letter, dated Linz, 27 May 1868; the original is in the *Wiener Stadt-
und Landesbibliothek*. The article in the *Neue Freie Presse* (19 May) was Hanslick's (?) which had
obviously embarrassed Bruckner because it referred to his 'forthcoming appointment' at the
Conservatory. Josef Ozlberger was a Linz businessman.

160 See *HSABB* 1, 87f. for this letter, dated Steyr, 2 June 1868; the original is in St. Florian.

to Vienna, can I urge you, before you take this step irrevocably, to consider most seriously whether your possible position here, which will be largely concerned with teaching, is commensurate with your inclination and aptitude to impart your great knowledge to others and, above all, whether you will feel happy in a new situation in which, I must repeat, your main source of income will be teaching, since by far the greatest part of your income at present is derived from organ playing and conducting.

If your decision to move still remains firm after you have given all that your serious consideration, please never forget that you have taken this step of your own volition and at your own risk, that I have only assisted in being able to offer you this excellent position which is by no means attractive materially and is not absolutely secure, and that if there should come some unexpected and disappointing bad news or, God forbid, an accident which resulted in your being unfit to work, I cannot under any circumstances assume responsibility or liability of a moral or material nature.

I am not in a position at the moment to say whether it would be possible to accede to your request for an increase in salary by a few hundred florins in return for an extension to the proposed teaching duties; however, I will raise this point at the next board meeting and inform you of the outcome immediately. (To effect an intervention on the Ministry's part is, in my view, a virtual impossibility.)

Reflect on the matter until then, and , even if I am able to give you encouraging news about an increase in salary, keep on examining the situation from all sides before giving your answer - carefully considered and of your own volition. I strongly advise you to take your time!

With best wishes and the best of intentions,

Joh. Herbeck[161]

---

161 See *HSABB* 1, 89 for this letter, dated Vienna, 10 June 1868. The location of the original is unknown; it was first printed in Ludwig Herbeck, *Johann Herbeck. Ein Lebensbild von seinem Sohne* (Vienna, 1885), Appendix, 78. See page 122 and footnote 137 for Bruckner's letter to Imhof. During his meeting with Bruckner on 24 May, Herbeck had promised to ask Imhof about the possibilities of a pension or some other kind of future financial security for the composer.

Herbeck's well-meaning letter seems to have intensified Bruckner's feelings of isolation and uncertainty. A report in the *Neue Freie Presse* on 17 June that the *Gesellschaft der Musikfreunde* had appointed Leopold Alexander Zellner, a music teacher, composer and acoustician, to the vacant position at the Conservatory no doubt convinced him that a move to Vienna was now more or less out of the question.[162] He gave full vent to his feelings in a letter to Weinwurm:

Dear friend,

No doubt you know what has happened and how it happened. After you wrote I made many requests in a letter to Mr. v. Herbeck, but these were by no means intended to suggest that I did not accept the original conditions. I should have gratefully accepted the position at any price.

I was waiting for the contract documents - and then it happened. I am dreadfully unhappy about the whole thing, can neither eat nor drink, and expect that I will have to make abject apologies. If only I had seized the opportunity immediately, wretched fellow that I am! Mr. v. Herbeck's intentions were so generous! Why did I give way to certain misgivings?

Just think of this prestigious position! Where and when will there be another opportunity like it? I am heartbroken. Everything gets on my nerves. If I had dreamt that anything like this would happen, I would have travelled to Vienna every day. Take pity on me, Weinwurm - I am in a hopeless position, perhaps abandoned for ever.

---

162 In fact, a later report which appeared in both the *Wiener Zeitung* and *Neue Freie Presse* on 14 July 1868 makes it clear that at least three new appointments either had been or were about to be made for the beginning of the new session in October 1868. According to Richard von Perger and Robert Hirschfeld, *Geschichte der k.k. Gesellschaft der Musikfreunde in Wien* (Vienna, 1912), 323f.,

Zellner was appointed to teach harmony, Franz Krenn to teach harmony, counterpoint and composition, and Bruckner to teach harmony, counterpoint and organ. Zellner was subsequently appointed secretary-general of the *Gesellschaft der Musikfreunde*. See Elisabeth Maier, *ABDS* 2, 181 (also footnotes 124 and 125). See also *G-A* IV/1 (1936), 72ff. for further information about Leopold Alexander Zellner (1823-1894).

And so all is perhaps lost!!! You can have no idea of my torment and dreadful sorrow; my only wish is that this will not affect your own happiness.

If I had imagined that this would happen, I would not have written a single syllable. Now I am distressed.

But I have only myself to blame for my stupidity and the resulting torment - bitter torment. How could this have happened? I only wanted to explore the possibilities of improving the salary, but should have accepted with alacrity; after all, 600 florins and many lessons etc. would have provided sufficient security.

Farewell, and think often about your grief-stricken friend.

Anton Bruckner[163]

On the same day (20 June), Bruckner, apparently convinced that he had ruined his chances of obtaining a post in Vienna and anxious not to stay in Linz for the rest of his life, wrote a remarkably undiplomatic letter to Hans von Bülow in Munich. It was patently the act of a confused and emotionally overwrought man.

N.B. My address: Anton Bruckner, cathedral organist and choirmaster in Linz.

Dear, highly esteemed Court Director,

I am extremely sorry, Sir, to have to trouble you with a request, particularly at a time when every moment is precious to you. I have been compelled to do so by pressing circumstances.

I have been fortunate enough to make a name for myself in Austria through my organ playing. In Vienna I have repeatedly been called the best organist in Austria. I am qualified as a Conservatory teacher

163 See *HSABB* 1, 90 for this letter, dated Linz, 20 June 1868. The original is in the *Wiener Stadt- und Landesbibliothek*; there is a facsimile of the first page in Hans C. Fischer, op.cit., 122. The letter which Bruckner sent to Herbeck is presumably the one mentioned by Herbeck himself in his reply to Bruckner (also on 20 June; see below); the original of this letter has not been found - it was perhaps destroyed by Herbeck?

(a pupil of Sechter's). I have written several large Masses, the first of which was performed in the Court Chapel in Vienna with such success that a second was commissioned by the Lord Chamberlain. You were good enough, Sir, to examine some movements of my C minor symphony a few years ago. Permit me to make, in confidence, the following request: if I am passed over in my own country, as I cannot stay for ever in Linz, could I, on your recommendation and on the recommendation of Mr. Wagner, be granted an audience with the king and play the organ to His Majesty with a view, perhaps, to obtaining a position as court organist and assistant court director either in the church or the court theatre in return for a better and assured salary? Would this be possible, or is it completely out of the question at present? I am confident that Mr. Wagner, who wrote affectionately to me a short time ago, would gladly do all he could for me if there was any possibility at the present time. Please be good enough to ask Mr. Wagner. And then, I beseech you, send me your own response and that of Mr. Wagner as soon as possible. If this is a possibility, how much could I expect as an annual income? I await your reply most eagerly.

I humbly beseech you to treat this request of mine in the strictest confidence and, in particular, not to divulge it to anyone in Vienna.

Will the third and final performance be on the 29th? If there is the slightest possibility, I would like to come to Munich to share with Mr. Wagner, my illustrious model, in the great pleasure and joy inspired by this superlative work. My congratulations and deepest respect! Please be so kind as to reply.

Your grateful servant,

Anton Bruckner[164]

---

164   See *HSABB* 1, 90f. for this letter, dated Linz, 20 June 1868. The original is in the *Wiener Stadt- und Landesbibliothek*; there is a facsimile of the final page of the letter in Hans C. Fischer, op.cit., 122. Bruckner showed his C minor Symphony to von Bülow in June 1865 when he was in Munich to see a performance of Wagner's *Tristan und Isolde*. The king referred to is King Ludwig II of Bavaria (1845-86), a patron of Wagner and his music. The first performance of *Die Meistersinger* was conducted by von Bülow in Munich on 21 June 1868, the day after this letter was sent. The third performance, originally intended for 29 June, was postponed until 2 July.

Bruckner was probably able to withdraw this request when he travelled to Munich for the third performance of *Die Meistersinger* at the beginning of July. In the meantime, Herbeck had been extremely active on his behalf and was able to inform him of a new, improved offer and to reassure him that there was no need for further impassioned outbursts of despair:

My dear Mr. Bruckner,

Everything is going well! So calm yourself! Do you place so little trust in my given word that you feel constrained to indulge in such wretched outbursts? It is not true that there is no place for you anywhere and that your own country rejects you. You must surely realise that it is not possible to dismiss a question of subsistence with a gesture of the hand, particularly when important and well-grounded fears are expressed by the person concerned. And now, to reassure you, I am able to inform you that the governing body of the *Gesellschaft* is prepared to increase your income to 800 florins (in return for an extra three hours' teaching each week), and that your eventual appointment as an imperial court organist (designate) is only a formality. Your appointment at the Conservatory must first be settled by contract (and this can be effected in a very short time), of course, before your appointment as a court organist can be recommended to His Majesty the Emperor.

I am not yet able to send you the text of the contract because that cannot be finalized until the next board meeting. (I am expecting notification of a meeting in the next few days.) Do not forget that all information concerning your appointment as a court organist must remain a secret.

And so, if you are pleased with today's information, write me a couple of lines - but let there be no distress or despair, as there is no justification for it in your present position. Reflect on the fact that many a talented musician in Austria has not been able to attain your present position (not to mention your future one), that we are prepared to do all that we can for you under the present circumstances, and that, as already mentioned, the entirely natural questions about provision in the event of illness which you raised and which I sanctioned, together with your request for an increase in salary, have caused a delay - due to no fault of mine.

Your affairs will now take an uninterrupted, straightforward and favourable course. No one can spoil them, apart from you yourself, that is if you were to send the same kind of emotional letters to others as the one I received from you today. So do not go 'out of the world' but 'into the world'. Let there be unworthy despondency in a man and artist of your calibre. You have no occasion for it.

Kind regards, and sincerely yours.

Joh. Herbeck[165]

After the uncertainties and emotional upheavals of the preceding weeks, Bruckner's affairs now proceeded more calmly and assumed a 'straightforward, uninterrupted' course, as Herbeck had predicted. On 28 June he wrote to the administrative body of the Conservatory, accepting the appointment 'with gratitude', and asked that it be 'finalized' and made official.[166] The appointment was duly made official on 6 July, and Bruckner wrote a second letter to the Conservatory, formally accepting the position:

> ... I wish to thank you most sincerely for the written reassurances, and, trusting in the assurances which have been made, to inform you that I have finally resolved to accept the teaching posts offered me, and so, God willing, will be ready to take up this highly prestigious position in Vienna at the beginning of October.
>
> Yours faithfully,
> Anton Bruckner[167]

---

165 See *HSABB* 1, 92 for this letter, dated Vienna, 20 June 1868. The original is not extant; it was first printed in Ludwig Herbeck, op.cit., Appendix, 78f.

166 See *HSABB* 1, 93 for the text of this letter. The original is in the *Gesellschaft der Musikfreunde* library; there is a facsimile in Leopold Nowak, *Anton Bruckner. Musik und Leben* (Linz, 1973), 130.

167 See *HSABB* 1, 93 for this letter, dated Linz, 23 July 1868. The original can be found in the *Gesellschaft der Musikfreunde* library; there is a facsimile in Manfred Wagner, *Bruckner* (Mainz,

At the end of July Bruckner informed the church authorities in Linz that he had accepted a position at the Vienna Conservatory. Just as he had earlier asked Mayr at St. Florian to hold his old organist post in reserve until he had become firmly established in Linz, he now requested that his Linz position be held in reserve for some time, adding that it would bring him 'great comfort' and 'great peace of mind' if his request was granted. Thanks to the supportive intervention of Bishop Rudigier, Bruckner was able to leave Linz without any nagging doubts about his future security.[168]

A letter from Ignaz Dorn throws some further light on Bruckner's ambivalent feelings during the summer of 1868. Dorn had written an earlier letter congratulating Bruckner on his new appointment, and Bruckner had apparently misinterpreted Dorn's words. Dorn now attempted to clear up the misunderstanding.

> Dear friend,
>
> I cannot understand why you should have found my letter so disquieting as to have second thoughts about your decision. To see a danger in it for you was far from my intention - on the contrary, I congratulate you on your new sphere of activity. The fact that I alluded to your previous position, which was by no means

---

1983), 84. See *G-A* III/1, 459ff. for the text of the official contract sent to Bruckner on 6 July; the original is in the *ÖNB*.

168 See *HSABB* 1, 93f. for Bruckner's letter to the church authorities, dated Linz, 24 July 1868. The location of the original is unknown; it was first printed in *G-A* III/1, 457f. See *HSABB* 1, 96f. for Bishop Rudigier's letter to the Government offices in Linz, dated Linz, 25 August 1868, in which the bishop draws attention to Bruckner's 'excellent qualities and merits'; the original of this letter is in the *Ordinariatsarchiv*, Linz. Karl Waldeck, one of Bruckner's former pupils, was his provisional replacement as organist of Linz Cathedral. After Bruckner wrote to the church authorities on 18 July 1870, formally resigning from his former position and thanking them for holding it in reserve, Waldeck was formally appointed. See *HSABB* 1, 119 for this letter. The location of the original is unknown; it was first printed in *ABB*, 113.

unimportant, and even highlighted it, because there are so few of them available, was not intended to make you doubt your move. I was simply surprised that, after spending such a long time in Linz, you are leaving it so decisively. Otherwise, do not have any further scruples.

As you have already perceived, what I wrote was certainly of no particular moment -

Or do you feel that I was not justified in attaching so much importance to your previous position in Linz? Could I have ignored it? To me its significance was such that I could not avoid mentioning it, if only on account of the long duration of your activities which still revive happy memories, e.g. your Mass, Symphony etc. Because you have improved your position, however, and I congratulated you on it in my first letter and congratulate you again in this one, I can put your mind at rest and, in accordance with your wishes, completely reassure you here and now. So cast away all your doubts and be convinced that all of us who know you delight in the knowledge that you are a professor in Vienna! As you are so often the topic of conversation here, I cannot refrain from talking about your two compositions (Mass and Symphony) and from drawing particular attention to your virtuoso organ playing and fugal extemporization. That is certainly the truth! Ask my colleague Kitzler. We often sit and chat with a bunch of musicians. Have you heard Wagner's *Die Meistersinger*? I consider it to be his greatest work! His other operas are so marvellously beautiful, of course - fine polyphonic works - but counterpoint is particularly prominent in *Die Meistersinger*. Be sure to have a good look at the score. You will find that it confirms what I said.

And so, farewell. I have run out of space. May the doubts that you have entertained also come to an end. Let me hear from you again soon.

Best wishes, dear Professor, from

Your friend
Dorn,
Music director

I addressed my first letter to Vienna because I thought that you were there already. As you have written to tell me that you will be in Linz until October, I am sending this letter to Linz. My first letter was obviously forwarded to you from Vienna.[169]

The only matter which was still not fully resolved was Bruckner's appointment as an organist-designate at the Court Chapel. Once again Herbeck intervened on Bruckner's behalf and wrote a letter of recommendation to the Lord Chamberlain:

> ... Your obedient servant wishes to support the request made by Anton Bruckner, cathedral organist in Linz, that he be graciously offered the position of organist-designate in the *Hofmusikkapelle*.
> As an organ virtuoso Bruckner has no equal in the Empire. He has been appointed by the 'Gesellschaft der Musikfreunde' in Vienna, commencing next session, Professor of Counterpoint and Organ Playing at the Conservatory in place of Professor Sechter, the deceased court organist and one of the most renowned celebrities in the area of music theory - and this speaks volumes for Bruckner's outstanding ability - and, in his present position in Linz, has an excellent reputation as a man and artist.
> The circle of outstanding artists in the Court Chapel would be desirably enriched by Bruckner's appointment and there would be absolutely no financial outgoings on the part of the court treasury.
> My Lord, I trust that this information will help to reassure you that you are not dealing with an unworthy applicant, should you speak to His Majesty the Emperor on his behalf.[170]

---

169 See *HSABB* 1, 94 for this letter, dated Brno, 6 August 1868. The location of the original is unknown; it was first printed in *ABB*, 302ff. The works referred to by Dorn are the D minor Mass and the Symphony no. 1 in C minor.

170 See *HSABB* 1, 95 for this letter, dated Vienna, 8 August 1868; the original is in the Hofburg archives, Vienna. Also see earlier and footnote 134 for Bruckner's application to the Lord Chamberlain in October 1867 for the post of either court organist or supernumerary unpaid assistant music director. Herbeck obviously considered that he would stand a better chance if he set his sights somewhat lower. In fact, Bruckner's appointment was to be as second organist-designate, as Rudolf Bibl had been first organist-designate since February 1863. Bibl eventually obtained a permanent position in June 1875 and Bruckner at the beginning of 1878.

In his formal report to the Emperor, Prince Hohenlohe-Schillingsfürst enclosed Herbeck's request and added the further recommendation:

> ... As it has always been customary to secure artists of outstanding reputation for the court music chapel, and Bruckner is certainly described as such, as, in addition, there is a greater need for organists to be employed not only in Vienna but also in Your Majesty's other residences, and, finally, as Bruckner's appointment as unpaid organist-designate would not incur any extra expense, may I ask Your Majesty's permission to have the customary designate authorization made out for Anton Bruckner?[171]

Emperor Franz Josef duly ratified Bruckner's appointment, and Herbeck was informed a few days later. Herbeck immediately contacted Bruckner by telegram to give him the good news and then wrote an official letter to advise him that he had been appointed an organist-designate at the court chapel and was entitled to use the title 'Imperial Court Organist'. He was also a candidate for a definitive post in the future, and, in the meantime, would be required to act as a substitute organist as often as necessary.[172]

While Bruckner was making preparations for his move to Vienna, he was also active as a choirmaster in Linz. The two main Linz choirs, *Frohsinn* and *Sängerbund*, were asked to take part in a charity concert on 17 August for the benefit

---

171 See *ABDS* 1, 47 for the full text of this report, dated 30 August 1868; the original is in the Hofburg archives, Vienna.

172 See *ABDS* 1, 48 for the Emperor's letter of authorization, dated Ischl, 4 September 1868; see also *ABDS* 2, 185 for a facsimile of the original. See also *ABDS* 1, 50 for the letter from the Lord Chamberlain's office to the Court Chapel, dated 8 September 1868; the original is in the Court Chapel archives, Vienna. For Herbeck's letter to Bruckner, dated 9 September 1868, see *ABDS* 1, 51. There is a facsimile of this letter in *G-A* III/1, between pages 462 and 463; a draft of the letter can be found in the Court Chapel archives, Vienna.

144

of the people of Ulrichsberg which had suffered extensive fire damage, and Mathias Weißmann, the secretary of *Frohsinn*, wrote to Bruckner asking him to attend a joint rehearsal. At the end of September, a special informal soirée was organized by *Frohsinn* in the *Stadt Frankfurt* hotel in Linz to bid farewell to Bruckner and Weißmann wrote him an official letter of appreciation for his excellent achievements as choirmaster.[173]

After moving to Vienna, Bruckner maintained contact with his friends in Linz. Letters from Alois Weinwurm and Moritz von Mayfeld indicate that Bruckner had already written to them commenting enthusiastically and favourably on musical life in Vienna. Alois urged him to make sure that he obtained sufficient financial remuneration for his artistic endeavours:

> Dear friend,
>
> I was very happy to read your welcome lines and to learn that all is extremely well with you. I congratulate you - it must be good for you to be able to associate with true artists. Your successor in the choral society, whom I have not met yet, is enjoying tremendous praise...
> Otherwise everything is as it always has been in our neck of the woods. The great artistic delights have already started - *Musikverein* - *Frohsinn* - *Sängerbund* - *Eintracht* - and several other artistic societies; in short, the poor public will have to be pretty thick-skinned. There is something that I would urge you to do. Make use of your patrons while the iron is hot. Those who secured the court appointment for you almost certainly have the power to obtain an income for you. There are enough funds to ensure that a worthy artist such as you is supported in a most generous manner. So give these gentlemen no peace - it must happen, and I am convinced that

---

173 See *HSABB* 1, 96ff. for the texts of both letters, dated Linz, 13 August and 29 September respectively. The originals can be found in the 'Frohsinn-Archiv' of the *Linzer Singakademie*; also in the 'Frohsinn-Archiv' is another letter of appreciation from *Frohsinn* to Bruckner, dated Linz, 25 October 1868.

it can and will happen.

When you give me pleasure by writing a few lines to me again, enclose your address.

Best wishes from
Your true friend
A. Weinwurm[174]

Moritz von Mayfeld was clearly delighted that Bruckner had not taken long to find his feet in Vienna:

Most illustrious maestro!

I am very pleased to hear that you are having a good time in Vienna, and that circumstances are beginning to turn out favourably as I predicted they would. That there now appears to be the possibility of triumphs in 'foreign parts' for you surpasses even my own expectations. I hope that you will give me further information about this Nancy opportunity in due course.

My wife sends her very best wishes to you and, as you are already aware, takes the keenest interest in your artistic endeavours. As she is travelling with her sisters to Vienna next Friday in any case, she will hear your Mass if it is actually to be performed in the Court Chapel on the 22nd (or perhaps on the 29th). She is very much looking forward to it, but, as she is concerned that she will not be able to get a seat in the small chapel, would be most grateful to you if you could perhaps be of some assistance to her in this matter. I also hope to be able to come, and to extricate myself from my duties here for this one day. Could I ask you, therefore, to write or send a telegram to me in any case and tell me if the performance is to take place.

I am very envious of the many beautiful things you are able to hear in Vienna in contrast to the very meagre fare which one is served here.

I have also to inform you that a certain Miss v. Lucam, a harmony student, will contact you sometime this month about lessons. She is

---

174 See *HSABB* 1, 98 for this letter, dated Linz, 8 November 1868; the original is in St. Florian. Bruckner's successor as conductor of *Frohsinn* was Franz Behr.

a very good pianist and an enthusiastic musician.
And so until we probably meet again on the 22nd!

Yours sincerely,

Mayfeld

If you should see Dr. Hanslick, Laub or Körer, please convey my best wishes to them.[175]

As 1868 drew to a close Bruckner looked forward to spending Christmas with his friends in Linz. J.B. Schiedermayr, dean of Linz Cathedral, was the recipient of the following letter:

Dear Dean,

Above all I must thank you for all the kindness you have shown me. I will never, never forget it! For the sake of my nerves I will not describe how difficult it was for me to take leave of you, Your Grace. I can find no words to describe how much I miss you. I also sorely miss every spiritual contact, with the exception of Father Schneeweiß who visited me recently. Otherwise I am well and in very good health; moreover, everyone is well disposed towards me. The churches I normally attend are the chapel of the *Bürger-Versorgungshaus*, St. Stephen's and the court chapel. I have free admission to concerts and to the Court Opera. My Mass is to be performed in January, as further rehearsals are needed and Imhof has

---

175 See *HSABB* 1, 99 for this letter, dated Linz, 14 November 1868. The location of the original is unknown; it was first printed in *ABB*, 330f. The 'Nancy opportunity' is a reference to Bruckner's invitation to play the organ at a festival in Nancy; see chapter 4 for further information. A performance of Bruckner's new F minor Mass was originally scheduled for 22 November and was advertised in the *Neue Freie Presse* 1520; the first rehearsal evidently took place on 20 November. It was then postponed until 29 November, but was not performed then - there was a second rehearsal of the Mass on 16 January 1869. According to Bruckner, Herbeck found the Mass 'too long and unsingable'; see *G-A* IV/1(1936), 78.

not been available. I certainly hope that it will be possible for me to spend Christmas in Linz. Then Your Grace will not be able to get rid of me. In looking forward to it, I take comfort in the knowledge that Your Grace will have some idea of the pleasure I derive from being in your company. I also look forward very much to seeing His Grace the Bishop again. I beg you to convey my deepest respects to him; I certainly prayed - but did not write - on 3 December. I do not know the address and don't have the confidence to find out.

Please give my regards to your sisters. With the deepest respect, Your Grace, from your grateful servant

Anton Bruckner

N.B. My address is Währingerstraße 41.[176]

During 1869 Bruckner kept in regular touch with his friends in Linz, informing them of his successes as an organist in Nancy and Paris and making arrangements for the first performance of E minor Mass at the special dedication service of the Votive Chapel of the new cathedral on 29 September.[177] His successes abroad

---

176 See *HSABB* 1, 99f. for this letter, dated Vienna, 8 December 1868; the original of the letter is privately owned. Father Schneeweiß (1810-1886) was Bruckner's father confessor. A performance of the F minor Mass (or, possibly, the D minor Mass) in the court chapel was scheduled for 17 January 1869 but was replaced by a work written by Johann Baptist Gänsbacher (1778-1844), formerly director of music at St. Stephen's. 3 December was Bishop Rudigier's name-day.

177 Bruckner's letters to Schiedermayr are of particular interest, as two of them (Vienna, 20 May 1869 and Vienna, 19 June 1869) were originally owned by Alois Weissgärber, Schiedermayr's great-nephew, and are still privately owned by the family today. See *HSABB* 1, 105 and 108 for the texts of these letters. Bertha Barghesi was the illegitimate daughter of Karoline Barghesi who lived for some time with Dr. Josef Schiedermayr, Johann Schiedermayr's brother, in Vienna. Bertha had five children, two sons and three daughters. Because of certain facial likenesses to Bruckner in the two sons, Alois (who became an officer in the Austrian army) and Maximilian (who became one of the leaders of the Vienna Philharmonic), the suggestion has been made that Bruckner was Bertha's

prompted three choral societies to elect him an honorary member - the Wels *Männergesangverein* (20 May), *Frohsinn* (9 June) and the Linz *Diözesan-Kunstverein* (21 October). After 1869 he maintained a less regular contact with Linz but was occasionally asked to write works for specific occasions or to play at important services. His choral piece, *Mitternacht* WAB 80, was written for *Frohsinn*'s anniversary concert on 15 May 1870. On 4 June 1878 his motet, *Tota pulchra es* WAB 46, was given its first performance at a special ceremony in honour of Bishop Rudigier's twenty-five year tenure as bishop of the Linz diocese. Six years later, on 4 December 1884, Bruckner played the organ in the performance of Mozart's *Requiem* at Rudigier's funeral service; Cardinal Ganglbauer from Vienna officiated. The following year Bruckner's imposing *Ecce sacerdos magnus* WAB 13 was written for the centenary celebrations of the Linz diocese.[178] At the request of Rudigier's successor, Bishop Müller, Bruckner's *Te Deum* was performed in September 1887 at a special event to mark the 25th anniversary of the laying of the foundation stone and the dedication of the organ of the new cathedral. In the spring of 1886, the *Frohsinn* choral society decided to mount a special Bruckner concert to commemorate its 41st anniversary. A special poetic greeting to Bruckner by Karl Kerschbaum, a local poet, appeared in the Linz *Tagespost* on Tuesday 13 April, and the concert took place two days later. It was certainly a most ambitious concert by Linz standards, consisting of *Germanenzug* WAB 70, *Um Mitternacht* WAB 90, the Adagio from his Third Symphony and the *Te Deum*. Wilhelm Floderer conducted and Bruckner, who was present, later wrote to *Frohsinn* to express his heartfelt

---

father! See two articles under the general title 'Familienerinnerungen an Anton Bruckner': Fröhlich-Weissgärber, 'Vorfahren meines Vaters' and Renate Bronnen, 'Die Weissgärber-Geschwister. Ein Kapitel aus dem Leben Anton Bruckners?' in *BJ 1984/85/86* (Linz, 1988), 25f. and 27-52. Facsimiles of the two letters mentioned above can also be found in *BJ 1984/85/86*, 28 and 40f.

178 In the event, two pieces scheduled to be performed during the centenary celebrations (26 September - 4 October), *Virga Jesse* WAB 85 and *Ecce sacerdos magnus* WAB 13, were found to be too difficult and were replaced by other pieces.

gratitude. A special ceremony was held in his honour after the concert, and glowing reports appeared in the *Tagespost*, the *Linzer Zeitung* and the *Volksblatt*.[179] In May 1889 Bruckner was invited to play the organ at the enthronement of the new bishop, Franz Maria Doppelbauer. On 21 December 1890 the Linz *Musikverein* orchestra, conducted by Adalbert Schreyer, performed the second (1877) version of Bruckner's Third Symphony. This was an unfortunate piece of programme planning - Bruckner was unable to attend because the recently completed third version of the same symphony was being performed in Vienna on the same day by the Philharmonic Orchestra conducted by Hans Richter!

At the request of Bishop Doppelbauer, Bruckner played the organ in Linz Cathedral on Easter Sunday 1891. This was to be the last time that he played the organ in Linz. As a token of gratitude and as a gesture of recognition of Bruckner's many years of service to the region, Doppelbauer arranged for the composer to be granted an annual stipend of 400 florins from the Upper Austrian Parliament. He was in effect able to achieve what Bruckner had not been able to accomplish seventeen years earlier when he petitioned the Upper Austrian Parliament for an annual endowment to provide him with some additional financial security. This had been refused on the grounds that Bruckner was already receiving a significant salary from the Vienna Conservatory and was not in exceptional need of financial help.[180]

When Bruckner died in 1896, the musical director in Linz was August Göllerich, the composer's first biographer. He was responsible for initiating the first regular cycle of Bruckner concerts in Austria. With the foundation of a most important centre for Bruckner research - the *Anton Bruckner Institut Linz* - in the late 1970s, the city can be said to have fully repaid its debt to one of its greatest sons.

---

179 See *HSABB* 1, 299 for Bruckner's letter to *Frohsinn*, dated Vienna, 20 April 1886; the original has been lost; it was first printed in the *Linzer Zeitung*, 30 April 1886. It is also printed in *G-A* III/1, together with a full report of the concert, ceremony and reviews (pp. 593-604).

180 See *G-A* III/1, 564ff. for further details.

3.3 The Music

In this brief assessment of the compositional output of the Linz years, the main emphasis will be on those works written after Bruckner's long period of study with Sechter which came to a successful conclusion at the end of 1861. Very few works were written in the years 1856-61 as a result of a stringent self-imposed moratorium on original compositions. The 'student works' written under Kitzler's supervision in the years 1861-63 show the gradual emergence of an original voice, and the Mass in D minor WAB 26 (1864) is the first work in which Bruckner's true stature is fully displayed.

3.3.1 Secular choral works

Two issues of the *Linzer Zeitung* in June 1863 included the official announcement that there was to be a composition competition as part of the first *Upper Austrian Singing Festival* to take place in Linz on 14 and 15 August 1864.[181] Applicants were invited to submit their works by 30 November 1863, and eight compositions would be chosen for performance at the festival, their composers receiving 50 florins each. At the festival itself, additional prizes of 100, 60 and 40 florins would be given to the composers of the pieces adjudged first, second and third in order of merit. At some point during 1864 the festival was postponed until June 1865 and was re-named the *Oberösterreichisches-salzburgisches Sängerbundesfest*.

We first learn of Bruckner's interest in the competition in a letter sent to him by the poet August Silberstein which suggests that he had already contacted the poet

---

181   Issues of 18 June, p. 574 and 28 June, p. 612.

about a suitable poem. Silberstein enclosed his poem *Germanenzug*, commented on its structure, made some suggestions about a possible musical setting, wished him good luck, and included a glossary of mythological names which might be new to him.[182] In his reply Bruckner, after thanking him for the poem, asked for Silberstein's advice about the metre of the piece which, in his own opinion, ought to be 4/4 to correspond with the mood of the poem.[183] His reference at the end of the letter to the 3/4 metre of *Zigeuner-Waldlied* WAB 135 as being unsuitable would suggest that Bruckner's original intention was to use this choral piece, which is now lost, as the basis for his competition entry:

> ... He was unhappy with the text, perhaps because he felt a gypsy song was unsuitable for a male-chorus festival, and asked Silberstein for something more appropriate. When Bruckner saw the new text and recognised that triple metre was no longer appropriate, he wrote a new piece in duple metre using material from the *Zigeuner-Waldlied* and discarded the earlier composition.[184]

---

182 See *HSABB* 1, 35 for this letter, dated Vienna, 27 July 1863. The original of the letter has been lost; it was first printed in *ABB*, 348-49. The autograph copy of Silberstein's poem is in the *ÖNB*; there is a facsimile in *G-A* III/1, between pages 208 and 209. Dr. August Silberstein (1825-1900, a poet and journalist in Vienna, was a member of the *Wiener Männergesangverein* and, from 1866, an honorary member of the *Wiener Schubertbund*. He also provided Bruckner with the texts for *Helgoland* WAB 71, *Vaterlandslied* WAB 92, and *Vaterländisches Weinlied* WAB 91.

183 See *HSABB* 1, 36 for this letter, dated Linz, 29 July 1863; the original is in the *Wiener Stadt- und Landesbibliothek*.

184 Paul Hawkshaw, 'From Zigeunerwald to Valhalla in Common Time. The Genesis of Anton Bruckner's Germanenzug' in *BJ 1987/88* (Linz, 1990), 21f. See also Uwe Harten, '"Germanen durchstreiten des Urwaldes Nacht". Zu Anton Bruckners Chorwerk Germanenzug' in *Österreichische Musik - Musik in Österreich: Beiträge zur Musikgeschichte Mitteleuropas: Theophil Antonicek zum 60. Geburtstag* (Tutzing, 1998), 395-402.

As the postscript to Bruckner's letter to Rudolf Weinwurm of 1 September makes clear - 'I have just written a chorus (Germanenzug) for the Upper Austrian Festival' - he spent August composing the work or at least the first version of the work.[185] We next hear of the choral piece in January 1864. An article in the edition of the *Linzer Zeitung* for 20 January stated that Bruckner's *Germanenzug* was one of the eight successful compositions that had been chosen from an entry of 120 works at a meeting of the festival committee on 10 January. Bruckner himself was one of the judges, two of the others being Hans Schläger from Salzburg and Anton Storch from Vienna, but the identities of the composers were deliberately concealed during the selection process.[186]

Bruckner's correspondence with the publisher Kränzl and with his friend Rudolf Weinwurm in Vienna between January and August indicates that he was still making alterations to the work as late as the summer of 1864. As Hawkshaw points out, the first three of his four letters to Kränzl

> ... deal with routine composer / publisher matters: on 28 January Bruckner granted publishing rights to Kränzl's firm; on 5 February he sent Kränzl a piano reduction; and on 9 May he asked the publisher to ensure that, in the full score, the first horn had a D sharp in measure 56.[187]

Although Bruckner sent a piano reduction to Kränzl on 5 February, he was still

---

185 See page 98 and footnote 84.

186 From the information provided in *G-A* III/1, 210, it would appear that the initial entry had been no less than 331 works. These were presumably narrowed down to 120 and finally pruned to the eight successful choruses which were allowed to go forward to the festival.

187 Hawkshaw, op.cit., 22. See *HSABB* 1, 40 and 42f. for Bruckner's four letters to Josef Leopold Kränzl (1825-1907), dated Linz, 28 January, 5 February, 9 May and 13 August 1864 respectively; the originals are in the *Museum Innviertler Volkskundehaus*, Ried im Innkreis where Kränzl had his publishing business. Publication of the successful competition pieces was obviously part of the prize.

considering, at Weinwurm's suggestion, a change of instrumentation in the middle section of the chorus (a harp to replace the horn quartet) in late February and early March. This is the gist of his two letters to Weinwurm (25 February and 1 March) from which we also glean the information that Weinwurm was likewise involved in making some alterations in the scoring of his own piece which had also been successful in the competition.[188] Even as late as 13 August when Bruckner returned the proofs to Kränzl, he was eager to point out that he had not only made corrections but also added several new changes.

Of the three manuscript scores of *Germanenzug* WAB 70 in Kremsmünster abbey, the earliest - an autograph score of the instrumental parts only - is possibly the version mentioned in the letter Bruckner sent to Weinwurm on 1 September 1863. The other two scores are a full score and a piano reduction, mainly of the instrumental accompaniment, both of which Bruckner prepared in collaboration with Franz Schimatschek, his Linz copyist.[189] Bruckner's letters to Kränzl and Weinwurm in February and March 1864 allude to this version of the work which differs in several respects from the earlier autograph score. In addition, there is almost certainly a 'lost intermediate version, which must have existed in manuscripts of the full score and piano reduction.'[190] This intermediate version would have been written in October or November 1863 before the composition deadline of 30 November. The other missing layers of the compositional process are the engraver's copies of the full score and the piano reduction which Bruckner referred to in his letter to Kränzl on 13 August. We can surmise, however, that they contained the 'many changes' which

---

188 See pages 99f. and footnotes 86 and 87.

189 For a fuller description of these manuscripts, see Hawkshaw, op.cit., 22ff, *HMSAB*, 198ff., and Franz Burkhardt, 'Anton Bruckner und sein Germanenzug', *IBG Mitteilungsblatt* 14 (1978), 19-23. Franz Schimatschek (1812-1877), a horn player in the Linz theatre orchestra and the National Guard band, was also well known as an excellent copyist and Bruckner had an extremely high opinion of him.

190 Hawkshaw, op.cit., 26.

appeared in the first edition.[191]

The eight successful choruses which had reached the final stages of the competition were conducted by their own composers at the Festival in Linz on 5 June 1865. First, second and third prizes were awarded according to the volume of applause - surely a risky business without a 'clapometer'? - and Bruckner's *Germanenzug* had to take second place to Weinwurm's *Germania*, a result which, as we have seen, seems to have somewhat soured the relationship between the two friends for a time. The *Linzer Zeitung* contained the following review of Bruckner's work:

> Mr. Bruckner is an epic composer in this chorus. The poem is spirited and sublime, but requires so much declamatory accent that we cannot regard it as being very suitable for a musical setting and must judge it at least as a very dangerous stumbling-block for the composer. The composition as such has verve and provides fresh proof of Mr. Bruckner's great talent for the higher style and his powerful and secure mastery of the entire descriptive material. Both the opening and closing sections make an excellent, impressive effect. The entry of the solo quartet has a singular beauty. The poet, who was at the festival, will no doubt have given the composer some assistance in his setting of the poem and we cannot raise any objection to that. Nevertheless, now that the poem has been set to music, we have to express our opinion that *inter alia* the end of the first movement which is marked *forte*: 'as the watchful escort of Valkyries hovers around the heroes and sings of the battle' and the solo

---

191 This was the first of Bruckner's works to be published. The exact date of publication is not known but was presumably during the late summer or autumn of 1864. Later in the century (1892?) an edition of the score and parts was published by A. Robitschek (Vienna and Leipzig), and Eduard Kremser prepared an edition of the work for chorus and orchestra. There is a modern edition in both full score and study score format, ed. Franz Burkhardt et al., in *ABSW* 22/2 / 22/7 (Vienna, Musikwissenschaftlicher Verlag, 1987 / 1998), 179-212 / 1-32. The original scoring of the work is for male-voice choir accompanied by a brass ensemble comprising four horns, two cornets, four trumpets, three trombones, a tenor horn (euphonium) and tuba.

quartet which enters immediately afterwards *piano* are not entirely successful.[192]

In spite of this critic's reservations, *Germanenzug* was performed several times during the composer's lifetime. Its slower middle section was sung by the *Wiener Akademischer Gesangsverein* accompanied by a horn quartet from the Vienna *Staatsoper* at Bruckner's funeral on 14 October 1896.

While working on *Germanenzug*, Bruckner wrote two other accompanied secular choral works, *Um Mitternacht* WAB 89 and *Herbstlied* WAB 73. *Um Mitternacht*, for male-voice choir, solo alto and piano, was completed on 12 April 1864. Bruckner set the same text by Robert Prutz again in Vienna more than twenty years later (*Um Mitternacht* WAB 90), writing for similar forces but replacing the solo alto with a solo tenor. The autograph score has no dedication, but Schimatschek's copy has a dedication to the Linz *Sängerbund* on the title page signed and dated by Bruckner, 15 April 1864.[193] Bruckner conducted the first performance of the piece in Linz on 11 December 1864 at the anniversary celebrations of *Sängerbund*. The reviewer of the work in the *Linzer Zeitung* referred to its 'unusually sombre mood' at the beginning but singled out the solo alto entry in E major and 'its truly delightful conclusion' for particular mention.[194] *Herbstlied*, a setting of a poem by Friedrich

---

192 This review (critic unknown) appeared in the *Linzer Zeitung* 129 on 7 June 1865; see Susanna Taub, op.cit., 28f. for facsimiles of this report and the report of the festival procession in the *Linzer Abendbote*, 7 June 1865. Bruckner's *Germanenzug* was also mentioned in the report of the festival which appeared in the *Neue Freie Presse* 277 on 8 June.

193 The autograph score, formerly in the private possession of Anton Dermota, is now in the *ÖNB*. Schimatschek's copy, as described in *G-A* III/1, 252, is in the archives of the *Linz Singakademie*. The work was first published by U.E. Vienna in 1911, edited and with a foreword by V. Keldorfer.

194 See *G-A* III/1, 254 for an extract from this review (possibly by Franz Gamon) in the *Linzer Zeitung* 287, 16 December 1864. See Susanna Taub, op.cit., 44f. for facsimiles of this review and

v. Sallet for male-voice choir, two soprano soloists and piano, was composed in March 1864 and dedicated to Josef Hafferl, who was the chairman of the *Frohsinn* choir at the time. The Viennese copyist, Franz Hlawaczek, prepared two copies. Both have dedications but only one has autograph entries by the composer with his signature and the date 19 March 1864.[195] As there is no surviving autograph score, Hawkshaw surmises that Bruckner wanted to keep one of the copies for his own use because the autograph 'was for some reason impractical to use'. Why Bruckner should have employed a Viennese copyist is a mystery, but it is possible that Rudolf Weinwurm hired Hlawaczek on his behalf.[196] The chorus was first performed by *Frohsinn* at a special ladies' evening in Linz on 24 November 1864. One of the two soprano soloists was Marie Schimatschek, the eldest daughter of Franz Schimatschek. The reviewer in the *Linzer Zeitung* on 2 December considered the piece to be well composed but found the initial soprano entries too prominent above the *pianissimo* choral description of the echoes of earlier nightingale singing.[197]

While the accompanied secular choral works were confined to the years 1863-65, the unaccompanied works spanned almost the entire Linz period. According to the date at the end of the autograph score, *Das edle Herz* WAB 66 was completed in December 1857.[198] It was Bruckner's second setting of a poem by Ernst Marinelli, a St. Florian priest. Whereas the earlier setting (WAB 65, c.1851) is for male voices, the Linz setting is for mixed voices. One of the first pieces Bruckner wrote after

---

another review which appeared in the *Linzer Abendbote* 284, 13 December 1864.

195 Both copies are now in the archives of the Linz *Singakademie*. The work was first published by U.E. Vienna in 1911, edited and with a foreword by V. Keldorfer.

196 See *HMSAB*, 149 and 327f.

197 See Susanna Taub, op.cit., 25 for a facsimile of this review in the *Linzer Zeitung* 276, 2 December 1864.

198 This autograph score is located in Wels municipal library. Renate Grasberger's dating of 1861 in *Werkverzeichnis Anton Bruckners* (Tutzing, 1977), 72 is clearly wrong. The piece is discussed in *G-A* III/1, 91f. and printed in *G-A* III/2, 13-17. See also *HMSAB*, 255 and 262.

completing his theoretical studies with Sechter was a setting for mixed-voice quartet of Heine's poem *Du bist wie eine Blume* WAB 64. There are two autograph scores, the second of which is dated Linz, 5 December 1861 at the end.[199] Bruckner dedicated this piece to the *Sängerbund* choir and it was performed at the choir's fourth anniversary concert on 15 December. Bruckner composed the first of his two settings of Zedlitz's *Der Abendhimmel* WAB 55 in January 1862 for male-voice quartet. According to Göllerich, a fair copy of the manuscript bore the dedication: 'Dedicated to my dear friends, P.T. Munsch 1. Tenor, Dr. Stifler 2. Tenor, Dr. Benoni 1. Bass, Dr. Weinmann 2. Bass. Anton Bruckner. January 1862'.[200] The second setting, WAB 56, for male-voice choir, was completed on 6 December 1866, nearly five years later, and reveals just how much richer Bruckner's harmonic language had become during this time.[201]

Towards the end of 1866, A. M. Storch, the conductor of the *Niederösterreichische Sängerbund*, asked Bruckner to send him a chorus for male voices. The composer made reference to this request in a letter to Weinwurm of 2 December in which he also mentioned that he had just completed the E minor Mass.[202] On 11 December Bruckner thanked Storch profusely for his request, and

---

199 The first of these, now in the *ÖNB*, is a composition score and is reproduced in *G-A* III/2, 193-96. The second, now in the archives of the Linz *Singakademie*, is a fair copy and is reproduced in Appendix 5 of *HMSAB*. See also *G-A* III/1, 124 and *HMSAB*, 266f.

200 A facsimile of the autograph composition score in the *ÖNB* is reproduced in *HMSAB*, 112ff., but the fair copy, as described by Göllerich in *G-A* III/1, 124f. and to which he must have had access, is missing. See also *G-A* III/2, 18ff. for a printed copy of the work, and *HMSAB*, 112ff. and 268f. for further discussion.

201 The autograph is in the *ÖNB*. See *G-A* III/1, 361f. and *HMSAB*, 291 for further discussion. The work was first published by U.E. Vienna (chorus parts 1899, score 1902) as the second of *Zwei Männerchöre*, the first being *O könnt' ich dich beglücken* WAB 92.

202 See page 112 and footnote 115.

158

continued:

> ... I had nothing at all ready, but composed these choruses in the last two weeks. I am making two of them - 'Abendhimmel' and 'Weinlied' - available to you to do with as you wish. But I have been so bold (please forgive me) as to dedicate a third piece, Silberstein's 'O könnt' ich dich beglücken', to your excellent choir because I considered it to be the most substantial of the three... I am not interested at all in any honorarium. I will be sufficiently rewarded if the good Lord permits one of my works to be performed...[203]

The *Weinlied* referred to in this letter is Bruckner's setting of another poem by August Silberstein, *Vaterländisches Weinlied* WAB 91, a short twelve-bar piece.[204] *O könnt' ich dich beglücken* WAB 92, a setting of a four-verse patriotic poem for tenor and baritone soloists in addition to male-voice choir, is the most extended of these unaccompanied works.[205]

The remaining unaccompanied secular works written during the Linz period are of uncertain date, but it is probable that the short motto, *Das Frauenherz, die Mannesbrust* WAB 95a, was given its first performance by the combined *Frohsinn* men's and women's choirs during a spring outing to the Kiernberger forest on 17 May 1868. The words are by Karl Kerschbaum, a friend of Bruckner and chairman

---

203 See *HSABB* 1, 64 for the text of this letter; the original is in the *Gesellschaft der Musikfreunde* library.

204 The autograph of this chorus has been lost. See *HMSAB*, 289f. for details of two copy scores. See also *G-A* III/1, 358-61 and F. Racek, 'Ein neuer Text zu Bruckners "Vaterländisches Weinlied" in Franz Grasberger, ed., *Bruckner-Studien* (Vienna, 1964), 83-86. The work was first published as *Vaterländisch* by Emil Berté and Co. in *Wiener Componistenalbum* (Vienna, 1892). It is also printed in *G-A* III/2, 139.

205 The autograph of this chorus has been lost. See *HMSAB*, 290, *G-A* III/1, 358 and 362-65, and footnote 201.

of *Frohsinn*.[206] According to Göllerich, the motto *Des Höchsten Preis* WAB 95b, with words by A. Mittermayr, was written for the *Liedertafel Sierning* near Steyr. Its simpler harmonic style suggests an earlier date.[207] The two versions of the *Volkslied: Anheben lasst uns all' zusamm'* WAB 94, the first for male voices unaccompanied and the second for voice and piano, were probably written during the Vienna period.[208]

3.3.2 Sacred choral works

From the beginning of the Linz period comes an *Ave Maria* WAB 5 for four-part mixed-voice choir, cello and organ. It provides a good example of Bruckner's contrapuntal knowledge shortly after the beginning of his marathon course in harmony and counterpoint and, as Göllerich points out, is the last of his sacred works to contain a figured bass.[209] Towards the end of his period of study with

---

206 There is neither an autograph nor a copy score of this work. It is printed in *G-A* III/2, 158 and discussed in *G-A* III/1, 516 and *HMSAB*, 301.

207 There is no autograph score available. The three copy scores extant do not have specific connections with the Linz period. See *G-A* III/1, 516 and *HMSAB*, 12 and 300. The work is printed in *G-A* III/2, 159.

208 There are facsimiles of both versions in *G-A* III/2, 191f. Both Göllerich (III/1, 105f.) and Renate Grasberger, op.cit., 100) suggest a Linz date, c. 1861 in the latter case. Alfred Orel, 'Ein vergessener Preis-Chor von Anton Bruckner' in *Wiener Volkszeitung*, January 1941, 11-16, however, gives the date 1882. As Paul Hawkshaw observes, 'there is nothing in the physical characteristics of the sources which would contradict this dating and there is certainly no physical evidence that *Volkslied* is a Linz composition' (*HMSAB*, 12; see also 259). For further information about Bruckner's secular choral works, see Angela Pachovsky, 'Bruckners weltliche Chöre' in *Bruckner-Vorträge, Bruckner-Tagung Wien 1999 Bericht* (Vienna, 2000), 35-46.

209 *G-A* III/1, 34. The work is discussed in some detail in pp. 33-40. It was first published in Bruckner's lifetime by J. Groß of Innsbruck (1893). For a modern edition, see *ABSW* XXI/1, 75-81

Sechter, Bruckner wrote *Am Grabe* WAB 2 for a special occasion - the funeral on 11 February 1861 of Josefine Hafferl, the mother of the chairman of *Frohsinn*. As he had to write this piece at short notice, he made use of the same text as *Vor Arneths Grabe* WAB 53 written seven years earlier, but omitted the final verse. The review of the piece in the *Linzer Zeitung* on 12 February highlighted the 'atmosphere of gentle feeling' which pervaded the work. Although Bruckner borrowed an earlier text he avoided providing an identical musical treatment. *Am Grabe* displays a more mature handling of the text and a more expansive harmonic treatment, and Hawkshaw appositely asserts that it was 'not so much a revision designed to update an earlier work as it was a new composition using material from an older one'.[210]

The *Ave Maria* WAB 6 for unaccompanied seven-part mixed-voice choir (SAATTBB) is one of Bruckner's most appealing works. It was composed in May 1861 and first performed on 12 May by *Frohsinn* as the offertory hymn during a Mass by Lotti in the cathedral as part of the choir's anniversary celebrations. Like the contemporary *Afferentur regi* WAB 1, it was frequently included in later performances of the Mass in D minor.[211] Bruckner also rehearsed the motet with the *Singakademie* in Salzburg in September 1861 when he applied for the vacant post of music director. Although he was unsuccessful, the *Ave Maria* evidently made a favourable impression - as it had done after its first performance earlier in the year when the reporter for the *Linzer Zeitung* described it as 'a strictly contrapuntal work imbued with religious feeling' which had provided 'shining proof of his intensive

---

(also foreword, xi) with critical report in *ABSW* XXI/2, 57f.

210 *HMSAB*, 221-26, 223 in particular; see also 264. The work is also discussed in *G-A* III/1, 92ff. It was first published by Friedrich Eckstein in his *Erinnerungen an Anton Bruckner* (Vienna, 1923). See Susanna Taub, 22 for a facsimile of the review of the piece in the *Linzer Zeitung* 35.

211 Later performances of the motet in the context of the Mass in D minor include those in Linz (20 November 1864) and Vienna (10 February 1867). It was also conducted by Joseph Schalk during one of the private evenings of the *Wagner-Verein* in Vienna (8 November, 1888).

studies... and his particular aptitude for composing church music'.[212] *Afferentur regi* for four-part mixed-voice choir was written in Linz on 7 November and first performed at St. Florian on 13 December 1861. It was unaccompanied originally, but Bruckner added three optional trombone parts later. The autograph sketch in Kremsmünster, which does not have trombone parts, 'looks very much like a composition score for an *a cappella* motet for four mixed voices' and possibly represents 'the earliest stages of the work's composition' rather than being 'the first of two versions of the motet'.[213]

Four years elapsed before Bruckner wrote his next small-scale sacred piece. Indeed *Trauungslied* WAB 49, set to a German text by Dr. Franz I. Proschko, is really a semi-sacred composition, an occasional work for male-voice choir and organ written in January 1865 to celebrate the wedding of Karl Kerschbaum, chairman of *Frohsinn*, and Marie Schimatschek, a concert singer and daughter of Franz Schimatschek. The *Frohsinn* choir, with Bruckner at the organ, gave it its first

---

212 This report in the *Linzer Zeitung* 112 was on 15 May 1861; see Susanna Taub, op.cit., 22 for facsimile. See earlier and footnote 37 for Bruckner's own account (to Rudolf Weinwurm) of his Salzburg experience. *Ave Maria* was first published by Emil Wetzler (Vienna, 1887). For further discussion of the motet, see *G-A* III/1, 97, *HMSAB*, 230-34, *ABSW* XXI/1, 184 and 188, and *ABSW* XXI/2, 58-63. For a modern edition, see *ABSW* XXI/1, 82-85.

213 *HMSAB*, 152; see also 267f. There is a facsimile of the autograph in Max Auer, *Anton Bruckner als Kirchenmusiker* (Regensburg: Bosse, 1927), 64. This offertory motet was first published by Universal Edition (U.E. 4978) in 1922 as a supplement to the November / December (11/12) issue of *Musica Divina*. The editor, J.V. von Wöss, replaced the three trombones with an organ. For further discussion, see *G-A* III/1, 122f. and *ABSW* XXI/2, 64-72. For a modern edition, see the latter's companion volume, *ABSW* XXI/1, 86f.

performance in Linz Parish Church on 6 February.[214]

Just as the *Afferentur regi* and *Ave Maria* motets are closely associated with the D minor Mass, a motet written near the end of the Linz period - *Pange lingua* WAB 33 - has modal (Phrygian) and thematic connections with the E minor Mass. It was composed on 31 January 1868 and Bruckner's original intention was to have it performed at the same time as the first performance of his Mass in Linz on 29 September 1869, but he had to wait twenty years before hearing it. Writing to his friend Oddo Loidol in Kremsmünster on 18 October 1892, he enclosed copies of *Iam locis orto sidere* WAB 18 and the 1868 *Pange lingua*, referring to the latter as 'my favourite *Tantum ergo*' which was already in print and which he had already heard three times in Steyr. Bruckner directed that it was to be performed 'very slowly and solemnly'.[215] In the 1880s Franz Witt, one of the leaders of the Caecilian reform movement in Catholic church music in the second half of the 19th century, included this small motet in a collection of 'Eucharistic Songs' and, to Bruckner's great annoyance, 'corrected' the ending of the piece which presumably offended his over-sensitive ears. This 'correction' was amended in the Groß edition of 1895 and subsequent editions of the piece.[216]

---

214 The piece is discussed in *G-A* III/1, 309ff. and *HMSAB*, 280f. Göllerich's discussion includes a factual report of the performance in the *Linzer Zeitung* 31, 8 February 1865; see Susanna Taub, op.cit., 26 for a facsimile of this report. There is a facsimile of the autograph, which is in the archives of the Linz *Singakademie*, in *G-A* III/2, 219-24.

215 See *ABB*, 264f. for the text of this letter. Franz Bayer, who was director of the church choir at Steyr, made a copy of this work. It is now in the *ÖNB*, as is Bruckner's autograph. See also Altman Kellner, *Musikgeschichte des Stiftes Kremsmünster* (Kassel, 1956), 756f.

216 Prior to its publication in Franz X. Witt, *Eucharistische Gesänge* 5 (1888), it appeared in the supplement of Witt, ed., *Musica Sacra* 18 (1885), 44. Witt also made some rhythmical changes in bars 9-11. For an account of Bruckner's reaction, see Friedrich Eckstein, *Erinnerungen*, 13-17. There is a facsimile of the autograph of this motet in *G-A* III/1, 500. For further discussion of the work, see *G-A* III/1, 499-503, *ABSW* XXI/1, foreword (xi) and 184, and *ABSW* XXI/2, 72-76. For

For the anniversary celebrations of *Frohsinn* in 1868, Bruckner wrote an offertory motet, *Inveni David* WAB 19, for male voices and four trombones, completing it in Linz on 21 April and directing the first performance on 10 May.[217] The last of the small sacred pieces from the Linz period is *Iam lucis orto sidere* WAB 18, a hymn for mixed-voice choir *a cappella* probably written during the summer months of 1868. It is a simple, modally inspired piece and homophonic throughout. Its dedicatee, Professor Adolf Dorfer, was the abbot of Wilhering abbey, and Robert Riepl, one of the priests working at the abbey, supplied the text. On October 15, 1867 Riepl wrote to the bishop's office in Linz requesting approval for the text to be kept in the Wilhering monastery library. Riepl also paid the costs of the first edition in 1868.[218] When Bruckner was asked in 1892 to play the organ in the student chapel for a school service in Kremsmünster, he had to decline because of a badly swollen foot, but he remembered this hymn and sent it, together with a copy of the contemporary *Pange lingua*, to Father Oddo Loidol.[219] A rather intriguing transposed version of the hymn was published in the Viennese magazine *An der*

---

a modern edition, see *ABSW* XXI/1, 88f.

217   The work is discussed in *G-A* III/1, 441ff. and *ABSW* XXI/2, 76-80. A facsimile of the autograph, which is located in the archives of the Linz *Singakademie*, can be found after page 64 in Max Auer, *Anton Bruckner als Kirchenmusiker* (Regensburg: Bosse, 1927), and in *G-A* III/2, 239-44. There is a modern edition of the work in *ABSW* XXI/1, 90-93.

218   G.K. Mitterschiffthaler refers to this work in his article, 'Die Beziehungen Anton Bruckners zum Stift Wilhering', *Bruckner Studien* (Vienna, 1975), 128. There is no autograph extant and the probable engraver's copy differs in some respects from the first edition (Linz: Feichtingers Erben, 1868). See *G-A* III/1, 496-99 and, for more accurate information, *ABSW* XXI/1, 184, *ABSW* XXI/2, 80-85, and *HMSAB*, 292f. For the musical text of this first version, see *G-A* III/2, 142f. and *ABSW* XXI/1, 94-97 (including arrangement with organ accompaniment).

219   See footnote 215.

schönen blauen Donau in May 1886.[220]

One small sacred piece which has been lost is a *Litanei* WAB 132. Our sole source of knowledge about it is the beginning of a letter from Sechter to Bruckner in September 1858:

> ... Yesterday I received your letter of the 22nd, together with the parcel containing the *Litanei*, and I am pleased that it has been successful. Please convey my respects to music director Zappe...[221]

From this we can deduce that the piece was written and performed in Linz in 1858, probably conducted by Karl Zappe, the cathedral music director, during a church service.

The first of the larger sacred works and one which may well have been written in St. Florian before 1856 is a setting of *Psalm 146* WAB 37 for soloists, double choir and an orchestra consisting of one flute, two oboes, two clarinets, two bassoons, four horns, two trumpets, three trombones, timpani and strings. Paul Hawkshaw asserts correctly that there is 'no documentary evidence that it was composed in Linz' and adds that there is 'every reason to believe Bruckner would have shied away from writing such a large piece while he was studying with Sechter'. Max Graf's dating of 1860 is almost certainly wrong.[222]

---

220 It was transposed up a minor third to G minor, and verses 3-6 of the original eight verses were omitted. See *ABSW* XXI/1, 185 and 188, and *ABSW* XXI/2, 134f. for further information. The most recent editions of the piece are (a) G.K. Mitterschiffthaler, ed., music supplement of *Singende Kirche* 21/4 (1973-74); (b) *ABSW* XXI/1, 146f.

221 See *HSABB* 1, 13f. for the text of this letter, dated Vienna, 26 September 1858; it was first printed in *ABB*, 350f. The originals of both Bruckner's letter of 22 September and Sechter's reply are not extant.

222 See *HMSAB* 82, footnote 1 for Hawkshaw's comments; see also 298 and 323f. for further information about the sources, including a copy with autograph entries in the *ÖNB*. There is no

Bishop Rudigier asked Bruckner to write a festival cantata for the special ceremony on 1 May 1862 at which the foundation stone of the new Linz Cathedral was laid. The *Fest-Cantate 'Preiset den Herrn'* WAB 16 was written between 26 March and 25 April and was scored for four-part male-voice choir, male solo quartet, bass soloist, wind band and timpani. It was performed by *Frohsinn* and invited guest singers accompanied by a military band conducted by Engelbert Lanz.[223]

Bruckner's setting of *Psalm 112* WAB 35, scored for double choir and an orchestra comprising double woodwind, two horns, two trumpets, three trombones, timpani and strings, was composed in Linz in 1863 shortly after the completion of the Symphony in F minor and the termination of his course of studies with Kitzler. Dates in the autograph score suggest that the work was begun in June and completed on

---

original autograph extant. For Graf's dating, see his article 'Anton Bruckner: der Entwicklungsgang' in *Die Musik* 1 (January 1902), 581. Göllerich's view was that the piece was begun in St. Florian and completed in Linz, but he also suggested a completion date of 1860 - see *G-A* III/1, 71 and 658. Renate Grasberger gives the place and period of composition as 'St. Florian oder Linz, Juli 1860' in her *Werkzeichnis*, 41. The first modern edition, edited Paul Hawkshaw, is in *ABSW* XX/4 (Vienna: Musikwissenschaftlicher Verlag, 1996). The text of Psalm 146, in Allioli's German translation, is equivalent to verses 1-11 of Psalm 147 in the Lutheran translation and in the Authorized Version.

223 The text of the cantata was supplied by Dr. Maximilian Pammesberger (1820-1864), a priest, theologian and editor of the *Christliche Kunstblätter* in Linz. The work is discussed in *G-A* III/1, 135-39. The autograph score, in which Schimatschek copied all the voice parts and Bruckner wrote all the instrumental parts, and the autograph vocal score are in the Linz Cathedral archives. There are also autograph sketches in the *ÖNB*. See *HMSAB* 167, 189-92 and 269f. There is a facsimile of the autograph score in *G-A* III/2, 197-216. The first edition of the full score, edited by Karl Etti, was published by Doblinger in 1955. The cantata has also been published in both full score and study score format, ed. Franz Burkhart, Rudolf H. Führer and Leopold Nowak, in *ABSW* XXII/2 (Vienna: Musikwissenschaftlicher Verlag, 1987), 148-77; *ABSW* XXII/6 (Vienna, 1998). There were reports of the first performance in the *Linzer Zeitung* on 2 and 3 May 1862; see Susanna Taub, op.cit., 25 for a facsimile of the second report.

5 July but there is also an annotation in Bruckner's hand in the *Kitzler Studienbuch* -
'Ouverture - dann Symphonie u Psalm beschlossen / 10. Juli 1863' - which provides
a slightly later finishing date. According to Gräflinger, the Psalm was originally
conceived for the laying of the foundation stone of the General Hospital in Linz on
15 September 1863, but there is no report of its performance. Indeed the first
recorded performance of the work did not take place until 14 March 1926 when it
was conducted by Max Auer in Vöcklabruck.[224]

Psalm 112 was the final preparation for the three great Mass settings - in D minor,
E minor and F minor. His increasing confidence in writing for large choral and
orchestral forces is seen in the motivic working, rich harmonic colouring and
impressive symphonic technique of these works. These are derived from Beethoven
and the early Romantics and there are only a few echoes of the late eighteenth-
century sacred style which he consciously cultivated in his early works and which are
still present, albeit not so noticeably, in the B flat minor Mass and Psalm settings.

The first information about Bruckner's *Mass in D minor* WAB 26, scored for
soloists, chorus and an orchestra comprising double woodwind, two horns, two
trumpets, three trombones, timpani, strings and organ, was provided by the *Linzer
Zeitung* on 4 June 1864:

---

224 For Gräflinger's comments, see *GrBL*, 34. The autograph score of the Psalm is in the *ÖNB*.
It was first published in 1926, edited J.V. Wöss, by U.E. Vienna (full score U.E. 6685). The work
is discussed in *G-A* III/1, 190-203 and there is a facsimile of a page from the score between pages
200 and 201. There is a facsimile of another page from the score in Robert Haas, *Anton Bruckner*
(Potsdam, 1934), 47. See also *HMSAB*, 275. The first modern edition, edited Paul Hawkshaw, is
in *ABSW* XX/5 (Vienna: Musikwissenschaftlicher Verlag, 1996). See Paul Hawkshaw's article,
'Bruckners Psalmen', in *Bruckner-Vorträge* (Vienna, 2000) for a facsimile of a page from the
autograph. The text of Psalm 112, in Allioli's German translation, is equivalent to that of Psalm 113
in the Lutheran translation and in the Authorized Version.

... Mr. Anton Bruckner is working most assiduously at the composition of a Mass which is to receive its first performance in Ischl during this summer.

According to the autograph score, the *Kyrie* of the Mass was finished on 4 July, the *Credo*, begun during July, was completed on 1 September, and the *Sanctus*, *Agnus*, and *Benedictus* were also completed in September - on the 6th, 22nd and 29th (at '7 o'clock in the evening') respectively. The *Gloria* is not dated but, in view of the dates on which the other movements were commenced, it is probable that Bruckner began work on it in June or July. Bruckner's copyist, Schimatschek, wrote the parts, and the Mass was performed for the first time, not in Ischl, but in the old Linz Cathedral, on 20 November 1864.[225] It found favour with the critics, the *Linzer Abendbote* reporting the following day that 'Bruckner's Mass in D major (sic) performed yesterday in the Cathedral is the finest of its kind which has been produced for a long time, according to the judgment of our most worthy connoisseurs'.[226]

It obviously made sufficient impression for Moritz von Mayfeld to feel justified in organizing a repeat of the performance at a 'Concert spirituel' in the *Redoutensaal* on 18 December. In a letter to Rudolf Weinwurm on 26 December, Bruckner gave details of both performances:

... Through the good offices of several music patrons my Mass was

225 See *HMSAB*, 168 and 278ff. for details of autograph sketches in Kremsmünster and other material, including the autograph score, in the *ÖNB*. The Mass is fully discussed in *G-A* III/1, 259-306 and there is a facsimile of a page from the autograph of the *Credo* between pages 264 and 265. It was first published by Groß of Innsbruck in 1892. The first modern edition is *ABSW* XVI (Vienna, 1957) which includes an informative foreword by Leopold Nowak.

226 From review in the *Linzer Abendbote*; see Susanna Taub, op.cit., 46 for a facsimile of the review in the *Linzer Zeitung*.

performed in the Cathedral on 20 November and at a 'Concert spirituel' in the Linz Redoutensaal on 18 December. The fact that the attendance at the latter was exceptional, even to overflowing, will prove to you just what effect it had in church; and this surprises me all the more as the mood of the work is very serious and its form very free.[227]

A further detail of the second performance in the *Redoutensaal* is provided by Bruckner in his letter to Weinwurm on 21 January 1865. As there was no organ in the hall and because 'the organs are usually too deep', the organ solo before 'Et resurrexit' in the *Credo* was transferred to the woodwind (two clarinets and two bassoons) probably by the composer himself. Bruckner mentioned to Weinwurm, who had expressed an interest in performing the work in Vienna, that he would pay for any expense involved in altering the parts.[228]

In the *Linzer Zeitung* Franz Gamon contributed a series in five weekly instalments on the development of the Mass from the end of the fifteenth century until Bruckner's time and, in the fourth and fifth instalments, he discussed the D minor Mass, describing it as 'the most important modern work in the realm of church music', pointing to Bruckner's 'predilection for the polyphonic style' which he employed

certainly not to appear competent or out of mere pleasure in self-imposed difficulties but because it alone is worthy of the highest thoughts. The realization of the artistic ideal is seen at its most admirable in the strict forms of complex counterpoint, as these admit depth and strength of characterisation in a flexible conception.

Gamon concluded his discussion by giving special mention to the *Gloria* and

---

227   See p. 103 and footnote 93.

228   See p. 105 and footnote 95.

Credo movements:

> ... it is the *Gloria* and *Credo* in particular which testify to Bruckner's great talent insofar as the instrumental writing, while conditioned by the nature of the vocal writing, nonetheless leads an independent existence. These two movements can be ranked justifiably among the best in the domain of church music. The other movements are not on the same high level, although the *Benedictus* and the *Dona nobis pacem* are outstanding, the former in its voice-leading, the latter in its soothing translucence.[229]

Bruckner's unconcealed delight at the prospect of Weinwurm performing the Mass during the 500th-anniversary celebrations of Vienna University is revealed in a letter to his friend at the beginning of 1865 in which he advised him of the difficulties of the work and the need to set aside adequate rehearsal time. Bruckner sent the score to Weinwurm on 21 January and, in an accompanying letter, mooted the possibility of his 'showing it to Dr. Hanslick and perhaps other people in the same profession'.[230] Weinwurm's plan did not materialise but Hanslick provided a sympathetic second-hand account of the Linz performance of the Mass in the *Neue freie Presse* on 1 April 1865. It was Herbeck who was responsible for the first Viennese performance of the D minor Mass in the Court Chapel on 10 February 1867 and, as we have seen, this set in train a whole series of events which culminated in Bruckner's eventual move to Vienna in the autumn of 1868.

In performances of the Mass before 1876, which included another Linz performance on 6 January 1868, a performance in Salzburg Cathedral on 11

---

229   Gamon's five articles appeared weekly in the *Linzer Zeitung* from 30 November to 29 December. See *GrBL*, 36ff. for the complete text of Gamon's discussion of the D minor Mass, which constituted the fourth and fifth articles, 20 and 29 December respectively; facsimiles of substantial parts of the articles can be found in Susanna Taub, op.cit., 47-58.

230   See earlier and footnotes 94 and 95 for these two letters.

September 1870 and another Vienna performance on 18 July 1875, the work was given in its original form. During the summer of 1876, however, Bruckner worked on all three of his mature Masses and, after scrutinizing their periodic structure, made 'rhythmical' adjustments. A few places in the D minor Mass were altered in this way, and the orchestration also underwent some revision. Further corrections, particularly in the *Credo*, were made in the winter of 1881/82.[231] The first complete performance of the Mass outside Austria was conducted by Mahler in Hamburg on 31 March 1893. Franz Bayer, who conducted two performances of the work in Steyr in April 1893 and April 1896, was one of Bruckner's most enthusiastic devotees and gave tangible expression to his support by directing performances of the composer's works in the town. Bruckner himself played the organ in the 1893 performance and paid tribute to the performers at a reception in his honour held afterwards. In a letter to Bayer he remarked that the Mass had been 'performed astonishingly well'.[232] Keen interest in the work was also shown by Father Georg Huemer, director of music at Kremsmünster abbey. Oddo Loidol, a pupil in Bruckner's Harmony and Counterpoint class at the Vienna Conservatory during the 1879/1880 session, became a Benedictine priest at the abbey. Writing to Loidol on 17 October 1880, Bruckner congratulated his ex-pupil on his move to Kremsmünster and asked him to procure the score of the Mass, which he had evidently lent to Huemer, and return it to Vienna 'as this Mass is now being performed more often again and is beginning to find exceptional favour'.[233]

---

231 See *HMSAB*, 278f. for details of Bruckner's later annotations in the autograph score (in the *ÖNB*) and Schimatschek's copy score (also in the *ÖNB*).

232 This letter is dated Vienna, 22 April 1893, and its text can be found in *ABB*, 271f. The original of the letter is in St. Florian; there is a facsimile in *GrBL*, after page 58.

233 The text of this letter can be found in Altman Kellner, *Musikgeschichte des Stiftes Kremsmünster* (1956), 751ff. See footnote 47 in Chapter 2 for details of the correspondence between Simon Ledermüller in St. Florian and Loidol in Kremsmünster. There are two autograph sketches

The *Mass in E minor* WAB 27, scored for eight-part choir and a wind band consisting of two oboes, two clarinets, two bassoons, four horns, two trumpets and three trombones, was composed in Linz between August / September and November 1866.[234] The work was dedicated to Bishop Rudigier who had commissioned it earlier in the year for the consecration ceremony of the *Votivkapelle*. It was completed on 25 November, and Bruckner wrote to Weinwurm a week later:

> ... The Mass for voices in eight parts with wind accompaniment [written] for the dedication of the Votivkapelle, is finished.[235]

As the consecration ceremony did not take place until 29 September 1869, Bruckner had to wait almost three years for the first performance of the Mass. By this time he was in Vienna and he had to ask Johann Schiedermayr, the dean of the Cathedral, to arrange preliminary rehearsals of the work. In a letter dated 20 May 1869 he suggested that the *Frohsinn* and *Musikverein* choirs would have to start rehearsing immediately because of the great difficulty of the Mass. A further letter of 19 June was more urgent in tone:

---

of the Mass, viz. a continuity draft of part of the *Credo* (bars 225 - end) and a score sketch of five bars of the *Credo* (bars 176-80), in the Kremsmünster abbey library.

234 The autograph score, with some entries by an anonymous hand, in the Linz Cathedral library has dates at the end of the *Credo*, *Sanctus*, *Benedictus* and *Agnus*, but no dates at the end of the *Kyrie* and *Gloria*. See *HMSAB*, 268f. for details of the autograph score, autograph sketches, copy scores and parts. A facsimile of the dedication page appears between pages 552 and 553 in *G-A* III/1 and after the foreword in *ABSW* XVII/2 (Vienna, 1959). The work was first published by Doblinger (Vienna, 1896). There are modern editions of the original 1866 version in *ABSW* XVII/1 (ed. Nowak, Vienna, 1977) and of the 1882/83 revised version in *ABSW* XVII/2 (ed. Nowak, Vienna, 1959).

235 See earlier and footnote 115.

> ... Weilnböck wrote to me that Waldeck had said that if the Mass was not studied now with the *Musikverein* students, its performance was out of the question; and they cannot postpone rehearsal until later, as it is difficult.[236]

Bruckner, who conducted the first performance at the end of September, had to spend a good part of his summer vacation in Linz, rehearsing the Mass 28 times during August and September. On 9 August he received a letter of thanks from the bishop for his sterling efforts.[237] At the open-air performance on 29 September, members of the *Frohsinn, Sängerbund* and *Musikverein* choirs were accompanied by the military band of the Austro-Hungarian infantry regiment *Ernst Ludwig, Grossherzog von Hessen und bei Rhein Nr. 14.* The press reviews were largely favourable. In his review of the Mass, which appeared in three issues of the *Linzer Volksblatt,* J.E. Habert discussed the work and its performance in some detail, extolling its many fine points but finding fault with what he considered to be oppressive chromaticism in the *Benedictus.* There were also some difficulties of ensemble and balance at times, noticeably in the *Sanctus.*[238] The reviewer for the *Linzer Zeitung,* probably Moritz von Mayfeld, also provided a detailed account of the work, singling out many beauties of detail - the 'quiet, sorrowful tones' of the

---

236 See *G-A* III/1, 545f. and footnote 177 earlier in this chapter.

237 See *HSABB,* 110f. for the text of this letter, the original of which is in the *ÖNB.* There is a facsimile of the letter between pages 548 and 549 in *G-A* III/1.

238 The full text of this review, which appeared in the *Linzer Volksblatt* on 6, 7 and 9 October 1869, is printed in *G-A* III/1, 551-57; there are facsimiles in Susanna Taub, op.cit., 85ff. Göllerich surmises that a report of the first performance by Josef Seiberl (*G-A* III/1, 549ff.), which was not published at the time, was probably intended for the *Volksblatt* but was superseded by Habert's review. Also see Karl Pfannhauser, 'Zu Anton Bruckners Mess-Vertonungen (2. Teil)' in *IBG Mitteilungsblatt* 26 (October 1985), 16f. for extracts from another article by Habert in the *Zeitschrift für katholische Kirchenmusik* 11 and 12 (November and December 1869[?]), 98ff.

'Et incarnatus est', the 'whispered "passus et sepultus est" vividly expressing the soul expiring with contrition', and the 'enchanting beauty' of the *Benedictus* - and praising the execution:

> ... Naturally, and with justification, we dismiss several small points occasioned by difficulties arising from the nature of the place, and this would make us all the more desirous of hearing this work in a suitable hall so that its rich beauties could be more fully displayed.[239]

Bruckner received fees amounting to 225 florins after the performance and, in letters to Bishop Rudigier and Schiedermayr, expressed his gratitude in moving terms.[240] One of the singers at the first performance, Linda Schönbeck, later recalled the event and the rehearsals preceding it. Bruckner was evidently so pleased with the Linz performance that he conceived the idea of hiring a special train to take all the performers to Vienna so that the Mass could be heard there. This project did not materialize![241]

The E minor Mass did not escape the inevitable revision process! Bruckner used a copy of the work made by Schimatschek to carry out his 'rhythmical modifications' in 1876 and to enter further changes in 1882. At the end of September 1882, at Bruckner's request, Johann Noll, the copyist of the Vienna Court Chapel, began to prepare a new score; he completed it on 24 January 1883.[242] In 1885 Bruckner was

---

239 From the review in the *Linzer Zeitung*, 6 October 1869. For full text, see *G-A* III/1, 557ff.; there is a facsimile in Susanna Taub, op.cit., 88f.

240 See *HSABB* 1, 112f. for the texts of these letters, dated Vienna, 19 October and 18 October 1869 respectively; the location of the original, first printed in *ABB*, 109f., is unknown, and the original of the latter, first printed in the *Neues Wiener Tagblatt* (16 June 1916) is owned privately.

241 See *GrBL*, 94.

242 See *HMSAB*, 288f. for further details of Schimatschek's and Noll's copies, both in the *ÖNB*. For more detailed information about the changes, see *G-A* III/1, 366-71, the forewords to *ABSW*

174

asked to write a setting of *Ecce sacerdos magnus* WAB 13 for the centennial celebrations of Linz diocese (26 September - 4 October). The musical highlight of the festival, however, was to be a performance in the cathedral of Bruckner's E minor Mass. On 18 May 1885, Bruckner sent a copy of the *Ecce sacerdos* to Johann Burgstaller, the Linz Cathedral choir director, and also referred to some revisions he had made to the Mass:

> ... The Mass is dedicated to the late Right Reverend Bishop and is the property of the Cathedral Chapter. I have made alterations, and perhaps these should be copied into the parts now that we have a new bishop. The Mass is for a choir with woodwind and brass accompaniment but without strings. In 1869 I rehearsed it and then conducted it on the greatest day of my life at the consecration of the Votive Chapel. The bishop and the Emperor's representative drank a toast to me at the episcopal banquet.[243]

Adalbert Schreyer, director of the Linz *Musikverein*, was responsible for the second Linz performance of the Mass on 4 October 1885, Emperor Franz Josef's name-day. Göllerich reports that Bruckner not only provided an organ prelude and postlude but also accompanied the Mass at times.[244] One of the handwritten annotations which Bruckner added to the Noll copy was 'NB Sanctus 4/4 Tact' at the beginning of the *Sanctus* which suggests that the composer wanted the

---

XVII/1 and XVII/2 and the appendix to the latter. The Mass was not performed in the *Hofkapelle* until October 1907, however. Its earliest recorded Vienna performance is 17 March 1899 at a concert of the *Akademisches Gesangverein* conducted by Neubauer.

243   See *HSABB* 1, 264 for the text of this letter; the original is in the possession of the *Dombauverein*, Linz. Johann Baptist Burgstaller (1840-1925) was choir director at the new cathedral in Linz from 1869 to 1909.

244   See *G-A* III/1, 591. There is no autograph organ part, however. See also the foreword to *ABSW* XVII/1.

movement to be sung slowly regardless of intonation difficulties. Adalbert Schreyer's report to Gräflinger of the 1885 performance throws some light on this:

> ... Bruckner would have liked the *Sanctus*, which begins *a cappella* but in strict polyphony according to the Palestrinian style, even slower still. However, he certainly understood that for important reasons, namely to avoid a vacillating intonation, I could not reduce the tempo any further. Bruckner appeared particularly pleased not only with the precise execution of the work but also with the expressive rendering in which the performers displayed their understanding and inner comprehension.[245]

Writing to Schreyer from Vienna on 28 October 1885, Bruckner expressed his delight at the 'heroic performance' and asked Schreyer to pass on his grateful thanks to all the participants.[246] On the same day he wrote a letter of thanks to Burgstaller and asked him if he would become the dedicatee of the motet *Afferentur regi*. He also enclosed the score of the Mass with a note containing some alterations he had made to performance directions. He gave Burgstaller about three weeks to mark up his own score and then return both Bruckner's score and the note to Vienna.[247]

The original version of the *Mass in F minor* WAB 28, scored for soloists, chorus and orchestra, was written between 14 September 1867 and 9 September 1868, shortly before Bruckner's move to Vienna. The existence of two bifolios of sketches containing a continuity draft for the first 296 bars of the *Credo* as well as some E minor Mass sketches might suggest an earlier conception of the movement, but it is more likely that Bruckner, having begun sketching the *Kyrie* in September 1867

---

245 See *GrBL*, 98f.

246 See *HSABB* 1, 277f. for the text of this letter; the original is in the *Oberösterreichisches Landesmuseum*, Linz.

247 See *HSABB* 1, 277 for the text of this letter. The original, which contains details of Bruckner's alterations in another hand, is in the *ÖNB*.

after the treatment of his illness at Bad Kreuzen, sketched the other movements in order.[248] Annotations in the autograph score reveal that the sketches for the *Kyrie* were completed on 19 October 1867 and those for the *Gloria* were begun on 6 November. On 30 December, Bruckner wrote to Herbeck in Vienna, sending greetings for the New Year and referring to current progress in composing the Mass:

> ... The *Credo* of my new Mass will soon be ready. *Kyrie* and *Gloria* are sketched. I am gathering my strength.[249]

Bruckner conveyed the same information to his friend Weinwurm a week later.[250] Moritz von Mayfeld's second report of the Linz performance of the D minor Mass in January 1868 contained a reference to the new Mass:

> ... According to reports Mr. Bruckner, the cathedral organist, is fully occupied at present with a new Mass which has already progressed as far as the *Credo*, and upon which we place our highest hopes.[251]

---

248   See *HMSAB*, 294-97 and Paul Hawkshaw, 'Anton Bruckner's revisions to the Mass in F minor' in *Bruckner Studies* (Cambridge: CUP, 1997), 3-31 for details of other source material. There is a facsimile of the *Credo* continuity draft, with commentary, between pages 114 and 115 of *GrBL*. Facsimiles of other sketches can be found in (1) *G-A* III/1 (*Gloria* sketches, between pages 480 and 481; fragment of the autograph score of the end of the *Credo*, 465-69; (2) foreword to H.F. Redlich's edition of the work [Eulenburg E.E. 961, 1968] (fragment of the autograph score at the end of the *Credo*); (3) Paul Hawkshaw's article in *Bruckner Studies* (sketches of the *Credo*: 6f. and 14f., *Kyrie*: 11, *Gloria*, 12f.)

249   See page 122 and footnote 137.

250   See page 123 and footnote 138.

251   From Mayfeld's article in the *Linzer Zeitung* 9, 11 January 1868. See *G-A* III/1, 421f.; there is a facsimile in Susanna Taub, op.cit., 69.

The events of 1868 prevented Bruckner from working intensively on the Mass again until his future employment at Vienna had been secured. Almost certainly wishing to finish the work before moving from Linz, he spent August and the early part of September completing the *Benedictus* and writing the *Sanctus* and *Agnus Dei*.

Bruckner's original intention, no doubt encouraged by Herbeck, was to establish his position in Vienna by having the work performed as early as possible. According to Mayfeld's letter to Bruckner of 14 November 1868 a performance of the Mass was scheduled for either the 22nd or 29th of November.[252] The performance was postponed initially until January 1869 and a rehearsal took place on 16 January. It was further postponed and there was another rehearsal on 18 June. In spite of several changes which Bruckner made, Herbeck considered the Mass to be too long and unsingable in places and performed a Mass by Gänsbacher in its place on the Sunday for which it was scheduled.[253] Its first performance was not in the *Hofkapelle* but in the *Augustinerkirche* on 16 June 1872. Bruckner wrote to Mayfeld a few days before the performance, informing him that he himself would be conducting the Court Opera chorus and orchestra led by Hellmesberger, and inviting him to be

---

252 See *HSABB* 1, 99 for the text of this letter. There was a rehearsal of the Mass on 20 November but the planned November performance in the *Hofkapelle* did not take place.

253 See Bruckner's letters to Schiedermayr, dated Vienna, 8 December 1868, and Mayfeld, dated Vienna, 13 July 1869, in *HSABB* 1, 99f. and 110. The Gänsbacher Mass was sung in the *Hofkapelle* on 17 January 1869. While it is possible that the performances of the Mass initially scheduled for November 1868 and then postponed until January refer to the D minor Mass, there is no doubt that the Mass mentioned in Bruckner's letter to Mayfeld is the F minor Mass. The rehearsal had evidently pleased Herbeck and a performance was now scheduled for the autumn of 1869. See also Bruckner's own version of events, in a statement to Göllerich in later years, in *G-A* IV/1, 77ff.

present.[254] The first performance in the *Hofkapelle*, also conducted by Bruckner, took place on 8 December 1873, and Bruckner conducted other performances of the work in the same venue during the 1870s and 1880s. The Mass appears to have made a powerful impression, and there were reports in the most influential Viennese newspapers after its first performance in the *Augustinerkirche*. Writing in the *Fremdenblatt*, Ludwig Speidel considered the work to be

> ... a composition which bears the most eloquent testimony to the composer's powers of invention and unusual ability. He has immersed himself with poetical understanding in the situations created by the Mass text, and his enormous grasp of counterpoint makes it easy for him to take the most difficult problems in his stride. Moreover, the excellent composer could not withstand the temptation of following the text as far as the smallest detail, a dangerous procedure which leads him all too often into longueurs and threatens the general structure of the movement (as in the *Credo*, for example). And then he allows the dramatic content of the text to seduce him into bordering on the theatrical at times, again in the *Credo* where one imagines oneself in the midst of a sacred 'Wolf's Glen' at one point. Viewed as a whole, however, Bruckner's Mass is a work which inspires great respect for the composer's learning and ability.[255]

Hanslick, writing in the *Neue Freie Presse*, also provided a positive and favourable review:

---

254 See *HSABB* 1, 134 for the text of this letter, dated Vienna, 11 June 1872. It was first printed in *ABB*, 120; the location of the original is not extant.

255 See *G-A* IV/1, 202 for the text of this review in the *Fremdenblatt*, 20 June 1872.

... [Bruckner's F minor Mass] caused a considerable stir on account of its artistic handling of contrapuntal and fugal material, as well as several strikingly original beauties. In style and conception - not only because of its great dimensions and performance difficulties - it points to the *Missa solemnis* as its model but also displays strong Wagnerian influences. It would be interesting if the Mass were granted a good concert performance and thereby brought to the notice of a larger public.[256]

Shortly after its first performance Bruckner wrote to J.B. Schiedermayr in Linz:

... It is only a week ago that the Mass in F no. 3, the most difficult of all Masses, was performed for the first time in the *Augustinerkirche*. (It cost more than 300 florins, as I had the forces of the court theatre at my disposal.) It was written in praise of the Highest and I wanted its first performance to be in a church. The response from both performers and audience was tremendous.[257]

The Mass underwent various changes of revision before if was eventually printed in 1894.[258] It was 'rhythmically altered' in 1876 and some changes were made in the string figuration in 1876 and 1877, particularly in the *Credo*. The original autograph score also has traces of a further revision of the *Credo* which Bruckner made in 1881, probably in preparation for a performance of the Mass in the *Hofkapelle* on 30 April 1882.[259]

---

256 See *G-A* IV/1, 202 ff. for the text of this review, which appeared in the *Neue Freie Presse* 2812, 29 June 1872.

257 See *HSABB* 1, 134 for the text of this letter, dated Vienna, 23 June 1872. It was first printed in the *Neues Wiener Tagblatt*, 16 June 1916; the location of the original is not extant.

258 Doblinger, Vienna (full score pl. no. D.1866). This includes the changes made by Joseph Schalk.

259 Also consult the forewords to the Robert Haas edition, *Anton Bruckner Sämtliche Werke* XIV (Leipzig: Brucknerverlag, 1944) and the Hans Ferdinand Redlich edition (London: Eulenburg, 1968)

About two months before a further performance of the Mass in the *Hofkapelle* on 8 December 1885, Bruckner wrote to Loidol in Kremsmünster with the request that Father Georg Huemer, music director at the abbey, make a copy of the Mass and return the score as soon as possible. It is possible that he required it for rehearsal purposes.[260]

Between 1890 and 1893 Bruckner inserted changes in another copy of the Mass. These include the addition of both horns in the fugue of the *Gloria* (bars 292-300) and alterations in the woodwind and two solo string parts in the 'Et incarnatus est' section of the *Credo*. Apart from the second clarinet part in the second half of bar 138, these were incorporated in the first edition.[261] But the first edition also contains many changes for which Bruckner was not responsible. Along with his brother Franz and Ferdinand Löwe, Joseph Schalk had been closely associated with Bruckner and his music since the late 1870s. Joseph in particular had championed the composer through the 1880s by making arrangements of the symphonies for two pianos and performing them in meetings of the *Akademischer Wagner-Verein* in Vienna.[262]

---

both of which are based on the autograph, as well as Paul Hawkshaw's article in *Bruckner Studies* (1997).

260   See *HSABB* 1, 275 for this letter, dated Vienna, 25 September 1885; the original is in Kremsmünster abbey.

261   This copy score (Mus. Hs. 6015 in the *ÖNB*) was the work of two unknown copyists. It belonged originally to the *Hofkapelle*. Nowak's edition of the Mass, *ABSW* XVIII (Vienna, 1960), with its informative foreword, includes all the changes made by Bruckner himself from 1868 to 1893.

262   For further information, see Thomas Leibnitz, *Die Brüder Schalk und Anton Bruckner* [*LBSAB* hereafter] (Tutzing; Schneider, 1988) and 'Anton Bruckner and "German music": Josef Schalk and the establishment of Bruckner as a national composer' in *Perspectives on Anton Bruckner* (Aldershot: Ashgate, 2001), 338-50; also Andrea Harrandt, 'Students and friends as "prophets" and "promoters": the reception of Bruckner's works in the *Wiener Akademische Wagner-Verein*', in *ibid.*, 338-350.

Unfortunately, in his zealous endeavours to achieve a breakthrough for Bruckner's works he did not always appreciate the dividing line between assistance and independent action when helping the composer to prepare the scores of Symphonies nos. 3 and 8 and the F minor Mass for printing in the late 1880s and early 1890s. In his work on the Mass between 1890 and 1893 he changed the instrumentation in places, adding third and fourth horns, filling out the woodwind texture, 'revising' the brass parts and altering the dynamics.[263] Schalk's immediate intention was to conduct a performance of this revised version of the Mass in 1893. As on a previous occasion (the two-piano performance of Symphony no. 5 in the spring of 1887), he left it rather late to inform Bruckner of his intention, with the result that there were some unpleasant scenes at the final rehearsals which the composer attended.[264] In spite of self-doubts Joseph completed his revision of the orchestration of the Mass during February 1893 but sent his work to Franz for correction.[265] The performance, organised by the *Wagner-Verein*, took place in the large *Musikverein* hall on 23 March and was successful, although Hanslick and Heuberger, as usual, were more critical. Bruckner was obviously delighted, Hans Richter congratulated Schalk on his fine conducting and Brahms, who was also present, visibly joined in the applause at the end.

Max von Oberleithner, one of Bruckner's private pupils, helped Schalk to prepare the printer's proof copy of the Mass in 1894 and hoped to include certain of his own revisions in the printed version. Oberleithner and Schalk had already collaborated in the first edition of Symphony no. 8 in 1892 and certain 'corrections' had been

---

263   These and other alterations were inserted in pencil by Schalk in a copy of the Mass which Johann Noll, the *Hofkapelle* copyist, had made in 1883 (Mus. Hs 29.302 in the *ÖNB*).

264   See *ABB*, 268f. for Bruckner's letter to Göllerich, dated Vienna, 10 May 1893 and *LBSAB*, 177f. for Joseph's letter to Franz, dated Vienna, 15 April 1893. See also Chapter 6 and footnotes 323-26 in that chapter for further information.

265   See *LBSAB*, 176 for Joseph's letter to Franz, dated Vienna, 1 March 1893. Franz himself was busy working on a revised version of Bruckner's Symphony no. 5 which he intended to perform in Graz the following year.

made which had not been noticed by Bruckner. In the case of the F minor Mass, however, there was an altercation between Bruckner, Schalk and Oberleithner concerning changes in the proof copy which had been made without his knowledge. Writing to his brother Franz on 25 May 1894 and, incidentally, thanking him for sending a copy of the revised Symphony no. 5 which he had conducted with great success in Graz in April, Joseph referred to the impasse and hoped that Franz might be able to act as an intermediary.[266] There was undoubtedly a breach in the Schalk-Bruckner relationship at this point, but certainly not the 'final breach' suggested in the Göllerich-Auer biography.[267] Indeed the Schalk correspondence reveals that, after an interruption of a few months, relationships with Bruckner returned to a reasonably amicable level. Joseph mentions intended visits to Bruckner in two letters to his brother.[268] Bruckner himself wrote to Joseph on 6 October (albeit with the formal greeting 'Hochverehrter Herr Professor') to ask him if he would act as his representative in forthcoming rehearsals of the F minor Mass and, before that, play through the work for Gericke, who was to conduct it, as he was too ill to leave his flat.[269] This was hardly the act of a man who had lost trust in his young colleague.

The performance of the F minor Mass at a *Gesellschaft* concert in Vienna on 4 November 1894 was intended as a 70th birthday celebration and, in fact, was one of

---

266 See *LBSAB*, 191f.

267 See *G-A* IV/3, 527. However, there is a footnote which refers to several visits which Joseph Schalk paid Bruckner, as related in Lili Schalk, *Franz Schalk. Briefe und Betrachtungen mit einem Lebensabriss von Victor Junk* [hereafter *FSBB*] (Vienna: Musikwissenschaftlichter Verlag, 1935), 64. See also chapter 6 and footnotes 413f.

268 These letters are dated 1 August and 3 October 1894 respectively; see *LBSAB*, 195.

269 See *LBSAB*, 195.

Bruckner's last public appearances.[270]   His health deteriorated rapidly in mid-November and, although there was a partial recovery, the remaining months of his life were a continual swing between relapse and slight improvement. Bruckner's last words on the Mass are contained in a letter of Siegfried Ochs, the conductor of the Berlin Philharmonic choir, who had directed two very successful performances of the *Te Deum* in May 1891 and January 1894 and was now contemplating a possible performance of the Mass:

> ... Bruckner is getting old and would really like to hear the F minor Mass again! Please, please! That would be the highpoint of my life. But there are many changes which don't appear in the score. At the D flat major passage in the *Credo* - 'Deum verum de Deo vero' - full organ, please! Spare no stops! And the cellist should be prominent with a very rich, warm tone at the beginning of the *Benedictus*. When shall I hear it? Please reply.
>   In humble admiration and with greetings to the excellent orchestra, the wonderful choir, and you, their great director...[271]

Anton Meißner's entries in Bruckner's *Österreichische Professoren- und Lehrerkalender* for April-June 1895 indicate that the composer was missing the autograph of the Mass and the copy of the work which had been used for engraving purposes. The entry for June was more specific:

> Dr. Speidel relinquished the original score of the Mass in F immediately after the performance [on 4 November 1894]; it was

---

270   For Bruckner's own account of the performance (and his recollection of Karl Waldeck's criticism of the original 'Et incarnatus est') during his penultimate University lecture on 5 November, see *G-A* IV/3, 444f. See also *GrBL*, 114 for Waldeck's own recollection of his criticism, and Stephen Johnson, *Bruckner Remembered* (London: Faber and Faber, 1998), 109 for an English translation.

271   See *ABB*, 283f. for this letter, dated Vienna, 14 April 1895.

184

probably collected by the publisher.[272]

The autograph, one of many bequeathed to the *Österreichisches Nationalbibliothek* by Bruckner in his will, was finally traced to a Mrs. Winkler and purchased from her in 1922, 26 years after the composer's death![273]

3.3.3 Solo and chamber works

The dating of all four songs Bruckner wrote during the Linz period is uncertain. On 30 October 1858, the composer wrote to Weinwurm that he had composed 'a little song'.[274] Auer surmised that this was a reference to *Wie bist du, Frühling, gut und treu*, a setting of five verses from Oskar von Redwitz's *Amaranths Waldeslieder* WAB 58, intended for one of Abbot Mayr's musical evenings at St. Florian.[275] But it is more likely that it was composed in 1856 as Bruckner's 'farewell present to his music-loving patron on leaving St. Florian abbey'.[276] A handwritten note attached to the autograph in the *Stadt- und Landesbibliothek*, Vienna indicates that Josef Reiter, the son of Franz Reiter who was a friend of Bruckner's, made a gift of it to Max Morold. It was evidently this autograph score, with some slight modifications,

---

272   See *G-A* IV/3, 544.

273   The full account of the re-discovery and purchase is related in Robert Haas, 'Die Originalpartitur von Bruckners Messe in f-Moll', *Der Auftakt* 4 (1924), 106.

274   See *HSABB* 1, 14 for the text of this letter; the original is in the *ÖNB*.

275   *G-A* III/1, 56.

276   Preface to Angela Pachovsky, ed., *Lieder für Gesang und Klavier*, *ABSW* XXIII/1 (Vienna, 1997), vii.

which was used as the basis for the first edition in 1902.[277] Franz Reiter adapted the piece for soprano, ladies' choir and string orchestra / piano accompaniment and performed it in Linz on 11 April 1886.[278] Far superior in its word setting and resourceful use of piano accompaniment is *Im April* WAB 75, a setting of words by Emanuel Geibel which Bruckner conceived in the early 1860s and dedicated to Helene Hofmann, one of his piano pupils.[279] In his discussion of *Mein Herz und deine Stimme* WAB 79, a setting of a poem by Platen, and *Herbstkummer* WAB 72, a setting of a poem by Ernst, Auer remarks that 'both songs have only curiosity value' and casts doubts on the authenticity of the former which was dedicated to Pauline Hofmann, Helene's sister.[280] The latter's date (April 1864) is supported by stylistic features such as a more mature grasp of harmony, no doubt the result of experience gained in his work with Kitzler.[281]

---

277 This first edition, ed., M. Marschalk, was printed as a supplement to *Die Musik* I/17 (1902), 1591ff. See *G-A* III/1, 56-59 and *HMSAB*, 262f. A facsimile of the autograph is printed in *G-A* III/2, 183-88. There is a modern edition of the song in *ABSW* XXIII/1, 3-11. This volume also contains a critical report, 33ff., and a facsimile of the autograph, 44-48.

278 According to *G-A* III/1, 57, this version also appeared in print in Linz. There is no reference to his arrangement, however, in *ABSW* XXIII/1.

279 There is no autograph extant, only two copy scores, one in St. Florian and the other in the *ÖNB*; the first of these has an autograph dedication to Helene Hofmann. See also *G-A* III/1, 511ff., *HMSAB*, 299 and 324, and *ABSW* XXIII/1, vii and 39f. The song was first published by Doblinger, Vienna in 1898. There is a modern edition in *ABSW* XXIII/1, 23-27.

280 There is no autograph of *Mein Herz und deine Stimme* extant, only three copy scores, one in private ownership and two in the *ÖNB* (Mus. Hs. 19.783 and Mus. Hs. 19.784). See *G-A* III/1, 514, *HMSAB*, 299f., and *ABSW* XXIII/1, vii and 37ff. The song is printed in *G-A* III/2, 144-50. There is also a modern edition in *ABSW* XXIII/1, 18-22.

281 Again there is no autograph of *Herbstkummer* extant, but a copy score in the *ÖNB* (Mus. Hs. 19.781) has a note on the title page indicating that it was copied in 1891 from another copy dated 4 October 1867. See *G-A* III/1, 515, *HMSAB*, 291, and *ABSW* XXIII/1, vii and 35ff. The work is

During the period Christmas 1861 - August 1862, Bruckner also completed a number of song exercises as part of his studies in musical form with Kitzler. They range from incomplete sketches to complete compositions and are contained in the *Kitzler Studienbuch*.[282]

There is also some uncertainty about the precise dating of some of the works for piano Bruckner wrote during the Linz period. A detailed study of the autograph of the *Klavierstück* in E flat WAB 119, in particular a comparison with the exercises in the *Kitzler Studienbuch*, has led Hawkshaw to assign to it a date of 1862 or early 1863, much later than the c. 1856 given in the Grasberger *Werkverzeichnis* and repeated by Walburga Litschauer, who correctly draws attention to the piece's Mendelssohnian qualities and makes a perceptive comparison with the latter's *Song without Words* op. 53 no. 4.[283] At the end of the autograph score of *Stille Betrachtung an einem Herbstabend* WAB 123, Bruckner added the date 10 October 1863 and the name of its dedicatee, Emma Thaner, one of his piano pupils from 1857 to 1863. There is also an autograph sketch of the work which, according to Hawkshaw,

> bears a remarkable resemblance to the *Kitzler Studienbuch* exercises. It is a melody-bass continuity draft with some chordal and contrapuntal passages filled in. The melody is complete and the bass

---

printed in *G-A* III/2, 152-57. There is also a modern edition in *ABSW* XXIII/1, 12-17.

282 Brief descriptions of these twelve songs, including musical incipits, can be found in the Appendix to *ABSW* XXIII/1, 49-52.

283 See *HMSAB*, 75 for a discussion of the manuscript paper, the shape of the treble clef, and a comparison with one of the exercises in the *Kitzler Studienbuch*; also 272. For further discussion, see *G-A* III/1, 43, Walburga Litschauer, ed., *Anton Bruckner Werke für Klavier zu zwei Händen*, *ABSW* XII/2 (Vienna, 1988/2000), foreword and *Revisionsbericht*, 37, and Litschauer, 'Bruckner und das romantische Klavierstück' in *BSL 1987* (Linz, 1989), 109. There is a facsimile of the autograph in *G-A* III/2, 182. There is also a modern edition in *ABSW* XII/2, 12.

only partially worked out. At times stemless notes are used to outline the bass.[284]

The Mendelssohnian connection is also striking in this piece. Previous commentators have already drawn attention to its similarity in many respects with Mendelssohn's *Venetianisches Gondellied* in F sharp minor, op. 30 no. 6.[285] Its dedicatee later recalled her years of study with Bruckner, describing him as a 'strict teacher who took a great deal of trouble with his pupils' and mentioning *inter alia* his occasional vanity and keen eye for feminine beauty. She was by her own confession not a particularly talented pupil and never learned to play *Stille Betrachtung* which she found too difficult.[286]

The *Kitzler Studienbuch* includes the sketch of the first movement of a *Sonata in G minor*, dated '29 June 1862', a composition exercise begun after Bruckner had done some preparatory work on the component parts of sonata first movement form. Only the right hand part was notated for bars 25-28 and 134-37 and bars 148-54 were written again as an appendix in an alternative version in G major. Various entries in Bruckner's hand, such as names of keys, comments on form and remarks about compositional technique identify the sketch as no more than an exercise.[287]

---

284 *HMSAB*, 157; see also 275f. For further discussion, see *G-A* III, 215, *ABSW* XII/2, foreword and *Revisionsbericht*, 37ff., and Litschauer, op.cit., 109. There are facsimiles of the autograph in *G-A* III/2, 217f., and of a sketch of bars 1-44 in *ABSW* XII/2, 38. There is also a modern edition in *ABSW* XII/2, 13f.

285 See Litschauer, op.cit., and Othmar Wessely, 'Bruckners Mendelssohn-Kenntnis' in *Bruckner-Studien* (Vienna, 1975), 109.

286 See *G-A* III/1, 215-20 for a fuller account.

287 See *HMSAB*, 100, *ABSW* XII/2, foreword and *Revisionsbericht*, 41-44, and Litschauer, op.cit., 110 for further details. The piece is printed in *ABSW* XII/2, 29-39.

At the very end of his time in Linz, on 10 September 1868, Bruckner completed a *Fantasie* WAB 118 and dedicated it to another of his pupils, Alexandrine Soika, the daughter of a high-ranking officer in the army.[288] Like Emma Thaner, Alexandrine Soika later recalled her experiences of Bruckner the man and the musician:

> ... one day I was taken by friends to the cathedral to see and hear Bruckner playing the organ. My interest as a child was at its maximum. We ascended the mysterious dark steps and my heart beat wildly. When I saw the plump man with his powerful shoulders and broad smiling face standing before me, however, I had an immediate desire to laugh which I could only suppress with great difficulty. But now he sat down at the organ - and there was no more laughing! I was overwhelmed by the atmosphere of solemn earnestness and silent awe, because it was now giants, now angels who appeared to inhabit the instrument. I was speechless, overcome...[289]

The most substantial of these piano pieces is *Erinnerung* WAB 117 which almost certainly dates from the end of the Linz period in spite of Bruckner's alleged information to the contrary. As there is no autograph date this cannot be corroborated, but its style and harmonic texture suggest a later rather than earlier date.[290]

---

288 Hawkshaw, in *HMSAB*, 297f., describes it as two separate fantasias, but see *G-A* III/1, 506ff., *ABSW* XII/2, foreword and *Revisionsbericht*, 39f., and Litschauer, op.cit., 109. There is a facsimile in *G-A* III/2, 245-49. The piece is printed in *ABSW* XII/2, 15-20.

289 *G-A* III/1, 504f.

290 In his foreword to the first edition of the piece (Vienna: Doblinger, 1900), August Stradal did not question Bruckner's no doubt faulty memory and surmised that it was written at the beginning of the Linz period. If this is the second of the two pieces written for Alexandrine Soika, however, it belongs to 1868. For further discussion, see *G-A* III/1, 508-11, *HMSAB*, 300, *ABSW* XII/2, foreword and *Revisionsbericht*, 40f., and Litschauer, op.cit., 109f. The piece is printed in *ABSW* XII/2, 21-24.

Like many skilled improvisers, Bruckner provided practically no written record of what he played. Only one organ piece - a *Fugue in D minor* WAB 125 - survives from the Linz period. It was composed at the same time as the offertory motet, *Afferentur regi* WAB 1. The sketch is dated Wednesday 6 and Thursday 7 November, and the autograph fair copy bears the date 8 November. Bruckner dedicated it to Ferdinand Kerschbaum on the occasion of the latter's ordination as a priest in Linz Cathedral on 30 July 1862. He played the organ during the ceremony and may well have performed this fugue. It is an academically 'correct' fugue, abiding by all the rules in a manner which would no doubt have brought great pleasure to Sechter, but is otherwise unexceptional.[291]

After completing work on the first movement of the Sonata in G minor for piano, Bruckner continued his compositional / analytical studies with Kitzler by writing a complete four-movement *String Quartet in C minor* WAB 111 as well as an alternative *Rondo* Finale. This occupied his attention during July and August 1862. The autograph includes several references to structure. On the first page of the third movement, for instance, Bruckner posed the question: 'Would the song-form here

291 Ferdinand Kerschbaum (1838-1901) was the brother of Karl Kerschbaum, one of Bruckner's Linz associates. For further information about Kerschbaum, see H. Zappe, 'Anton Bruckner, die Familie Zappe und die Musik' in *BJ 1982/83* (Linz, 1984), 151. The fugue, almost certainly one of the compositions which Bruckner submitted to the examination panel in Vienna later in the month, is discussed in *G-A* III/1, 121f., *HMSAB*, 128-33 and in the foreword of Erwin Horn, ed., *Werke für Orgel, ABSW* XII/6 (Vienna, 1999), vii There is a facsimile of the autograph (Mus. Hs. 3167 in the *ÖNB*) in *G-A* III/2, 189f. and of part of the autograph in *HMSAB*, 126; see also ibid , 266. The work was first published in *GrBL*, between pages 88 and 90. Other editions include Hans Haselböck, ed., *Anton Bruckner Orgelwerke* (Vienna / Munich: Doblinger, 1970), 14ff. and Erwin Horn, ed., *ABSW* XII/6, 9-15 (fair copy, transcription of the sketch, and the exposition with alternative countersubjects), See also Erwin Horn, 'Zwischen Interpretation und Improvisation. Anton Bruckner als Organist' in *BSL 1995* (Linz, 1997), 129f. and 'Anton Bruckner - Genie an der Orgel' in *BJ 1994/95/96* (Linz, 1997), 211-22.

also be in three parts if the second part up to the repetition is eight bars long?...
Would it be in three parts if the unrepeated second part forms a self-sufficient whole?'
At the beginning of the succeeding Trio he wrote down the keys which he could
possibly use: 'also: G minor, E flat major, E minor, B minor, C minor, D major, C
major' and then scored out with pencil E flat major, B minor and C minor. In the
event he chose G major, the same key as the Scherzo. The overall structure of the
first movement was also outlined in some detail, and Bruckner paid particular
attention to the part-writing in places. All four movements exhibit a clear grasp and
mature handling of the forms involved, viz. sonata form (first movement), rondo form
(second movement), sonata rondo form (fourth movement) and scherzo and trio
(third movement). However, ninety years were to elapse before the first known
performance and subsequent publication of the Quartet.[292]

Abendklänge WAB 110, Bruckner's only composition for violin and piano duo,
was originally dated 1836 by Göllerich who believed that the words 'an P.T. Herrn
Vater' added after the title in the original manuscript referred to Bruckner's own
father who died in that year. Subsequent research by Auer, however, uncovered an
autograph fair copy of the work dated 7 June 1866 and dedicated to Hugo v.
Grienberger, a civil servant in the district court, in which the title appears simply as
'Abendklänge'.[293]

---

292 The four movements and alternative Finale (fols. 83r - 103v in the *Kitzler Studienbuch*) were
completed on 15 August 1862. See *HMSAB* 88, 255 and 270 for precise dating. The work, together
with a short preface and copious *Revisionsbericht*, was first published, ed. Leopold Nowak, as *ABSW*
XIII/1 (Vienna, 1956). The alternative Rondo finale was published, ed. Nowak, as *ABSW* XIII/1
Separatdruck (Vienna, 1985). The first known performance was given by the Koeckert Quartet in
Berlin on 15 February 1951.

293 See *G-A* I, 106ff. for Göllerich's discussion of the piece and 104f. for a facsimile of the
autograph (Mus. Hs. 3159 in the *ÖNB*). See *G-A* II/1, 231f. and III/1, 357f. for a discussion of the
fair copy (Mus. Hs. 2121 in the *ÖNB*); also *HMSAB*, 156f. and 287. For a modern edition of the

3.3.4 Orchestral music

The next stage in Bruckner's systematic studies with Kitzler was the orchestral realization of some of the forms he had already studied, and there is a natural progression from four short pieces for orchestra to symphony by way of an overture. The *Apollo-Marsch* WAB 115 is undoubtedly spurious. There is no direct evidence that Bruckner composed this military band piece which is scored for two flutes, four clarinets, two flugelhorns, three euphoniums, four horns, six trumpets, three trombones, side drum and bass drum. There is no autograph score and the copy score extant was not necessarily made during the Linz years.[294] The first authentic orchestral works are the *March* in D minor WAB 96 for double woodwind, two horns, two trumpets, three trombones, timpani and strings, and the *Three Orchestral Pieces* (in E flat major, E minor and F major) WAB 97 for the same forces, except that only one trombone is used. The *March* was completed on 12 October 1862 and the *Orchestral Pieces* were composed in October and November, the second and third being completed on 10 and 16 November respectively. Auer suggests that they were probably inspired by the orchestral interludes which Kitzler used in his job as a theatre conductor.[295]

---

piece, including preface and critical commentary, see Walburga Litschauer, ed., *Abendklänge für Violine und Klavier*, ABSW XII/7 (Vienna, 1995).

294 See *HAMSB*, 13 (footnote 4) and 302. The work is also discussed in *G-A* III/1, 144f. and there is a piano arrangement in *G-A* III/2, 21-25. Max Auer, however, first cast doubts on the authenticity of the March in his *Anton Bruckner* (Vienna, 1947), 132, footnote 1, and Werner Probst identified it as Kéler Béla's *Mazzuchelli-Marsch* op. 22 (1857) in his article, 'Der "Apollomarsch" - wirklich von Bruckner?', *Österreichische Blasmusik* 32 (1984). It was first published as an Appendix to the edition of the *March in E flat major*, ed., Rüdiger Bornhöft, *ABSW* XII/8 (Vienna, 1996).

295 The works are discussed in *G-A* III/1, 145-51. There is a piano arrangement of the *March* in *G-A* III/2, 29-32, but the *Three Orchestral Pieces* are published in full score in *G-A* III/2, 33-60.

192

Immediately after completing the third of his Three Orchestral Pieces, Bruckner set to work on an *Overture in G minor* WAB 98. He completed the first version of the work on 4 January 1863 and composed the second, definitive version between 6 and 22 January. The autograph sketches of this work, conceived as a symphony first movement with slow introduction, bears witness to intensive activity during the Christmas / New Year period.[296]

The logical *terminus ad quem* of all this student work was a symphony - the *Symphony in F minor* WAB 99 - which Bruckner wrote between 7 January and 26 May 1863. There is a wealth of thematic sketch material for this work, some of which was discarded when Bruckner completed the autograph score.[297] The copy

---

They were subsequently published together with the *March*, ed. Orel as a 'Sonderdruck aus dem 11. Band' of the first complete edition (Vienna, 1934) and, more recently, ed. Hans Jancik and Rüdiger Bornhöft, as *Vier Orchesterstücke, ABSW* XII/4 (Vienna, 1996). The autograph sketches and score of the *March* occupies fols. 126r - 133r and the autograph score of the *Three Orchestral Pieces* occupies fols. 133v - 143v of the *Kitzler Studienbuch*. See *HMSAB*, 167 and 270ff. and the Preface and Revision Report to *ABSW* XII/4. According to Grasberger, *WVAB*, 106, the first performance of all four pieces was conducted by Franz Moißl in Klosterneuburg on 12 October 1924.

296   These autograph sketches, fols. 144r - 151r of the *Kitzler Studienbuch*, are owned privately. There is an autograph score with entries by Otto Kitzler and Göllerich-Auer in Kremsmünster (KR C56.5) and a copy in the *Stadt- und Landesbibliothek*, Vienna. For further information, see *HMSAB*, 167 and 272f. The work is also discussed in *G-A* III/1, 156-65. The Overture was first published by Universal Edition (U.E. 6570), ed. A. Orel (Vienna, 1921) - in conjunction with the study *Unbekannte Frühwerke Anton Bruckners* (U.E. 6570a). Other editions include a study score, ed. J.V. von Wöss (U.E 7048, 1921), a miniature score, ed. A.D. Walker (E.E 6488, 1969), and a study score (including Preface and Revision Report), ed. Jancik and Bornhöft, *ABSW* XII/5 (Vienna, 1996). The first known performance of the work was conducted by Franz Moißl in Klosterneuburg on 8 September 1921.

297   These autograph sketches, fols 152r - 159v, and continuity drafts, fols 160r - 163v in the *Kitzler Studienbuch*, are in private possession in Munich. There is an autograph score with entries

with autograph entries in the *Stadt- und Landesbibliothek*, Vienna has Bruckner's own annotation 'Schularbeit 863' which is a clear indication that the composer considered it to be an 'exercise' rather than a fully-fledged composition. The fact that there are very few agogic, dynamic or phrase marks (although Kitzler added some of his own in the first movement) also suggests that Bruckner's main concerns were to find an adequate and convincing structure for his thematic ideas and to clothe them in appropriate orchestral colours.

Bruckner visited the Munich festival in September 1863. Before leaving Linz he wrote to his friend Rudolf Weinwurm that he had completed his studies with Kitzler and had written both a symphony and a Psalm for double choir and orchestra.[298] While in Munich he met the royal music director, Franz Lachner, and showed him some of his works which included the F minor symphony. Lachner evidently promised that he would perform it in a future concert.[299] But it was another 50 years before there was a performance of the work, the slow movement only, not in Munich, but in Vienna on 31 October 1913. The conductor was Ferdinand Löwe and the review in the *Neue Freie Presse* commented on his affectionate interpretation but was rather lukewarm in its assessment of the movement itself.[300]

---

by Otto Kitzler in Kremsmünster and a copy score with autograph entries in the *Stadt- und Landesbibliothek*, Vienna. For further information ,see *HMSAB*, 167f. and 274ff. The symphony is also discussed in *G-A* III/1, 170-90, and in the foreword to Leopold Nowak, ed., *Symphony in F minor, ABSW* X (Vienna, 1973) as well as Leopold Nowak, ed., *ABSW* X *Revisionsbericht* (Vienna, 1982). A score of the Andante movement only, ed. Cyrill Hynais, was published by Universal Edition, Vienna (U.E. 5255) in 1913. There is a piano score of the entire work, ed. Hynais and Auer, in *G-A* III/2, 61-124. See also Wolfgang Grandjean, 'Anton Bruckners frühe Scherzi' in *BJ 1994/95/96* (Linz, 1997), 47-66.

298 Letter dated Linz, 1 September 1863. See earlier, page 98 and footnote 84.

299 According to a report in the *Linzer Zeitung* 236 (15 October 1863), 1001, and Bruckner's letter to Weinwurm, dated 8 October 1863. See earlier, page 98 and footnote 85.

300 *Neue Freie Presse* 17,671 (3 November 1913), 1/c in 'Music' section.

The first performance of the work in its entirety was given by the Berlin Philharmonic under the direction of Franz Moißl on 19 February 1925. In his review of the performance, Kurt Singer recognized one or two glimpses of the mature Bruckner and considered the outer movements to be more successful than the middle movements whose authenticity he would have doubted had it not been established by 'men of the calibre of Moißl, Springer and Orel'.[301]

Bruckner's next orchestral work - the *Symphony no. 1 in C minor* WAB 101 - marks a significant step forward in his career as a symphonist.[302] While writing this work, he composed a *March in E flat major* WAB 116 for military band, an occasional work dedicated to the band of the *Jäger-Truppe* in Linz as a gesture of appreciation for its participation in performances of two of his works, the cantata *Preiset den Herrn* WAB 16 and *Germanenzug* WAB 70. It is an unexceptional piece but illustrates a much greater assurance and fluency in Bruckner's harmonic language.[303]

Bruckner took a break in his ongoing work on the Symphony in C minor, composed between January 1865 and April 1866, to write the March. His progress on the symphony is outlined in some of his letters to Weinwurm during this period. At the end of January 1865 he wrote to his friend to tell him that he was working

---

301 Review in the morning edition of the Berlin paper *Vorwärts* (26 February 1925), 2.

302 It has now been firmly established that Symphony no. 'O' in D minor WAB 100 belongs entirely to the year 1869. The view prevailing until about 10-15 years ago (see, for instance, Nowak's foreword to *ABSW* 11) was that it was conceived between October 1863 and May 1864 and revised in 1869. It will be discussed in the next chapter.

303 The work is dated Linz, 12 August 1865. Both the autograph score (Mus. Hs. 3168) and a copy of the score made by Franz Schimatschek and signed by Bruckner (Mus. Hs. 6027) are in the *ÖNB*. See *HMSAB*, 281f. for further information. The work is discussed briefly in *G-A* III/1, 322 and is printed in *G-A* III/2 (piano score only, 26ff.; facsimile of the autograph, 225-33) and in Rüdiger Bornhöft, ed., *ABSW* XII/8 (Vienna, 1996).

on a Symphony in C minor which he referred to as 'No. 2'. A year later, Bruckner informed Weinwurm that he was working on the Adagio movement of the symphony and that the other movements, including a new Scherzo, were finished. In this letter and in another letter to Rudolf, written in March 1866, Bruckner also expressed the wish that he could come to Linz and see how his work was progressing.[304] Dates on the sketches and continuity drafts of the symphony indicate that he had made sufficient progress by the end of May 1865 - he finished scoring the Trio in Munich on 25 May - to be able to show his work to Anton Rubinstein and Hans von Bülow who were also in Munich for the first performances of Wagner's *Tristan und Isolde*. After putting the finishing touches to the work by making some extensive changes to the Adagio on 13 and 14 April 1866, Bruckner arranged for his copyist Schimatschek to prepare a copy of the score and parts and sent them to Dessoff and Herbeck in Vienna in the hope of a performance. But two years were to elapse before the première of the work conducted by Bruckner himself in Linz on 9 May 1868. Public and critical reaction was favourable. Mayfeld, writing in the *Linzer Zeitung*, had some reservations about the 'slight trace of striving for effect' but praised its many beauties and expressed the hope that the composer would soon 'find a position in Vienna commensurate with his ability and musical knowledge in order to give proper expression to his creative powers'. The reviewer in the *Tagespost* also had some reservations about the orchestration in places, detecting what he considered to be a discrepancy between Bruckner's intentions and the end result which sometimes obscured beautiful details in the work. He considered the first movement and the Scherzo to be the most successful movements. Hanslick's report in the Viennese *Neue Freie Presse* ensured that Bruckner's name came to the notice of a wider

---

304 Letters dated Linz, 29 January 1865, 27 January 1866 and 25 March 1866 respectively. See earlier, pages 105 and 107 and footnotes 96, 101 and 102.

public.[305]

With his First Symphony Bruckner signalled to the musical world that he was a force to be reckoned with. In accepting a post in Vienna 'commensurate with his

---

305 See earlier, pages 129-30 and footnotes 155 and 156. Source material, including the autograph score, autograph score fragments and sketches (Mus. Hs. 40.400), other autograph sketches (Mus. Hs. 6012), an autograph score fragment (Mus. Hs. 6019) and Franz Schimatschek's copy of the score with Bruckner's insertions (Mus. Hs. 3190) is in the *ÖNB*. An earlier version of the Adagio was composed in the latter part of 1865, and the definitive version was written between the end of January and the middle of April 1866. Auer's piano reduction of the earlier version is printed in *G-A* III/2, 125-35. The two versions are essentially different, although the same material is used. Mus. Hs. 6012 is the continuity draft of the first version of the Scherzo and Trio, composed between March and May 1865, and Mus. Hs. 6019 is the autograph score bifolio of the same Scherzo. There is a facsimile of the former in *G-A* III/2, 234-37, and Auer's piano score of the latter in *G-A* III/2, 136ff. The second Scherzo (mentioned by Bruckner in his letter to Weinwurm) was probably begun at the end of 1865 and was completed on 23 January, 1866. The original Trio was retained. See also *HMSAB*, 255, 282-87 and three articles by Wolfgang Grandjean: 'Konzeptionen des langsamen Satzes. Zum Adagio von Anton Bruckners Erster Symphonie' in *BJ 1991/92/93* (Linz, 1995), 13-24, 'Zur Aufführung der ergänzten Urfassung des Adagio und des ursprünglichen Scherzo der Ersten Symphonie von Anton Bruckner' in *IBG Mitteilungsblatt* 41 (1993), 34-37, and 'Anton Bruckners frühe Scherzi' in *BJ 1994/95/96* (Linz, 1997), 47-66.

The symphony was revised in May 1877 ('rhythmical' revision), 1884 and 1889/90 but there was a more extensive revision between 12 March 1890 and 18 April 1891 which resulted in the writing of a new score ('Vienna' version) which was performed for the first time in Vienna on 13 December 1891 and first published by Doblinger in 1893 (D.1868). The work is discussed in *G-A* III/1, 322-48 ('Linz' version), *G-A* IV/3, 204-17 ('Vienna' version) and in the forewords to the scores edited by Haas (Vienna, 1935), Nowak (*ABSW* I/1, Vienna, 1955), Brosche (*ABSW* I/2, Vienna, 1980) and Grandjean (*ABSW zu Band I/1* - original versions of the Adagio and Scherzo movements, Vienna, 1995). The latter also includes facsimiles of two pages from Mus. Hs. 40.400 and one page from Mus. Hs. 6019 as well as an extensive *Critical Report*, 61-68. The essential differences between the 'Linz' and 'Vienna' versions are discussed by Thomas Schipperges in 'Zur Wiener Fassung von Anton Bruckners Erster Sinfonie' in *Archiv für Musikwissenschaft* 47 (1990), 272-85.

ability and musical knowledge' he embarked on a journey which was to bring fulfilment, but not without misunderstanding, opposition and a long struggle for recognition. But a sure foundation had been laid in Linz. The transition from Mass to Symphony had been begun and, after years of painstaking study, an original voice was gradually emerging. There was to be no turning back.

CHAPTER 4

Bruckner in Vienna: The First Ten Years (1868-1877)

Bruckner's move to Vienna in the early autumn of 1868 came at a time when both Austria and its capital city were experiencing profound changes. After Austria's defeat by Prussia at Königgratz in 1866 there was a half a century of comparative freedom from warfare. An uneasy political alliance between Austria, Germany and Russia was sealed in October 1873 by the *Dreikaiserbund* and renewed in June 1881, at Bismarck's instigation, as the *Dreikaiserbündnis*, the signatories agreeing to remain neutral if one of them went to war with another nation. Although this 'Three Emperors' Alliance' broke down in the mid-1880s when Austria and Russia almost went to war over trouble in the Balkans, Bismarck again attempted to patch up differences by negotiating a 'Reinsurance Treaty'. By the beginning of the 1890s, however, Russia was developing a relationship with France, while Austria and Germany maintained an alliance which 'somehow developed into a relationship of special indissolubility, as between brothers who may fret against their blood-tie but have to accept the fruit of its existence'.[1]

Within her own territories Austria negotiated a 'Compromise' with Hungary in 1867 which resulted in the establishment of the Austro-Hungarian monarchy, Franz Josef and his pro-Hungarian wife Elisabeth being crowned with much pomp and

---

1 C.A. Macartney, *The House of Austria* (Edinburgh: EUP, 1978), 175.

ceremony in Budapest on 7 June.[2] The new era of political and economic liberalism, in which the ordinary citizen took advantage of the loosening of governmental control, and growth in capital and an expansion of credit facilities were encouraged, was rudely interrupted by the stock market crash of 'Black Friday', 9 May 1873. The crash came as a particular shock, happening as it did only a week after Franz Josef had opened, with several foreign rulers and dignitaries present, Vienna's World Exhibition, a monument to the splendours of industrial growth. Shares dropped by up to 70 per cent, many small businesses were ruined, a large number of small investors were demoralised, thousands lost their jobs and there were many suicides. Bruckner, who had his own personal insurance policy, must have viewed the situation with some alarm:

> Bruckner's anxiety to ensure financial security for himself in Vienna, which clearly exasperated Herbeck during the negotiations in 1868 for Bruckner's appointment to the staff of the Conservatory of the Gesellschaft der Musikfreunde and which may well have been founded on memories of 1857 [American/European financial crisis] and perhaps even folk-memories of the virtual state bankruptcy of 1811, proved to be all too justified.[3]

In December 1857, during the period when Bruckner was making regular visits to Vienna to pursue his course in Harmony and Counterpoint with Simon Sechter, Franz Josef issued a decree that the city walls be removed. The main parts were removed by 1864 and in 1865 the *Ringstrasse*, a spacious boulevard, eighty two feet wide, which follows the outlines of the old ramparts of the city, was ready for use. Both public buildings and private dwellings were gradually built along this

---

2 Liszt wrote his *Coronation Mass* for this occasion.

3 Paul Banks, 'Vienna: Absolutism and Nostalgia' in Jim Samson, ed., *The Late Romantic Era* (London:Macmillan, 1991), 84.

magnificent road. The private dwellings belonged to financiers, factory owners, important businessmen and the *nouveaux riches*. The public buildings, in a variety of architectural styles, celebrated the political, educational and cultural life of Vienna:

> The contrast between the old inner city and the Ring area inevitably widened as a result of the political change. The inner city was dominated architecturally by the symbols of the first and second estates: the Baroque Hofburg, residence of the Emperor; the elegant palais of the aristocracy; the Gothic cathedral of St. Stephen and a host of smaller churches scattered through the narrow streets. In the new Ringstrasse development, the third estate celebrated in architecture the triumph of constitutional *Recht* over imperial *Macht*, of secular culture over religious faith. Not palaces, garrisons and churches, but centres of constitutional government and higher culture dominated the Ring.[4]

The first of the new buildings to be completed was the Opera House which opened in 1869 with a performance of Mozart's *Don Giovanni*. Two museums in a neo-Renaissance style, one for the History of Art, the other for Natural History, were build further along but on the opposite side of the *Ringstrasse* between 1872 and 1881. Still further along and more or less directly opposite the old Hofburg is the neo-Classical *House of Parliament*, an imposing white edifice completed in 1883 by the Danish architect, Theophil Hansen.[5] The *Rathaus* (Town Hall), a neo-Gothic structure, was also completed in 1883. In front of but towards the right of the *Rathaus*, the new University building was constructed in a neo-Renaissance style

---

4 Carl E. Schorske, *Fin-de-siècle Vienna* (London: Weidenfeld and Nicolson, 4/1979), 31.

5 Hansen was also responsible for the concert hall of the *Musikverein* (1869), the *Stock Exchange* building (1877), the *Academy of Fine Arts* and the *Evangelical School*.

between 1872 and 1884.[6] Across from the *Rathaus* and the University and next to the *Volksgarten* is the *Burgtheater*, also in a neo-Renaissance style. It took sixteen years to build (1872-1888).

The population increase in Vienna from about 500,000 to a million inhabitants during the second half of the century necessitated a proportionate increase in health and safety facilities. The ruling Liberal party was responsible in the 1860s and 1870s for such measures as the re-channelling of the Danube to prevent flooding, the development of an excellent water supply and a first-rate public health system, the opening (in 1873) of the first city hospital, and the provision of spacious public parks. In his great novel *Der Mann ohne Eigenschaften*, Robert Musil captures something of the labyrinthine quality of social life in the capital, the seeds of rebellion underneath the surface glitter, as he paints a satirical picture of late nineteenth-century Vienna, describing it as 'this vanished Kakania':

> All in all, how many amazing things might be said about this vanished Kakania! Everything and every person in it, for instance, bore the label of *kaiserlich-königlich* (Imperial-Royal) or *kaiserlich and königlich* (Imperial *and* Royal), abbreviated as "k.k." or "k.& k.," but to be sure which institutions and which persons were to be designated by "k.k." and which by "k.& k." required the mastery of a secret science. On paper it was called the Austro-Hungarian Monarchy, but in conversation it was called Austria, a name solemnly abjured officially while stubbornly retained emotionally, just to show that feelings are quite as important as constitutional law and that regulations are one thing but real life something else entirely. Liberal in its constitution, it was administered clerically. The government was clerical, but everyday life was liberal. All citizens were equal before the law, but not everyone was a citizen. There was a Parliament, which asserted its freedom so forcefully that it was

---

6 Its architect was Heinrich Ferstel who also built several of the private dwellings along the Ring. His outstanding achievement, however, is the *Votivkirche*.

usually kept shut; there was also an Emergency Powers Act that enabled the government to get along without Parliament, but then, when everyone had happily settled for absolutism, the Crown decreed that it was time to go back to parliamentary rule. The country was full of such goings-on, among them the sort of nationalist movements that rightly attracted so much attention in Europe and are so thoroughly misunderstood today. They were so violent that they jammed the machinery of government and brought it to a dead stop several times a year, but in the intervals and during the deadlocks people got along perfectly well and acted as if nothing had happened. And in fact, nothing really *had* happened.[7]

Be that as it may, there is no doubt that Vienna came to assume the position of musical capital of Europe in the last thirty years of the century, a position which she had held at the beginning of the century but which had been ceded to Paris in the intervening period. It was the permanent home of both Brahms and Bruckner, and many other leading musicians resided in the city for long or short periods of time. Both Gustav Mahler and Hugo Wolf came to study at the Vienna Conservatory in the mid-1870s. While Wolf remained in the city and established a reputation as a composer of *Lieder* and a virulent anti-Brahms music critic, Mahler occupied various conducting posts throughout the Habsburg Empire and Germany before returning triumphantly to Vienna as the director of the Opera in April 1897, six months after Bruckner's death.

Brahms came to Vienna initially in 1862 and made his first public appearance in the city on 16 November when he played the piano part in his own Piano Quartet in G minor op. 25 (with the Hellmesberger Quartet). In May 1863 he was asked to become the conductor of the *Singakademie*, a mixed-voice choir, and he stayed in this post for a year. In the mid-1860s, however, he went on several concert tours

---

7 Robert Musil, *Der Mann ohne Eigenschaften* (Reinbeck bei Hamburg: Rowohlt Verlag GmBH, 1978); English translation by Sophie Wilkins as *The Man without Qualities* (London: Picador, 1995, 2/1997), 29f..

204

either alone or with Joseph Joachim (violin) and Julius Stockhausen (singer) and travelled extensively throughout Germany and Austria and to the main musical centres of Hungary, Switzerland, Denmark and the Netherlands. He was also hoping for some kind of recognition from his own native city of Hamburg, specifically the post of conductor of the Hamburg Philharmonic concerts, but was passed over on two occasions - in 1863 and 1867. Although he spent a good part of each year in Vienna from 1862 onwards, he had not bought an apartment of his own, preferring to stay at hotels or with friends. In May 1869 his father wrote to him that Vienna was 'too important to exchange... for Hamburg where everybody's mind is only on business' and suggested that he finally settle there - a city where he was understood and recognized. Brahms appears to have taken his advice. He moved into an apartment in the Prater and then two years later, in December 1871, rented some rooms from the Vogl family at Karlsgasse 4. These rooms were situated near the *Karlskirche* and not far from the *Gesellschaft der Musikfreunde* building and Brahms stayed here for the rest of his life. In 1872, after the death of his father and his acceptance of the directorship of the *Gesellschaft* concerts, he put his roots firmly down in the city.

Brahms and Bruckner moved in different social circles. Brahms was 'gladly received by well established society',[8] was deeply involved in Vienna's concert life, had friendships with several members of the *Gesellschaft der Musikfreunde* and fairly secure relationships with well-established publishers such as Breitkopf & Härtel and Simrock. Bruckner's involvement in Vienna's concert life was, by dint of his employment as a Harmony and Counterpoint teacher at the Conservatory and, later, at the University and his appointment as an organist at the *Hofkapelle*, more restricted. Although, thanks largely to successful visits to Nancy, Paris and London

---

8 Franz Endler, transl. L. Jecny, *Vienna. A Guide to its Music and Musicians* (Portland, Oregon: Amadeus Press, 1989), 56.

as a performer in the late 1860s and early 1870s, he had an international reputation as an organ virtuoso, he had to struggle for many years to gain recognition as a symphonist. Devoted pupils like Joseph Schalk and Ferdinand Löwe gave performances of their own piano arrangements of the symphonies in the somewhat rarefied atmosphere of the *Akademischer Wagner-Verein* meetings in Vienna.[9] The only publisher who took any interest in him initially - and rather surprisingly, after the disastrous first performance of the second version of Symphony no. 3 in 1877 - was Theodor Rättig, by no means in the 'same league' as Breitkopf & Härtel or Simrock. Later Emperor Franz Josef subsidised the publication of two of his symphonies, the third version of Symphony no. 3 and the second version of Symphony no. 8.

Although quite different temperamentally and in their backgrounds and aspirations, Brahms and Bruckner seem to have maintained a distant but respectful relationship. We know, for instance, that Bruckner played the organ part in a performance of Handel's *Te Deum* conducted by Brahms in the *Musikvereinssaal* on 10 November 1872 and that he had a high regard for Brahms's technical skill as a composer while sometimes criticising what he found to be a dearth of musical invention in his works. Brahms possessed scores of Bruckner's Seventh and Eighth Symphonies and the piano score of the *Te Deum*, a work which he particularly admired. Nevertheless he was of the opinion that Bruckner had 'no idea of an ordered musical structure'.[10] Brahms and Bruckner had their own favourite

---

9 The Vienna branch, one of several European branches of the Society, was founded in 1872 by Felix Mottl, Guido Adler and Karl Wolff. See Helmut Kowar, 'Vereine für die Neudeutschen in Wien' in *BSL 1984* (Linz, 1986), 81-90.

10 See Brahms's references to Bruckner in various conversations recorded by Max Kalbeck, in his *Johannes Brahms* (Berlin, 3/1912-20), 403-10, Elisabeth von Herzogenberg's exchange of letters with Brahms apropos the Leipzig premiere of Bruckner's Seventh Symphony on 30 December 1884 in *G-A* IV/2, 239-41, and a letter to Clara Schumann, written on 22 February 1893, in Berthold Litzmann, *Briefwechsel Clara Schumann-Johannes Brahms* II (Leipzig, 1927), 501f. Two of Bruckner's pupils from the 1880s recalled some of his opinions of Brahms's music. According to Franz Marschner, one of his University students, Bruckner once said that 'he who wants to be

Gasthäuser but they met socially on at least one occasion.[11] Unfortunately the rival claims of their 'supporters' or 'disciples' as to the supremacy of programme or absolute music led at the time to an unnatural and overblown emphasis on the obvious stylistic differences between the composers. As Hilde Spiel observes:

> During the 1880s the musical world of the capital was riven by the conflict between Wagnerians and Brahmsians - inadequately described as believers in progressive forms of this art on the one hand and established ones on the other... In fact, despite the deep gulf and acrimonious controversies which at that time divided Vienna's music-lovers... no strict boundaries can be discerned between one school and the other.[12]

Bruckner's deep admiration for Wagner was no secret and this 'deep gulf' became even more pronounced after the latter's death in 1883. Bruckner now

---

comforted by music will be a follower of Brahms, but he who wants to be stirred will not be satisfied with his music'. In response to a question from Anton Meißner, Bruckner said: 'You know, Anton, that the two of us are Catholics and have fiery temperaments. Brahms is for cool temperaments and Protestants'; see *G-A* 4/2, 131f. and 135. See also Stephen Johnson, *Bruckner Remembered* (London: Faber and Faber, 1998), 153ff.

11 See Friedrich Klose, *Meine Lehrjahre bei Bruckner* (Regensburg , 1927), 147, and August Stradal's reminiscence as reported in *G-A* 4/2, 690. See also Stephen Johnson, op.cit., 151ff.

12 Hilde Spiel, *Vienna's Golden Autumn* (London: Weidenfeld and Nicolson, 1987), 161-62. For further discussion about stylistic similarities and differences between Brahms and Bruckner, see Guido Adler, 'Johannes Brahms. Wirken, Wesen und Stellung' in *Studien zur Musikwissenschaft* xx (1930), 26; Hans Gal, *Johannes Brahms* (London: Weidenfeld and Nicolson, 1963), 151-54; Werner Korte, *Bruckner und Brahms. Die spätromantische Lösung der autonomen Konzeption* (Tutzing: Schneider, 1963); Constantin Floros, *Brahms und Bruckner. Studien zur musikalischen Exegetik* (Wiesbaden, 1980); idem, 'Zur Gegensätzlichkeit der Symphonik Brahms und Bruckners' in *BSL 1983* (Linz, 1985), 145-53.

unwittingly became the standard-bearer of the pro-Wagner faction. During the last twenty years of his life Wagner made several extended visits to Vienna. In the early 1860s he conducted concerts including excerpts from his operas at the *Theater an der Wien* and supervised rehearsals for the planned premiere of *Tristan und Isolde* at the Opera, a project that was abandoned in March 1864. In the 1870s, however, several of his operas had their Viennese premieres - *Die Meistersinger* (late February 1870), *Die Walküre* (early March 1877), *Das Rheingold* (end of January 1878), *Götterdämmerung* (February 1879) and the complete *Ring* (May 1879). In May 1872 Wagner came to Vienna to conduct a concert sponsored by the newly-formed *Wagner Society* to help raise funds for the Bayreuth project. According to Göllerich, Wagner went out of his way to greet Bruckner who was one of the deputation to meet him at the station.[13] During Bruckner's visit to Bayreuth in 1873 Wagner accepted the dedication of the Third Symphony. The two composers met again in Vienna at the end of February 1875 when Wagner returned to the city to raise more money for Bayreuth. On March 1, he conducted a performance of his own works - the *Kaisermarsch* and excerpts from *The Ring* - and received a very warm reception. During his stay Wagner invited Bruckner to a soirée. After singing through the whole of the final act of *Götterdämmerung*, he made a point of thanking Bruckner for the dedication of the symphony and described him as a worthy successor of Beethoven.[14] Wagner was in Vienna again from the end of October until mid-December 1875 to attend performances of his *Tannhäuser* and *Lohengrin* at the Opera. He was so impressed by the singing of the chorus that he returned to Vienna in May of the following year to conduct a performance of *Lohengrin* himself.

---

13 See *G-A* IV/1, 199.

14 See *G-A* IV/1, 358f.

The two leading artistic directors in Viennese musical life in the second half of the nineteenth century were Johann Ritter von Herbeck and Joseph Hellmesberger. We have already encountered Herbeck as the man largely responsible for persuading Bruckner to move from Linz to Vienna in 1868. He continued to encourage the composer up to his untimely death in 1877. As director of the *Singverein* attached to the *Gesellschaft der Musikfreunde* he introduced several new works to the repertoire, including Schumann's *Manfred, Der Rose Pilgerfahrt* and *Szenen aus Goethe's Faust*, Liszt's *Legende von der heiligen Elisabeth* and parts of Brahms's *German Requiem*. He became court music director during the first period of Bruckner's stay in Vienna.[15] Hellmesberger, who was also to be involved with Bruckner on many occasions, succeeded Herbeck as court music director in 1877. As leader of a fine string quartet, he extended the public's awareness of the chamber music repertoire to include the late Beethoven and the Schubert quartets, not to mention works by Brahms and the Bruckner Quintet in F.[16]

---

15 Johann Ritter von Herbeck (1831-77) came from a singing background. A former choirboy at the *Heiligenkreuz* monastery, he became choir director at the *Piaristenkirche* in Vienna and then obtained the more prestigious post of conductor of the Vienna *Männergesangverein* in 1856. His other appointments included the posts of conductor of the *Gesellschaft* concerts (from 1859), associate conductor of the Opera (from 1863) and director of the Opera (1870-75). For further information about Herbeck, see Ludwig Herbeck, *Johann Herbeck. Ein Lebensbild* (Vienna: Gutmann, 1885; Leopold Nowak, 'Herbeck' in *MGG* 6 (1957), cols. 186-89; Othmar Wessely, 'Herbeck' in *The New Grove* 8 (1980), 498f.

16 Joseph Hellmesberger (1828-1893) came to conducting from an instrumental background. His first important appointment was director of the *Gesellschaft der Musikfreunde* (from 1849). He also conducted the *Gesellschaft* concerts from 1851 to 1859 and in the years 1870-71 and was leader of the court opera orchestra from 1860. He founded the *Hellmesberger String Quartet* in 1849 and remained its leader until 1891. Both his father Georg (1800-1873) and his son Joseph (1855-1907) were distinguished violinists. For further information, see R.M. Prosl, *Die Hellmesberger* (Vienna: Gerlach & Weidling, 1947); Alfred Orel, 'Josef Hellmesberger d.Ä' in *MGG* 6 (1957), cols. 114-15;

The new Opera House on the Ring was the focal point of musical activities in Vienna from 1870 onwards. Its directors were Franz von Dingelstedt (1867-70) who successfully negotiated the transfer from the old *Kärntnertortheater*, Johann Herbeck (1870-75) who put on fine productions of Wagner's *Der fliegende Holländer* and *Rienzi*, Verdi's *Aida* (1874) and Goldmark's *Königin von Saba* as well as performances of Mozart's *Cosi fan Tutte*, Weber's *Oberon* and Schumann's *Genoveva*, and Franz Jauner (1875-1880), a non-musician who engaged Wilhelm Gericke to conduct French and Italian operas and Hans Richter to conduct German operas. Highlights of Jauner's directorship were productions of *Carmen* in 1875, Verdi's visit to Vienna and the performances of his *Requiem* and *Aida* in 1875, as well as productions of Beethoven's *Fidelio*, a Mozart cycle which included the rarely performed *Idomeneo* and *La Clemenza di Tito*, and the complete *Ring* (1877-79). During the 1880s, thanks largely to Richter, Wagner's popularity soared in Vienna.[17] Wilhelm Jahn, director from 1881 to 1897, was an excellent conductor of French and Italian opera and a perfect foil for Richter. He brought productions of Massenet's *Manon* and *Werther* to Vienna in the early 1890s. *Verismo* opera was also popular in Vienna at this time. Mascagni came to conduct his *Cavalleria Rusticana* in 1891 and Leoncavallo's *Bajazzo* was produced. National operas like Moniuszko's *Halka*, Smetana's *The Bartered Bride* and *Dalibor* were also popular. Vienna became the focal point of the musical world in 1892 when it hosted the *International Exhibition of Theatre and Music*. The Opera assumed a major role in this Exhibition.

The Viennese operetta, essentially a transplant of the French *opéra bouffe* as

---

Richard Evidon, 'Joseph Hellmesberger' in *The New Grove* 8 (1980), 463f.

17 For further information about Richter, see Richard Schaal, 'Hans Richter' in *MGG* 11(1963), cols. 460f.; Hans-Hubert Schönzeler, 'Hans Richter' in *The New Grove* 15 (1980), 847f.; Christopher Fifield, *True Artist and True Friend. A Biography of Hans Richter* (Oxford: Clarendon Press, 1993).

developed by Offenbach, was enormously popular. Its home was the *Theater an der Wien* where thirteen of Johann Strauss's fifteen operettas had their first performances between 1871 and 1897. Strauss's *Die Fledermaus*, first produced there in 1874, achieved the distinction of being the first operetta to be performed in the Opera twenty years later. Berlioz, Wagner, Liszt, Brahms, Bruckner, Mahler and Schoenberg all had the highest regard for the 'waltz king' whom they recognised as encapsulating the spirit of Vienna. Brahms, frequently a guest at Strauss's home, gave the most eloquent testimony to his admiration in the two sets of *Liebeslieder* waltzes opp. 52 and 65. Strauss, in the audience at the first Vienna performance of Bruckner's Symphony no. 7 on 21 March 1886, sent the composer a telegram of congratulations and invited him to one of his soirées. Reluctant to go at first, Bruckner was finally persuaded when he was reassured that one or two of his friends would also be present. Bruckner greeted Strauss as a 'great composer' and Strauss returned the compliment, describing himself modestly as 'only a suburban composer' in comparison with the creator of the 'wonderful' Seventh Symphony.[18]   The two main concert-giving institutions in Vienna were the *Gesellschaft der Musikfreunde*, founded in 1812 but reorganized after 1848, and the *Philharmonische Konzerte*, instituted in 1842, but there were a number of fairly new concert-giving bodies, for instance the *Akademischer Gesangverein*, the *Singakademie*, the *Schubertbund*, the *Kaufmännischer Gesangverein* and the *Orchesterverein für klassische Musik*. The differences between *Hofoper*, *Hofkapelle*, *Gesellschaft der Musikfreunde* and *Philharmonische Konzerte* concerned function, internal structure funding and sponsorship. Although there was a clear distinction between those activities which were court-sponsored and those which were *Gesellschaft*-sponsored, there was very little to choose between them artistically, as many of the most prominent

---

18 See *G-A* IV/2, 433 and 467f. For further information about the popular culture of the period, see Camille Crittenden, *Johann Strauss and Vienna: operetta and the politics of popular culture* (Cambridge, 2000)

musicians were active in all of them, Otto Dessoff, for instance, was conductor of the Philharmonic Concerts from 1860 to 1875 and was also active as a conductor at the Opera, as an occasional conductor at the *Gesellschaft* concerts and as a professor of harmony and counterpoint at the Conservatory. Hans Richter, who succeeded him as Philharmonic conductor (1875-1898), was one of the principal conductors of the Opera and was artistic director of the *Musikverein* from 1884 to 1890. In addition he was assistant director of music at the court from 1877 to 1893 and became principal music director from 1893 to 1900. The Philharmonic Orchestra was also the Opera orchestra and most of its members additionally played in the *Gesellschaft* concerts.

Although the first concert to be given in the newly constructed *Gesellschaft der Musikfreunde* building in 1870 was a fairly conservative affair,[19] there was, generally speaking, more openness to novelty at the *Gesellschaft* concerts than at the Philharmonic concerts.[20] A number of works for chorus and orchestra were performed, for instance Beethoven's Symphony no. 9 and *Missa solemnis*, Brahms's *German Requiem*, Liszt's *Christus* and Bruckner's *Psalm 150*. The *Gesellschaft* had its own large chorus - the *Singverein* - to participate in these large-scale works. Brahms directed the *Gesellschaft* concerts during the 1872-73 season.

On the lighter side, a distinctive type of popular music was offered by the Schrammel brothers (Joseph and Johann) from 1877 onwards. The 'Schrammel Quartet' consisted of two violins, bass guitar (later a 'button concertina') and a small, high-pitched clarinet. The Schrammel brothers wrote most of the music they played and their quartet was in demand to provide musical entertainment for the nobility

---

19 The concert, which took place on 6 January, was conducted by Herbeck and included works by Bach, Haydn, Mozart, Beethoven and Schubert.

20 A situation which still exists today when one compares the type of concert given by the Vienna Symphony Orchestra or at the *Konzerthaus* attached to the Academy with the Vienna Philharmonic Concerts which are by subscription only.

and the royal family. It was admired by serious musicians and, as time went on, almost all Viennese light music for a small ensemble was simply called *Schrammelmusik.* An orchestral player did not think it beneath him to join with a colleague involved in light music entertainment to form such a folk music group. One of Bruckner's social pursuits, certainly during his first years in Vienna, was to attend balls in the pre-Lenten carnival period. In the *Krakauer Schreibkalender* - one of the diaries which he used from 1877 onwards as a kind of notebook and in which he jotted down *inter alia* the times of his lectures at the Conservatory and University and the times of lessons given to private pupils - he recorded the names of the ladies with whom he had danced at three balls he attended in January and February 1877! Bruckner, whose eye for feminine beauty often led him into bizarre situations and occasioned several rash proposals of marriage, had obviously been suitably impressed. The music at those balls would no doubt have been provided by a dance orchestra or an early form of the 'Schrammel quartet'.

No survey of the musical scene in Vienna during the second half of the century is complete without some mention of Eduard Hanslick who was without doubt the city's most formidable music critic. He contributed music reviews to several papers, for instance the *Allgemeine Wiener Musikzeitung* and the *Wiener Zeitung,* until 1864 when he became the music critic of the prestigious *Neue freie Presse.* Hanslick's major book on musical aesthetics, in which he espoused the cause of autonomous absolute music as distinct from heteronomous programme music, was entitled *Vom Musikalisch-Schönen* (*The Beautiful in Music,* 1854). It was highly regarded and went through several editions in his lifetime. On the strength of it he received an honorary readership from the University of Vienna in 1856 and was appointed a full professor of music history and aesthetics in 1870. Hanslick's relationship with Brahms was fairly cool initially (in the 1860s) but he later became one of his stoutest advocates. On the other hand, while welcoming Bruckner's appointment to the Vienna Conservatory in 1868, he took a strong stand against his applications for a similar appointment at the University and was one of a group of three or four reviewers who regularly castigated the composer for his Wagnerian leanings.[21]

Other important music critics who contributed to the 'reception history' of Bruckner's music both during his time in Vienna and posthumously were Ludwig Speidel who worked for the *Fremdenblatt* and was a 'mild and modest man, a critic who would rather remain on friendly terms with the actors of the *Hofburgtheater* than treat them harshly when they had failed in their parts' and whose dictum was 'a feuilleton is the immortality of one day',[22] Robert Hirschfeld who worked for the *Wiener Abendpost*, Theodor Helm who worked for the *Deutsche Zeitung*, Richard Specht who worked for *Der Merker*, Max Kalbeck and Ernst Decsey, both of whom worked for the *Neues Wiener Tagblatt*, Max Graf who worked for *Die Zeit* and Hugo Wolf who deliberately adopted a polemical anti-Brahms and pro-Wagner stance in his reviews for the *Salonblatt*.[23] Recent Bruckner scholarship has helped to provide a more balanced view of Bruckner's treatment by the Austrian press. While critical

---

21 Eduard Hanslick (1825-1904) was born in Prague and trained as both a musician and a lawyer. He eventually settled in Vienna in the late 1840s. His main critical writings are embodied in the *Geschichte des Concertwesens in Wien* (Vienna, 1869) and *Die moderne Oper* (1875-1900). English translations of some of them are contained in Henry Pleasants, ed., *Eduard Hanslick. Music Criticisms 1846-1899* (London: Penguin Books, 2/1963). For further information, see Friedrich Blume, 'Hanslick' in *MGG* 5 (1956), cols. 1482-1493 and Eric Sams, 'Hanslick' in *The New Grove* 8 (1980), 151ff.. Bruckner attended Hanslick's history lectures at the University during his first years in Vienna.

22 Spiel, op.cit., 103.

23 For accounts of Max Kalbeck's activities as a critic, see Sandra McColl, 'Max Kalbeck and Gustav Mahler', *Nineteenth-Century Music* 20/2 (1996), 167-83, and idem, 'Karl Kraus and Musical Criticism: The Case of Max Kalbeck', *The Musical Quarterly* 82/2 (Summer 1998), 279-308. Hugo Wolf contributed reviews to the *Salonblatt* from 1884 to 1887. An English translation of several of these reviews can be found in Henry Pleasants, transl. and ed., *The Music Criticism of Hugo Wolf* (London and New York: Holmes and Meier, 1978).

214

opinion may have been divided so far as his music was concerned, he was an established musical figure by the beginning of the 1880s:

> Bruckner took about ten years to be established as a 'very important person' in the Austrian press. During that time there were the occasional articles which were concerned essentially with events such as organ concerts and first performances, and there were also a few caricatures (for instance, in the Viennese comic paper *Die Bombe* on 22 October 1872) as well as the friendly if occasionally scandal-mongering mention of Bruckner in provincial papers, particularly regarding the question of his dismissal or non-dismissal from the *Staatsanstalt für Bildung von Lehrerinnen* in Vienna in 1871.
> From 1880, however, the composer was well enough known for his name to be found frequently in reports, commentaries and reviews not only on the occasion of performances of his works but also independently of those...[24]

How much Bruckner would have imbibed of the cultural atmosphere in Vienna is uncertain. Most of his time seems to have been spent teaching and composing and he used his vacations to visit Bayreuth, Steyr, St. Florian (where his brother Ignaz worked) and Vöcklabruck (where his sister Rosalie lived with her husband and two sons). There is no record of his showing any particular interest in dramatic productions at either the *Burgtheater* or the *Volkstheater* or of his being aware of the major developments in painting and sculpture which led to the Vienna Secession in the mid-1890s. On the other hand, his *Hochschulkalender* for 1880 reveals that he kept up to date with an event of national interest at the time - the Austrian North

---

24 Manfred Wagner, 'Bruckner in Wien', *ABDS* 2 (Linz, 1980), 41. A typical example of a writer well-disposed towards Bruckner is the 'C.B.' who wrote an article entitled 'Porträt eines Wiener Musikers' in the *Deutsche Zeitung*, 4 February 1880. It is reprinted in full in *ABDS* 2, 41-44. See also Norbert Tschulik, 'Anton Bruckner in der Wiener Zeitung. Ein Beitrag über die zeitgenössische Bruckner-Berichterstattung' in *BJ 1981* (Linz, 1982), 171-79.

Pole expedition.[25]

Bruckner took some time to settle and establish himself in Vienna. The contrast between life in the city and life in a provincial town like Linz was much greater than that between life in Linz and life in St. Florian. He was no longer in a fairly sheltered church music environment. His occasional organ duties at the *Hofkapelle* were but a small part of his weekly routine. One suspects that his organ tours at the beginning of his time in Vienna were an attempt to impress his more cultured colleagues and to make his name known in the city. He may have been naive in some matters but he was shrewd enough and had a sufficient amount of 'peasant cunning' to survive the particularly difficult early years and to sustain him thereafter. Much has been made of his lack of social graces which did not mix well with the etiquette of Viennese high society, the court circle in particular. But it would appear that, generally speaking, Bruckner's occasional unsocial behaviour was not a deterrent to his being accepted as a fine musician, and that he had his advocates in court circles after Herbeck's death in 1877. The Lord Chamberlain, Prince Constantin zu Hohenlohe-Schillingsfürst, to whom he dedicated his Symphony no. 4, was a keen music-lover and well-disposed towards him. His wife Princess Marie zu Sayn-Wittgenstein-Berleburg, whose mother was Liszt's lover and companion for many years, was convinced, however, that Bruckner was frequently 'economical with the truth' in his accounts of his relationship with the court:

> ... My husband made a clear distinction between Bruckner the artist to whom as an indigenous composer he wished to give due recognition, and Bruckner the man who was very popular in some court circles. This was in keeping with certain traditions from the 'good old days' of the patriarchal Emperor Franz - when an artist's little gaucheries met with more approval than his elegant, gentlemanly bearing... my husband and I also discovered that Bruckner knew how to promote himself well in his court

---

25 The diary entries for 1880 are printed in *G-A* IV/1, 621f. and *ABDS* 2, 24f.

relationships. Many of his comments about this which were voiced publicly lack any semblance of truth... Excuse me if our point of view is at variance with your admiration for the composer. You will naturally have had the opportunity of seeing him at his most unaffected - and such a mighty talent must also have had its earthy side. Unfortunately, we saw him in nasty disguise - a certain amount of calculated, self-satisfied clumsiness lay behind his court etiquette.[26]

This is a necessary corrective to the apocryphal accounts of Bruckner as a beleaguered figure and a 'fish out of water' in Vienna. The many difficulties and setbacks must not be minimized but his strong faith helped him to surmount them.[27] The reminiscences of his friends and pupils show that he had the healthy respect and loyalty of many young amateur and professional musicians.[28] Towards the end of his life Bruckner gradually obtained the more substantial recognition he so richly deserved. In November 1891 the honorary degree of Doctor of Philosophy was conferred on him by the University of Vienna in recognition of his achievements and, from July 1895 until his death, Emperor Franz Josef, to whom he dedicated his Symphony no. 8 and from whom he received the *Franz Josef Order* in July 1886, put at his disposal the *Kustodenstöckl*, a sort of porter's lodge in the grounds of the

---

26 From Princess Marie's letter to August Göllerich. See *G-A* IV/2, 506f.

27 See Johannes-Leopold Mayer, 'Musik als Gesellschaftliches Ärgernis...' in *ABDS* 2, 75-156, 109ff. in particular, for a revealing sociological study of Bruckner's Vienna years.

28 Of the many reminiscences, the most important are Friedrich Eckstein, *Erinnerungen an Anton Bruckner* (Vienna: Universal Edition, 1923); Carl Hruby, *Meine Erinnerungen an Anton Bruckner* (Vienna: Friedrich Schalk, 1901); Friedrich Klose, *Meine Lehrjahre bei Bruckner. Erinnerungen und Betrachtungen* (Regensburg: Bosse, 1927); Max v. Oberleithner, *Meine Erinnerungen an Bruckner* (Regensburg: Bosse, 1933); Lili Schalk, ed., *Franz Schalk. Briefe und Betrachtungen* (Vienna: Musikwissenschaftlicher Verlag, 1935); August Stradal, 'Erinnerungen an Anton Bruckner' in *Neue Musik-Zeitung* 34 (1913), 125-128 and 165-68; idem, 'Erinnerungen aus Bruckners letzter Zeit' in *Zeitschrift für Musik* 99 (1932), 835-60, 971-78 and 1071-75.

Schloss Belvedere.

Other long-held views of Bruckner's life-style have been challenged recently. Manfred Wagner, for instance, counters the typical statement that 'he retained his baggy country clothes' when in Vienna by referring us to oil paintings and photographs of the composer which reveal that he had a good sartorial sense.[29] His preference of trousers which were wide and did not quite reach his ankles was purely a convenience measure - to facilitate organ playing! Wagner's conclusion that 'no representation, either photographic or artistic, reveals anything that can be ridiculed' can hardly be disputed.[30] Bruckner's eating and drinking habits were by no means unusual. He had a hearty but hardly intemperate appetite for beer. The timing of his meals was determined, of course, by his teaching hours which on some days stretched to mid-evening. Finally, his lodgings were of above-average comfort for a person of his social standing at the time. His first apartment, for which he paid an annual rent of 200 florins, was at Währingerstrasse 41, 2nd floor, in the ninth district. He chose it deliberately because of its good view and its proximity to both the *Hofkapelle* and the Conservatory. In 1877 he moved to an apartment on the fourth floor of Hessgasse 7 near the Schottenring and commanding a fine view of the Kahlenberg. His landlord was Dr. Anton Oelzelt von Newin, a young philosopher who attended some of Bruckner's Harmony and Counterpoint classes while studying at the University and was a great admirer of his organ playing.[31] Bruckner had been

---

29 This 'typical' statement can be found in Deryck Cooke, 'Bruckner', *The New Grove Late Romantic Masters* (London: Macmillan, 1985), 24. Copies of some of the paintings and photographs mentioned by Wagner can be found throughout the Bruckner literature. The most useful and informative collection is provided by Renate Grasberger, 'Bruckner-Ikonographie. Teil 1: Um 1854 bis 1924', *ABDS* 7 (Linz , 1990).

30 Wagner, loc.cit., *ABDS* 2, 22.

31 See *G-A* IV/1, 460ff. for details of Bruckner's organ playing at Klosterneuburg on 4 October 1876 which Oelzelt von Newin heard.

promised this apartment at the end of 1876 but the removal was delayed owing to difficulties raised by some of Oelzelt von Newin's relatives. Oelzelt von Newin wrote to Bruckner in February 1877 to apologize for the delay and to assure him that the promise would be fulfilled.[32] The composer was immensely grateful to his young friend for allowing him to have the apartment at a very reasonable rent, and later gave tangible expression of his gratitude by dedicating his Sixth Symphony to him.[33] Friedrich Eckstein provides us with a vivid description of this apartment:

> How vividly I can still recall the beautiful, bright and spacious apartment in the Hessgasse near the Schottenring. That latticed anteroom with dark green curtains near the staircase and the large tidy kitchen which Bruckner probably never used. Then the brightly painted study near the street with the huge pedal harmonium at the window which was permanently closed and served only as a book stand. Opposite this, in the middle of the room, the huge, long and ancient Bösendorfer piano with its thin, whirring spinet-like tone, also buried beneath scores, piles of manuscripts and music paper, either empty or covered with sketches and workings-out.
>
> In the middle of this study stood the small, unassuming, thin-legged little table, painted green but worn at the edges and covered with numerous ink splashes, at which Bruckner worked many hours each day, often until late at night, and where he also gave lessons - the pupil sitting opposite him, eager to complete the set exercises and then to have them returned after the master had taken the utmost care to correct them. Most of the time here was spent discussing in painstaking detail all the conceivable workings of an exercise - first

---

32 See *HSABB* 1, 169 for the text of this letter. It was printed for the first time in *G-A* IV/1, 463f.

33 Bruckner paid the same rent (200 florins) that he had paid for the apartment in Währingerstrasse. Several letters from Oelzelt von Newin to Bruckner have survived. In one of them, dated 15 June 1891, he again expressed gratitude to his 'patron' and mentioned that he had just returned from Berlin where his *Te Deum* was successfully performed. See *ABB* 247, 248. An undated visiting card and the originals of six letters to Oelzelt von Newin, dated 7 February 1877, 11 June 1877, 19 November 1891, New Year 1892, 11 June 1892 and 13 June 1894, can be found in the *Gesellschaft der Musikfreunde* library.

of all, strictly according to the rules; and then, finally, very free methods of treatment were carefully examined. Next to Bruckner's study was his bedroom in which there was no other furniture apart from his bed. The floor was painted in brown enamel varnish and the walls in a deep ultramarine blue, a colour combination which I encountered later only in Scandinavian and Russian farm cottages. On the floor piled high against the walls were quantities of music, music paper, sketches, books, correspondence etc., and frequently, whenever a sketch, a letter or an important document went missing, I had to crawl along the floor on all fours in order to find what I was looking for.[34]

Bruckner's favourite sister Anna moved with him to Vienna to act as his housekeeper. When she died in January 1870, nearly ten years after the death of their mother, Katherina Kachelmayr was recommended to him. Her duties included house cleaning, making the occasional meal, and being at the apartment at 7 a.m. most mornings to brew him some coffee. As she remained with him as a faithful housekeeper for the next 26 years she was often the confidante of his numerous brief 'affairs of the heart'. Their relationship was cordial but had its inevitable tensions. When composing he would often lose all sense of time, and she was under strict instructions neither to clean nor to admit any visitors to his study during these periods. He frequently left a lovingly prepared dish uneaten, preferring to keep working until late in the evening when he would go to a local inn and enjoy a substantial supper. When his health gradually declined in the last three or four years of his life, 'Frau Kathi' helped to nurse him through various illnesses. In July 1895, when Bruckner was no longer able to cope with the exertion of climbing up and down stairs, she was at hand when he moved to the *Kustodenstöckl* in the Belvedere grounds. During the final months of his life when he required round-the-clock help, she brought her daughter to assist her and cared for the ailing composer with great

---

34 Friedrich Eckstein, op.cit. See also Friedrich Klose, op.cit. 10 - there are English translations of this in Paul Banks, loc.cit., 85 and Stephen Johnson, op.cit., 43f. - and *G-A* IV/1, 465-67.

220

devotion.[35]

Bruckner remained at the Conservatory for 23 years and stayed in the same post during that time.[36] Although the possibility of an organ-teaching post had been mooted in the mid-1860s, Bruckner was the first to give organ instruction at the Conservatory. In fact there was no organ available for lessons at first; a piano andthen a pedal harmonium were put at his disposal. When an organ was finally installed Bruckner bought the harmonium for his own use. Significantly, Bruckner

---

35 Katherine Kachelmayr died in 1911. Towards the end of her life when she was in a mental institution in Vienna, she received some financial help from Bruckner's brother Ignaz.

As well as the books and articles already cited, the following will provide a more detailed account of Vienna and musical life in the city during Bruckner's time there:

A. Böhm, *Geschichte des Singvereins der Gesellschaft der Musikfreunde in Wien* (Vienna, 1908); R.V. Perger and R. Hirschfeld, *Geschichte des k.k. Gesellschaft der Musikfreunde in Wien*, 2 vols. (Vienna, 1912); Heinrich Kralik, *Die Wiener Philharmoniker und ihre Dirigenten* (Vienna, 1960); Arthur J. May, *The Hapsburg Monarchy 1867-1914* (Cambridge, Mass: Harvard UP, 1960); Ilsa Barea, *Vienna. Legend and Reality* (London: Secker and Wartburg, 1966); Alfred Orel, 'Wien VII. Das 19. Jahrhundert' in *MGG* 14 (1968), cols. 611-15; F. Hadamowsky, *Die Wiener Hoftheater (Staatsoper), Part 2: Die Wiener Hofoper (Staatsoper) 1811-1974* (Vienna, 1975); R.A. Kahn, *A History of the Habsburg Empire 1526-1918* (Berkeley, 1977); R. Flotzinger and G. Gruber, eds., *Musikgeschichte Österreichs II. Vom Barock zur Gegenwart* (Graz, 1979); Mosco Carner and Rudolf Klein, 'Vienna 5: 1830-1945' in *The New Grove* 19 (1980), 723-36; John W. Boyer, *Political Radicalism in Late Imperial Vienna* (Chicago and London: The University of Chicago Press, 1981); H. Herrmann-Schneider, *Status und Funktion des Hofkapellmeisters in Wien (1848-1918)* (Graz, 1981); D.J. Olsen, *The City as a Work of Art: London, Paris ,Vienna* (New Haven and London, 1986); Alfred Planyavsky, 'Die Wiener Philharmoniker im Rückblick' in *ÖMZ* 47/2-3 (February-March 1992), 86-110, 95f. and 98ff. in particular; Andrew Wheatcroft, *The Habsburgs* (London: Viking, 1995).

36 The original 1868 contract obliged him to teach theory for six hours a week and organ for six hours a week. This was changed in 1869 to nine hours of theory and three hours of organ. Bruckner retired on 15 January 1891after taking six months' leave because of illness.

never taught composition at the Conservatory.[37] According to the reminiscences of many of his pupils, Bruckner brought to his theory teaching the same rigid discipline that he had experienced during his studies with Sechter. Nevertheless he frequently introduced a lighter touch to proceedings by using a colourful illustration to underline the point he wished to make. His text books were the same ones that he himself had used, namely Dürrnberger's *Elementar-Lehrbuch der Harmonie- und Generalbasslehre* (1841) and Sechter's *Grundsätze der musikalischen Komposition* (1853).[38] The following account of Bruckner's teaching - by the philosopher Dr. Franz Marschner, one of his Counterpoint pupils at the Conservatory from 1883 to

---

37 Composition was taught by Otto Dessoff (1861-1875), Franz Krenn (1869-1891), Robert Fuchs (1874-1909), Hermann Grädener (1875-1909) and Johann Nepomuk Fuchs (1888-1894).

38 See *G-A* IV/1, 43-62 for Viktor Christ's notes on his theory lessons at the Conservatory. Further information about Bruckner's teaching methods at the Conservatory, later at the University, and on a one-to-one basis with his private pupils is provided by the following: Friedrich Eckstein, op.cit. (1923) [Eckstein was a private pupil from 1881 to 1884 as well as attending Bruckner's University lectures from 1884 to 1886. His notes on Bruckner's teaching are preserved in the *ÖNB* - Mus. Hs. 28.443-47 and Miscellanea 70]; Friedrich Klose, op.cit. (1927) [Klose was a private pupil from 1886 to 1889]; Alfred Orel, *Ein Harmonielehrekolleg bei Bruckner* (Berlin-Vienna-Zurich, 1940) [containing Carl Speiser's notes on the harmony lectures during the winter semester 1889/90]; Ernst Schwanzara, ed., *Anton Bruckner. Vorlesungen über Harmonielehre und Kontrapunkt in der Universität Wien* (Vienna: Österreichischer Bundesverlag, 1950) [covering the period 1891-94]; William Waldstein, 'Bruckner als Lehrer' in Franz Grasberger, ed., *Bruckner-Studien. Leopold Nowak zum 60. Geburtstag* (Vienna: Musikwissenschaftlicher Verlag, 1964), 113-20; Erich Schenk and Gernot Gruber, '"Die ganzen Studien" zu Josef Vockners Theorieunterricht bei Anton Bruckner' in Othmar Wessely, ed., *Bruckner Studien* (Vienna, 1975), 349-77 [Vockner was a private pupil from 1876 to 1888]; Rudolf Flotzinger, 'Rafael Loidols Theoriekolleg bei Bruckner 1879/1880' in Wessely, op.cit., 379-431. See also Theophil Antonicek, 'Bruckner's Universitätsschüler in den Nationalien der Philosophischen Fakultät' in Wessely, op.cit., 433-87 for a complete list and some biographical details of the students who attended the University music lectures given by Bruckner and his colleagues, including Hanslick and Guido Adler, from 1875 to 1897.

1885 - is typical of many:

> In his teaching he was a strict technician but kindly as a person. I already had the impression that he was an excellent teacher of Counterpoint. In order to understand his teaching method, however, one had to be adequately trained; fortunately that was the case as far as I was concerned. He presented the vast material of Sechter's theories in a simple and cogent manner and could be held up as a model teacher, enabling his pupil to keep on assimilating a relatively limited number of maxims and rules in a logical manner... He told me himself that he had studied Counterpoint seven hours a day for seven years, but under the personal supervision of his teacher Sechter only during holiday periods. I ascribed his abnormal nervous condition to this extended period of highly concentrated study. To write counterpoint in the way that he was accustomed to was an extremely strenuous undertaking even for someone with the greatest aptitude and facility. He worked alone with us, proceeding at a very slow pace but as thoroughly as possible. We often brought him only a couple of lines of work.
>
> 'People work far too quickly for me', he once said; 'I work very slowly, much more slowly than they do, but I also reflect upon everything that I am considering'. His own contrapuntal inventions, particularly his counter-themes, were wonderful. The time devoted to the teaching of Harmony and Counterpoint at the Conservatory seemed to him to be far too short. When I asked him once how he would plan the teaching, his expressed opinion was that a harmony course should definitely last three years, whereas a few months would be sufficient for Composition teaching as Composition was not really a subject that could be taught. As a teacher Bruckner had the excellent habit of playing corrections on the piano and of using them as aural tests for us to write down.[39]

From the outset of his time in Vienna Bruckner was particularly concerned that he would have enough material resources to enable him to devote more time to

---

39 From *G-A* IV/1, 70ff . See also Stephen Johnson, op.cit., 82-100 for other reminiscences of Bruckner's individual teaching methods (Ernst Decsey, Friedrich Klose, Ferdinand Löwe, Friedrich Eckstein, Max von Oberleithner, Gustav Mahler, Felix von Kraus and Guido Adler).

composition, and he made several requests for financial aid to the Ministry of Culture and Education. At the end of 1868 he was given a grant of 500 florins to enable him to produce 'large symphonic works'.[40]

Although Bruckner's duties at the *Hofkapelle* were initially no more than those of an unpaid supernumerary organist, in which he alternated with the other two organists, Rudolf Bibl and Pius Richter, he occasionally received fees for 'services rendered'. On 13 July 1869 he confided to his friend Moritz von Mayfeld in Linz that Herbeck had promised he would receive some holiday money from the court (treasury); he received official notification of the payment of 60 florins a fortnight later.[41] Almost 18 months later, in November 1870, Bruckner was granted a sum of 100 florins.[42]

The payment in July was possibly in recognition of Bruckner's success in representing Austria as an organist in Nancy and Paris at the end of April and beginning of May. A new Merklin organ had been installed in the church of St. Epvre in Nancy and the Hapsburg court had been invited to send an organist to participate in a kind of organ festival. Rudolf Bibl had been approached first but had declined, and Bruckner was the next choice. Moritz von Mayfeld had already alluded to this 'Nancy opportunity' and the possibility of 'triumphs in foreign parts' in a letter to Bruckner in November 1868, and Bruckner himself referred to his imminent

---

40 'zur Herstellung grösserer symphonischer Werke'. The money was made available officially on 20 December and the letter of corroboration, dated Vienna, 28 December 1868, was addressed to 'Mr Anton Bruckner, composer and professor at the Vienna Conservatory'. See *G-A* IV/1, 79f.

41 See *HSABB* 1, 110 for Bruckner's letter to Mayfeld, and *ABDS* 1, 52ff. for the official letter from the court treasury, dated Vienna, 27 July 1869. The originals of both letters are in the *ÖNB*.

42 See *ABDS* 1, 56f. The money was officially released on 18 November and Bruckner informed on 23 November; the original of the letter to Bruckner is privately owned.

departure for France in a letter to Dr. Rudolf Prohaska on 15 April 1869.[43] On the same day he wrote to the Conservatory to obtain official permission for time off to travel to Nancy, promising to make up the teaching hours that he would miss.[44] Bruckner left Vienna on 24 April and played the organ in Nancy on Wednesday 28 April and Thursday 29 April.[45] On the first day he played a Prelude and Fugue by Bach and a free improvisation. On the second day he improvised on the 'Emperor hymn', the theme of the slow movement from Haydn's String Quartet op. 76 no. 3.[46] Bruckner was pleased with his performances and reported to Herbeck that the audience reaction had been extremely favourable:

> ... The concerts are over... There was a lot of ceremony. During my first days here and even at the first concert a Parisian organist (Mr. Vilbac) seemed to me to be the clear favourite with the Germans among us. But I had the connoisseurs on my side already at the first

43 See *HSABB* 1, 99 for Mayfeld's letter to Bruckner, dated Linz, 14 November 1868, and *HSABB* 1, 102f. for Bruckner's letter to Prohaska; the originals of both letters are not extant. Dr. Rudolf Prohaska (1839-1909) was a lawyer in Linz and chairman of the *Musikverein*. He had asked Bruckner for some information about a piece of music and Bruckner was able to tell him that it would be cheaper for him to order it directly from Gotthardt in Vienna than indirectly through a music dealer in Linz.

44 Bruckner was granted leave of absence from 24 April to 3 May. In the letter from Leopold Zellner, the secretary general of the Conservatory, Bruckner was also informed that his request for his weekly organ teaching to be reduced by three hours and his harmony and counterpoint teaching to be increased by three hours had been granted. He has also been successful in his request for a pedal harmonium to be made available for organ lessons. See *HSABB* 1, 103 for Bruckner's letter and Zellner's reply, dated Vienna, 23 April 1869; the originals of both letters can be found in the *Gesellschaft der Musikfreunde* library.

45 There were previews of the Nancy concerts in the *Revue et gazette musicale* 36 (18 April 1869), 135, *Le ménestrel* 37 (18 April 1869), 158 and *La France musicale* 33 (25 April 1869), 131

46 See *G-A* IV/1, 85ff. for the programme of the concert which included soprano solos and choral pieces.

concert. I couldn't fail to be moved by the reception given to my playing at the second concert (yesterday, 29th April); I cannot begin to describe it. The aristocrats, the Parisians, the Germans and the Belgians vied with each other in paying me their respects, and this was all the more surprising after Vilbac (a very dear, fine French artist and a friend of Thomas) played some very well prepared French pieces. There is no doubt that he has an extremely sympathetic following in Nancy as he comes here frequently. I have no idea what will be reported in the papers - unfortunately, I won't be able to understand it! I have only the verbal opinions of experts - modesty compels me to be silent about those - and the reception and applause of the public. Amiable young ladies from the highest nobility even came up to the organ to show their appreciation...[47]

None of the newspaper reports of the two concerts went into any detail about the individual performances. The reviewer for L'Espérance, however, had the following to say about Bruckner's contributions to the two concerts:

... Mr. Bruckner, organist of His Majesty the Emperor of Austria and Professor of Organ at the Conservatory of Music in Vienna, ended the concert [on 28 April] in a suitable manner with an elegant and skilful improvisation in which the most serious qualities of the true artist were revealed. On the following day, 29 April, a large sympathetic number of people re-gathered for another concert in the beautiful nave of St. Epvre. The Viennese artist, Mr. Bruckner, developed the Austrian national hymn with an uncommon richness of harmony and vigour of execution.[48]

47 See HSABB 1, 104 for this extract from Bruckner's letter to Herbeck, dated Nancy, 30 April 1869; the original is in the Gesellschaft der Musikfreunde library. Alphonse Vilbac (1829-1884) was organist at the church of Saint-Eugène in Paris.

48 From a report in the edition of 2 May; see G-A IV/1, 90f. for a German translation. There was also a general report of the official installation of the organ and the organ concerts two days earlier in L'Espérance (on 30 April).

The reporter for the *Journal de la Meurthe et des Vosges* described Bruckner as 'one of the best organists we have ever heard, a man of the highest taste, of the most comprehensive and most prolific knowledge' and added that the Austrian court was fortunate to possess such an artist.[49]

In the letter to Herbeck mentioned earlier Bruckner also requested three days' extension to his leave as the 'gentlemen who are paying for me' were insistent that he travel to Paris and try out a new organ there. Bruckner asked Herbeck to pass this information on to his students. The firm of Merklin-Schütze clearly wanted to make as much use of Bruckner as possible in the short time available, and Bruckner for his part saw it as an opportunity not to be missed![50]

On Monday 3 May Bruckner gave a concert to an invited audience in Merklin-Schütze's own building. He improvised on a theme from his First Symphony. His most ambitious playing, however, was reserved for a concert on the five-manual Cavaillé-Coll organ in Notre Dame Cathedral, where he improvised on a theme submitted by a Parisian organist, C.A. Chauvet, and evidently impressed some of the leading French composers who were present and congratulated him warmly after the concert. While in Paris he also played on the organs of the churches of St. Sulpice and St. Trinité and visited Auber, Gounod and the firm of Cavaillé-Coll.[51] As his concerts in Paris were not advertised widely and were private rather than public affairs, there were very few reviews, but a report of the first concert in the *Revue et Gazette musicale* drew attention to the high quality of his playing which combined

---

49 From a report in the edition of 1 May; see *G-A* IV/1, 92 for a German translation.

50 See footnote 47.

51 See *HSABB* 1, 109 for a letter from August Neuberger, the managing director of the firm, offering Bruckner assistance in any future tours. The originals of both this letter, dated Paris, 23 June 1869, and Bruckner's letter to Cavaillé-Coll referred to by Neuberger, dated Vienna, 7 June 1869, have been lost.

'enormous skill' with 'much taste' and 'great vigour'.[52]

Bruckner broke his return journey to Vienna by stopping off at Wels where he was elected an honorary member of the *Male Voice Society* and, in a gesture of gratitude, gave an organ recital at the parish church.[53] On his return to Vienna he wrote to his friend Schiedermayr in Linz describing his successful visit and giving a more detailed account of his 'triumph' at Notre Dame where 'one of the greatest organists in Paris' gave him a theme for improvisation which he duly developed in three sections. He also suggested that rehearsals for the premiere of his E minor Mass in Linz later in the year commence immediately.[54]

Bruckner's French successes naturally aroused great interest in both Linz and Vienna and there were several newspaper reports. The reviewer for the *Linzer Zeitung* regarded these successes as an honour not only for Bruckner himself but also:

> ... for the land and place where this affable and unassuming artist was born. The mayor of St. Florian sent Mr. Bruckner the following note to mark this occasion: 'With our heartiest congratulations on your most prestigious successes in Nancy and Paris which are an

---

52 From report in *Revue et gazette musicale* 36 (9 May 1869). There were further reports in *Le ménestrel* 37 (9 May) and *La France musicale*. For further information about Bruckner's French visit, see Josef Burg, 'Anton Bruckners Begegnungen mit der zeitgenössischen Orgel- und Musikwelt in Frankreich' in *Musica sacra* 98 (1978), vol. 2, 80-94; idem, 'Anton Bruckners musikalische Begegnungen in Frankreich' in *MIBG* 14 (1978), 2-19 and 15 (1979), 2-23. For later French critical reaction to Bruckner as a composer, see Josef Burg, 'Der Komponist Anton Bruckner im Spiegelbild der französischen Musikpresse seiner Zeit' in *BJ 1987/88* (Linz, 1990), 95-112. See also footnote 57.

53 Bruckner was sent official confirmation of this honour by August Göllerich senior, the father of Bruckner's later biographer, who was president of the society. See *HSABB* 1, 106 for Göllerich's letter, dated Wels, 23 May 1869; the original is in St. Florian abbey.

54 See *HSABB* 1, 105 for this letter, dated Vienna, 20 May 1869; the original is privately owned. Bruckner was given the theme for improvisation by Charles Alexis Chauvet, the organist of St. Trinité.

enduring credit not only to you and your Austrian fatherland but also to Upper Austria, where you were born, and St. Florian in particular'.[55]

On 20 May there was a short report by Ludwig Speidel in the *Wiener Fremdenblatt*, and on 13 June Hanslick's article, 'Erfolge eines österreichischen Organisten in Frankreich' appeared in the *Neue freie Presse*. As it was Bruckner's intention at this time to pursue his organ-playing career both in Germany / Austria and further afield, he used the opportunity to send a copy of Hanslick's article, in which his organ playing was described as having 'made a huge impression, putting almost all the other performances in the shade' to Barthold Senff, the editor of the *Signale für die musikalische Welt*, in Leipzig.[56] Senff duly obliged and Bruckner's successes were reported in the *Signale* on 24 June. There was a further report in the June issue of J.E. Habert's *Zeitschrift für katholische Kirchenmusik*.[57]

It must have given Bruckner great pleasure to be unanimously elected an honorary member of the *Frohsinn* choral society in June. He was informed of this honour on 9 June and replied a week later with a letter of thanks in which he looked forward to occasions in the future when he would be able to give personal expression

---

55 Extract from report of Bruckner's visits to Nancy and Paris in the *Linzer Zeitung* 118 (26 May 1869), 501. See *G-A* IV/1, 99-102 for full report. See *HSABB* 1, 106 for the letter from Andreas Schlager, the mayor of St. Florian (dated 'before 26 May 1869 by Harrandt).

56 See *G-A* IV/1, 104f. for the complete text of Hanslick's report.

57 For other general information about Bruckner's visits to Nancy and Paris in 1869 and London in 1871, see Mosco Carner, 'Anton Bruckner's Organ Recitals in France and England' in *The Musical Times* 78 (1937), 117ff.; Franz Grasberger, 'Anton Bruckners Auslandreisen' in *ÖMZ* 24 (1969), 630-35; A.C. Howie, 'Bruckner - the travelling virtuoso' in *Perspectives on Anton Bruckner* (Aldershot: Ashgate, 2001), in preparation.

to his gratitude.[58] Later in the year, about a month after the first performance of his E minor Mass in Linz, he was also elected an honorary member of the Linz *Diözesan-Kunstverein*.[59]

The performance of the E minor Mass, part of the consecration ceremony of the Votive Chapel of the new cathedral in Linz on 29 September, was the second major event of the year for Bruckner. But its significance was quite different. While the organ-playing successes marked the beginning of a new chapter in which national and, eventually, international recognition were the end results, the performance of the E minor Mass signalled the end of an old chapter. In spite of the occasional longing glances he cast backwards to Linz in 1869 and in spite of the immense trouble he took over the preparations for this performance, he knew that he had taken a decisive step and that his future lay in Vienna.

Bruckner had completed his Mass in E minor WAB 27, scored for eight-part choir and a wind band consisting of two oboes, two clarinets, two bassoons, four horns, two trumpets and three trombones, three years earlier in November 1866. Its dedicatee was Bishop Rudigier who had commissioned it for the consecration of the *Votivkapelle*, an event which had been postponed from 1866. As Bruckner was now in Vienna he had to ask Johann Baptist Schiedermayr, the dean of Linz Cathedral, to arrange preliminary rehearsals of the work. Writing to him on 20 May, he suggested that the *Frohsinn* and *Musikverein* choirs would have to start rehearsing immediately because of the great difficulty of the Mass.[60] A second letter written a month later was more urgent in tone:

---

58 See *HSABB* 1, 107 for the official letter from *Frohsinn*, signed by Dr. Mathias Weißmann and Dr. Wilhelm Habilhd, and for Bruckner's reply, dated Vienna, 16 June 1869. The original of the former is not extant; the original of the latter is in the *Frohsinn* archive of the Linz *Singakademie*.

59 See *HSABB* 1, 113f. for the letter from the Diocesan Society to Bruckner, dated Linz, 26 October 1869; the original is in St. Florian.

60 See footnote 54.

...Weilnböck wrote to me that Waldeck had said that if the Mass was not studied now with the *Musikverein* students, its performance was out of the question - and they cannot delay rehearsing it until later...[61]

Bruckner was so concerned about the performance of his Mass that he spent a good part of his summer vacation in Linz, rehearsing the work no fewer than 28 times during the months of August and September. On 9 August he received a letter of thanks from the bishop for his sterling efforts in preparing the Mass for its first performance. Rudigier was able to tell Bruckner that the entire *Sängerbund*, some members of *Frohsinn* and other individuals in the town had offered their services.[62] Bruckner had to obtain official permission for a few days' leave from Conservatory duties so that he could direct the final rehearsals of his work. He made this request indirectly through Herbeck when he wrote to him to acknowledge receipt of an honorarium from the Lord Chancellor and to convey Rudigier's invitation to attend the consecration ceremony and the official dinner afterwards.[63] At the open-air performance conducted by Bruckner on 29 September a choir made up of members of *Frohsinn*, *Sängerbund* and the *Musikverein* was accompanied by the military band of the Austro-Hungarian infantry regiment *Ernst Ludwig, Grossherzog von Hessen und bei Rhein Nr. 14*. The press reviews were largely favourable. In his review of the Mass, which appeared in three issues of the *Linzer Volksblatt*, J.E. Habert discussed the work and its performance in some detail, extolling its many fine points but finding fault with what he considered to be oppressive chromaticism

---

61 See *HSABB* 1, 108 for this letter, dated Vienna, 19 June 1869; the original is privately owned. Much of the letter is an outpouring of gratitude to Schiedermayr for his support particularly during his illness two years earlier. See also Chapter 3, pp. 171-72.

62 See *HSABB* 1, 110f. for this letter from Rudigier to Bruckner; the original is in the *ÖNB*.

63 See *HSABB* 1, 111 for this letter, dated Linz, 13 September 1869; the original is in the *ÖNB*. Bruckner said that he was 'terribly harassed' by the rehearsals. We do not know if Herbeck took up the invitation.

in the *Benedictus*. He also observed that there were some difficulties of ensemble and balance at times, noticeably in the *Sanctus*.[64] The reviewer for the *Linzer Zeitung*, probably Moritz von Mayfeld, also provided a detailed account of the work, singling out many fine details of word-setting in the *Credo* movement, drawing particular attention to the "enchanting beauty" of the *Benedictus*, and praising the performance. He was aware that there were several blemishes and miscalculations which were the direct result of the location; all the more reason, however, for an opportunity to hear it 'in a suitable hall so that its rich beauties could be more fully displayed'.[65]

Bruckner received fees amounting to 225 florins after the performance and, in letters to J.B. Schiedermayr and Bishop Rudigier, gave eloquent expression to his gratitude.[66] One of the singers at the first performance, Linda Schönbeck, later recalled the event and the rehearsals preceding it. Bruckner was evidently so pleased with the Linz performance that he conceived the idea of hiring a special train to take all the performers to Vienna so that the Mass could be heard there - but this project did not materialise![67] Sixteen years later, when he sent a copy of his newly completed motet *Ecce sacerdos magnus* WAB 13 to Johann Burgstaller, the Linz Cathedral choir director, Bruckner referred to some revisions he had made to the Mass and

---

64 The full text of the review, which appeared in the *Linzer Volksblatt* on 6,7 and 9 October, is printed in *G-A* III/1, 551-57. See also Chapter 3, page 172, footnote 238 for Göllerich's reference to a report of the first performance by Josef Seiberl (*G-A* III/1, 549ff.) which was not published at the time. Facsimiles of Habert's review can be found in Susanna Taub, *Zeitgenössische Bruckner-Rezeption in der Linzer Printmedien (1855-1869)* (Salzburg, 1987), 85ff.

65 See *G-A* III/1, 557ff. for full text of the report in the *Linzer Zeitung* (6 October 1869), and Susanna Taub, op.cit., 88f. for facsimile. See also Chapter 3, pp. 172-73.

66 See *HSABB* 1, 112f. for these two letters, dated Vienna, 18 and 19 October 1869 respectively; the originals are not extant. See also Chapter 3, page 173, and footnote 240.

67 See *GrBL*, 94. See also Chapter 3, page 173.

recalled that 'the bishop and the Emperor's representative drank a toast to me at the episcopal banquet'.[68]

Bruckner also provided a new work for the consecration ceremony, the gradual *Locus iste* WAB 23 for unaccompanied mixed voices. It was composed on 11 August 1869 and later dedicated to his friend and pupil Oddo Loidol.[69] The motet, a setting of the text from the Mass for the Dedication of the Church, begins with Mozartian phrases but soon introduces characteristic Brucknerian progressions, for instance a striking sequence at the words 'inaestimabile sacramentum' which ends with a descending melodic gesture reminiscent of some phrases in the *Gloria* and *Agnus* movements of the E minor Mass.

Bruckner's third major undertaking of the year was the composition of his Symphony no. "0" WAB 100. Although the dates on the autograph are quite clear, the earliest date being 24 January 1869 and the finishing date 12 September 1869, the accepted view among scholars until the late 20th century was that the work was originally conceived in Linz between October 1863 and May 1864, that is before Symphony no. 1, and that the autograph dates refer to Bruckner's revision of the work during his first year in Vienna.[70] This view appears to have been strengthened by the critical report of the symphony in the Complete Edition which did not appear

---

68 See chapter 5, footnote 253; the complete text of this letter can be found in *HSABB* 1, 264; see also Chapter 3, pp. 173-74 and footnote 243.

69 The gradual was first published as no. 2 of *Vier Graduale* by Theodor Rättig in Vienna in 1886. For a modern edition, see *ABSW* XXI/1, 98f. Further information about this piece is provided in *G-A* IV/1, 108ff. and *ABSW* XXI/2, 86-89.

70 See, for instance, the discussion of the symphony in *G-A* III/1, 226-45 and IV/1, 112. The autograph is in the *Oberösterreichisches Landesmuseum*, Linz, Signatur V17. There are facsimiles of pages from the first movement and final movement in *ABSW* XI/2, 6 and 9.

until thirteen years after the publication of the work in this particular edition.[71] In the past a few commentators had doubts about this chronology, doubts confirmed by more recent studies of the manuscript which have shown that the autograph is not a fair copy of earlier work but represents work carried out in 1869 and, unlike Symphonies 1-4, not revised subsequently.[72]

Bruckner referred to the steady progress he was making on the symphony in a letter to Mayfeld. He also indicated that he had revised the entire middle section of the Andante in accordance with Mayfeld's suggestions. As we know that Bruckner spent Easter in Linz, it is possible that he played the completed parts of the work, including the slow movement, to his friend at that time. A significant amount of work on the symphony was undertaken in Linz during the summer vacation.[73] Bruckner had the score and parts of the work copied in 1870 and he presented it to the Ministry of Culture and Education when he wrote to them in May requesting a grant.[74] Bruckner also showed the work to the court music director, Otto Dessoff,

---

71   Leopold Nowak, ed., *Symphonie D-Moll "Nullte"*, ABSW XI/2 (Vienna, 1981) and XI/1 (Vienna, 1968). Nowak, however, seems to have come to accept the later dating of the symphony.

72   See Alfred Orel, *Anton Bruckner. Das Werk - Der Künstler - Die Zeit* (Leipzig, 1925), 136f.; Hans F. Redlich, 'Bruckner's Forgotten Symphony "No. 0"' in *Music Survey* 2 (1949), 14-20; Paul Hawkshaw, 'The Date of Bruckner's "Nullified" Symphony in D minor' in *19th-Century Music* vi/3 (1982-83), 252-63; Ludwig Finscher, 'Zur Stellung der "Nullten" Symphonie in Bruckners Werk' in Christoph-Hellmut Mahling, ed., *Anton Bruckner. Studien zu Werk und Wirkung. Walter Wiora zum 30 Dezember 1986* (Tutzing: Schneider, 1988), 63-79; Bo Marschner, 'Die chronologischen Probleme der "Nullten" Symphonie Bruckners' in *BJ 1987/88* (Linz, 1990), 53-62; Constantin Floros, 'Zu Bruckners frühen symphonischen Schaffen' in *BSL 1988* (Linz, 1992), 178-90.

73   See *HSABB* 1, 110 for the text of Bruckner's letter to Mayfeld, dated Vienna, 13 July 1869; the original is in the *ÖNB*. In a postscript to his letter to Herbeck in September (see footnote 63), Bruckner wrote that he had 'just finished' his D minor Symphony.

74   See *HSABB* 1, 117 for the text of this letter, dated Vienna, 11 May 1870; the original is in the *Österr. Verwaltungsarchiv*, Vienna

234

before the end of 1872 and there was possibly a 'private' performance. Dessoff is reported to have been astounded by the opening of the symphony and to have commented, 'Where is the main theme then?' His reaction was probably one of the reasons, if not the main one, for Bruckner's setting the work aside at the time and 'nullifying' it later when he organized his manuscripts in 1895. Paul Hawkshaw provides another possible explanation:

> Even though there is no doubt that the opening movement of the Third Symphony [in D minor, begun October 1872] is quite a different work from its counterpart in the nullified D minor symphony, it is certainly possible that the similarity between the two movements has a bearing on the question of when Bruckner decided to reject the earlier one. This similarity may even have been part of his reason for making that decision.[75]

Just as there are echoes of this symphony in later works, the Third, Fifth and Sixth in particular, so no. "0" also draws on ideas from the E minor and F minor Masses and some of the shorter sacred works of the 1860-68 period. Hans Redlich draws attention to one of these reminiscences to bolster his argument that the Symphony was conceived in 1869:

> ... perhaps the most convincing proof, albeit adduced only from internal evidence, of the Symphony's late origin is the twice-repeated quotation (in the Andante) of a mournful motive sung to the words 'Qui tollis peccata mundi' in the *Gloria* of the E minor Mass (composed in 1866). This quotation, surely, would lose much of its significance if it were merely anticipated in an early sketch of 1863-64, i.e. long before the Mass was composed; on the other hand it is very significant if understood as the outcome of Bruckner's spiritual and mental crisis during 1866-7. Indeed, the after-effects of that crisis may have determined the conceptual pattern of the whole work which, if composed after Symphony 1 and the E minor and F minor Masses,

75 Paul Hawkshaw, op.cit., 263.

appears in many respects like a retrograde step after the boldness of Symphony no. 1...[76]

Allusions to the *Benedictus* of the F minor Mass can be found in the coda of the first movement and the beginning of the slow movement; the latter also contains references to the 'Et incarnatus est' from the *Credo*.

No sooner had Bruckner put the finishing touches to the D minor Symphony than he began work on a Symphony in B flat major WAB 142. A page of sketches for a first movement, dated 29 and 31 October 1869, has survived. On the reverse side, dated 1 February 1870, there are other sketches, probably preliminary sketches for the Finale of the Symphony no. 2 in C minor. The sketches of the projected B flat major symphony first movement, which go some way into the second theme group, also show some similarity to the first movement of this C minor symphony to which Bruckner began to give serious attention in October 1871.[77]

1870 did not begin happily for Bruckner. His sister Anna, who had been acting as his housekeeper, died of tuberculosis on 16 January. A week earlier Bruckner wrote to his other sister Rosalie in Vöcklabruck asking her to come to be with Anna as she did not have long to live:

> ... NB. Nani longs to see you. Don't be put off by the cost of travelling. Ignaz and I will do all we can to help you. If you don't come immediately, it will be too late and you will go through the same torment that you experienced when our dear mother died...[78]

---

76 Hans F. Redlich, *Bruckner and Mahler*, in *The Master Musicians* series (London: Dent, rev. ed. 1963), 83.

77 These sketches, Mus. Hs. 6018 in the *ÖNB*, are discussed and transcribed in *G-A* IV/1, 112-18. There is a facsimile of both sides of the sheet between pages 112 and 113.

78 See *HSABB* 1, 115 for this letter, dated Vienna, 9 January 1870; the original is owned privately.

We do not know if Rosalie made the journey from Vöcklabruck. On 16 January Bruckner wrote to her again to give her the sad news of Anna's death and to tell her that the funeral would be two days later, on Tuesday 18 January.[79] Bruckner was able to express something of his grief when he wrote to Johann Schiedermayr, the dean of Linz Cathedral, a few days later:

> ... I am greatly to blame for having allowed her to do all the housework. If I had suspected this, under no circumstances would I have brought my sorely missed dear sister with me to Vienna; indeed I would rather have remained in Linz. As Your Grace is aware of my nervous condition, you will be able to understand better than anyone what I have suffered. If only I could now spend some time away from Vienna...[80]

When Bruckner wrote to Schiedermayr later in the year to send him name-day greetings, he was in a much better frame of mind. He looked forward to spending some time with him in Linz after the end of July when the Conservatory term ended.[81]

There was a considerable improvement in Bruckner's financial position in 1870. On 11 May he wrote to the Ministry of Culture and Education requesting a grant to enable him to devote more time to composition:

---

79 This letter can also be found in *HSABB* 1, 115; the original is privately owned. Maria Anna Bruckner (1836-70) was buried in the Währinger Friedhof, Vienna. Her body was transferred to St. Florian on 18 May 1901. In her article 'Bruckneriana in Vöcklabruck' in *Studien zur Musikwissenschaft* 42 (Tutzing, 1993), 283-322, Elisabeth Maier mentions two photographs of Maria Anna owned by the Hueber family in Vöcklabruck; there is a reproduction of the second photograph on p. 322.

80 See *HSABB* 1, 116 for this letter, dated Vienna, 23 January 1870; the original is privately owned.

81 See *HSABB* 1, 118f. for this letter, dated Vienna, 21 June 1870; the original is in the *ÖNB*.

... The applicant earlier completed a long period of study without any [financial] support. He was fortunate to receive a grant for the first time when he came to Vienna two years ago. A long-lasting nervous illness three years ago, a more recent illness and the death of his youngest sister has burdened him with substantial financial liabilities which that small grant has not cleared. In addition, your humble servant (who has the great honour of being Sechter's successor at the Conservatory) does less private teaching, particularly in the spring, summer and autumn months, because he feels a great urge to compose. Consequently, he ventures to make, albeit with a heavy heart, another urgent request for a grant like the first one. He also takes the liberty of humbly presenting you with his attempt at a new symphony and of respectfully drawing your attention to his recent successes at the organ contest in Nancy and at concerts in Paris.[82]

Karl von Stremayr, who had been appointed Minister of Education in 1870, seems to have been well-disposed towards Bruckner. He allocated him a grant of 400 florins on 7 November, and Bruckner received the money a week later. On 18 October, possibly on Stremayr's recommendation, Bruckner was appointed teacher of theory, piano and organ at the *St. Anna Teacher Training Institute for Men and Women* in Vienna.[83] This resulted in an increase in Bruckner's annual income of 540 florins. Thanks to Herbeck, Bruckner received another 100 florins' remuneration the following month for his services to the *Hofkapelle*.[84]

Bruckner also considered that an improvement in the teaching arrangements at the Conservatory could possibly result in an increased income. Towards the end of the academic year he wrote to the administration asking them to create a second year for the teaching of Harmony (which had been the case previously), because, in his

---

82 See footnote 74.

83 Bruckner's impending appointment is mentioned by Moritz Anton von Becker, who was on the board of the *Gesellschaft der Musikfreunde*, in a letter sent to a friend on 9 July 1870; the original of this letter is in the *ÖNB*. See *HSABB* 1, 117.

84 Herbeck informed Bruckner of this extra income on 20 November; see *ABDS* 1, 54-57.

opinion, it was impossible to get through the syllabus satisfactorily in one year. He also asked that prospective Counterpoint students be allocated to him from the outset and the Counterpoint syllabus be changed so that simple, double, triple and quadruple counterpoint was taught in the first year, and canon and fugue in the final year. Finally, in a postscript, he recommended an increase in the organ teaching hours, using the Berlin Conservatory as a representative example (six hours per week over three years).[85]

Although Bruckner had been made an honorary member of the *Dommusikverein und Mozarteum* in Salzburg in 1868 after his second unsuccessful application for the musical directorship, the promised performance of his Mass in D minor did not materialize until 11 September 1870. According to Auer, some of the annotations in the instrumental parts of the work used for the performance provide an interesting glimpse of players' typical reactions to music they had never seen or heard before, but hardly amount to what Auer described as a 'lack of understanding, indeed hostility with which some of the musicians accompanied the performance under Bruckner's direction'.[86] Auer was also incorrect in asserting that there was 'no review whatsoever of the performance in the Salzburg papers'.[87] Gerhard Walterskirchen quotes from a newspaper report which was by no means negative:

---

85 See *HSABB* 1, 118 for Bruckner's letter to the Conservatory, dated Vienna, 4 June 1870; the original is in the *Gesellschaft der Musikfreunde* library.

86 See *G-A* IV/1, 132. According to Auer, Schimatschek wrote a set of parts in 1867 specifically for Salzburg, and these were no doubt used in 1870. The instrumental parts with annotations 'Linz 1867/68' by the Viennese double bassists Franz Braun and Franz Simandl were those used for the original Linz performances in 1864, the Viennese performance in February 1867 and the Linz performance in January 1868 and were then kept in the *Hofkapelle* for later performances there. The parts used for Salzburg have not been located. My thanks to Paul Hawkshaw for helping to clarify this.

87 See *G-A* IV/1, 132f.

... Although the work as a whole is obviously written from the standpoint of the current direction of modern music and favours the dramatic interpretation and rendering of the sacred mass text throughout, its stylistic unity and, in part, concise musical language are to be praised. As the outstanding parts of the Mass in every respect we would single out the *Kyrie* with its dark, brooding and mysterious atmosphere, the powerful *Credo*, the 'Incarnatus' of which appears to us to be suffused with truly divine inspiration, and the gripping *Agnus Dei* in which the whole of sinful mankind pleads for redemption. The instrumentation of the work requires the full dedication of the entire orchestra, and the performance of this exceedingly difficult Mass was extremely laudable in the short time available in which, to our knowledge, only one rehearsal was possible.[88]

Bruckner had also been active earlier in the year as organist at a concert given by the *Wiener Männergesangsverein* in the *Augustinerkirche* on 14 April, and at concerts in the Vienna *Piaristenkirche*, Linz and Wels.[89] His reply to a letter sent by Th. Mann at the beginning of September is of particular interest because it corroborates information we are able to glean from his recitals in France in 1869 and London in 1871, namely that his recitals consisted largely of improvisations on given themes. Mann, an organist from North Germany, had evidently written to Bruckner for details of the concert he had given in the *Piaristenkirche* on 10 June. Bruckner began by apologizing for not replying sooner - he had just returned from holiday:

---

88 This extract from a review of the Mass which appeared in the *Salzburger Zeitung* 205 (12 September 1870) is quoted by Walterskirchen in 'Bruckner in Salzburg - Bruckner - Erstaufführungen in Salzburg', *IBG Mitteilungsblatt* 16 (1979), 16. Walterskirchen also quotes from a favourable review (in the *Salzburger Chronik* 106, 14 September 1870) of an organ recital which Bruckner gave at the Cathedral on 12 September

89 See *HSABB* 1, 116 for Bruckner's letter to the *Wiener Männergesangsverein*, dated Vienna, 29 March 1870, in which he thanked the male voice choir for their invitation to participate in the concert; the original is in the *Germanisches Nationalmuseum*, Nuremberg. As well as being provisional organist in the *Hofkapelle*, Bruckner played the organ about twice a month at services in the *Augustinerkirche* from 1870 until the late 1880s. Leopold Eder (1823-1902) was music director of the church at the time. For further information, see Walburga Litschauer, 'Bruckner und die Wiener Kirchenmusiker', in *BSL 1985* (Linz, 1988), 99ff.

.. Apart from the five-part Fugue in C minor by Sebastian Bach I improvised everything and so wrote nothing down. First of all I attempted to improvise an introduction from the theme of the Bach fugue, then the Andante in a free style in which I used quiet registration; finally, at the request of many teachers, I improvised a further two movements, the first in free style, the other contrapuntal and fugue-like. That was all. I usually do not prepare anything beforehand but have the theme given to me; this procedure brought me success at the organ congress in Nancy last year as well as in the concerts in Paris, in Notre Dame...[90]

At the request of his friend Karl Waldeck, who had been appointed provisional organist of Linz Cathedral when Bruckner left in 1868, Bruckner formally resigned from the post which had been kept open for him.[91] His last official connection with Linz was now severed but he still visited the town regularly. Indeed, his only composition of the year was written in response to a request from the *Liedertafel Frohsinn* for a choral piece for the anniversary celebrations in 1870. In November 1869 Bruckner had written to the choir committee thanking them for their invitation and informing them that Rudolf Weinwurm had helped him to find a suitable text, a poem by Joseph Mendelssohn.[92] Bruckner provided *Frohsinn* with a highly effective piece for male voices and piano accompaniment, *Mitternacht* WAB 80, which was

---

90 See *HSABB* 1, 119f. for Bruckner's letter to Mann, undated but probably written towards the end of September; the originals of Mann's letter, dated 8 September, and Bruckner's reply are not extant.

91 See *HSABB* 1, 119 for Bruckner's letter to the diocesan authorities in Linz - dated Vienna, 18 July 1870 - in which he thanked them for holding the post open; the original is not extant. See also *HSABB* 1, 120 for a letter from Bruckner probably to Waldeck on his name-day; it is dated Vienna, 4 November 1870, and the original can be found in the *National Museum*, Prague.

92 See *HSABB*, 114 for this letter, dated Vienna, 24 November 1869. The originals of this letter and the initial invitation from Brosch and Weißmann, dated Linz, 13 August 1869, are in the Linz *Singakademie* library. Bruckner was mistaken in believing that Joseph Mendelssohn (1817-56) was Felix Mendelssohn's grandfather.

given its first performance in Linz on 15 May.[93]   Bruckner complemented the atmospheric words - flowers and trees bathed in moonlight, and a gentle breeze - with a pulsating repeated quaver right-hand part in the accompaniment.

On 22 November Bruckner received the news from Ansfelden that he had been granted honorary citizenship of his native village. The letter from the village council referred to his increasing European reputation, some of the lustre of which shone 'in that place where your esteemed father worked tirelessly and conscientiously as a teacher... where you passed the happy days of your youth'.[94] A fortnight later Bruckner received an invitation from the *Währinger Liedertafel* to attend an anniversary meeting of the choir at the *Zum wilden Mann* inn where he would receive a certificate of honorary membership.[95]   And so a year which had begun tragically for Bruckner ended on a much happier note.

For Bruckner the main event of 1871 was undoubtedly his visit to London. First, he had to take part in a competition to determine who would represent Austria in a series of demonstration concerts of the newly installed Willis organ in the Albert Hall. Although it was probably a foregone conclusion that he would win this competition, Bruckner had to abide by the rules. The competition took place on 18 April and he was informed on 24 April that he had been successful. A further official letter from the Chamber of Trade and Industry reminded Bruckner that, starting on

---

93 The autograph of this choral piece, which bears the dedication "gewidmet der Liedertafel 'Frohsinn' in Linz zur Jubiläumsfeier von ihrem Ehrenmitgliede Anton Bruckner", is in the Linz *Singakademie* library. It was first published in 1903 by Doblinger, plate no. D. 2861 The first performance was reviewed in the *Linzer Zeitung*.

94 See *HSABB* 1, 120f. for this letter, dated 'Ansfelden, am Feste der hl. Caecilia, 1870'; reference is also made to a visit to Ansfelden by Bruckner the previous year. The original is in St. Florian.

95 See *HSABB*, 121f. for this letter, dated Währing [a suburb of Vienna], 6 December 1870; the original is in St. Florian. For many years Bruckner played the organ at the special Mass held every year in Währing Parish Church to commemorate the founding of this choral society.

2 August, he would be required to perform 'two programmes each of at least one hour's duration daily between 10 in the morning and 6 in the evening at times specified by the committee'. The fee would be £50 which was inclusive of travel and accommodation costs and would be given to him at the end of his concerts.[96] Although Auer specifies that Bruckner 'received his travelling expenses from Herbeck who had given him advice about the journey', there is no record of this money coming from the *Hofkapelle*. The Lord Chamberlain granted him official leave from the middle of July until the end of September, however.[97] When Bruckner wrote to his former teacher, August Dürrnberger, to inform him that he was using his theory book, *Elementar-Lehrbuch der Harmonie-und Generalbaß-Lehre*, in his new teaching post at St. Anna's Teacher Training Institute, he took it for granted that Dürrnberger would have heard that he was going to London.[98]

Bruckner could not speak a word of English but he knew that a prominent Linz businessman, Anton Reißleitner, was intending to travel to England and he wrote to him on 13 July, suggesting that they travel together. Bruckner planned to leave Vienna on Thursday 20 July, spend an overnight in Linz and travel from there at 9.00 pm on Friday 21 July:

> ... My organ playing in London is scheduled to begin on 2 August. I must be there a week before this, of course, and so I intend to travel from here to Linz next week, Thursday at the latest, and to continue my journey from Linz the following day at 9 in the evening. Please

---

96 See *HSABB* 1, 122ff. for three letters from the Chamber of Trade and Industry (*Handels- und Gewerbekammer für Österreich unter der Enns*) to Bruckner, dated Vienna, 28 March, 24 April and 10 July 1871 resp. The originals of the first two are in St. Florian; the original of the third is in the *ÖNB*.

97 See *ABDS* 1, 57ff.

98 See *HSABB* 1, 123 for this letter, dated Vienna, 16 May 1871 [and not 16 March 1871, as stated in both *ABB*, 114 and *GrBB*, 28]; the original is not extant.

be certain to come and travel with me. I can usually be found on Sundays at the organ in the *Musikverein*. We will be able to make a splendid return journey through Switzerland...[99]

But Reißleitner did not accompany him to England. Bruckner changed his itinerary and travelled to Nuremberg to visit the Zimmermann family whose acquaintance he had made ten years earlier during the 1861 Choir Festival. One of the family, Franz Zimmermann, became his travelling companion and they arrived in London on Saturday 29 July, booking in at Seyd's Hotel in Finsbury Square. The Austrian ambassador in London, Count Apponyi, was contacted about Bruckner's visit and asked to provide all the support necessary.[100]

On the evening of his arrival in London Bruckner went to the Royal Albert Hall to practise. Although work had finished for the day and the steam engines working the bellows could no longer be heated, the manager of the hall allowed Bruckner to play for as long as there was enough steam left. Apparently the manager was so impressed when he heard Bruckner playing and experimenting with the different stops that he gave orders for the engines to be heated again. A number of people gathered round the organ to listen to Bruckner who played on until late evening.

We have very little idea of what Bruckner thought of the Albert Hall organ or how it compared, in his judgment, with the magnificent St. Florian organ.[101] On the

---

99 See *HSABB* 1, 125; the original is in the *ÖNB*.

100 The rough draft of the letter from the Lord Chamberlain's office to Apponyi, dated Vienna, 5 August 1871, is printed in *ABDS* 1, 59f.

101 The new Albert Hall organ, with a specification of 111 stops, was built by Henry Willis (1821-1901), one of the leading English organ builders in the 19th century. Willis, who also supplied organs for the Alexandra Palace, St. Paul's Cathedral (1872), Salisbury Cathedral (1877), Truro Cathedral (1887), Hereford Cathedral (1893) and Lincoln Cathedral (1898), was a great admirer of Cavaillé-Coll whom he met in the late 1840s, and there is a certain amount of French influence in his organs, for instance use of pneumatic levers (in spite of his preference for tracker action), ventils

other hand, the organ recitals at the Royal Albert Hall received a fair amount of coverage from the leading music journals. The following paragraph appeared in the 'Table Talk' column of *The Musical Standard* on 5 August:

> Herr Anton Bruckner, court organist at Vienna, and Professor in the Conservatorium of that city, has arrived in London to play on the great organ of the Royal Albert Hall. Herr Bruckner is celebrated for his classical improvisations on the works of Handel, Bach and Mendelssohn.[102]

The Choir included details of the concerts and programmes from the end of July to the end of September. In the edition for 19 August there is a full list of concerts and programmes from Monday 31 July to Wednesday 16 August, including Bruckner's recitals which contained a mixture of pieces by Bach, Handel and Mendelssohn and a number of improvisations as already intimated in *The Musical Standard*. The details are as follows:

First recital, Wednesday 2 August, 12.00

1 Bach: Toccata in F major
2 Improvisation upon the foregoing
3 Handel: Fugue in D minor
4 Improvisation (original)
5 Bach: Improvisation on Fugue in E major
6 Improvisation on English melodies

Second recital, Thursday 3 August, 3.00

1 Mendelssohn: Sonata no. 1
2 Improvisation upon the foregoing

---

and a predominance of reeds in the full choruses.

102 *The Musical Standard*, vol. I, New Series, no. 366 (London, Saturday 5 August, 1871), 167. There was a similar preview in *The Musical World* 49 / 22 (5 August 1871).

3 Improvisation (original)
4 Bach: Fugue in C sharp minor
5 Improvisation upon the Austrian national anthem
6 Improvisation upon the 'Hallelujah Chorus'

Third recital, Friday 4 August, 3.00

1 Bach: Concerto in A minor
2 Improvisation
3 Improvisation on Weber's 'Freischütz'
4 Bach: Fugue in G minor
5 Improvisation
6 Improvisation on the English national anthem

Fourth recital, Saturday 5 August, 12.00

1 Bach: Concerto in C major
2 Improvisation
3 Improvisation on the song 'Lorelei'
4 Bach: Fugue in G minor
5 Improvisation on Schubert's song 'Fremd bin ich eingezogen'
6 Improvisation upon the 'Hallelujah Chorus'

Fifth recital, Monday 7 August

1 Bach: Toccata
2 Improvisation
3 Improvisation on a theme of Mendelssohn
4 Improvisation on melodies of Schubert
5 Improvisation on Mendelssohn's 'Hunter's Farewell'

Sixth recital, Tuesday 8 August

1 Bach: Fugue in E
2 Improvisation
3 Improvisation on a German melody
4 Improvisation on a theme of Schubert
5 Fugue, improvised
6 Improvisation on the 'Hallelujah Chorus'[103]

---

103 *The Choir* xii / 247 (Saturday 19 August, 1871), 116.

All six programmes have a similar shape - no more than two original pieces, and a preponderance of improvisation on well-known melodies. Significantly, Handel's 'Hallelujah Chorus' appears three times. It is revealing to compare a programme such as this (and it was typical of the English organ recital of the time, in which the emphasis was on both instruction and entertainment and a wide range of transcriptions of orchestral, instrumental, vocal and choral music was juxtaposed with original organ music) with a modern organ recital! There is no doubt that Bruckner had a small and fairly limited repertoire, which, according to Erwin Horn, was a 'shocking limitation for an organist who was acknowledged as Austria's most important representative of his instrument'.[104] But this was a deliberate choice on Bruckner's part. Seven years earlier, when he was contemplating giving organ recitals in Dresden and Leipzig, he had made his position absolutely clear in a letter to Rudolf Weinwurm. There was no point, he said, in going to any particular trouble to prepare a repertoire - 'organists are always poorly paid... it's best to play for nothing and to perform only fantasias etc. without having to memorise anything'.[105]

There is no reason to believe that Bruckner changed his attitude in the intervening years. On the other hand, it would be wrong to assume that Bruckner did not make the necessary technical preparations for his London concerts. Even for his improvisations Bruckner would not have relied completely on the inspiration of the moment. Several of the themes were chosen regularly and the improvisations would have adhered to a similar overall structure each time, although the details would have changed from performance to performance. The *Fugue in D minor* WAB 125, one of the contrapuntal exercises which Bruckner submitted to the *Gesellschaft der Musikfreunde* ten years earlier, in November 1861, gives us some idea, albeit in embryonic form, of what a Bruckner improvised fugue would have been

---

104 Erwin Horn, *BSL 1995* (Linz, 1997), 112.

105 From letter dated Linz, 1 March 1864. See *HSABB* 1, 41f.

like, containing as it does examples of 'false entries', diminution, augmentation, inversion and organ points.

The only English organist to play during this recital series was William T. Best who, like Bruckner, was renowned for his improvisations and virtuoso playing and was greatly admired for his impressive pedal technique particularly in Bach's organ works. In fact, Best gave the inaugural recital on 18 July.[106] Other foreign organists included Heintze, Lohr, Mailly, Saint-Saëns, Lindemann, Lux, Tod and Henrici.[107] It is clear that Bruckner was misinformed when he was advised that he would have to play twice daily. Although there is no mention in the English press of an organ competition being held as part of this recital series, Bruckner's later report to Göllerich suggests that there must have been some kind of unofficial improvisation contest.[108] There is a high degree of chauvinism in the press reports of the recitals. The main criticism, understandably, concerned the lack of any British representative apart from Best. In his review of the first series of recitals, the reporter for *The Musical Standard* was extremely critical of the foreign organists, although Bruckner fared better than Heintze or Lohr:

---

106 The recital by William Best (1826-1897), which included Bach's Prelude and Fugue ('St. Anne's') BWV 552, Best's arrangement of Handel's Organ Concerto no. 1, Mendelssohn's Organ Sonata no. 1, and pieces by S.S. Wesley, Edward Hopkins and Henry Smart, was reviewed in *The Musical Times* xv / 342 (1 August 1871), 171. The report of the same recital in *The Choir* xii / 245 (Saturday 5 August, 1871), 88, referred to a review in the *Guardian* - '... though it evidently afforded extreme pleasure to a tolerably numerous audience in the low-priced parts of the hall, from a musical point of view, it would have been more satisfactory had Mr. Best thought more of the music before him than upon the instrument upon which he was playing...'

107 Details of their programmes can be found in *The Choir* xii / 248, 249, 251 and 254 (Saturday 26 August, Saturday 2 September, Saturday 16 September and Saturday 7 October, 1871).

108 See *G-A* IV/1, 147f.

Upon the completion of Mr. Willis's organ at the Albert Hall we were promised a series of performances by professors of high standing, both British and foreign. To what extent this promise has been fulfilled we propose now to print out. In the first place, the inaugural performance was given nearly a month ago, yet the sole representative of our native professors has been Mr. W.T. Best. It is hardly necessary to state that a better could not be found, nor that the most refined taste could take the least exception to any part of Mr. Best's ten or twelve programmes. Nevertheless England can boast of other performers of deservedly high repute, men who have in some cases made a certain branch of the art their 'speciality'. Will the London amateurs and the foreign visitors to the Exhibition have no opportunity of hearing the renowned improvisations of one professor or the equally celebrated fugue playing of another before the season quite dies out and no auditors are left for any music but the dash of the waves on the shingle or the sound of the wind through the pine branches? To this extent the Council has failed to fulfil its organ programme. Another part of the scheme, however - the presentation of foreign organ-players - has been carried out to the letter if not in the spirit. Recitals have been given by Mr. G.W. Heintze from the Conservatorium, Stockholm, by Herr Johann Löhr [sic] of Pesth and by Herr Anton Brückner [sic], court organist at Vienna. Of these performances it may be said that, if they failed to satisfy the critic, they must have gladdened the heart of the true born Briton. Unfortunately in England artistic sympathies cannot always blend with patriotic feelings, but we confess to have experienced emotions of thankfulness, not to say glorification, at hearing a performance by Mr. Best at 3 o'clock, after attending a recital by one of his continental rivals at 12. Modest mediocrity may be briefly passed over - we advert therefore no more definitely to Mr. Heintze or Herr Löhr [sic] - but the playing of Herr Anton Brückner [sic] deserves a word or two. We were advised by the official programme that Herr Brückner's [sic] 'strong points were classical improvisations on the works of Handel, Bach and Mendelssohn'. We were therefore not altogether unprepared to find that the playing of Mendelssohn's No. 1 Sonata was a 'weak point', and such indeed was the case. It is only charitable to suppose that Herr Brückner [sic] had not the advantage of a previous trial of the organ, especially as he evinced rather more control over the instrument in his succeeding improvisations. But in the course of our struggles after musical experience we have been present at more than one competitive performance for a church organistship; to the exhibitions of certain of the candidates there may be likened more or less the recitals of the eminent foreign professors at the Albert Hall. We trust the authorities will not disregard these remarks - that they will bring forward some of our good English organists, and a more careful selection from those eminent in other countries.[109]

In the 'Table Talk' column in the same issue of *The Musical Standard* the following report appeared:

> The foreign organists of note who have given performances on the Albert Hall instrument are Herr J. Lohr, from Pesth, Herr C.W. Heintze, from Stockholm, Herr A. Bruckner, from Vienna, and M. Mailly, from Belgium. Bach's preludes and fugues have formed an important item in all the programmes.[110]

In the following issue of *The Musical Standard*, the reporter renewed his attack on the choice of foreign artists in the 'Table Talk' column:

> It is stated that the selection of organists for the public performances on the organ at the Albert Hall is made by the Hon. Seymour Egerton, the well-known conductor of the Wandering Minstrels. Whether this gentleman possesses any aptitude for this special duty is a matter of serious doubt, when the *fiasco* of the foreign organists who have already played is taken into consideration. The so-called 'International Congress of Organists' will, we fear, be an entire

---

109 From the article 'Organ Recitals at the Albert Hall' in *The Musical Standard*, vol. I, New Series, no. 367 (London, Saturday 12 August, 1871), 188f. See earlier (p. 258) , however, for a report of Bruckner's earlier practice on the organ. The reviewer for *The Musical World* 49 / 33 (August 1871) was equally unfriendly. Michael Musgrave remarks that 'Bruckner was clearly a victim of anti-German feeling'; see his *The Musical Life of the Crystal Palace* (Cambridge, 1995), 256, footnote 19.

110 Ibid., 197.

failure.[111]

The reporter had not got his facts right, however. A letter in *The Orchestra* from Col. Henry Y.D. Scott, the secretary of the Royal Commissioners specially appointed by Queen Victoria to supervise the International Exhibition in London, was specifically intended to correct faulty information and clear up misunderstandings:

> ... Her Majesty's Commissioners did not, as you imagine, issue any advertisement inviting foreign organists to play. It was the wish of the Commissioners that the opening of the organ should be signalised by performances by artists representing the various musical schools of Europe. With this view they requested each foreign Government taking part in the International Exhibition to name an organist to represent his country on the occasion, and all the gentlemen with whom engagements have been made were nominated by their respective Governments in compliance with this request.[112]

In any case one has to put a question mark against the musical judgment of *The Musical Standard* reporter. While he had more positive things to say about Lux's recitals,[113] he failed to mention Saint-Saëns's recitals. The writer of a letter to the editor in the 'Correspondence' column of the September 30 issue of *The Choir* also suggested that a 'congress of *English organists* would... have yielded more satisfactory results' but conceded that the foreign organists had not had the same opportunity as Best of becoming acquainted with the organ:

---

111 From the 'Table Talk' column in *The Musical Standard* vol. I, New Series, no. 368 (London, Saturday 19 August, 1871), 209.

112 From *The Orchestra* xvi / 412 (Friday 18 August, 1871), 315.

113 'Reports' in *The Musical Standard* Vol. I, New Series, no. 371 (London, Saturday 9 September, 1871), 239.

... it must be mentioned that their only chance of making themselves acquainted with the organ, or preparing for their performances, has been during an hour or two after six o'clock in the evening...[114]

The reporter for *The Orchestra*, on the other hand, spoke of these recitals in glowing terms.[115] In an earlier article he provided a much more sympathetic account of the respective merits of Heintze, Lohr and Bruckner and showed that he had some knowledge of the organ:

... The first who has played was Herr Heintze of Stockholm, a young man still *in statu pupillari*. He executed some of the masterpieces of Sebastian Bach, some of the sonatas by Mendelssohn, some fugues and fantasias by Topfer, Merkel, Hesse, Kohler [sic], Kuhmstedt, Markul [sic] and others of the modern German school. His performances were marked by much truth and considerable precision; but he failed in that iron, *staccato* touch which is essential for clear part-playing in the Albert Hall...

In Herr Johann Lohr, of Pesth, we meet with a good musician and a player of considerable power. He is a combination of the new and the old schools. He gave us extracts from the symphonies of Liszt, marches by Chopin, songs by Schubert, pieces by Gottschalk, Markul [sic], Pitoch and many others, interspersed with compositions by Beethoven and Mozart, together with the more distinctive organ music of Handel and Bach. Herr Lohr had great executive capabilities, and his ambitious attacks on the sonatas of Beethoven, and more especially so on the monstrous vagaries of the Abbé Liszt, proved in the end more astonishing than pleasing. He suffered from the same disadvantages as Herr Heintze, and certainly did not meet the requirements of the Hall, nor those of the instrument. There was much good playing, but nothing perfect.

The Court Organist of Vienna, Anton Bruckner, was third at the organ, and announced specially as great in 'extemporaneous

---

114 The letter, dated London, 20 September 1871 and signed 'A Lover of Justice', was printed in *The Choir* xii / 253, 214.

115 Article in *The Orchestra* xvi / 413 (Friday 25 August, 1871), 329f.

252

performances'. We were told that 'Herr Bruckner's strong points are classical improvisations on the works of Handel, Bach and Mendelssohn'. He has given us a grand extempore Fantasia, which although not very original in thought or design, was clever, remarkable for its canonic counterpoint, and for the surmounting of much difficulty in the pedal passages. There can be nothing said extemporaneously upon the National Anthem of Austria, and still less upon the Hallelujah Chorus of Handel, nor do we think any improvisation with any effect can be given upon the toccatas of Bach or the sonatas of Mendelssohn. Great composers exhaust their themes. Nothing can be added to the Hallelujah Chorus, nothing to a toccata of Sebastian Bach...[116]

According to Göllerich, a letter sent from the Austrian embassy in London to the Chamber of Commerce in Vienna after Bruckner's third concert spoke of the 'extraordinary successes of the court organist Professor Bruckner sent by you'.[117] Professor Paul Stöving, who carried out some research on Bruckner's organ recitals in London for another of Bruckner's biographers, Franz Gräflinger, made the point that 'none of the important newspapers - *Times, Standard, Daily News*' - mentioned the composer or even the recitals, but added that this was hardly surprising since 'August is the quietest month for music in London, and the newspapers and people were concerned with more important matters - political controversies, the aftermath of the Franco-Prussian War'.[118] Bruckner seems to have been sufficiently concerned about the lack of a report in the leading newspaper, *The Times*, whose music critic was in Germany at the time, to make an approach through the vice-consul, Dr. von Pinsio, to the exhibition committee with the purpose of rectifying this 'anomaly'. When Dr. von Pinsio replied, inviting him to submit an article of his own, Bruckner

---

116 From article 'Concert-Organ Playing at the Royal Albert Hall' in *The Orchestra* xvi, 411 (Friday August 11, 1871), 297f.

117 See *G-A* IV/1, 157.

118 See *GrBL*, 78.

clearly had second thoughts.

Bruckner's visit to London included some engagements at the Crystal Palace. He did some sight-seeing in his 'free' week between the Albert Hall and Crystal Palace concerts and particularly enjoyed travelling on the large London buses.

The Crystal Palace had been erected by Joseph Paxton for the Great Exhibition in Hyde Park in 1851 and had then been removed to a new site at Sydenham, about ten miles away, and officially 're-opened' there by Queen Victoria on 10 June 1854. The fourteen organs which had been built specifically for the 1851 Great Exhibition had also been relocated elsewhere. The instrument played by Bruckner when he gave his recitals there in the second half of August 1871 had been built by Gray and Davison for the first of the annual Handel Festivals in 1857. Some new steps were added in 1871 and 1882. Like the Royal Albert Hall organ, the influence of Cavaillé-Coll was clearly discernible, in the use of combination pedals, the introduction of modern French stops and the employment of several mixtures and reeds. According to Anthony Bird,

> The purpose of the rebuilt Crystal Palace was to combine recreation with education in a manner which the late twentieth century might consider daunting. A vast concert hall with room for an audience of 4,000, and almost as many performers, dominated by a huge organ... occupied the central space at the intersection of nave and main transept'.[119]

In his description of the organ in 1857 George Macfarren commented that the aim

---

119 Anthony Bird, *Paxton's Palace* (London, 1976), 130f. The specification of the large organ, first published in *The Musical World* 35 (1857), 391ff., is also printed in Nicholas Thistlethwaite, *The making of the Victorian organ* (Cambridge, 2/1993), 477ff. and Musgrave, op.cit., 148f. The specification of a second, smaller but still substantial, instrument installed by J.M. Walker and Sons in the Concert Room of the Crystal Palace in 1868 is given in Musgrave, op.cit., 156ff. It was evidently intended for participation in choral and orchestral music, also soloistically and in concertos.

254

of the organ builders 'has been to produce an instrument, the varied qualities of which should combine all desirable musical beauty with force and grandeur of tone sufficient to qualify it for the part it is specially designed to bear in this great commemoration'.[120]

Bruckner's recitals in the Crystal Palace on 19, 21, 22, 23 and 28 August were in the context of lengthy popular concerts. A report of the final concert (28 August) in *The Musical Standard* mentions a recital by 'Herr Anton Bruckner, Court Organist of Vienna, who has already played in the Albert Hall. One of Mendelssohn's sonatas opened the programme, which included Bach's Fugue in E major and an improvisation on Handel's "Hallelujah"...'[121]

The second Crystal Palace concert, on 21 August, took the form of a 'Great National German Festival'. It began at 2 pm with Weber's *Oberon* overture, continued with songs by Abt, Meyerbeer, Handel, Speyer, Mozart and Schubert, after which Bruckner played an improvisation on Schubert's song 'Leise flehen meine Lieder' and, by popular request, an improvisation on the popular German song, 'Nacht am Rhein' which, according to Bruckner's own account, resulted in a tumultuous reception and even a proposal of marriage from an admiring female member of the audience![122]

There was an estimated audience of 70,000 at his third recital on Tuesday 22

120 G.A. Macfarren, *Programme of Arrangements for the Handel Festival, 1857*; quoted by Musgrave in op.cit., 145f.

121 From 'Reports' in *The Musical Standard*, Vol. I, New Series, no. 370 (London, Saturday 2 September, 1871), 229.

122 See *G-A* IV/1, 162. See also Käthe Braun-Prager, 'Mei liabe Lady, dös ist nix!', *Neues Österreich*, 4 August 1957, and 'Anton Bruckner in London', *Wiener Zeitung*, 15 August 1958. Evidently the lady in question asked Bruckner to return soon but to learn English in the meantime. Bruckner's retort was that he was too old to learn English and that, if she wished to speak to him again, she should learn German!

August. After his fourth recital, on Wednesday 23 August, Bruckner wrote to his Linz colleague, Moritz von Mayfeld, from Seyd's hotel:

> ... Just finished. Have given ten concerts, six in the Albert Hall, four in the Crystal Palace. Tremendous applause, always unending. Encores required, i.e. often I had to play two extra improvisations at the end... Many compliments, congratulations, invitations. Manns, the conductor of the Crystal Palace concerts, told me that he was amazed and that I must come again soon and send him some of my compositions. Dr. Spinsio [sic] sends his greetings. I will soon be returning by way of Brussels, but I will not be playing any more as I am too tired and overwrought. I will keep Germany, Berlin, also Holland and Switzerland for later...

As a postscript he added:

> Yesterday I played to an audience of 70,000 and had to give an encore, at the Committee's request. I wanted to give due respect to such great applause. On Monday I played with similar success in the concert...
> NB Unfortunately, the 'Times' critic is in Germany, with the result that hardly anything has been written about me yet. Please be so good as to inform the 'Linzer Zeitung', i.e. Dr. Dutschek.[123]

Although Bruckner informed Mayfeld that he did not intend to give any more concerts, the report in *The Musical Standard* alluded to above makes it clear that he played for a fifth time at the Crystal Palace on Monday 28 August. A programme of the 'Popular Ballad Concert' which consisted of ballads and duets mainly by English composers includes the following:

---

123 See *HSABB* 1, 126 for this letter. There is a facsimile of the original (which is not extant) in *G-A* IV/1, between pages 160 and 161.

At Three o'clock,

Performance on the Festival Organ

By Herr Anton Bruckner

(Court Organist of Vienna)

1. Sonata .... Mendelssohn
2. Improvisation .... Bruckner
3. Fugue, E major.. Bach
4. Improvisation, 'Halleluja'.. Handel
5 Improvisation .... Bruckner[124]

From Bruckner's own recollections as related to Göllerich, it would appear that he might even have played a sixth time at the Crystal Palace - but there is no reference to this in any programme. It was suggested that he undertake a concert tour throughout England either then or the following year. At that point, however - as his letter to Mayfeld makes clear - he was understandably exhausted and his only wish was to return to Vienna. During his time in London he made several English friends and obviously earned the respect of several English organists including W.T. Best, who gave him a copy of his *Collection of Organ Pieces composed for Church Use* as a gift, and James Coward, the resident Crystal Palace organist, who presented him with a copy of his *Ten Glees and a Madrigal* with the dedication 'Anton Bruckner from James Coward with best wishes. Organist of the Crystal Palace and Sacred Harmonic Society'.[125] He was most impressed with the friendliness of his English hosts and showed a great interest in English organs with their concave pedal

---

124 A copy of this programme as well as a copy of Mendelssohn's F minor Sonata with an indication of the registration in the Adagio and the additional note 'Kryst.' were part of Bruckner's estate. See *G-A* IV/1, 164f.

125 According to *G-A* II/1, 338 and 340 and IV/1, 157 and 160, these gifts from Best and Coward were part of Bruckner's estate.

arrangement.

At the end of his series of English recitals there was an extremely complimentary review in *The Morning Advertiser*:

> Professor Bruckner from Vienna.
>
> When the International Exhibition and Royal Albert Hall were opened, the Council issued an invitation to artists of all nations to come over and test the excellence of the great organ. Amongst those who accepted this invitation was Herr Anton Bruckner, Court Organist and Professor at the Conservatoire. The executions by this disciple of art are truly excellent, and quite worthy of the father-land of Haydn and Mozart. Herr Bruckner executes the classical compositions of Bach, Mendelssohn and others with great easiness which leaves the hearer nothing to desire, and which would certainly even satisfy the composers themselves in the highest degree. But where Herr Bruckner excels is in his improvisations, in which you will find a great easiness and abundance of idea, and the ingenious method by which such idea is carried out - grave or solemn, melodious or charming, brilliant or grand - is very remarkable. The London public has fully acknowledged Herr Bruckner's perfect execution, and many have expressed a hope that this first visit may not be the last. We join in. Bruckner may publish some of his most successful compositions for the benefit and enjoyment of the musical public who, we are sure, would be very pleased to become better acquainted with the works of this thorough artist.[126]

In its report of Bruckner's successful London visit, the *Linzer Zeitung* reproduced *The Morning Advertiser* review as a typical example of the friendly reception of Bruckner on the part of the English press.[127]

Pursuing Manns's suggestion that he should send some of his own music to be

---

126 From *The Morning Advertiser* (1 September, 1871); reprinted in *G-A* IV/1, 168f.

127 *Linzer Zeitung* (16 September, 1871); see *G-A* IV/1, 170ff.

performed in London, Bruckner wrote an exploratory letter to the Committee of the International Exhibition on 3 January 1872. In his reply, Colonel Henry Scott, the secretary of the Committee, asked Bruckner to send the score and parts of one of his works so that it could be considered for performance at the opening of the Exhibition.[128] Bruckner decided to send the D minor Mass to England. Although the score was accessible (in St. Florian), the parts were still in Salzburg where the Mass had been performed two years earlier. Bruckner had to write to the *Dom-Musikverein und Mozarteum* to request the return of the parts.[129] On 30 April Bruckner informed the Exhibition's Executive Committee that he had sent the score of the Mass to England, and its receipt was acknowledged by J.A. Wright, the Committee secretary.[130] But the work was not performed and there are no records of any preliminary rehearsals. Four (!) years after his London recitals Bruckner eventually received a medal from the Exhibition Committee in belated recognition of his efforts.[131] Reports that he had been awarded a prize by Queen Victoria were totally unfounded.

Bruckner maintained contact with his travelling companion, Franz Zimmermann, for some time. Zimmermann wrote to him on 1 December 1871, recalling their stay in London and mentioning that, on a recent business trip, he had opened a copy of the *Illustrierte Zeitung* by chance and read an article on the Albert Hall organ in

128 See *HSABB* 1, 132 for Scott's reply to Bruckner's letter, dated 12 March 1872; it was first published in *G-A* IV/1, 173. The originals of both letters are not extant.

129 See *HSABB* 1, 132f. for this letter, dated Vienna, 23 March 1872; the original is in the *Konsistorialarchiv*, Salzburg. It was first published in the *IBG-Mitteilungsblatt* 16 (December 1979).

130 See *HSABB* 1, 133 for Wright's letter, dated 10 June 1872; it was first published in *G-A* IV/1, 174. The originals of both letters are not extant.

131 See *HSABB* 1, 157 for the letter from the Austrian Chamber of Commerce, dated 13 July 1875, enclosing the medal; it was first published in *G-A* IV/1, 167f. The original is not extant.

which Bruckner's name was mentioned.[132]   In another letter to Bruckner the following year, Zimmermann thanked him for his kind invitation to stay in his apartment during the forthcoming Vienna World Exhibition and wished him every success with his plans to undertake a concert tour of England. There is no indication that the correspondence between them continued beyond August 1873 when Zimmermann wrote again in response to a letter from Bruckner, who was intending to visit him and his family on his way back to Vienna from Bayreuth.[133]

At the end of his exhausting but stimulating visit to London Bruckner returned to Vienna by way of Brussels, not Switzerland as originally planned. Part of September was spent at St. Florian, a haven of peace and quiet after his busy concert schedule, and he resumed his duties at the Conservatory and the *Hofkapelle* at the end of the month. The remaining months of 1871 were clouded by the repercussions of what appears to have been an innocent remark Bruckner had made to one of the young women students at St. Anna's in Vienna earlier in the year. Evidently he had addressed her as 'lieber Schatz', stroked her hand gently and praised her work. Her colleague whom he had scolded in a fit of bad temper had spitefully reported the matter to the school authorities. Disciplinary action was commenced and there were moves to dismiss him and allow Eduard Kremser, who was already employed by the Institute, to take his classes.[134]   He was completely exonerated, however, and Stremayr, the Minister of Education, made it clear that there was no reason why 'the well-known organist Bruckner' should be dismissed from organ and piano teaching.

132 See *HSABB* 1, 131f. The original of this letter has not survived; it was first printed in *G-A* IV/1, 174f. The article appeared in the 18 November 1871 issue of the Leipzig paper.

133 See *HSABB* 1, 136 and 138 for Zimmermann's letters to Bruckner, dated Nuremberg, 19 September 1872 and 7 August 1873; they were first printed in *G-A* IV/1, 176ff. Bruckner's letters have not survived and the originals of Zimmermann's letters are not extant.

134 See *G-A* IV/1, 180ff. for a letter, possibly from Moritz Alois von Becker (1812-1887), the school superintendent, to Karl von Stremayr, dated 5 October 1871.

260

There is an implied rebuke of Vernaleken, a director of the Institute, in the postscript of Stremayr's letter:

> With the removal of Bruckner, a leading organ celebrity and reliable teacher at the Conservatory, nothing would be accomplished as it is most probable that his teaching duties would be transferred to Kremser. It is not even known if he [Kremser] can play the organ. Vernaleken appears to have made light of the whole matter.[135]

Bruckner seems to have felt it necessary to procure a reference from Joseph Hellmesberger, the director of the Conservatory, in the midst of this affair. Hellmesberger's reference underlined Bruckner's fine teaching, the first-rate examination results of his pupils and the excellent discipline he maintained in his classes.[136]

Unfortunately, the 'St. Anna affair' was reported in several newspapers, for instance the Linz *Tagespost* on 12 October and the Steyr *Alpen-Bote* on 15 October, without any indication that Bruckner had been completely exonerated of any wrongdoing. As he was understandably concerned that the whole picture should be presented, he wrote to the editor of the *Tagespost*, enclosing a copy of a testimonial he had received from Robert Niedergesäß, another director of the Institute:

> The directors have pleasure in declaring that in the Training Institute for Women Teachers during the school year 1870/71 Mr. Anton Bruckner, the imperial court organist, fulfilled his piano teaching duties with outstanding success, demonstrated excellent teaching skills and distinguished himself at all times in adopting a strict moral

---

135 Theodor Vernaleken (1812 - c.1897) worked for the Ministry of Education until 1870 and was responsible for the organization of secondary schools. He was appointed a director at St. Anna's in 1870. See *G-A* IV/1, 186ff. for the text of Stremayr's letter, dated Vienna, 17 October 1871.

136 See *G-A* IV/1, 191 for the text of this reference, dated Vienna, 12 October 1871.

behaviour, demonstrating a devotion and enthusiasm for the job and revealing those qualities which bring credit to artists and teachers.[137]

The article in the Linz *Tagespost* also contained an erroneous assertion that Bruckner, anxious about his future, had written to the King of Bavaria enquiring about a position at a Munich Institute. Writing to his friend Schiedermayr in Linz on 21 October, Bruckner stated categorically that he had not 'petitioned Munich'. Although a letter from Hermann Heiß, the Privy Councillor, to Herbeck had made it perfectly clear that he had been completely exonerated, and Bruckner had been informed earlier that he could resume teaching in the male section of the Institute, he had no desire now to continue teaching in the female section as a result of what had happened, in spite of the loss of income. He had informed the Minister of Education accordingly.[138]

In a letter to another Linz friend, Karl Waldeck, written on the same day, he thanked him for his support during what had been an extremely difficult time and added: 'better 500 florins less than to have to put up with such villainy'.[139] A week later Bruckner wrote again to Waldeck to reassure him that, in spite of what had happened, he had no intention of returning to Linz with a view to becoming cathedral organist again![140]

---

137 This testimonial is dated Vienna, 17 October 1871. See *G-A* IV/1, 182-85 for extracts from the newspaper articles and for the testimonial. See *HSABB* 1, 129 for the text of Bruckner's letter to the *Tagespost* (undated) which also appeared in the *Alpen-Bote* on 22 October.

138 See *HSABB* 1, 126f. for Bruckner's letter to Schiedermayr; the original is in the *ÖNB*. Also see *HSABB* 1, 128 for Heiß's letter to Herbeck, dated Vienna, 21 October 1871; the original is also in the *ÖNB*.

139 See *HSABB* 1, 127f. for this letter; the original is not extant. It was first printed in the *Neue musikalische Presse* 14 (1905), no. 17.

140 See *HSABB* 1, 129 for this letter, dated Vienna, 28 October 1871; the original is in the *ÖNB*.

262

At the beginning of November Bruckner gave a fuller account of the whole affair to Moritz v. Mayfeld, providing the more recent information that

> ... yesterday Herbeck told me he had received a second letter from Privy Councillor Hermann which states that the Ministry has not dismissed me from the female section of the Institute and hopes that I will keep my position there, although I have made it clear that I have lost all desire to stay.

The events of October had demoralized him, teaching at the moment was a greater strain than usual, and the need to do so much teaching in order to make ends meet left him little time to compose.[141]

The events of 1871 stimulated great interest within church music circles in Germany and Austria. Franz Xaver Witt, the leading figure in the German Caecilian reform movement in Catholic church music, considered that Bruckner's organ success in London had overshadowed the contribution made by the equally fine German representative, Eduard Tod from Stuttgart, and wished to scotch the rumour that Queen Victoria had granted first prize to the Austrian organist. He also mentioned the St. Anna affair in the first of two articles. J.E. Habert, the founder of the Austrian Caecilian Society but, incidentally, not on good terms with Witt, said that he had no part in the rumour of Bruckner's 'prize-winning' exploits and chided Witt for not making it clear that Bruckner had been completely exonerated of any misdemeanour. Witt, to his credit, did this in a second article. Ignaz Traumihler from St. Florian, a keen Caecilian, had sent him a copy of Niedergesäß's testimonial which had already been printed in Austrian newspapers.[142]

---

141 See *HSABB* 1, 130 for this letter, dated Vienna, 2 November 1871; the original is in the *ÖNB*.

142 Witt's two articles appeared in the *Fliegende Blätter für katholische Kirchenmusik*, vols. 2 and 5 (October 1871), and Habert's article in the *Zeitschrift für katholische Kirchenmusik* (October 1871).

It is hardly surprising that Bruckner wrote very little, if anything at all, during the first nine months of 1871. A performance of the F minor Mass had not yet materialized and the St. Anna affair had clouded what had otherwise been a very successful year for him as an organ virtuoso.[143] The fact that he was still feeling somewhat raw emotionally would explain his reaction to a caricature of himself which appeared in a Viennese cartoon paper, *Die Bombe*, on 22 October and caused some amusement among his colleagues, including Herbeck.[144] Nevertheless he began work, or resumed work if one regards an earlier sketch dated 1 February 1870 as the first workings of the Finale, on his Symphony no. 2 in C minor WAB 102 in October, commencing with the first movement on the 11th of the month. This symphony occupied him for the best part of a year. In the meantime, he had to settle once again into the regular routine of a Conservatory teacher and occasional *Hofkapelle* organist. His reputation as an organist had grown enormously, of course, and a letter sent to him by the Moravian organ builder, Franz von Pistrich, in October/November is probably typical of many others he would have received soliciting his advice and opinion. His reply suggests that he was either not particularly impressed or had other more pressing matters on his mind:

> ... I did not return to Vienna until October. Perhaps you should approach the Vienna Musikverein with your new artistic invention. In my opinion, it would be more advantageous to make contact with the general secretary, Julius Zellner. I would also be able to see it there...[145]

---

143 In the first part of his letter to Mayfeld (see footnote 139 above), Bruckner stated that the *Singverein* would not be able to rehearse the Mass before 21 November.

144 Bruckner also makes reference to this in his letter to Mayfekl (see footnotes 139 and 141).

145 See *HSABB* 1, 131 for this letter, dated Vienna, 3 November 1871. It was first published in *BJ 1980* (Linz 1980), 129, where there is also a facsimile of the original (located in the *Moravian Museum*, Brno). Pistrich's letter to Bruckner is not extant.

264

At the end of the year, on 31 December, Bruckner played the organ part in a performance of the first part of Liszt's oratorio, *Christus*, conducted by Anton Rubinstein in the large *Musikverein* hall. Liszt was present and, according to remarks allegedly made to Göllerich, was not happy with Bruckner's playing.[146]

One of the highlights of 1872 for Bruckner was undoubtedly Richard Wagner's visit to Vienna in May to raise funds for his Bayreuth project. Bruckner was a member of the deputation which met Wagner at the *Westbahnhof* station on 6 May and, accompanied by Otto Kitzler and Ignaz Dorn,[147] attended the concert given by Wagner on 12 May which included performances of Beethoven's 'Eroica' Symphony and excerpts from *Die Walküre*, *Tannhäuser* and *Tristan*. The following month, on the 16th, Bruckner conducted the first performance of his F minor Mass in the *Augustinerkirche*. He had to pay the cost involved, 300 florins, out of his own pocket and experienced many difficulties in rehearsal but no doubt considered all the effort and money well spent in view of the favourable critical and public reaction.[148]

Bruckner spent the rest of the summer working on his Second Symphony and completed it in St. Florian in September.[149] He also visited the Mayfelds' country

---

146   See August Göllerich, *Franz Liszt* (Berlin, 1908[?]), 152f.

147   Dorn died about a fortnight later. A special memorial service was held in the *Bürger-Versorgungshaus Kapelle* in Vienna on 25 June. See *HSABB* 1, 135 for Bruckner's letter to Eduard Kremser, dated Vienna, 25 June 1872, in which he thanks Kremser for his obituary of Dorn in *Vaterland* (20 June 1872). See also Chapter 3, pp. 87f. for further information about Dorn and his relationship with Bruckner.

148   See Chapter 3, pp. 175-79 for further details about the composition and performance of the F minor Mass. Bruckner conducted a second performance of the Mass in the *Hofkapelle* later in the year, on Sunday 8 December.

149   The autograph of the score is in the *ÖNB* (Mus.Hs. 19.474) and it provides a clear picture of the progress made on the work. The first movement was begun on 11 October 1871 and completed on 8 July 1872 in Vienna. The Trio was sketched on 16 July and completed on 18 July; no dates are

home in Schwanenstadt during the summer vacation. He and Betty v. Mayfeld played through the work at the piano and the composer was delighted with his partner's contribution. After the parts had been copied, the Vienna Philharmonic conducted by Otto Dessoff, with some assistance from Bruckner, gave the symphony a trial run. The reaction among the players was mixed. The cellist David Popper was enthusiastic, but there was a hostile response from the conductor and the majority of the musicians and the work was not accepted for performance in the 1872/73 season. Bruckner made a note of this as '1st rejection' ('I. Ablehnung') in his copy of the *Krakauer Schreibkalender* which he used as a diary-cum-organizer at the time.[150]

On 10 November Bruckner and Brahms made a rare joint appearance in the large *Musikverein* hall when the newly installed organ was heard for the first time in a concert which included Handel's *Te Deum*. Brahms conducted and Bruckner played Brahms's realisation of the basso continuo part on the organ. Five days later, on 15

given for the Scherzo, but we can assume that it was written between 8 and 16 July. The Adagio was begun on 18 July and completed a week later, on 25 July. Work on the Finale was begun in Vienna on 28 July, continued in Linz and completed at St. Florian on 11 September. See *G-A* IV/1, 208f. for a facsimile of a page from the Adagio, and 206-225 for a discussion of the work. See also Franz Grasberger, 'Anton Bruckners Zweite Symphonie' in Othmar Wessely, ed., *Bruckner-Studien* (Vienna, 1975), 303-21 which includes facsimiles of two pages from the autograph between pp. 308 and 309.

150 According to Carl F. Pohl, the librarian of the *Gesellschaft der Musikfreunde*, who wrote to Josef Seiberl in St. Florian in November, Franz Liszt may have been present at this rehearsal as he was 'quite delighted' with the symphony. See *G-A* IV/1, 224. The copy score used in this trial run, begun by the Viennese copyist Tenschert and completed by the Linz copyist Carda, is in the ÖNB (Mus. Hs. 6035). The manuscript parts are located in St. Florian abbey. See William Carragan, 'The early version of the Second Symphony' in Howie, Jackson and Hawkshaw, eds., *Perspectives on Anton Bruckner* (Aldershot: Ashgate, 2001), in preparation, for more detailed information about the sources.

November, Bruckner improvised on the organ for 30 minutes and Brahms conducted the *Singverein* in performances of unaccompanied choral pieces by Eccard and Isaac.[151]

At the beginning of 1873 Bruckner made a further attempt to secure funding in order to reduce his teaching load. He wrote to Stremayr, requesting an annual subsidy so that he would be in a position to do less teaching (both institutional and private) and devote more of his time to composition. To strengthen his case, he added that Liszt had encouraged him to pursue his compositional career. He was grateful for Stremayr's help in the past but was concerned that his 30-40 hours' teaching each week was 'significantly paralysing' his creative activity.[152] There is no record of Stremayr's reply to the request. Indeed, it is more than likely that he felt that he had done enough already to help Bruckner.

Although he was now working on the Symphony no. 3 in D minor WAB 103, Bruckner's immediate concern was to organize a performance of his Symphony no. 2. At the end of March he wrote to the directorate of the *Gesellschaft der Musikfreunde*, requesting the use of the large hall for a concert on 8 June at midday. His intention was to 'perform a new symphony' and play some pieces on the organ;[153] but the first performance of the symphony was postponed until October, probably in order to coincide with the end of the World Exhibition in Vienna and the beginning of a new concert season. Bruckner had to arrange the concert himself and wrote once again to the *Gesellschaft* directorate and the police department,

---

151   This concert was reviewed by several critics, including Ambros in the *Wiener Zeitung* (17 November), Hanslick in the *Neue Freie Presse* 2960 (19 November) and Pyllemann in the *Allgemeine Musikalische Zeitung* vi (27 November), 771.

152   See *HSABB* 1, 136f. for this letter, dated Vienna, 27 January 1873. The original is not extant; it was first printed in the *Neues Wiener Journal*, 16 June 1933. See also *G-A* IV/1, 227ff.

153   See *HSABB* 1, 137 for this letter, dated Vienna, 30 March 1873; the original is in the *Gesellschaft der Musikfreunde* library.

asking for permission to hold the concert on Sunday 26 October at 12.30.[154] He reckoned that the total cost of the enterprise, which included the hiring of the Philharmonic orchestra for rehearsals and performance and the copying of parts, amounted to 700 florins. Fortunately, he received some financial assistance from a sympathetic patron, Prince Johann Liechtenstein.

After playing a Bach Toccata and Fugue in C major and a free improvisation on the organ, Bruckner conducted the first performance of his C minor symphony. The critical reaction was mixed. In his review in the *Neue Freie Presse*, Hanslick commented on the many fine details but the overall structural weakness. Nevertheless, it had made a very favourable impression on the public:

> ... We content ourselves today with the report of this splendid public success which we heartily concede to this unassuming but energetic and ambitious composer. Mr. Bruckner received loud and continuous applause after his organ pieces and each movement of the symphony. The Philharmonic Orchestra gave a masterly performance of this unusually difficult composition (under the personal direction of the composer).[155]

Ludwig Speidel, writing in the *Fremdenblatt*, made similar comments but was more specific in his criticism, contrasting the beauties of the Andante movement with the lack of structural cohesion in the outer movements:

---

154 See *HSABB* 1, 140f. for the texts of these letters, both dated Vienna, 18 October 1873, and for the permission granted by the *Gesellschaft* and the police department, 18 October and 21 October respectively; the originals are in St. Florian. Bruckner also wrote to the *Gesellschaft* committee on 17 November to thank them for the use of the hall. See *HSABB* 1, 144; the original is in the *Gesellschaft* library.

155 *Neue Freie Presse* 5298 (28 October 1873), 6. Quoted in *G-A* IV/1, 245f.

... The motives follow each other rather than being organically set off one against the other; the development of the motives lacks the necessary clarity; the movements do not have overall cohesion but are disjointed. There is often some wonderful detailed work and the first part of the Scherzo - the least original section as far as content is concerned - is artistically shaped with a secure hand. As regards the stylistic direction of the symphony, there has been an attempt to fuse the new and most recent musical achievements with classical tradition. In this sense Bruckner's work contains some really splendid passages even if one cannot say that the whole piece presents a successful solution to the problem set.

Nevertheless in this symphony we encounter a musical personality whose shoe-laces the numerous opponents that have emerged are not worthy to untie. He can smile at his antagonists because in knowledge and ability he leaves them infinitely far behind...[156]

The reviewer for the *Wiener Sonn- und Montags-Zeitung* also praised the originality of the score and singled out 'details full of... artistic nobility' and the masterly 'blending of tone colours'.[157] Speidel's observation that Bruckner had many detractors, on the other hand, is borne out by an extremely unfavourable review of the symphony, written by one of his Conservatory colleagues, the historian A.W. Ambros, whose main criticism was that the composer's obvious devotion to Wagner had led him astray, particularly in the outer movements:

...It would be worth the trouble to count the number of general pauses in the work, a device which the great composers quite rightly have used only infrequently. Where we desire and expect a musical language that is coherent, well-organized and motivically inter-connected, we hear nothing but suspensions, interjections, musical question- and exclamation-marks and parentheses which are neither preceded nor followed by anything of substance. Where we expect a firm musical structure we are harried until we are made breathless

---

156 *Fremdenblatt* (28 October 1873). Quoted in *G-A* IV/1, 246ff.

157 *Wiener Sonn- und Montags-Zeitung, Beilage zu Nr. 89* (2 November 1873), 5.

by sound patterns that are strung together in a random fashion...

Ambros argued that a true measure of the composition's worth would be gauged not from performing it in front of a partisan Viennese audience but from playing it to an unprejudiced, objective audience in Berlin or Leipzig. If it succeeded there it would truly have survived the test of fire. Ambros showed his true arch-conservative colours in the final paragraph of his review, however:

> We have found in the new work features which cause us deeply to regret that a man of such talent, instead of taking the path to the temple of fame boldly and courageously on his own two feet, prefers to jump on to the mounting-board of the Wagnerian chariot of triumph and allow himself to be carried along - provided that the chariot does not throw him off along the way... If we could presume that he would not close his ears to a sincere (but perhaps unwelcome) voice, we would say to him: moderation, restraint, self-control... Our contemporary music suffers from lack of moderation... As things stand it appears that we are not on the threshold of a glorious new musical epoch but have arrived at the end of all music.[158]

Bruckner appears to have been more than satisfied with the performance. On 27 October he wrote an official letter of appreciation to the Philharmonic committee in which he made the rather quaint statement that, just as a 'father seeks the best possible place for his child', so he would like to dedicate the symphony to the

---

158 *Wiener Abendpost*, the evening edition of the *Wiener Zeitung* (28 October 1873); quoted in *G-A* IV/1, 249-54. Ambros provided another review of the Second Symphony in the *Wiener Abendpost* on 26 February 1876. For further information about August Wilhelm Ambros (1816-1876), see Norbert Tschulik, 'August Wilhelm Ambros und das Wagner-Problem. Ein Beitrag zur Geschichte der Musikkritik und der Wagner-Rezeption' in *Studien zur Musikwissenschaft* 29 (1979), 155-69. Tschulik has also provided a survey of reviews of Bruckner in the *Wiener Zeitung* in *BJ 1981* (Linz, 1982), 171-79. Other reviews of the first performance of the Second Symphony can be found in Leopold Nowak and William Carragan, eds., *ABSW* 2: *II Symphonie C-Moll* (Vienna, forthcoming).

orchestra; a week later he thanked the *Liedertafel Frohsinn* for their congratulatory letter, saying that the Philharmonic musicians had 'played like gods' and that he had received a tremendous ovation.[159] The orchestra evidently did not accept the dedication and, eleven years later, Franz Liszt, who had shown interest in the work initially, was asked to be its dedicatee.[160] Liszt eventually replied in the affirmative and hoped for an early opportunity of hearing the work again, but his lack of real interest can be gauged from the fact that he did not take the score with him when he left Vienna to visit Budapest and apparently forgot all about it![161] When Bruckner came across the dedication score by chance again a year later, he withdrew his dedication, and the work was eventually published by Doblinger without dedication in 1892.[162] Between its first performance in October 1873 and its publication in 1892, Bruckner made several cuts and alterations in scoring, albeit not as extensive as the changes made in some of the later symphonies. He also eliminated some of the general pauses which he included in the original version in order to make the musical architecture clearer and thus avoid one of the criticisms of the First Symphony, namely that it was shapeless and structurally incoherent.[163] The Second Symphony

---

159 See *HSABB* 1, 141 and 142 for these two letters, dated Vienna, 27 October and 4 November 1873 respectively. The original of the former is in the *Vienna Philharmonic Archive*; the original of the latter is in the *Linzer Singakademie, Frohsinn-Archiv*.

160 A letter accepting the dedication was in fact drafted at the beginning of October 1875, but it appears that it was not sent to Bruckner. It can also be found in the *Vienna Philharmonic Archive*.

161 See *HSABB* 1, 223 for Liszt's letter to Bruckner, dated Vienna, 29 October 1884. There is a facsimile of this letter in *ABB*, between pages 272 and 273.

162 The work was published in score (D.1769) and parts (D.1770), also in a piano reduction for four hands, edited by Joseph Schalk (D.1806).

163 The Finale contains the most changes. Some of them were evidently suggested by Herbeck and made before the second performance of the symphony conducted by Bruckner in a *Gesellschaft* concert on 20 February 1876. There was a more thorough revision in 1877 and some important pre-

marks a significant development in Bruckner's symphonic thinking. There is a much closer thematic / motivic relationship within and between the movements. Significantly, the close proximity in time between the gestation of the symphony and the first performance of the F minor Mass is underlined by quotations from the latter in the slow movement and Finale.[164]

On the strength of the successful first performance of the symphony on 26 October Bruckner felt justified in renewing his request for an annual grant. In his official letter he mentioned not only the enthusiastic public response and the favourable press reviews but also his successes as an organ virtuoso in Nancy, Paris and London as well as Liszt's and Wagner's high estimation of his works. Wagner, for instance, had recently accepted the dedication of his Symphony no. 3 in D minor. As in his previous letter he ended by stressing that he lost 'much precious time and energy' for composition because he was obliged to supplement his Conservatory income by

---

publication changes were made in 1892. For further information, see Robert Haas, ed., *ABSW* 2: *II.Symphonie C-Moll* (Leipzig, 1938) [including critical apparatus]; Leopold Nowak, ed., *ABSW* 2: *II. Symphonie C-Moll, Fassung von 1877, 2., revidierte Ausgabe* (Vienna, 1965); Franz Grasberger, 'Anton Bruckners Zweite Symphonie', op.cit. (Vienna, 1975), 309; Timothy L. Jackson, 'Bruckner's Metrical Numbers' in *19th-Century Music* xiv/2 (1990), 107-14; Timothy L. Jackson, 'Bruckner's Rhythm. Syncopated Hyperrhythm and Diachronic Transformation in the Second Symphony' in *BSL 1992* (Linz, 1995), 93-106; Timothy L. Jackson, 'Schubert as "John the Baptist to Wagner-Jesus"' in *BJ 1991/92/93* (Vienna, 1995), 61-107; William Carragan, ed., *ABSW* II/1: *II. Symphonie C-Moll, Fassung von 1872* (Vienna, forthcoming); Leopold Nowak and William Carragan, eds., *ABSW* II/2: *II. Symphonie C-Moll, Fassung von 1877, 3. revidierte Ausgabe* (Vienna, forthcoming); William Carragan, ed., *ABSW* II: *II. Symphonie C-Moll, Revisionsbericht*; William Carragan, 'The early version of the Second Symphony' in *Perspectives on Anton Bruckner* (Aldershot, 2001)..

164   There are references to the *Benedictus* in the slow movement and to the *Kyrie* in the Finale. For further discussion, see Constantin Floros, 'Die Zitate in Bruckners Symphonik' in *BJ 1982/83* (Linz, 1984), 7-18. Floros goes so far as to say that the *Benedictus* quotations 'have an extremely personal significance' and are of autobiographical importance.

giving private lessons.[165] Once again he was unsuccessful.

Wagner's acceptance of the dedication of Symphony no. 3 in September crowned a year of fairly extensive work on the symphony which was begun, according to Josef Kluger, in October 1872 with the 'Andante' section of the slow movement and the theme of the following 'Misterioso' section.[166] Dates on the autograph score and on some separate autograph folios clearly indicate that Bruckner was occupied with the first version of the symphony throughout 1873, completing it literally at the end of the year.[167]

During August 1873 Bruckner spent some of his summer vacation at Carlsbad and Marienbad before going to St. Florian. The Finale of the symphony was begun in sketch form before he left Vienna. An outbreak of cholera in the city prompted him to make a quick departure. The sketches of the Finale were completed on 31 August just before Bruckner travelled to Bayreuth to visit Wagner and ask him which of the two symphonies - the Second or the Third - he would prefer to have dedicated to him. Bruckner later recalled the occasion for inclusion in Hans von Wolzogen's

---

165 See *HSABB* 1, 143 for this letter, dated Vienna, 9 November 1873. The original is not extant; it was first published in the *Neues Wiener Journal*, 16 June 1933. Bruckner entrusted his letter to Dr. Franz Gross (1815-1890), mayor of Wels and a member of parliament.

166 Josef Kluger (1865-1937), a young friend of the composer, was a priest and, later, provost at Klosterneuburg abbey. In a later conversation with Kluger, Bruckner recalled that the Andante was written on 15 October in memory of his mother Theresia whose name-day it was, and the 'Misterioso' came to him the following day. See *G-A* IV/1, 260f.

167 When preparing the 'second version' in 1877 Bruckner used the original autograph (Mus.Hs. 19.475 in the *ÖNB*), making alterations and discarding those sheets which he did not need. Hence there is no 'clean' autograph of the original version, apart from the Adagio and Scherzo movements. According to Bruckner's annotation at the end of the Finale, the work was completed during the night of 31 December. For a thorough survey of the source material and a revision report of the three printed versions of the symphony in the *Gesamtausgabe*, see Thomas Röder, ed., *ABSW* III/1-3: *III Symphonie D-Moll Revisionbericht* (Vienna, 1997).

reminiscences of Wagner:

> It was about the beginning of September 1873 when I asked the Master if I could let him see my 2nd (C minor) and 3rd (D minor) symphonies. He was unwilling because of lack of time (the building of the theatre) and said that he would not be able to examine the scores then as he had even had to put *The Ring* on one side. When I replied, 'Master, I have no right to take up even a quarter an hour of your time. I thought that with your quick eye a glance at the themes would be sufficient for you to get some idea of the music', the Master said, slapping me on the shoulder, 'Come with me into the drawing-room'. He looked at the 2nd Symphony and pronounced it 'really good', although it seemed to him to be too tame. He then began to look at the 3rd Symphony and, with the words, 'Ah, this is really something', examined the whole first section (he mentioned the trumpet in particular). 'Leave the work here', he said, 'and I will examine it more closely after lunch' (it was twelve o'clock). 'Should I make my request', I thought to myself, whereupon the Master encouraged me. Very timidly and with my heart pounding, I spoke to my dearly loved Master: 'Master, I have something on my heart which I dare not say'. The Master replied, 'Out with it. You must know how fond I am of you'. Then I made my request, but only in the event of the Master being completely satisfied, as I did not wish to bring dishonour to his illustrious name. Then the Master said, 'You are invited to Wahnfried for 5 o'clock in the evening. You can meet me there and, after I have been able to examine the D minor symphony thoroughly, we can talk more about this'. No sooner had I come to Wahnfried from the theatre at 5 o'clock than the Master of all masters met me with open arms, embraced me and said, 'Dear friend, I accept the dedication; you give me enormous pleasure with the work'. I stayed with the Master for two and a half very happy hours. He spoke to me about the musical situation in Vienna, plied me with beer, took me into the garden and showed me his grave!!!..[168]

---

168 From Hans von Wolzogen, *Erinnerungen an R. Wagner* (2/1891). The full text of Bruckner's undated letter to Wolzogen can be found in *ABB*, 166ff. and *G-A* IV/1, 239f. For Göllerich's account of the same episode, see *G-A* IV/1, 232-36 and Stephen Johnson's English translation in *Bruckner Remembered* (London: Faber and Faber, 1998), 131-34.

274

There is an amusing independent account of this episode by the sculptor, Gustav
Kietz, who was at Bayreuth at the time working on a bust of Cosima. According to
Kietz, Bruckner was so overwhelmed by the occasion and by the excess of beer that
he was unable to remember the following morning which symphony Wagner had
chosen for dedication![169] The piece of notepaper on which Bruckner scribbled a
message to Wagner to clarify matters - 'Symphony in D minor, where the trumpet
begins the theme' - and Wagner jotted down, 'Yes! Yes! Best wishes!' is, of course,
a well-known piece of Bruckner memorabilia.[170]

October marked the beginning of a new teaching session for Bruckner. He had
a narrow escape on a return journey from Linz to Vienna at the beginning of the
month. The train in which he was travelling was involved in an accident just outside
the *Westbahnhof* station. Fortunately for Bruckner, his carriage was not affected in
the impact of the collision with a spare engine and he was unhurt.[171]

In October Bruckner was accepted into membership of the Vienna branch of the
Akademischer Wagner-Verein and, in his letter of thanks, intimated that he would
be delighted to belong to a society in which 'intelligence and enthusiasm for the

---

169 See G.A. Kietz, *Richard Wagner in den Jahren 1842-49 und 1873-75* (Dresden, 1905), quoted
in *G-A* IV/1, 236ff. Translated by Stephen Johnson in op.cit., 135f. On pp. 134f. Johnson also
provides a translation of Max von Oberleithner's account (from *Meine Erinnerungen an Anton
Bruckner*).

170 See *HSABB* 1, 138. There is a facsimile in *G-A* IV/1, between pages 480 and 481. The
original is in the *Stadtbibliothek*, Vienna.

171 Bruckner mentioned this accident in a letter to Ignaz Pollmann, mayor of Tulln. Bruckner had
played at the successful inauguration of the new organ on 19 January and had been sent a silver
tobacco tin as a gift during the summer vacation. He wrote to Pollmann from Vienna on 8 October,
apologizing for the lateness of his reply. See *HSABB* 1, 138f.; the original is in the *Heimatmuseum*,
Tulln.

truly noble are so famously represented'.[172] Work on the realization of the sketches of the Finale of the D minor Symphony occupied him during the autumn and early winter months, and his prediction in a letter to the *Liedertafel Frohsinn* that 'the Wagner-Symphony (D minor)' would be completely finished in two months' time proved to be correct.[173]

With Bruckner's Symphony no. 3 we are confronted, perhaps more perplexingly than in any other of his symphonies, with the complex question of different 'versions'. Three examples from the last forty years clearly illustrate the particular confusion which surrounds this symphony. In his foreword to the Eulenburg miniature score of the work,[174] Hans Ferdinand Redlich specified no less than six versions of the work, namely the original version of 1873, a second version which was the result of some revision carried out in 1874, a third version which was the product of the thorough 'rhythmical' revisions undertaken in the years 1876/77 as embodied in the manuscript sources, a fourth version: the first edition of 1879, a fifth version which incorporated Bruckner's further revisions made in 1889/90 as embodied in the manuscript sources, and a sixth version: the second edition of 1890. In his foreword to the first edition of the 1873 original version of the symphony,[175]

Leopold Nowak cited five different versions which correspond with Redlich's first, third, fourth, fifth and sixth versions. A few years later, however, in his foreword

---

172 See *HSABB* 1, 139 for this letter, dated Vienna, 15 October 1873; the original is in the *Stadtbibliothek*, Vienna. The Vienna branch of the *Wagner-Verein* was founded on 20 February 1873.

173 See *HSABB* 1, 142 for this letter, dated Vienna, 4 November 1873; the original is in the *Linzer Singakademie, Frohsinn-Archiv*.

174 E.E.4553 (1961).

175 *ABSW* III/1: *III Symphonie d-Moll, 1. Fassung 1873* (Vienna, 1977).

to the edition of the '1877 version',[176] Nowak distinguished between the 1873 original version, a complete revision of the symphony towards the end of 1876 which included a new version of the slow movement which had been discovered,[177] the second version of 1877 which included a third version of the slow movement and a new coda to the Scherzo movement, and the third version of 1889 incorporated in the 1890 second edition.[178] By reducing the number of actual 'versions' to three, Nowak was no doubt adhering to the important conclusions agreed at a Bruckner symposium held in Linz in September 1980. The Austrian scholar, Manfred Wagner, was one of the leading contributors to this symposium and provided a clear appraisal of what exactly constitutes a separate 'version'.[179] This was later re-worked as an essay in a booklet accompanying the recordings of the original versions of the Third, Fourth and Eighth Symphonies.[180] Wagner's succinct summing-up is as follows:

> ... 'version' is now accepted as each preparation by Bruckner himself of the work as a whole. Thus Symphonies nos. 1-4 and no. 8 exist in at least two versions, whereas there is only one version each of Symphonies 5, 6, 7 and 9. In 1980, the term 'improvement' [Germ. 'Verbesserung'], which had been commonly used in relation to the

176 *ABSW* III/2: *III Symphonie d-Moll, 2. Fassung 1877* (Vienna, 1981).

177 Published separately as a supplement to *ABSW* III/1 - *Adagio Nr. 2 1876* (Vienna, 1980).

178 See also Leopold Nowak, ed., *ABSW* III/3: *III Symphonie d-Moll, 3. Fassung 1889* (Vienna, 1958), Preface; Arthur D. Walker, 'Bruckner's Works. A list of the published scores of the various versions', *Brio* III/2 (1966); Deryck Cooke, 'The Bruckner Problem Simplified' in *Vindications. Essays on Romantic Music* (London: Faber, 1982), 43-71, particularly 46 and 55-58.

179 Manfred Wagner, 'Bruckners Sinfonie-Fassungen - grundsätzlich referiert' in *BSL 1980: 'Die Fassungen'* (Linz, 1981), 15-24.

180 The three symphonies were played by the Frankfurt Radio Symphony Orchestra, conducted Eliahu Inbal, and recorded on Telefunken 635 64201-4 (1983).

new versions, was firmly rejected. The use of this term had resulted in summary aesthetic judgment being passed on the original versions, declaring them to be preliminary works and lumping together necessary corrections with alterations that had entirely different objectives. It also neglected the possibility that later changes in the symphonic design might have expressed different compositional conceptions, viz. alternative approaches to structural unity, a new view of dynamics in relation to climax building and contrasts, or a departure from organ texture in the direction of more idiomatic orchestral writing... Naturally, 'accommodation' [Germ. 'Anpassung'] played a significant part in the motivation which was responsible for later versions, primarily accommodation to Bruckner's personal style at the time. It is important to bear in mind in this connection that until he was approaching forty his handling of orchestral texture had been based almost exclusively on theoretical studies; in contrast to many famous composers of his day, he had not grown up in the orchestra-pit, but had acquired his first-hand experience, whether as a conductor or as a visitor to the musical world of Vienna, quite late in life. We do not know, and will probably never discover, just how far his personal opinion of that world differed from that of his friends and whether the influence of friends and interpreters was the deciding factor in the alterations which he made, or whether he himself made a conscious decision to conform with contemporary musical practice. It is not easy to determine what Bruckner truly felt about friends like the Schalk brothers, Löwe and Mahler, who were the elite of the musical establishment.[181]... He may have considered the solo piano

---

181 He welcomed their suggestions but was not always happy with the end-results. See Robert Simpson, 'The 1873 Version of Bruckner's Third Symphony' in *BJ 1982/83* (Linz, 1984), 27ff.; *LBSAB* (Tutzing, 1988; Benjamin M. Korstvedt, 'The First Published Edition of Anton Bruckner's Fourth Symphony: Collaboration and Authenticity' in *19th-Century Music* xx/1 (Summer 1996), 3-26; Paul Hawkshaw, 'The Bruckner Problem Revisited' in *19th-Century Music* xxi/1 (Summer 1997), 96-107; Korstvedt's response, 'The Bruckner Problem Revisited (A Reply)' in ibid., 108f.; Thomas Leibnitz, 'Anton Bruckner and "German Music". Josef Schalk and the establishment of Bruckner as a national composer' in *Perspectives on Anton Bruckner* (Aldershot: Ashgate, 2001), in preparation, for comments about the participation of others.

and piano duet arrangements made by the Schalk brothers and Löwe to be new versions of or corrections to his own work which he could reluctantly accept (Symphonies 4 and 5) and probably did accept provided that they helped him to achieve public success and recognition, but which subsequently gave him cause for concern when he considered the possibility that they might be handed down to posterity. I imagine that the presentation of his works to the Austrian National Library was less an act of devotion on his part to the Austrian state than a final act of self-defence for the future, a means of countering the danger that conceptions of his works which did not agree with his own might later become accepted or valid.

The chronology of Bruckner's methods of composition is the main evidence in support of the fact that he brought different conceptions to bear on identical thematic ideas. Each bout of creativity was typically followed first by a fallow period and then by a phase of examination and revision. The first spurt of activity resulted in the three Masses and Symphony no. 1, punctuated by exhaustion culminating in a nervous collapse,[182] the second (1871/76) produced Symphonies nos. 2,3, 4 and 5 in a row, and the third (1880/87) saw Symphonies nos. 6, 7 and 8, but the intervals between these periods of compositional activity were devoted not only to a re-orientation in Bruckner's professional commitments but also to a revision of these works which had evidently been created under tremendous pressure.[183]

---

182   This 'first spurt of activity' is dated 1867/68 by Wagner, but is more accurately 1863/64 - 1868.

183   From essay entitled 'The Concept of the First Versions of Bruckner's Symphonies' in the booklet. English translation by Lindsay Craig with some of my one amendments and additions. Other articles and books dealing *inter alia* with the original and subsequent versions of Symphony no. 3 include: J. Tröller, *Anton Bruckner, III Symphonie d-Moll* [*Meisterwerke der Musik* 13] (Munich, 1976); Manfred Wagner, *Der Wandel des Konzepts. Zu den verschiedenen Fassungen von Bruckners Dritter, Vierter und Achter Sinfonie* (Vienna: Musikwissenschaftlicher Verlag, 1980); Rudolf Stephan, 'Zu Anton Bruckners Dritter Symphonie' and 'Anton Bruckner: Dritte Symphonie d-Moll, erste und dritte Fassung in Ausschnitten einander gegenübergestellt' in *BSL 1980* (Linz, 1981), 65-73 and 91-96; Harry Halbreich, 'Bruckners Dritter Symphonie und ihre Fassungen' in op.cit., 75-83; Constantin Floros, 'Die Zitate in Bruckners Symphonik' in *BJ 1982/83* (Linz, 1984), 12ff.; Thomas Röder, *Auf dem Weg zur Bruckner Symphonie* (Stuttgart: Steiner, 1987); Gertrud

The original version of the D minor Symphony undoubtedly contains a much greater number of quotations, both from Wagner's *Tristan* and *Die Walküre* and his own music, than any other of his works. While both Auer and Oeser describe these Wagnerian quotations as an act of 'naive homage' to Wagner, Constantin Floros inclines more to the view that Bruckner's intention was anything but naive as he would have thought it self-evident that a 'Wagner Symphony' should include Wagner quotations.[184] After his visit to Bayreuth in September 1873 Bruckner inserted

Kubacsek-Steinhauer, 'Die vierhändigen Bearbeitungen der Dritten Symphonie von Anton Bruckner' in *BJ 1987/88* (Linz, 1990), 67-78; Bo Marschner, 'Die letzte (1889) Fassung von Anton Bruckners 3. Sinfonie. Ein Problemfall in der kritischen Gesamtausgabe' in *Neue berlinische Musikzeitung* viii/3, suppl. (1993), 22-32 [originally published in Danish: 'Anton Bruckners 3. symfoni i dens seneste version (1889)' in *Otte ekkoer af musikforschung i Arhus* (Aarhus, 1988), 135-57]; Gunnar Cohrs, 'Die Trompetenstimme in der Adagioklimax der Letztfassung der Dritten Symphonie' and Wolfgang Kühnen, 'Die Botschaft als Chiffre. Zur Syntax musikalischer Zitate in der ersten Fassung von Bruckners Dritter Symphonie' in *BJ 1991/92/93* (Vienna, 1995), 25-29 and 31-43; Gunnar Cohrs, 'Bruckner-Premiere in Bremen' in *MIBG* xlv (December 1995), 24f. (a discussion of the world premiere of the original version of the Third played on instruments of the period by the London Classical Players conducted by Roger Norrington, 15 September 1995); Thomas Röder, 'Zu Bruckners Scherzo: der "responsoriale" Thementyp, die Kadenz, die Coda und der Zyklus' in *BJ 1994/95/96* (Linz, 1997), 67-77; Elisabeth Reiter, 'Nochmals: Die "Wagner-Zitate" - Funktion und Kontext' in *BJ 1994/95/96* (Linz, 1997), 79-89; Thomas Röder, 'Die Dritte Symphonie - unfaßbar' in *BSL 1996* (Linx, 1998), 47-64; Thomas Röder, 'Master and disciple united: The 1889 Finale of the Third Symphony' in *Perspectives on Anton Bruckner* (Aldershot: Ashgate, 2001), in prep. In his *Anton Bruckner III Symphonie d-Moll Revisionsbericht* (Vienna, 1997), Röder has provided not only a substantial 'omnibus' volume of critical apparatus, identifying the many textual changes with commendable clarity, but also an extremely useful 'chronology' or compositional history of the symphony from October 1872 to 10 February 1895, the date of the last known performance of the work during the composer's lifetime.

184 See Max Auer, *Anton Bruckner. Sein Leben und Werk* (Vienna, 2/1934), 184, Fritz Oeser, introduction to his edition of *Anton Bruckner 3. Symphonie in D-Moll, 2. Fassung von 1878*

280

the *Tristan* and *Walküre* motives carefully and discreetly without interrupting the flow of the music. When he revised the symphony in 1876/77 he eliminated all but one of the Wagner quotations which he retained in the Adagio because it was woven organically into the musical texture. The self-quotations (the 'miserere' phrase from the *Gloria* of the D minor Mass; the head-motive from the first movement of the Second Symphony), on the other hand, were largely retained.

A sacred work, *Christus factus est* WAB 10, formerly dated 1879 by Auer, has been shown to belong to the latter part of 1873.[185] Scored for eight-part mixed-voice choir, three trombones and strings, it was notated on the same type of manuscript paper which Bruckner used for the Finale of his Symphony no. 3. There is also an entry in the *Hofkapelle* schedule for 8 December 1873 - 'Messe in F. Graduale: Christus factus est, Offertorium: Ave Maria' which clearly refers to this work: hence Nowak's dating 'vor dem 8. Dezember 1873'.[186]

A throat infection confined Bruckner to his apartment over the Christmas period. But he did not forget to send Herbeck name-day greetings in a letter which combines sentiments of deep respect and great affection.[187]

At the beginning of January 1874 Bruckner's petition to the Upper Austrian Parliament for an 'annual endowment for life' was rejected, in spite of support from Dr. Alois Bahr. The Finance Committee treated Bruckner's request sympathetically in view of his reputation, but considered that his Conservatory salary should be

---

(Wiesbaden: Brucknerverlag, 1950), iii, and Constantin Floros, 'Die Zitate in Bruckners Symphonik' in op.cit., 12.

185 See *G-A* IV/1, 591ff.

186 See *ABSW* XXI/1, viii, 185, 188 and *ABSW* XXI/2, 89-98; for musical text, see *ABSW* XXI/1, 100-06. It was first performed outside the *Hofkapelle* at a *Wagner Society* concert in Vienna on 20 April 1912. See also Imogen Fellinger, 'Die drei Fassungen des "Christus factus est" in Bruckners kirchenmusikalischen Schaffen' in *BSL 1985* (Linz, 1988), 145-53.

187 See *HSABB* 1, 144 for this letter, dated Vienna, 27 December 1873; the original is in the *ÖNB*.

sufficient to meet his needs.[188] Undeterred, Bruckner made an official application for a teaching post at the University of Vienna. An earlier application in 1867 had been unsuccessful, but Bruckner now hoped that his achievements since then would carry sufficient weight to impress the authorities. In his application to the Ministry of Education and Culture he began by referring to his successful visits to France and England, the encouragement of Liszt, Wagner and other important contemporary composers, and the performances of his F minor Mass and Symphony no. 2 which had been well received by the public and by the members of the Philharmonic who had given him 'a great ovation after the public had left'. He continued:

> Your obedient servant is already in his fiftieth year, and time for composition is very precious. In order to fulfil the task in front of him, to gain time and leisure for musical composition and be able to remain in his dear native Austria, the undersigned takes the liberty of making his humble petition for the establishment of a regular teaching post, with accompanying salary and pension facility, in the Theory of Music, Harmony etc. at the University, if possible, and open to all students at colleges, grammar schools etc.
>
> As the History of Music and Singing are taught at the University and a similar position was established recently at the University of Berlin for one colleague...and at Paris for another colleague, your obedient servant is confident that his petition to the highest state authority in his home country will not be without success because he is convinced that this highest authority which is headed by such a distinguished friend and connoisseur of art as Your Excellency [Stremayr] is a great supporter of art as well as of science.
>
> Because the objection that this is not a University subject has been dealt with elsewhere and, furthermore, it should be taught at all Universities, because those students taking the subject would almost certainly be the most serious and the most industrious (and there would be no need to fear that they would neglect their principal subject), because many very talented people are encouraged in this

---

188 See *HSABB* 1, 145 for the reply (signed by Moritz Ritter von Eigner, the party leader), dated Linz, 10 January 1874; see also *G-A* III/1, 564ff. and *G-A* IV/1, 287. Alois Bahr was a member of the Liberal party and a keen supporter of the *Liedertafel Frohsinn*.

manner and are steered away from useless and harmful entertainments, and because the majority of students normally do not have either the means or the time to attend the Conservatory, your obedient servant believes that he will not be knocking at the door of the Imperial Ministry in vain.[189]

Bruckner's letter was forwarded to the Faculty of Philosophy at the University on 21 April. Dr. Edward Sueß, the Dean of the Faculty, then gave it to Hanslick for his comments which he made to the Faculty on 4 May. Hanslick recalled a similar request for the establishment of a Harmony and Counterpoint teaching post at the University made in the early 1860s and the decision of the Faculty then that the University was not the place for such a post, particularly as Vienna was well supplied with music schools in which the subject could more fittingly be taught. It had been agreed in 1862 that Rudolf Weinwurm, the conductor of the *Akademischer Gesangverein*, could give singing lessons and provide enough basic theoretical instruction as was necessary for his students.[190] In Hanslick's opinion there was nothing in Bruckner's request to warrant a change in the earlier decision. But there was a 'sting in the tail' of Hanslick's submission to the Faculty:

Bruckner's personality provides even less justification for the establishment of such a subject, as his conspicuous lack of any intellectual background would appear to render him not in the least suitable for a University. I need touch on this point no further than to request the Faculty to observe the peculiar drafting of Bruckner's request...

---

189 See *HSABB* 1, 146f. for this letter, dated Vienna, 18 April 1874; the original is in the Vienna University Library. See also Robert Lach, *Die Bruckner-Akten des Wiener Universitäts-Archives* (Vienna: Strache, 1926) for a thorough account of Bruckner's relationship with the University, including the relevant documentation. There is also a concise discussion of Bruckner's applications for a lectureship in Ernst Schwanzara, *Anton Bruckner. Vorlesungen über Harmonielehre und Kontrapunkt an der Universität Wien* (Vienna: Österr. Bundesverlag, 1950), 40-47.

190 See Schwanzara, op.cit., 36-39.

Hanslick ended his submission by recommending that Bruckner's request be declined. Almost a week later Bruckner wrote directly to the Faculty of Philosophy. His opening statement that he had not pursued University studies himself, did not possess a doctorate and was not seeking a professorship but a teaching position in Musical Theory at the University suggests that he had some knowledge of the main drift of Hanslick's submission. He continued by stressing the point that there was an obvious need for such a position at the University. Many University students who did not have the opportunity at school to learn theory (only singing was an obligatory subject) and did not have the time to attend the Conservatory would welcome the opportunity of attending classes. Indeed it would be very useful preparation for the study of the History of Music![191] Sueß, the Dean of the Faculty, passed the letter on to Hanslick whose conclusion was that there was nothing in it to make him alter his earlier recommendation.[192]

Following Stremayr's advice that he strengthen his case by submitting certificates and examples of his own works to the Faculty, Bruckner wrote again on 15 July, enclosing scores of his F minor Mass, Symphony no. 2 and the first and second movements of his Symphony no. 4. He was unable to include the score of Symphony no. 3 because it had been sent to the Philharmonic for rehearsal purposes. He described the University as his 'last resort'; as the result of a change in the curriculum at St. Anna's, piano was no longer an obligatory subject and Rudolf Weinwurm had been appointed to oversee the music teaching there. 'As fencing and singing are taught [at the University]', he concluded, 'all the more reason for not rejecting my subject which aids the understanding of music history and, moreover, is of

---

191 See *HSABB* 1, 148f. for Bruckner's letter to the College of Professors of the Faculty of Philosophy, dated Vienna, 10 May 1874; the original is in the Vienna University Library. Hanslick's submission is dated 4 May; see *G-A* IV/1, 292ff.

192 Hanslick's verdict is dated 15 May 1874; see *G-A* IV/1, 298.

practical use.[193]

At a meeting of the Faculty on 31 October Bruckner's request was formally declined (13 for, 21 against). Hanslick's opposition is understandable to a degree. It was not simply a case of spiteful antagonism because Bruckner happened to mention the encouragement of Liszt and Wagner - like a red rag to a bull? - in one of his letters of application. He felt strongly that Music Theory / Harmony was not a University subject. Bruckner for his part did not help his case by drawing undue attention to his material needs and by resorting occasionally to undiplomatic turns of phrase such as the suggestion that the University was his 'last resort' as a source of income. What about his Conservatory earnings and the income from his private pupils? But Hanslick did use one unfortunate underhand tactic in his attempt to block Bruckner. He tried to drive a wedge between him and his old friend Rudolf Weinwurm. Weinwurm told Halatschka, a member of the *Akademischer Gesangverein*, that Hanslick had approached him with the suggestion that it would be to his benefit if he used his influence to dissuade Bruckner. Weinwurm's reply was that he would have nothing to do with it.[194] In a later letter to Dr. Adolf Weiß, Weinwurm provided further details:

> It was in 1875 [sic] that Hanslick asked me to visit him one day. He greeted me with the words: 'Bruckner is doing his utmost to get himself appointed as a music teacher at the University. He already has the Minister on his side and he is putting pressure on all the professors and Senate members and tormenting the life out of them. As you have worked at the University for such a long time, the only way of holding him back is for you to make an application to teach the subjects in question'. I took my leave of him with a bow but without saying a word. Of course I did not apply. There was no question

---

193 See *HSABB* 1, 151 for this letter to the Faculty of Philosophy, dated Vienna, 15 July 1874; the original is in the Vienna University Library.

194 See *G-A* IV/1, 313f.

of my being party to such deviousness or even of allowing myself to be used against another artist in this way...[195]

In the midst of all this Bruckner attempted unsuccessfully to persuade the Conservatory authorities that Fugue was too difficult a discipline to learn in the first year of a Counterpoint course and that the course should be changed accordingly.[196] Bruckner also tried to solicit help and support outside Austria and, recalling his successful visits to Nancy and Paris in 1869 and London in 1871, wrote to Baron Schwarz von Senborn:

> ... In order to obtain time to compose it is necessary to find a patron. Lord Dudley would perhaps not be averse to supporting art. The applicant would naturally place himself and his works at his [Lord Dudley's] disposal in return for a guaranteed fixed annual income.
> The applicant would also be happy with a position provided that the inability to speak English and French was not a hindrance. If Lord Dudley cannot be persuaded, perhaps there is someone else in England or America. But it would have to be officially guaranteed and for life even if the support proved to be very small...[197]

Although Bruckner's position at the *Hofkapelle* was secure, it was unpaid apart from the occasional disbursements made at the court's discretion. On 28 June,

---

195 Letter dated Prague, 27 January 1883; quoted by J. Frieben, *Rudolf Weinwurm* (unpublished typewritten thesis, Vienna, 1960)

196 See *HSABB* 1, 149 for Bruckner's letter to the Conservatory, dated Vienna, 28 May 1874; the original is in the *Gesellschaft der Musikfreunde* library.

197 See *HSABB* 1, 149f. for this letter, dated Vienna, 22 June 1874; the original is in the *Gesellschaft der Musikfreunde* library. Wilhelm Freiherr Schwarz von Senborn (1816-1903) was the Austrian government's chief representative at the second London World Exhibition in 1862, was in charge of the Vienna World Exhibition in 1873, and was the Austrian ambassador in Washington from September 1874 to the beginning of 1875.

however, he was informed by Herbeck that he was next in line for a paid organist's post.[198] This did not materialize for some time and, not surprisingly, his letter to Schwarz von Senborn did not produce any tangible results. A letter from Bayreuth, however, must have brought him considerable pleasure. Cosima Wagner, writing on behalf of her husband, acknowledged receipt of the dedication score of Symphony no. 3 which Bruckner sent to Wagner in May. Cosima said that Wagner had gone through the score with Hans Richter and was delighted with both the symphony and its dedication. As a gesture of thanks, he invited Bruckner to the projected performances of *The Ring* in Bayreuth in 1876 when he hoped to have an opportunity of spending a few moments with him.[199]

Bruckner spent a large part of the summer vacation in St. Florian and used some of the time to complete the sketch of the Finale of his Symphony no. 4. He also paid a short visit to his sister Rosalia and her family in Vöcklabruck and attended a rehearsal of the *Liedertafel* whose president, Dr. Alois Scherer, was a friend of his.

The change of teaching arrangements at St. Anna's resulted in a substantial loss of income, 1000 shillings per annum, for Bruckner. He communicated his concern to Bishop Rudigier in Linz who replied immediately to sympathise with the composer. Bruckner's former employer also took the opportunity to recall his achievements as

---

198 See *ABDS* 1, 66 and *G-A* IV/1, 316f. Herbeck was instrumental in introducing some necessary changes to the 'promotion system' in the *Hofkapelle*; see *ABDS*, 64f.

199 See *HSABB* 1, 150 for this letter from Cosima Wagner, dated Bayreuth, 24 June 1874; the original is in St. Florian. We do not know exactly when Bruckner sent this score, as its accompanying letter is not extant. The dedication page was engraved by Josef Maria Kaiser, an engraver and sign writer who taught at the Linz *Staatsgymnasium*, and Bruckner wrote to him on 14 February 1874 to give precise instructions at to the layout of the dedication. His own name was to be engraved simply but Richard Wagner's name was to be engraved 'with grandeur (but without detracting from the noble simplicity' of the whole. See *HSABB* 1, 145f. for this letter; the original is in the *ÖNB*.

a cathedral organist in Linz, and expressed the hope that the Minister for Education would be in a position to help.[200]

During a year in which his attempts to gain 'more time and leisure' to compose received further setbacks, Bruckner nevertheless worked on another symphony, the Symphony no. 4 in E flat major WAB 104, and wrote a small occasional piece, the motto *Freier Sinn und froher Mut* WAB 147, for the Grein *Liedertafel*.[201]

Bruckner completed the original version of his Symphony no. 4 in eleven months. The sketch of the first movement was begun on 2 January 1874 and the complete score was finished on 22 November.[202] The symphony was substantially altered in subsequent years, the most significant changes being a new Scherzo which was added in 1878, a second Finale, entitled *Volksfest*, written in August and September 1878,[203] and a third Finale (1879/1880).[204] Further changes were made after the first

---

200　See *HSABB* 1, 152 for Rudigier's letter, dated Linz, 7 October 1874; there is a copy (not the original) in St. Florian. Bruckner's letter of 6 October is not extant.

201　This piece is dated Vienna, 21 March 1874 and was first published in Linz in 1905 as one of a collection of *Wahl- und Sängersprüche* sung by *Frohsinn*. For further information, see the *IBG Mitteilungsblatt* 10 (December 1976), 9.

202　The autograph of the first version is in the *ÖNB* (Mus.Hs. 6082). It was published for the first time, ed. Leopold Nowak, as *IV. Symphonie Es-Dur, 1. Fassung 1874*, *ABSW* IV/1 (Vienna, 1975) and first performed in the *Brucknerhaus*, Linz on 20 September 1975 by the Munich Philharmonic conducted by Kurt Wöss. It is discussed in *G-A* IV/1, 321-53 and in the foreword to *ABSW* IV/1. See also footnote 204 below.

203　Mus.Hs. 3177 in the *ONB*, originally published by Haas in the appendix to the earlier Complete Edition IV (Vienna, 1936) and reissued, with some small corrections, ed. Nowak, as an Appendix to *ABSW* IV/2 (Vienna, 1981).

204　The autograph of the first three movements of the second version and the third Finale - Mus. Hs. 19.476 in the *ÖNB* - was published, ed. Nowak, as *IV. Symphonie Es-Dur, 2. Fassung 1878 mit Finale 1880*, *ABSW* IV/2 (Vienna, 1953). The first performance of the symphony in this form was given by the Vienna Philharmonic Orchestra under Hans Richter in Vienna on 20 February 1881.

performance in 1881; others were introduced, not all by Bruckner, prior to the publication of the first edition of the symphony by Gutmann in Vienna in September 1889.[205] The chequered history of the work is parallelled only by that of Symphony no. 3. The original versions of both symphonies are considerably longer than subsequent versions. The outer movements in particular underwent much structural tautening, with smooth transitions taking the place of abrupt pauses and caesuras, and textural 'thinning' in which over-elaborate inner parts and florid violin figuration were avoided. These 'improvements' are more convincing in the Fourth Symphony than in the Third where some of the grandeur of the original is undoubtedly lost. Bruckner himself sub-titled the symphony 'The Romantic' in its original version but there was no programmatic 'spelling out' of the term until later.[206]

---

205 This 'version' was first performed by the VPO under Richter in Vienna on 22 January 1888. The score was reissued in 1895 and was later published by Universal Edition and Eulenburg (E.E. 3636, including H.F. Redlich's edition of 1954)

206 For further information, see the forewords to *ABSW* IV/1, IV/2, IV/2 Appendix and H.F. Redlich's Eulenburg edition. See also Leopold Nowak, 'Anton Bruckner, der Romantiker' in *Mitteilungsblatt der IBG* 8 (1975), 2-10, repr. in *Über Anton Bruckner* (Vienna: Musikwissenschaftlicher Verlag, 1985), 153-59; Theodor Wünschmann, 'Zur Partitur der 4. Symphonie Anton Bruckners in der Fassung von 1874' (Vaduz, 1979); Leopold Nowak, 'Das Finale von 1878 zur IV. Symphonie von Anton Bruckner' in *Mitteilungsblatt der IBG* 18 (1980), 27ff., repr. in *Über Anton Bruckner* (Vienna, 1985), 225f.; Constantin Floros, 'Das Programm der "Romantischen" Symphonie' in *Brahms und Bruckner. Studien zur musikalischen Exegetik* (Wiesbaden: Breitkopf & Härtel, 1980), 171-81; Manfred Wagner, 'Zu den Fassungen von Bruckners Vierter Sinfonie in Es (Romantische)' in *Der Wandel des Konzepts. Zu den verschiedenen Fassungen von Bruckners Dritter, Vierter und Achter Sinfonie* (Vienna: Musikwissenschaftlicher Verlag, 1980), 21-38; Cornelis van Zwol, 'Bruckners Vierte Symphonie: nicht nur eine "Romantische"' in *BSL 1980. Die Fassungen* (Linz, 1981), 25-38; Leopold Nowak, 'Die drei Final-Sätze zur IV. Symphonie von Anton Bruckner' in *ÖMZ* 36 (Vienna, 1981), 2-11, repr. in *Über Anton Bruckner* (Vienna, 1985), 233-42; Thomas Röder, 'Motto und symphonischer Zyklus. Zu den Fassungen von Anton Bruckners Vierter Symphonie' in *Archiv f. Musikwissenschaft*

At the beginning of 1875 Bruckner was in a state of deep depression. He could see no way out of his difficult financial situation and, although positive things were being said about his Third Symphony which he had offered to the Vienna Philharmonic for rehearsal in the autumn of 1874, there was no immediate prospect of a performance. Bruckner was in downcast mood when he wrote to Moritz von Mayfeld:

> My 4th Symphony is finished. I have also made significant improvements in the Wagner Symphony (D minor). Hans Richter, the Wagner conductor, was in Vienna and let it be known in several circles how glowingly Wagner speaks about it. It is not going to be performed. Dessoff held some rehearsals in the holidays and raised my hopes but later announced (breaking the promise he made me at the beginning of October) that the programme was full.
> ... Brahms appears to have blocked my Symphony no. 2 in C minor in Leipzig. Richter is reported to have said that he would like to perform the D minor Symphony in Pest. What Hanslick has done to me can be read in the old 'Presse' of 25 December.
> Even Herbeck suggested that I should see whether I could get any help from Wagner. Now I have only the Conservatory and it is impossible for me to live on my income from there. Last September and again later I had to withdraw some money (700 shillings) so that I did not go hungry.
> No one is helping me. Stremayr makes promises - and does

---

xlii (1985), 166-77; Rudolf Stephan, 'Bruckners Romantische Sinfonie' in C-H Mahling, ed., *Anton Bruckner. Studien zu Werk und Wirkung* (Tutzing: Schneider, 1988), 171-87; Benjamin M. Korstvedt, *The First Printed Edition of Anton Bruckner's Fourth Symphony: Authorship, Production and Reception* (doctoral thesis, University of Pennsylvania, 1995); Benjamin M. Korstvedt, 'The First Published Edition of Anton Bruckner's Fourth Symphony: Collaboration and Authenticity' in *19th-Century Music* xx/1 (Summer 1996), 3-26; Bo Marschner, 'Schema und Individualität in der Formbildung Bruckners anhand seiner Reprisenkonzeption ab der Vierten Symphonie' in *BSL 1996* (Linz, 1998), 17-24; Edward Laufer, 'Continuity in the Fourth Symphony (first movement)' in *Perspectives on Anton Bruckner* (Aldershot: Ashgate, 2001), in preparation; Robert S. Hatten, 'The expressive role of disjunction: A semiotic approach to form and meaning in the Fourth and Fifth Symphonies' in *ibid.*, in preparation.

nothing. Fortunately a few foreigners have come to have lessons from me - otherwise I would have to beg.

Now listen. I asked all the principal piano teachers to pass over some teaching to me. Each one promised to do so but I got nothing apart from a few hours of theory. You can see, Sir, how serious the matter is. I would gladly go abroad if only I could obtain a position which would provide me with a good living. Where should I turn? Under no circumstances would I have allowed myself to be brought to Vienna had I suspected this. It would be an easy matter for my enemies to push me out of the Conservatory. It surprises me that this has not happened yet. The Conservatory students and even the domestic staff are shocked at how I am being treated. My life has lost all joy and motivation - for no reason. How gladly I would return to my old posts! When I think of the time I spent in England! This is how things stand... *What should I do?* [207]

A month later, Bruckner wrote again to Mayfeld who had replied to his first letter. In the meantime he had spoken at the court to Salzmann-Bienenfeld in the hope that a position might be vacant. But nothing had moved since Herbeck had written to him the previous June:

I have just returned from speaking with Councillor Salzmann after so many requests and delays. Although Herbeck had told me what the outcome would be a long time ago, I went ahead in compliance with your wish. Salzmann recited the old formula - as soon as something was free he would draw Herbeck's attention to me. In any case I already broached the matter with Herbeck a year ago. The post has been designated by Hohenlohe for Riedel [sic] for four years now.

---

207 See *HSABB* 1, 153f. for this letter, dated Vienna, 12 January 1875; the original is in the *Archiv der Stadt Linz*, Linz. Earlier in the letter Bruckner refers to an unsigned report of the Faculty meeting held on 31 October 1874 - entitled 'Der Generalbass im philosophischen Professoren-Collegium' - which appeared in the *Presse* and was sympathetic to Bruckner; see *G-A* IV/1, 302-05 for a copy of this report. Bruckner also mentioned his difficult financial situation in a letter to Julius Gartner, a Linz teacher and member of *Frohsinn*. See *HSABB* 1, 153 for this letter, dated Vienna, 31 December 1874. The original is in the *Oberösterreichisches Landesbibliothek*, Linz; see **Plate 2** for a facsimile.

I think I could have written a symphony in the time that I have used up in such an unprofitable way pursuing this matter. There were only two paths open to me - organ playing in England or musical director of a theatre in Austria. I did not understand what either entailed and I have never been sufficiently informed to pursue one of the two paths. Linz at least would have offered an opportunity so far as the latter is concerned.

I cannot ask Wagner for anything as I do not want to lose his goodwill.

And so only Liszt and Dönhof remain. I would like to throw the latter into the fire. Shouldn't the nobility be ashamed of themselves? As far as Wiesbaden is concerned I have made enquiries through a pupil from Frankfurt; no answer as yet. I have asked Richter about Pest, but he told me there was no money available.

My deepest gratitude for showing such interest and expending so much effort on my behalf!

It is all too late. To run up debts diligently and then to enjoy the fruits of my diligence and lament the stupidity of my move to Vienna in a debtors' prison - that could be my ultimate fate. I have lost 1000 shillings in annual income and as yet there has been nothing to compensate for it, not even a grant. I am not able to have my Fourth Symphony copied.

If only I had my Linz lessons here. How gladly I would give piano lessons. If I had remained in Linz, I would certainly have been appointed to Zappe's position as well as a teaching post at the Teacher Training Institute...[208]

It was during this state of depression, however, that Bruckner began work on his Symphony no. 5 in B flat, WAB 105, commencing with the Adagio movement on 14 February. Wagner's visit to Vienna at the end of February and beginning of March must have helped to lift Bruckner's depression. He was invited to attend a soiree

---

208 See *HSABB* 1, 154f. for this letter, dated Vienna, 13 February 1875. The original is in the *ÖNB* and there is a facsimile in **Plate 3**. Rudolph von Salzmann-Bienenfeld was an official in the court chancellery. Countess Marie Dönhoff (1848-1929) was the wife of Karl Dönhoff, the secretary of the German embassy in Vienna. Karl Zappe died in 1871. He was succeeded as music director of Linz Cathedral by his son Karl Zappe jr. (1837-1890). By Riedel Bruckner no doubt meant Hans Richter.

during which Wagner sang through the third act of *Götterdämmerung* with Rubinstein at the piano. Wagner is said to have given Bruckner a particularly warm welcome, referring to him as Beethoven's true successor as a symphonist.[209] There was an improvement in Bruckner's financial situation during the year. Rudolf Bibl's promotion to a salaried court organist's post left his former position as assistant librarian of the court chapel and singing teacher of the choirboys vacant. On 16 June Herbeck informed Bruckner that he had secured Bibl's former position and would receive an annual honorarium of 300 shillings, commencing 1 July.[210] Bruckner remained in this position until January 1878 when he was appointed a permanent member of the *Hofkapelle*. Of the several anecdotes about his kindly and not particularly strict attitude towards the choirboys under his charge, the following is fairly typical:

> My father came from Salzburg to Vienna in 1874 and was also a soloist in the Vienna choirboys. Every Sunday the children were brought from the Piarist school to the *Hofkapelle* in the imperial court coach. Whenever Bruckner, for whom my father, Max Keldorfer - himself an outstanding organist and composer - had the greatest respect, rehearsed one of his Masses with the boys and then performed it, he always had a gift ready for the boys when the time came for the return journey in the coach - a huge cake from Demel's. It happened once that the boys made some mistakes during the performance and went to the coach shamefacedly. The cake was there as always but Bruckner threw open the door and said, 'So, rascals, you don't sing correctly but you eat my cakes!'[211]

---

209 See *G-A* IV/1, 358f.

210 See *ABDS* 1, 68-71 for Herbeck's correspondence with the Chancellery, 31 May and 10 June, and 71f. for Herbeck's letter to Bruckner.

211 Grete Pietschmann (née Keldorfer) - reminiscence recorded by Austrian Radio as part of a special project in 1977.

Bruckner made another attempt to secure a lectureship at the University. He was encouraged to do so by August Göllerich sen., a member of parliament and a friend of both Stremayr, the Minister of Education, and Nikolaus Dumba, the president of the *Gesellschaft der Musikfreunde*. Bruckner's letter to the Ministry of Culture and Education, written in July, was more cogent and precise than his earlier applications and there may have been, as Maier suggests, 'a helping hand involved'.[212]

> As it of particular importance to me that the subjects of Harmony and Counterpoint are represented in our Universities just as they are in foreign Universities and as I have endeavoured for some years to bring this about, I take the liberty of making this humble request to the Ministry: that in view of the fact that the importance of these aforementioned subjects for education in general and musical education in particular - considering that they constitute almost the most vital elements without which all artistic understanding of and deep involvement in music are impossible - is not to be undervalued, a lectureship in Harmony and Counterpoint be established in the Faculty of Philosophy of this University, and I be appointed on the basis of my acknowledged expertise in these two subjects. If such a lectureship were to be established, those less well-off students who possess great talent but are not able to attend the Conservatory of Music would have the opportunity of receiving a complete musical education - which must be the purpose of a University.[213]

In October this application was forwarded to the Faculty for the consideration of its members. They were asked if 'lectures in Harmony and Counterpoint as a partial supplementation of Professor Hanslick's lectures in theory' could be recommended, and if 'there was any objection to Bruckner's appointment as a lecturer in these

---

212 Elisabeth Maier, loc. cit., *ABDS* 2, 196.

213 See *HSABB* 1, 156 for this letter, dated Vienna, 12 July 1875; the original is in the Vienna University Library.

294

subjects'.[214] Hanslick was now under pressure to state categorically that 'there was no objection to the appointment of Herr Bruckner as unpaid teacher of Harmony and Counterpoint at the University of Vienna' and to bring this recommendation to the meeting of the Faculty on 29 October. On 18 November Bruckner was informed officially of the appointment by Dr. Schneider, the Dean of the Faculty.[215] A week later he had already drafted the text of his inaugural lecture although it was apparently not delivered until 24 April 1876.[216]

At the beginning of June Bruckner wrote, in response to letter from his former teacher, Otto Kitzler, that he was working on his Fifth Symphony. He added:

> Wagner has declared that my D minor Symphony is a very important work. He invited me and Countess Dönhoff to supper and gave me a remarkable welcome. Liszt likewise.
> ... Could you not perform my C minor Symphony [no. 2] sometime?...[217]

Bruckner spent his summer vacation in Steyr and St. Florian.[218] On Thursday 26

214 See *G-A* IV/1, 365f.

215 See *G-A* IV/1, 366ff.

216 Theophil Antonicek suggests that Bruckner may have given some lectures during the winter semester of 1875. See Antonicek, 'Bruckners Universitätsschüler in den Nationalien der Philosophischen Fakultät' in Othmar Wessely, ed., *Bruckner-Studien* (Vienna, 1975), 442.

217 See *HSABB* 1, 155 for this letter, dated Vienna, 1 June 1875; the original is privately owned. It was printed for the first time in *Deutsches Volksblatt*, 25 October 1899.

218 As usual he applied to the Lord Chamberlain's department for official permission to be excused *Hofkapelle* duties. See *ABDS* 1, 73f. Bruckner directed a performance of his D minor Mass (together with *Christus factus est* [probably WAB 10] and *Ave Maria* [WAB 6]) in the *Hofkapelle* on Sunday 18 July. There was a review of this performance by Eduard Schelle in the *Presse* on 31 July.

August and Friday 27 August respectively he gave organ recitals in Steyr Parish Church and Linz Parish Church respectively, and, the following day (St. Augustine's day), played the organ as usual at St. Florian. Just before leaving Vienna at the beginning of August he made a further request to the Vienna Philharmonic committee that his D minor symphony be included in the 1875/76 season. No doubt wishing to add weight to his request, he mentioned its dedication to Wagner and the fact that both Wagner and Liszt considered it to be among the most important contemporary works. Bruckner was even prepared for the symphony to be performed piecemeal (half in one concert, half in another).[219] His request was turned down, in spite of the fact that a few players disagreed with the official verdict and Hans Richter, now at the helm of the orchestra, was well disposed towards him. Bruckner noted the rejection later in one of his diaries, the *Neuer Krakauer Schreibkalender* for 1877 - '2te Ablehnung durch die Philharmoniker im Herbst 1875 (Sinfonie Nr. 3).[220]

Bruckner returned to St. Florian in October. Several alterations were made to the main organ between 1873 and 1875, and Bruckner was invited to attend the dedication ceremony, no doubt because of his connections with the abbey and because he had an advisory role in the alterations which were carried out by Josef Mauracher. He practised on the new organ at the abbey on Sunday 17 October, and both he and Josef Seiberl performed at the official ceremony which took place on Abbot Ferdinand Moser's name-day, 19 October. There was a glowing report of

---

219 See *HSABB* 1, 157 for this letter, dated Vienna, 1 August 1875; the original is in the archives of the Vienna Philharmonic.

220 See *HSABB* 1, 158f. for the draft of a letter, dated 3 October 1875, which Hans Richter planned to send to Bruckner to thank him for his intended dedication of the Symphony no. 2 to the Philharmonic. This draft is in the Vienna Philharmonic archives. There is no indication that a fair copy was ever sent to Bruckner.

both Bruckner's and Seiberl's playing in the *Linzer Volksblatt*.[221]

As well as sketching a good part of Symphony no. 5 during the year, Bruckner began to write a *Requiem in D minor* WAB 141. The 18-bar sketch on three staves, dated 'Vienna, 18 September 1875', is probably the beginning of the instrumental opening of the *Introitus*. There is no external evidence to suggest that Bruckner was intending the work for a particular occasion, and no other sketches are extant.[222]

1876 is often called Bruckner's 'year of revisions'. This does not imply that other years were not characterized by intensive amendment to his first, second, even his third thoughts, but the zeal with which Bruckner applied himself to metrical studies of Beethoven's Third and Ninth Symphonies and Mozart's *Requiem* and 'rhythmical regulation' of some of his own works, including the D minor, E minor and F minor Masses and the Third and Fourth Symphonies, testifies to unusual activity in this area during 1876 and the year following..[223]

Bruckner exercised a similar type of scrupulousness in religious matters. A letter which he wrote to the Archbishop of Vienna in February 1876 provides one of the clearest illustrations of this. We know from entries in many pages of his diaries that

---

221 See *G-A* II/1, 253-57 for the specification of the organ and 258f. for the report. Mendelssohn's *Lobgesang* was performed. Bruckner played a Bach Toccata and Fugue and an improvisation on Handel's *Hallelujah Chorus*. Ferdinand Moser (1827-1901) became the new abbot of St. Florian on 27 November 1872.

222 The autograph of the sketch is in the *ÖNB* (Mus. Hs. 2105); see Robert Haas, *Anton Bruckner* (Potsdam, 1934), 59 for facsimile and *G-A* IV/1, 361f. for realization.

223 There are indications of his metrical study of the two Beethoven symphonies and Mozart's *Requiem*, as well as a detailed study of the periodic structure of the Fourth Symphony in two of Bruckner's diaries which he used as workbooks or notebooks, namely the *Oesterreichischer Volks- und Wirtschaftskalender für das Schaltjahr 1876* and the *Krakauer Schreibkalender* for 1877, both of which are located in the *ÖNB* (S.m. 3181 and 3182). Bruckner's annotated scores of the 'Eroica' and the Ninth are located in the *Gesellschaft der Musikfreunde* library.

he prayed regularly. It was a discipline which he maintained throughout his life, mainly in private but occasionally in public as some trustworthy anecdotes reveal. The diary entries in the *Akademischer Kalender der österreichischen Hochschulen, Fromme's österreichischer Hochschulenkalender* (1884/85 and 1885/86), *Fromme's österreichischer Professoren- und Lehrer-Kalender* (1886/87 1890/91 and 1894/95), the *Krakauer Schreibkalender für 1883* and *Formme's Neuer Auskunftskalender...1884* located in the Austrian National Library include lists of daily prayers from Ash Wednesday (22 February) 1882 until 1896.[224] The only days for which there are no entries are those in which Bruckner was elsewhere - on holiday or travelling - or handicapped by illness. The normal 'shorthand' symbols used are the capital letters R, V, A, S, Gl and the sign I with horizontal lines below the capital letters.[225] Although Bruckner's deeply religious nature was conditioned to some extent by his education and early surroundings, this was not the main reason for his lifelong devoutness. It was essentially something inborn which informed both his sacred works and his symphonies. There was no other 19th-century composer 'for whom prayer, confession, the sacraments and the creed were essentials of life to such a great extent.'[226] In his letter to the Archbishop he made it clear that, as a devout Catholic, he wished to observe fast days but was not always able to avoid eating meat because he had most of his meals in inns and restaurants where a fish dish was not always available. He requested dispensation or excusal from the observance of fast days other than Christmas Day, Good Friday and one of the three Ember days. The

---

224 The shelf nos. are S.m. 3178a, 3178b, 3179, 3182 and 3183.

225 For further information, see Franz Kosch, 'Der Beter Anton Bruckner' in *Bruckner-Studien* (Vienna, 1964), 67-73; Leopold M. Kantner, 'Die Frömmigkeit Anton Bruckners' in *ABDS* 2 (Vienna, 1980), 229-69; and Erich W. Partsch, 'Der "Musikant Gottes" - Zur Analyse eines Stereotyps' in *ABDS* 8 (Vienna, 1991), 235-55. For information of a more anecdotal nature, see *ABDS* 8, 59-68.

226 Friedrich Blume, 'Anton Bruckner' in *MGG* 2 (1952), col. 359.

dispensation was granted by the Archbishop, as was its renewal in 1884, 1885 and 1887.[227]

On 20 February Bruckner conducted a performance of his Symphony no. 2 as part of the Vienna Philharmonic's third *Gesellschaft* concert.[228] Between the earlier first performance in October 1873 and this performance Bruckner followed Herbeck's advice, albeit with some reluctance, and made some changes which particularly involved shortening the work in places. In spite of a less than perfect performance and, according to Herbeck's son, Bruckner's inadequate conducting, the symphony was applauded after each movement and at the end.[229] Hanslick's review in the *Neue Freie Presse* drew attention more to the rivalry between different factions in the audience than to the quality of the work itself:

> Each movement was applauded without opposition; at the end, however, when an enthusiastic faction in the hall carried its clapping and shouting to an excess and kept starting up again, the other part of the audience protested loudly and hissed repeatedly.[230]

---

227 See *HSABB* 1, 159 for Bruckner's letter to the Archbishop (Johann Rudolf Kutschker), dated Vienna, 23 February 1876. The original is in the *ÖNB*. There is a facsimile of this letter between pages 424 and 425 in *G-A* IV/1.

228 Johann Herbeck conducted the other items in the concert, including Beethoven's Triple Concerto in which Josef Hellmesberger, Friedrich Grützmacher and Julius Epstein were the violin, cello and piano soloists.

229 Ludwig Herbeck, op.cit., 398.

230 From Hanslick's review in the *Neue Freie Presse* 4128 (22 February 1876); quoted in *G-A* IV/1, 392. There were also reviews by Franz Gehring in the *Deutsche Zeitung* (22 February 1876), Laurencin d'Armond in the *Illustrirtes Musik- und Theater-Journal* 1 (1875/76), col. 691, Eduard Kremser in *Vaterland* (24 February 1876) and A.W. Ambros in the *Wiener Abendpost* (26 February 1876) as well as a reference to the performance in the French journal, *Revue et Gazette musicale* (12 March 1876).

In April Bruckner finally had the satisfaction of giving his inaugural lecture at Vienna University. He stressed the importance of Harmony and Counterpoint as academic subjects:

As you will know from various sources there have been colossal developments in music in the last two centuries. Its internal organization has been expanded and perfected to such an extent that today, as we cast a glance over this rich material, we stand in front of an already complete artistic edifice in which we can recognize both a clear structural regularity and a correspondence in its constituent parts to the whole. We see how the one grows out of the other, one cannot exist without the other, and yet each is self-sufficient. Just as each branch of science is responsible for arranging and sifting through its material by imposing rules and regulations, so the science of music - if I may take the liberty of describing it as such - has broken down its entire structure into atoms and has then grouped the elements together according to certain principles, thereby creating a discipline which can be called - to use another description - musical architecture. In this discipline the distinguished subjects of Harmony and Counterpoint form its foundation and its heart.

In view of what I have said, gentlemen, you will concede that a full understanding of what I have described as the musical architecture and of the foundation of this discipline is necessary for a proper appreciation and an exact assessment of a piece of music, first an evaluation of how and to what extent these rules are complied with, and then how the separate musical ideas serve to give life to the compositional process.

You may infer from this that the subjects 'Harmony' and 'Counterpoint' should find an essential place in intellectual life which has reached such an advanced stage of development; there they can be cultivated and taught as subjects in their own right without the exclusive aim of educating artists, because they belong - and rightly so- to the sustaining forces of our intellectual education. By means of them we are in the position of being able to give legitimate musical expression in an aesthetic manner to our thoughts and feelings.

The need to include these subjects in the curricula of universities in Germany, France, Russia etc. was already recognized some years ago, and this emphasized, in the most eloquent manner possible, the

300

importance of finding a place for them in intellectual life.

I would be going too far if I mentioned other factors which underline the importance of these subjects, but I believe I must draw attention to the fact that, through the knowledge of Harmony and Counterpoint, one can often arrive at the pleasant position of awakening public interest even with occasional compositions and, as a result, derive great benefit for oneself.

Having spoken about the importance and the significance of Harmony and Counterpoint, I will now turn briefly to the way in which I believe these subjects should be treated here.

As a result of my many years of study, the experience I have gained as a professor of these subjects in the Conservatory here and my knowledge of the relevant literature, I have decided not to restrict myself to any one of the currently available textbooks in my lectures so that, in the short time available, I will be able to present a true and clear picture to you by drawing on the best basic principles from the wealth of material extant. In the lectures I will continually strive to make myself understood by presenting my material clearly and by making the elements of theory interesting with the help of lucid examples, bearing in mind Goethe's words,

'All theory is grey.
Only the golden tree of life is green.'

I shall minimise many difficulties through practical exercises, thereby intimately combining theory and practice and steering you safely through this realm of knowledge from one boundary to the other where I will then leave you at the threshold of life with all its struggles, my one request being that you make faithful use of what you have learned and remember me with goodwill.

Although I have gone to great pains to create a space for these subjects at the University, it is my duty to express my gratitude publicly to the staff of the Faculty of Philosophy and to the Ministry of Education and Culture for their support in enabling the idea which I have long cherished to come to fruition at last.

In conclusion, esteemed gentlemen, may I make this request to you: make your own powerful contribution with your young and fresh minds so that these subjects may be properly acknowledged in the future here and musical learning may grow, blossom and prosper throughout the University. Dixit.[231]

---

231 There is some uncertainty as to the date of this lecture - possibly 24 April 1876, but see page 294, footnote 216. For the text, see *ABB*, 131-34 and *G-A* IV/1, 369-74. There is a facsimile of a

Bruckner's University lectures took place on Mondays from 5 to 7 (later from 6 to 8). The winter semester was devoted to Harmony and the summer semester to Counterpoint. From the outset they were well attended. In later years students often took the opportunity of appearing at the lectures and applauding him after a successful concert. Bruckner for his part seems to have relished his contact with the 'Herrn Gaudeamus' as he was fond of describing them. As he pointed out in his inaugural lecture, he did not have the time to teach the subjects as thoroughly as he did at the Conservatory and in his private lessons. Nevertheless, all those who recalled the lectures later were unanimous in agreeing that he had the ability to breathe life into potentially very dry material by way of an apt or, occasionally, very drastic illustration. He would also provide progress reports on his own compositions, sometimes playing extracts on the piano, and comment on recent performances of his works both at home and abroad. After his lectures he would invariably go to one of his favourite restaurants for an evening meal, accompanied by a few of his favourite students.

Bruckner made two further attempts to improve his financial circumstances and professional status during 1876. The position of assistant music director at the *Hofkapelle* had become vacant as a result of the retirement of Gottfried Preyer and Bruckner sent a letter of application to Hohenlohe-Schillingsfürst, the Lord Chamberlain, at the end of April, stressing in particular his knowledge of the church music repertoire and the favourable reception of his works by Wagner, Liszt, Herbeck and Hellmesberger.[232] His application was unsuccessful. Joseph

---

page from this handwritten speech between pp. 376 and 377 in *G-A* IV/1.

232 See *HSABB* 1, 160 for this letter, dated Vienna, 29 April 1876; the original is in the court archives, Vienna.

Hellmesberger was appointed to the position and Ludwig Rotter was also given the nominal title of 'assistant music director' in recognition of his 'excellent achievements in the realm of church music'.[233] Three months later Bruckner wrote an extremely polite, almost obsequious, letter to Hohenlohe-Schillingsfürst, asking for his unpaid lectureship at the University to be 'upgraded' to an associate professorship with an annual income.[234] Again Bruckner was unsuccessful, but in September he was granted a provisional sum of 200 shillings from the *Hofkapelle*.[235]

In spite of these discouragements Bruckner must have derived a great amount of satisfaction from conducting the first Viennese performance of his choral piece *Germanenzug* on 3 July in an open-air concert given in the *Volksgarten* by the *Akademischer Gesangverein*.[236] The choir's regular conductor, Richard Heuberger, directed the other works in the programme. Theodor Helm, the critic of the *Deutsche Zeitung*, provided a very objective review:

> ... The first half ended with the first performance [in Vienna] of Professor Bruckner's 'Germanenzug' conducted by the composer himself. The composition received loud applause and an encore was

---

233   See *ABDS* 1, 77 for Hohenlohe-Schillingfürst's recommendation (1 May 1876) and the Emperor's approval (3 May 1876). Joseph Hellmesberger (1828-1903) was the eldest son of Georg Hellmesberger, the famous violin virtuoso and teacher. Joseph himself was an outstanding violinist and, at the age of 23, was appointed Professor of Violin at the Conservatory and artistic director of the *Gesellschaft der Musikfreunde*. When the joint posts of Director of the Conservatory and Director of the *Gesellschaft* concerts were separated in 1859 Hellmesberger retained the former while Herbeck was appointed to the latter. Hellmesberger was appointed leader of the Court Opera Orchestra in 1860 and violinist at the *Hofkapelle* in 1863.

234   See *HSABB* 1, 160f. for this letter, dated Vienna, 26 July 1876; the incomplete original of this letter is in private possession in Vienna.

235   See *ABDS* 1, 79f. (26 September 1876).

236   The concert was advertised in two editions of the *WienerZeitung*, 2 June and 1 July.

demanded and given.[237]

Bruckner was granted leave from his *Hofkapelle* duties from 15 August until 15 September. He travelled to Bayreuth, arriving there on 23 August if not earlier, and probably attended some of the rehearsals and certainly the third complete performance of Wagner's *Ring* (27-30 August). The second part of his vacation was spent at St. Florian and he returned to Vienna in mid-September to resume his *Hofkapelle* commitments. During his stay at Bayreuth Bruckner made the acquaintance of Wilhelm Tappert, a German music journalist, who evidently expressed great interest in his music and held out the prospect of a performance of his Fourth Symphony in Berlin.[238] Shortly after returning to Vienna Bruckner wrote the first of several letters to Tappert apropos the symphony. The Bruckner-Tappert correspondence is a source of important and extremely interesting information about many details of the symphony. On 19 September he informed Tappert that a copy of the Fourth had just been completed and the parts were also ready. He hoped that Tappert would use his great influence to have the work performed 'in the residence of our great fatherland'.[239] Tappert was able to interest Benjamin Bilse, the music director of an orchestra in Berlin, in the symphony, and when Bruckner wrote again a fortnight later he enclosed a copy of the score (in two volumes). Although Hans Richter had requested that the score be returned the following March as there was a possibility of the symphony being performed in Vienna in April 1877, Bruckner's view was that 'a performance in Berlin would be of the greatest importance and a

---

237 See *G-A* IV/1, 413.

238 Wilhelm Tappert (1830 - 1907), an enthusiastic Wagnerian, was a music teacher and journalist and one of the leading figures in Berlin musical life.

239 See *HSABB* 1, 161 for this letter which was first published in *ABB*, 136. The original is privately owned, but the *Musikwissenschaftlicher Verlag*, Vienna possesses a photocopy.

thousand times better than one in Vienna' and he would be 'unbelievably happy' if it came to pass. Tappert had presumably asked Bruckner to send him some biographical details, as a 'curriculum vitae' was enclosed with this second letter. At the end Bruckner made a point of stressing the difficulties he was experiencing in Vienna. However, there is some suspicion of 'special pleading'!

> NB Private notice
>
> And so I have lived in Vienna since 1868 bitterly regretting that I moved here as I do not have any support, recognition or means of subsistence. On account of my position at the University as an unpaid lecturer in Harmony and Counterpoint, Dr. Hanslick has become a malicious enemy.
> I was responsible for introducing these subjects last December. Hanslick was always against it. I receive no salary either as a court organist.
> NB. When I started teaching my monthly salary was 10 shillings.[240]

In his third letter, written at the beginning of December, Bruckner said that he had read out Tappert's reply to his second letter to his Conservatory and University students and their response had been very enthusiastic.[241] If a performance did take place in Berlin, he would come to the final rehearsals. Bruckner then mentioned some changes he wished to be made in the score and hoped that they would not inconvenience Bilse unduly. He enclosed music examples to clarify these changes:

---

240 See *HSABB* 1, 162f. for this letter, dated Vienna, 1 October 1876; the original is not extant, but the *Musikwissenschaftlicher Verlag*, Vienna possesses a photocopy. Bruckner's caution in having his symphony first performed in Vienna can be compared with Brahms's apropos the first performance of his Symphony no. 1. The heading 'private notice' is presumably an indication that this was not to be published along with the rest of the information provided.

241 None of Tappert's replies to Bruckner's letters has survived.

... quaver rests to be added twice at letter C and letter H in the second movement, and the viola part to be slightly changed twice. (The horn part also to be deleted in bars 10-11 after C). To be billed to me, of course, and perhaps inserted in the parts by a member of the orchestra who is a copyist. Naturally I will understand if it does not meet with approval...[242]

Reference has already been made to Bruckner's close scrutiny of the periodic structure of several of his own works as well as Beethoven's Third and Ninth Symphonies and Mozart's *Requiem*.[243] Annotations in the autograph score of the Third Symphony, for instance 'Wien, 17 Juli 1876 letzte Verbesserung beendet' and 'Rhythmisch etc. geordnet 5. November 1876', also suggest intermittent activity on this work. The autograph score of Symphony no. 5 is also metrically numbered.[244] While there are metrical numbers in the autographs of the original versions of the Second, Third, Fourth and Fifth Symphonies, they are only sporadic and not always accurate. Discussing Bruckner's more frequent use of metrical numbers at this point

---

242 See *HSABB* 1, 164 for this letter, dated Vienna, 6 December 1876, which was first published in *ABB*, 140. The original is in private possession, but the *Musikwissenschaftlicher Verlag*, Vienna possesses a photocopy. There is a facsimile of the music examples in *HSABB* 1, 165.

243 See also Leopold Nowak, 'Metrische Studien von Anton Bruckner an Beethovens III. und IX. Symphonie' in Erich Schenk, ed., *Beethoven-Studien. Festgabe der Österreichischen Akademie der Wissenschaften zum 200. Geburtstag von Ludwig van Beethoven* (Vienna, 1970), 361-71, repr. in Leopold Nowak, *Über Anton Bruckner*, 105-15; and Leopold Nowak, 'Anton Bruckners Eroica-Studien' in op.cit., 257-65. For further discussion of Bruckner's study of Mozart's *Requiem*, concerning voice-leading and octave-doubling in particular, see Timothy Jackson, 'Bruckner's Oktaven. The problem of consecutives, doubling and orchestral voice-leading' in *Perspectives on Anton Bruckner* (Aldershot: Ashgate, 2001), in preparation.

244 See the facsimile of a page of the Adagio movement from the autograph, Mus. Hs. 19.477 fol. 45' in the *ÖNB*, in *ABSW* 5 (*V. Symphonie B-Dur. Revisionsbericht*), 59

in his compositional career, Timothy Jackson counters the argument that it is connected with Bruckner's numeromania, namely his fondness for counting all manner of things - from the number of leaves on a tree to the frequency of a particular prayer - by suggesting that there were more practical reasons:

> Surely the intense scrutiny of hostile critics and friends was a factor in Bruckner's compulsion to revise; ensuring metrical 'correctness' was part of this process... After 1876 Bruckner's compositional process becomes a complex dialogue oscillating between intuitive and analytical modes of thought - the latter represented by the metrical grid.[245]

Although the first draft of Symphony no. 5 was completed on 16 May, Bruckner spent the next twenty months making several changes and refinements and did not complete the final draft until January 1878. Nowak explains the genesis of the work as follows:

> One has spoken of two, even of three versions of the Fifth. It should be pointed out first of all that the first text was revised only insofar as the bass tuba was added later, but this was only within the framework of the first stage of composition which lasted from 1875 until the end of 1877 (or, rather, the first days of 1878). As the musical text took shape in different stages during this almost three-year period, and we have tangible evidence for this in the *Adagio* and *Finale*, we cannot justifiably speak of two different versions. There is no autograph evidence that Bruckner was responsible for the indisputable revision of the text in the first edition...[246]

---

245 Timothy L. Jackson, 'Bruckner's Metrical Numbers', in *19th-Century Music* XIV/2 (1990), 103.

246 Leopold Nowak, *V Symphonie B-Dur. Revisionsbericht* (Vienna, 1985), 7. See also Nowak's foreword to the score of the symphony, *ABSW* 5 (Vienna, 1951). The first edition was published by Doblinger (D.2080) in 1896. Franz Schalk, who conducted the first performance of the work (with

Some of the early stages in the compositional process are shown by preliminary workings of parts of the Adagio and Finale, as indicated by Nowak above.[247] Among the secondary source material is a particularly interesting copy of the Finale made by a Bruckner enthusiast, possibly Dr. Heinrich Schuster, who added the following comments at the end:

> This exceedingly splendid movement appears to me to be the greatest contrapuntal achievement, apart from *Die Meistersinger*, this century - indeed since Bach. An enthusiastic Brucknerian asks 1000 pardons for his impertinence.[248]

One work which was completed in 1876 was a piece for male-voice choir (including 'humming chorus') and soloists, *Das hohe Lied* WAB 74, a setting of words by Heinrich von der Mattig.[249] The autograph of the chorus has the date 'Vienna, 31 December 1876'.[250] Bruckner had the work copied and dedicated it to the *Akademischer Gesangverein*, possibly out of gratitude for their performance of his *Germanenzug* earlier in the year. Because of the difficulty of the humming chorus, the conductor Richard Heuberger suggested that the parts be doubled by a

---

an enlarged brass section in the Finale) in Graz in 1894, was largely responsible for this edition.

247 There are sketches of the beginning of the Finale (Mus. Hs. 6017) and a more substantial fair copy of bars 503-77 (Mus. Hs. 3162), corresponding to bars 503-70 in the final working, in the *ÖNB*. See *G-A* IV/1, 394-402 and *ABSW* 5 *Revisionsbericht*, 30-48. There is a facsimile of the first page of Mus. Hs. 6017, dated Vienna 10 May 1875, between pages 392 and 393 in *G-A* IV/1.

248 Mus. Hs. 6030 in the *ÖNB*. See *ABSW* 5 *Revisionsbericht*, 57 for a complete list of source material.

249 The pseudonym of Dr. Heinrich Wallmann (1827-1898), an army doctor, writer and journalist who was one of Bruckner's friends and provided him with other texts to set in the following years. An entry in Bruckner's 1876 diary gives Wallmann's addresss - 'Wahlman, Kriegsministerium 14 Abth. 3. Stock'.

250 Mus. Hs. 3188 in the *ÖNB*.

string quintet consisting of two violas, two cellos and double bass. Bruckner also took the opportunity of supporting the double choir with four horns, three trombones and bass tuba. Although he rehearsed the work in this revised form in December 1879 there is no evidence that it was performed publicly until 1902.[251] Bruckner dedicated the revised version of the chorus to the memory of Josef Seiberl, organist of St. Florian abbey.

Seiberl was almost certainly one of the friends he would have met when he spent part of his Christmas vacation at St. Florian. Bruckner would also have enjoyed spending some time with his brother Ignaz.[252]

On his return to Vienna, Bruckner began 1877 by making yet another attempt to improve his financial circumstances. In a letter to the Lower Austrian Parliament, he made an official application for the vacant position of director of music at the *Am Hof* church, listing five reasons why he was a suitable candidate: his experience as a church musician and Conservatory teacher, his theoretical studies with Sechter, his successes as an organist in Nancy, Paris and London, his growing recognition as a composer and his experience as a conductor. He added that Herbeck would be prepared to provide a reference, if necessary.[253] Bruckner had to wait nearly six months for the official reply that the 'post applied for had been granted to someone

---

251 It was edited for publication (Doblinger D. 2693, 1902) by Hans Wagner who dispensed with the humming parts and retained only one solo part, distributing the material of the other two parts among the chorus. Wagner conducted the first public performance of the work on 13 March 1902. See *G-A* IV/1, 422-27 and Andrea Harrandt, 'Bruckner und das bürgerliche Musiziergut seiner Jugendzeit' in *BSL 1987* (Linz, 1989), 101f.

252 A letter from Seiberl to Bruckner, written at the beginning of the year (precise date not given), mentions *inter alia* some difficulties Ignaz had been experiencing because of ill health. See*HSABB* 1, 166f.; the original is in St. Florian

253 See *HSABB* 1, 167f. for this letter, dated Vienna, 7 January 1877; the original is in St. Florian.

else'.[254] Bruckner's *curriculum vitae* was impressive, and it is possible that he was simply over-qualified for the post. The successful applicant was Josef Böhm

Also in January and largely as a result of the consistently good attendances at his University classes in 1876, Bruckner felt justified in making another appeal to the Ministry of Education and Culture for a modest annual income or, failing that, an annual honorarium, pointing out that universities in England and Germany recognised Harmony and Counterpoint as true academic disciplines and drawing a parallel with his friend Weinwurm's income as a singing teacher.[255] Bruckner's request was forwarded to Hanslick who, while stressing that Bruckner's and Weinwurm's posts were not comparable as remuneration for the latter was principally associated with Weinwurm's activities as conductor of the *Akademischer Gesangverein* and the resultant participation in academic functions, nevertheless recommended to the College of Professors that Bruckner be reimbursed in some way.[256] Hanslick's professorial colleagues turned down Bruckner's request, albeit with a rider to the effect that it be left to the discretion of the Minister of Education to decide whether some form of payment should be made on the submission of a further application at the end of the session. There is no evidence to suggest that such a submission was eventually made.

From the *Krakauer Schreibkalender* - the calendar which Bruckner used as a sort of diary, noting in it, *inter alia*, the times of lectures at the University and the Conservatory and the times of lessons given to private pupils - we can derive precise information about Bruckner's teaching responsibilities. In September 1877, at the

---

254 See *HSABB* 1, 168 for this letter, dated Vienna, 26 May 1877.

255 See *HSABB* 1, 168 for this letter, dated Vienna, 12 January 1877; the original is in the Vienna University library.

256 Hanslick's recommendation is dated Vienna, 18 January 1877. See Robert Lach, *Die Bruckner-Akten des Wiener Universitäts-Archives* (Vienna-Prague-Leipzig, 1926), 48f. and *G-A* IV/1, 437f.

beginning of a new session, his normal teaching load was two hours at the University, sixteen at the Conservatory and thirteen at home each week. There were also Court Chapel duties on Saturdays and Sundays. In later years, Bruckner re-arranged his timetable so that he would have days completely free for composition. This meant that he would occasionally have up to eleven hours' teaching on the same day. We also know, from the reminiscences of Decsey, Eckstein, Klose and others, that Bruckner, after a strenuous day's teaching or composing, preferred to relax in the evenings with a late meal in the company of a select number of his pupils and friends at one of his favourite *Gasthäuser*. The *Krakauer Schreibkalender*, however, affords us an amusing glimpse into one of Bruckner's other social pursuits. In January and February 1877, during the pre-Lenten carnival period, he attended three balls and noted down in his diary the names of the ladies with whom he had danced! Bruckner, whose eye for feminine beauty often led him into bizarre situations and occasioned several rash proposals of marriage, had obviously been suitably impressed.

Bruckner's revision work was just as intense in 1877. As well as revising the Third and Fifth Symphonies, he made 'rhythmical improvements' to his First and Second Symphonies. He entered metrical numbers in ink in the original manuscript of Symphony no. 1 and metrical numbers in both pencil and ink in copies of the score of Symphony no. 2 made by Carda and Tenschert.[257] Timothy Jackson describes the rhythmical changes made in the Andante of the Second Symphony as 'fine tuning' in comparison with the large cuts suggested by Herbeck for the 1876 performance.[258]

During the year Bruckner lost a close friend, Josef Seiberl, and a staunch ally,

---

257 Mus. Hs. 6034 and Mus. Hs. 6035 respectively in the *ÖNB*. Carda was based in Linz while Tenschert lived in Vienna.

258 Timothy Jackson, 'Bruckner's Metrical Numbers' in *19th-Century Music* xiv/2 (1990), 114.

Johann Herbeck. Seiberl was regarded as a worthy successor to Bruckner at St. Florian and, indeed, Bruckner's equal as an organist. The two friends had participated in the dedication of the renovated St. Florian organ in October 1875. In a letter to Ignaz Traumihler, the director of the St. Florian abbey choir, Bruckner not only expressed his feeling of shock at the tragic news but also took the opportunity of recommending one of his Conservatory pupils, Hans Rott, for the vacant position:

> ... He is the son of the famous actor at the *Theater an der Wien* and is a highly gifted musician and a most likeable, modest young man who plays Bach excellently and, for an eighteen-year-old, is an astonishing improviser.
> You will not find a better young man. He is my best pupil so far. He also studied counterpoint and composition with Krenn who is as fond of him as I am. At present he is the organist at the Piarist church in the Josefstadt...[259]

---

259 See *HSABB* 1, 174 for this letter, dated Vienna, 14 June 1877; the original is in St. Florian.

260 Hans Rott (1858-84) was a member of the *Wiener Akademischer Wagner-Verein* from 1875 to 1879 and a keen Wagnerian. He died tragically in a mental hospital in 1884. As a composer he had some influence on his friend, Gustav Mahler. Bruckner felt that Brahms's apparently harsh judgement on one of Rott's pieces had been one of the contributory factors to Rott's mental illness. See Franz Marschner's account, as related to Göllerich, in *G-A* IV/2, 131. For further information about Rott and his music, see Leopold Nowak, 'Die Kompositionen und Skizzen von Hans Rott in der Musiksammlung der Österreichischen Nationalbibliothek' in G. Brosche, ed., *Franz Grasberger zum 60. Geburtstag* (Tutzing: Schneider, 1975), 273-340; Paul Banks, 'Hans Rott' in *The New Grove* 16 (1980), 260; Paul Banks, 'Hans Rott' in *The Musical Times* cxxv (1984), 483ff.; Helmuth Kreysing and Frank Litterscheid, *Hans Rott. Der Begründer der neuen Symphonie* (*Musik-Konzepte* 103/104, ed. Heinz-Klaus Metzger and Rainer Riehn, Munich, 1999); Stephen McClatchie, 'Hans Rott, Gustav Mahler and the "New Symphony": New Evidence for a Pressing Question' in *Music and Letters* 81/3 (August 2000), 392-401.

312

Bruckner's recommendation was not followed up.[260] Later in the year Bruckner wrote his *Nachruf* WAB 88 for male voices and organ in Seiberl's memory and played the organ part during the unveiling of a memorial plaque for Seiberl at a special memorial service in St. Florian on 28 October.[261]

On the same day as this service, Johann Herbeck died. Herbeck had been one of the first to recognize Bruckner's stature, had been instrumental in bringing him from Linz to Vienna in 1868 and, since then, had consistently encouraged him and treated the often depressed and beleaguered composer with great sympathy and tact. Herbeck spent a few days at St. Florian towards the end of August and took the opportunity of visiting Bruckner at the abbey.[262] In his letter to Traumihler,

---

261 According to Auer *(G-A* IV/1, 456f.), the first performance was given by the St. Florian Abbey choir conducted by Traumihler. But according to Viktor Keldorfer, the editor of the first edition, *Nachruf* was given its first performance by the Linz *Sängerbund* conducted by Max Brava. See foreword to U.E. 3294 (1939 re-issue). This is corroborated by a letter which Bruckner wrote to Josef Neubauer, a notary's articled clerk and later bookkeeper in a savings bank at St. Florian. In this letter, dated 25 October 1877, Bruckner referred to the preparations being made for the performance of the work by *Sängerbund* and informed Neubauer that he intended to travel to St. Florian on the following Saturday in order to hold a rehearsal with all the participants on the Sunday. See *HSABB* 1, 176 for a précis of this letter which is owned privately in Vienna. As Bruckner later wished to make this work more widely available, he had the original text (by Heinrich Wallmann, pseud. Heinrich von der Mattig) changed by August Seuffert to one in which the sentiments were less specific. Under its new title, *Trösterin Musik*, it was given its first performance in Vienna on 11 April 1886 by the *Akademischer Gesangverein* conducted by Rudolf Weinwurm.

262 Herbeck wrote to Bruckner from Salzburg on 24 August, asking him to book two rooms at a guest house in St. Florian for the evening of Sunday 26 August, also to hire a coach and pick him and his family up from Linz. See *HSABB* 1, 175 for this letter, the original is in St. Florian.

Bruckner had intimated that he would be available to play the organ at St. Florian during his summer vacation.[263] This help would certainly have been invaluable at a time when the abbey was still seeking a permanent organist to take Seiberl's place.

During his stay at the abbey, Bruckner worked on the revision of his Third Symphony, and one of Herbeck's final acts was to arrange for the symphony, which was rejected by the Philharmonic after a rehearsal on 27 September, to be given a place in the programme of the December concert of the *Gesellschaft* series.[264] Bruckner later recalled his final meetings with Herbeck and paid tribute to him in an appreciation written for Ludwig Herbeck's biography of his father:

> I shall never forget how he cared for me most affectionately during performances of my Masses and symphonies and how flatteringly he spoke of these works. In September 1877, just before his death, we played through the second movement of my Fourth (Romantic) Symphony and he made the unforgettable comment: 'Schubert could have written that; one can have nothing but respect for a composer who can write something like that'. And at the end of August, seven weeks before he passed away, when, at his request, I collected him from Linz and accompanied him to St. Florian for the second time, he said to the abbey authorities after I had played for him on the newly-restored great organ: 'Gentlemen, you should be proud of him'.[265]

Bruckner's diary entries in October indicate that Herbeck died at 9.45 on the

---

263 See footnote 259. Bruckner had no *Hofkapelle* duties between 15 August and 15 September. See *HSABB* 1, 173 for his letter to the *Hofkapelle*, dated Vienna 7 June 1877, requesting leave. The original of this letter is in the *Hofkapelle* archives

264 See Otto Biba, 'Bruckner und die Wiener Orchester' in *Anton Bruckner. V. Internationales Gewandhaus- Symposion 1987* (Leipzig, 1988), 25.

265 Ludwig Herbeck, *Johann Herbeck. Ein Lebensbild* (Vienna: Gutmann, 1885), 233, footnote.

morning of 28 October. On 21 October Herbeck conducted Schubert's Mass in E flat major in the *Hofkapelle* while Bruckner was at Klosterneuburg, and he conducted a rehearsal of the *Singverein* for the last time the following day. His funeral was in the early afternoon of Tuesday 30 October.[266]

Either while he was staying at St. Florian or shortly before travelling there, Bruckner visited Kremsmünster abbey to participate in the 1100th anniversary celebrations. He had written earlier to Georg Huemer, director of the abbey choir, enclosing a copy of his D minor Mass, and it is possible that Huemer's original intention was to perform it during the church service which marked the beginning of the celebrations on 18 August. Perhaps he found it too difficult because, in the event, Beethoven's C major Mass was performed. Bruckner played the organ at the service and later gave a recital to a distinguished audience which included Stremayr, the Minister of Education, and the papal nuncio. It consisted of four improvisations, the first on the horn theme in the *Kyrie* of Beethoven's C major Mass, the second on the 'Hallelujah' chorus from Handel's *Messiah*, the third on the 'Alles was Odem hat' theme from Mendelssohn's *Hymn of Praise*, and the fourth on the *Kaiserlied* (18 August was also the Emperor's name-day).[267]

As well as seeking to augment his income by applying for the post at the *Am Hof* church and appealing to the Ministry of Education and Culture for a small income at the University, Bruckner also attempted to improve his position in the *Hofkapelle*. Since his unsuccessful application in April 1876 for the position of assistant musical director which had fallen vacant as a result of Gottfried Preyer's retirement, he had conducted two performances of his F minor Mass - on 30 July 1876 and 17 June

---

266 See Ludwig Herbeck, op.cit., 410ff.

267 See *HSABB* 1, 170 for Bruckner's letter to Huemer, dated Vienna, 1 March 1877; the original of this letter is in Kremsmünster abbey. See *G-A* IV/1, 454 for further information about Bruckner's visit to Kremsmünster.

1877.[268] Assuming quite correctly that Hellmesberger, who had been appointed assistant music director in 1876, would now succeed Herbeck as principal director, Bruckner made a fresh application for the assistant's post a few days after Herbeck's death. He referred once again to his 'serious financial situation'. His chances of success were fairly remote, however. Hans Richter, conductor of the Philharmonic and the Court Opera, was appointed assistant music director, and Pius Richter, a long-standing member of the *Hofkapelle*, was given the nominal title of assistant director in recognition of his services to church music. These appointments were advertised in two issues of the *Wiener Zeitung* and Bruckner, along with six other applicants, including Rudolf Weinwurm, was advised of his lack of success in a brief letter from the Lord Chamberlain's office.[269] Two months later, however, Bruckner received more heartening news. His status in the *Hofkapelle* was changed from temporary to permanent and there was a substantial increase in income.

In the autumn Bruckner's move to a larger apartment in Heßgasse 7, made available to him at a very reasonable rent by Dr. Anton Oelzelt von Newin, provided him with more space for his composition work and private teaching activities and offered him quick and easy access to both the Conservatory and the *Hofkapelle*.[270]

---

268   See earlier and footnote 232.

269   See *ABDS* 1, 81-89 for Bruckner's application (31 October), the Lord Chamberlain's recommendations (8 and 19 November) and the formal letter to unsuccessful applicants (27 November). Bruckner's application is also printed in *HSABB* 1, 177; the original is in the Hofburg archives. The two issues of the *Wiener Zeitung* were nos. 262 of 15 November and 270 of 23 November 1877.

270   Anton Oelzelt von Newin (1854-1925) was a young philosopher who had attended some of Bruckner's University lectures and was a great admirer of his organ playing. Bruckner had been promised the apartment at the end of 1876, but the removal was delayed owing to difficulties raised by some of Oelzelt von Newin's relatives. In February 1877, however, Oelzelt von Newin wrote to Bruckner to apologize for the delay and to assure him that the promise would be fulfilled. See

Bruckner was immensely grateful to his young friend for allowing him to have the apartment at a very reasonable rent, and later gave tangible expression to his gratitude in dedicating his Symphony no. 6 to him.

For Bruckner the most important musical event in 1877 was undoubtedly the first performance of his Third Symphony, the culmination of five years' work. Bruckner worked on an 'intermediate' version of the second movement of the symphony at some point between Autumn 1876 and 1877. It is 289 bars long, eleven bars longer than the Adagio of the original version and 38 bars longer than the Adagio of the second version, which replaced it. The most significant difference from the original occurs in the final reprise of the main subject material (bars 230ff.) where the syncopated violin figures are replaced by cascading broken chord figures, an undisguised homage to Wagner's *Tannhäuser* overture.[271] At the beginning of the year Bruckner began work on the definitive second version, commencing with the Finale on 27 January. Revision was completed on 28 April with the annotation 'ganz neue Umarbeitung fertig'. The autograph score of the second version is a composite of pages from the original version, the 1876 revision and the new sheets inserted in 1877.[272] The first movement was substantially cut from 746 to 652 bars, the Adagio

---

HSABB 1, 169f. and 173 for the correspondence between them in 1877. The location of the original of Oelzelt von Newin's undated letter to Bruckner is not known; it was first printed in *G-A* IV/1, 463f. The originals of Bruckner's two letters to Oelzelt von Newin, dated 7 February and 11 June 1877, are in the *Gesellschaft der Musikfreunde*.

271 In the parts used for the first performance of the symphony on 16 December 1877 two passages in the Adagio were pasted over with the notes of the second version of the work, written by the same copyist as the one who made the copy for the engraving in 1878. When these sheets were removed, this so-called 'intermediate' version of the movement was revealed. This version is described as 'Adagio nr. 2' in the *Bruckner Gesamtausgabe* published as a supplement (Vienna, 1980) to Nowak's earlier edition of the original version (*ABSW* 3/1, 1977). See Nowak's foreword and Thomas Röder, *III Symphonie D-Moll Revisionsbericht* (Vienna, 1997), 58.

272 This is located in the *ÖNB*, Mus. Hs. 19.475. Other material consulted by Nowak in his edition of the '1877 version' (*ABSW* 3/2, Vienna 1981) include the copy used for the 1878

from 278 (289) to 251 and the Finale from 764 to 638 bars. The Scherzo remained more or less intact until after the unsuccessful first performance of the work. On 30 January 1878 Bruckner composed a coda to this movement which increased its length by 41 bars.[273]

Bruckner's 'improvements' to the Third Symphony were not sufficient to impress the Philharmonic who rejected it once again after a rehearsal on 27 September.[274] Although Herbeck was able to use his influence to programme the work in a *Gesellschaft* concert, the composer was deeply offended by the rejection. He made his feelings abundantly clear when he wrote to Wilhelm Tappert on 12 October. In the earlier part of the letter he asked Tappert to return the score and parts of the Fourth Symphony which he had sent to Berlin in October 1876 as he had decided to revise the work:

> I have come to the firm conclusion that my Fourth (Romantic) Symphony is urgently in need of a thorough revision. In the Adagio, for instance, some of the violin figurations are too difficult, indeed unplayable, and the instrumentation here and there is too cumbersome and finicky. Herbeck, who likes this work very much, has made similar comments and confirmed me in my resolve to carry out fresh revision work on parts of the symphony. Would you be so good as to ask Music Director Bilse to return the score and parts together

engraving, the incomplete set of parts used for the first performance (located in the *Gesellschaft der Musikfreunde* library, XIII 26.428) and an autograph fragment of the Adagio also located in the *Gesellschaft* library (A 173). See also Thomas Röder, *III. Symphonie D-Moll Revisionbericht*, 18 and 201ff.

273 It was inserted in the parts but not printed; indeed it is marked 'not to be printed' and 'not in the score'. The copy used for the engraving does not include the coda. It was printed for the first time in *ABSW* 3/2 (Vienna, 1981). See Röder, op.cit., 212.

274 A diary entry in the *Krakauer Schreibkalender* for 1877 (Thursday 27 September) catalogues this rejection in the context of previous rejections. It reads '3te Ablehnung meiner Wagner-Sinfonie Nr. 3. 1. Ablehnung Herbst 1872. C moll Sinf. Nr. 2. 2. Ablehnung durch die Philharmoniker im Herbst 1875. Sinfonie nr. 3'.

318

with any bills outstanding.

My *Wagner Symphony*, no. 3 in D minor, is finished, and Herbeck
will perform it at a Musikverein concert on 16 December. If Director
Bilse is willing, and if you are agreeable, I shall send it to you
immediately after the performance in Vienna; this should leave
sufficient time. (Our Philharmonic players are totally hostile to the
new direction; I will not give them any more of my works, as I have
already experienced several rejections). I am completely bewildered
by Hans Richter's intimate dealings with Wagner's fiercest enemies.
Unfortunately, I have been forced to recognize him as a *generalissimo*
of double-dealing. Much of what Wagner said to me is beginning to
make sense now...[275]

Bruckner's criticism of Richter is understandable but not really justified. It was

an almost impossible task for any composer in Vienna at the time to steer a middle

course between the conservative and the radicals and Richter did it better than most.

Herbeck's sudden death a fortnight after this letter was written placed the

performance of the Third in jeopardy. In desperation he turned to August Göllerich

sen., the father of his future biographer, and asked him to use his influence with

Nikolaus Dumba, the president of the *Gesellschaft der Musikfreunde*, to have the

work retained in the programme. Although he had much more experience as a choral

than as an orchestral conductor, Bruckner had no option but to conduct the work

himself. According to eye-witness accounts and Bruckner's later reflections,

the orchestral rehearsals were something of a travesty with some of the players

openly laughing at the composer. Hellmesberger was allegedly one of the worst

---

275 See *HSABB* 1, 175f. for this letter, dated Vienna, 12 October 1877; there is a photocopy of the
original in the *Musikwissenschaftlicher Verlag*, Vienna. Bruckner had written earlier to Tappert that
'I... was shocked to see that I have damaged the work [4th Symphony] by using too many imitations
and have frequently destroyed the effectiveness of the best passages'. See *HSABB* 1, 172 for this
letter, dated Vienna, 1 May 1877; the original is in the *ÖNB*.

offenders.[276] The performance on 16 December was a debacle. It is not absolutely clear what caused the fiasco - whether it was Bruckner's nervous, insecure conducting, or the length of the work (albeit much shorter than the original version!), or sabotage on the part of a group hostile to the composer. The first three movements seem to have been fairly well received, but the audience began to drift out during the Finale and, at the end, only a few remained, including Bruckner's enthusiastically supportive young friends, Mahler, Krzyzanowski and Joseph Schalk. Bruckner described the public's misunderstanding in a letter to Tappert written ten months later.[277] Press reaction to the symphony was generally hostile. Writing in the *Neue freie Presse*, Hanslick made a distinction between Bruckner's honourable intentions as a composer and his realization of these intentions which were impractical and meaningless:

> ... As we would not wish to hurt the composer whom we esteem as a man and as an artist and whose artistic intentions are honourable albeit handled in an unusual fashion, we dispense with a review and make instead the humble confession that we did not understand his gigantic symphony. We were not able to make sense of his poetic intentions - perhaps a vision in which Beethoven's Ninth is joined in friendship with Wagner's *Walküre* only to come to grief under its horses' hooves at the end - or to comprehend the purely musical argument. The composer, who conducted his own work, was greeted with acclaim and comforted with enthusiastic applause at the end by a fraction of the audience who remained after the flight of the others.[278]

---

276 See *G-A* IV/1, 475, including an account by Rudolf Zöllner, one of the viola players in the orchestra, in the footnotes.

277 See *HSABB* 1, 179f. for this letter, dated Vienna, 9 October 1878; there is a photocopy of the original in the *Musikwissenschaftlicher Verlag*.

278 Review of 18 December 1877. See *G-A* IV/1, 479f., *ABDS* 2, 54, and Röder, op.cit., 387.

Other critics took Bruckner to task for the over-abundance of general pauses, the prolixity of the music and the lack of structural cohesion. Eduard Schelle, who reviewed the symphony in two issues of *Die Presse*, conceded that it 'provided an example of the composer's creative power' and 'contained many interesting ideas' but argued that its total effect was ruined by a 'lack of proportion, clear organization and logical structural development' and that it would benefit from a 'thorough reworking'. Schelle was obviously unaware of the fact that the work had already undergone extensive revision![279] Franz Gehring, the music critic of the *Deutsche Zeitung* described it as a 'most unusual work which could be called a colourful but shapeless patchwork of shreds of musical ideas rather than being given the potentially harmonious name of "symphony"',[280] while J.G. Woerz, the critic of the *Wiener Sonn- und Montagszeitung*, drew his readers' attention to comments which he had made four years earlier about Bruckner's use of the general pause in his Second Symphony, implying that the same was true of the Third Symphony, and rebuked the composer for his lack of structural 'tidiness':

> ... If his house had the same appearance as his symphony, a well-bred housewife would not be able to survive there for four days, and the public, who refuse to believe that true genius is to be found in formlessness, were equally unable to survive the four movements of Bruckner's musical creation...[281]

The reviewer for the *Wiener Abendpost* described the symphony as a 'monstrous work whose daring features and peculiarities cannot be adequately described in a few words'. It was a work in which there was evidence of an 'unbridled and untutored naturalism where no crudity is too large, no logical leap too wide' and 'the most

---

279 Reviews of 18 and 30 December 1877. See *ABDS* 2, 55, and Röder, op.cit., 386 and 391.

280 Review of 19 December. See *ABDS* 2, 56, and Röder, op.cit., 387

281 From review of 24 December 1877. See *ABDS* 2, 56 and Röder, op.cit., 390f.

outrageous things are done in a truly childlike good faith'. In spite of this, however, the symphony made a greater effect on him than 'many a well-designed and well-intentioned symphony written by a dry-as-dust pedant'.[282]

A more sympathetic observer of this unfortunate episode was the publisher Theodor Rättig, who was present at almost all of the orchestral rehearsals of the symphony as well as the first performance. In spite of the disastrous premiere, Rättig had sufficient faith in the composer and in the work to publish it at his own expense:

> As a member of the *Singverein* I was present at almost all of the orchestral rehearsals. For me it was altogether a distressing and shocking spectacle - to witness the younger members of the orchestra ridiculing the clumsy manner of direction adopted by the old man [sic!] who had absolutely no idea of how to conduct and who had to confine himself to giving tempo indications like a jumping jack. The composition itself appeared all the more imposing and I began to be convinced that here was one of the mightiest musical heroes of all times treading on the path of thorns which was the customary, one might say pre-ordained, fate of such spirits. The performance fully confirmed this view. A small group of at the most ten to twenty very young people of both sexes applauded but they were arrayed against a hissing, laughing crowd, and the expert commentators on current 'musical high fashion' gloated maliciously - a splendid topic for amusing conversation at dinner awaiting them at home. When the public had left the hall and the musicians the platform, the small group of his pupils and admirers gathered round the wretched composer to comfort him, but he cried, 'Leave me alone, the public don't want to have anything to do with me'. Then I joined the group, expressed my admiration in the warmest terms, and offered to publish the work which had just been hissed in a manner befitting its importance and at my own expense (c. 3000 florins). And, to the astonishment of the

---

282 From review, signed 'h', in the edition for 17 December 1877. See *ABDS* 2, 55 and Röder, op.cit., 386. Other reviews, including an extremely favourable one by Theodor Helm, can be found in Röder, op.cit., 387ff.

musical world, the work was published - an event which was almost certainly the first positive step towards a wider recognition of the composer. Great and naive spirits are not grateful, however, and probably no one made life more difficult for his closest friends and admirers than Anton Bruckner. When I presented him with the first beautifully printed and bound copy of the 'Third' he smiled and opened it enthusiastically, but then came the retort, 'In heaven's name! It says 'dedicated to Master Richard Wagner in deepest admiration'- and should say 'respect'. It was and continued to be very difficult to console him for this terrible mistake.[283]

Rättig published not only the full score but also a piano-duet arrangement of the symphony. Although the cover and title-page of this arrangement have Mahler's name only, it is believed that Mahler was responsible for the first three movements and his fellow-student Krzyzanowski for the Finale.[284] Julius Epstein, piano professor at the Vienna Conservatory and the teacher of both Mahler and Krzyzanowski, evidently edited his pupils' work.[285] It was without doubt an extremely

---

283 In the original German, the distinction is between 'Verehrung' and 'Ehrfurcht' respectively. See *G-A* IV/1, 477f. For an alternative English translation of this account, see Stephen Johnson, op.cit., 115f. For further information about Rättig, see Helene Rättig, 'Ein Wegbereiter Anton Bruckners', in *Gedanke und Tat. Zeitschrift für Freischaffende* 1 (1956), 1-7.

284 Stephen McClatchie mentions a letter from Hans Rott to Heinrich Krzyzanowski, Rudolf's brother (dated 3 October 1878) which 'confirms Rudolf Krzyzanowski's involvement with this arrangement... although Mahler's is the only name that appears on the title-page'. Rott wrote to Heinrich: 'Bruckner sends his greetings to Rudolf and asks him to please hurry along with the symphony; Rättig is pressing him...' (*ÖNB* Mus. Hs. 34.247/III/11). See Stephen McClatchie, 'Hans Rott, Gustav Mahler and the "New Symphony": New Evidence for a Pressing Question', in *Music and Letters* 81/3 (August 2000), 395, footnote 15.

285 The original manuscript(s) of the arrangement have been lost. Mahler and Krzyzanowski worked from Bruckner's autograph score of the second version (Mus. Hs. 19.475 in the *ÖNB*). Krzyzanowski returned the Finale to Bruckner and, on the composer's death in 1896, it formed part of his estate of manuscripts and scores which was bequeathed to the *ÖNB*. The first three

generous gesture on the part of Rättig, Mahler and Krzyzanowski.[286]

Gustav Mahler was never formally Bruckner's pupil at the Conservatory which he attended from 1875 to 1878. Although temperamentally quite different, Mahler obviously had a great respect for the older composer and was one of the first to recognise and appreciate his true stature. In an undated letter to Göllerich, Mahler later clarified his relationship with Bruckner:

> I was never Bruckner's pupil. The general belief that I was is probably attributable to the fact that I was regularly to be seen with Bruckner during my years as a student in Vienna and was always one of his greatest admirers and supporters. Indeed I believe that my friend Krzyzanowski (working in Weimar at present) and I were the only ones at the time. This would have been in the years 1875-1881. The letters which he sent me over a number of years are of very little interest... My involvement with him lasted until the completion of his Seventh Symphony. I still recall with pleasure that one beautiful morning during a lecture at the University he called to me from the lecture room (much to the astonishment of my colleagues) and played me the marvellous Adagio theme on a very old piano. In spite of the great difference in age between us, Bruckner's invariably happy, youthful and almost childlike disposition and his trusting nature made

---

movements, however, had a much more chequered career. They were retained by Mahler (who, according to Alma Mahler, regarded them as a gift from Bruckner). After Mahler's death they remained in Alma's possession until they were sold by auction to the *ÖNB* in 1948. Ferdinand Löwe and Joseph Schalk were responsible for the later piano-duet arrangement of the third version which was printed in 1890. See the informative article by Gertraud Kubacsek-Steinhauer, 'Die vierhändigen Bearbeitungen der Dritter Symphonie von Anton Bruckner', in *BJ 1987/88* (Linz, 1990), 67-78. See also Röder, op.cit., 232-40 for a detailed discussion of the arrangement, including the deviations from the autograph full score.

286   There were already concrete plans for printing the symphony by the autumn of 1878. In his letter to Wilhelm Tappert (Vienna, 9 October 1878; see footnote 275), Bruckner concludes by saying that 'Mr. Rättig wishes to have the piano scores of these Symphonies [that is, Symphonies 2,3 and 4] in order to publish them'. The symphony was definitely available in print in the early months of 1880 and was probably published in November 1879. For further information, see Röder, op.cit., 221.

our relationship a real friendship, and so it was natural that as I gradually came to appreciate and understand the trials and tribulations of his life my own development as a man and artist could not fail to be influenced by his. Indeed I feel that I have more right to call myself his 'pupil' than most of the others, and I shall always do so with respect and gratitude.[287]

From the early 1880s onwards contact between Bruckner and Mahler was restricted to the occasional visit and the occasional letter. An undated postcard sent by an apologetic Mahler to 'my dear, esteemed Master' indicates that he has not been in touch for some time because he has been 'somewhat buffeted by the waves of life' and is 'still on the high seas'. He reassures Bruckner, however, that it is one of his aims in life to contribute to the 'victorious breakthrough of your splendid and masterly art'.[288] Apart from a possible visit to Bruckner in 1884, we know for certain that Mahler met Bruckner on 15 June 1883.[289] Joseph Schalk's letters to his brother Franz in June and July 1888 apropos Bruckner's work on the third version of the Third Symphony also hint at another meeting between the two.[290] There is no doubt that Mahler kept his promise to 'contribute to the victorious breakthrough' of Bruckner's works and actively proselytized on his behalf. As early as 1886, for

---

287 See G-A IV/1, 448f., footnote.

288 Auer suggests early 1891 as a possible date. See ABB, 329.

289 A calendar entry on this date indicates that he lent Mahler the score of his Second Symphony. See G-A IV/2, 123 and Henry-Louis de la Grange, Mahler vol. 1 (London: Gollancz, 1974), 106.

290 See Lili Schalk, Franz Schalk. Briefe und Betrachtungen (Vienna and Leipzig: Musikwissenschaftlicher Verlag, 1935), Thomas Leibnitz, Die Brüder Schalk und Anton Bruckner (Tutzing: Schneider, 1988) [LBSAB] and the Schalk correspondence in the ÖNB, F18 Schalk 158/9/9 in particular.

291 See ABB, 329-30 for Mahler's letter to Bruckner, dated Hamburg, 16 April 1892; the original can be found in St. Florian.

instance, he conducted the Scherzo of the Third Symphony in Prague and, while he was chief conductor at the Hamburg Municipal Theatre (1891-97) and conductor of the Hamburg symphony concerts (1894-97), directed performances of Bruckner's Mass in D minor, the *Te Deum* and the Fourth Symphony. In April 1892 he was able to write enthusiastically to Bruckner about an extremely successful performance of the *Te Deum* during the Hamburg Opera's annual Good Friday concert of sacred music, a performance which evidently stirred both the public and the performers by 'the majesty of its architecture and the nobility of its ideas'.[291] This success was confirmed by Carl Wilhelm Zinne, music critic for the *Neue Hamburger Zeitung*, who wrote to Bruckner again the following year to inform him that Mahler was planning to conduct a repeat performance of the *Te Deum* as well as a performance of the D minor Mass as part of the Good Friday concert.[292] Bruckner expressed his gratitude to Mahler in a letter written to him in March 1893.[293] Mahler's profound admiration for the *Te Deum* led him to cross out the words 'for soli, chorus, organ and orchestra' in his copy of the score and replace them with 'for the tongues of heaven-blessed angels, chastened hearts and souls purified by fire'.

After Bruckner's death Mahler continued to perform his symphonies, in spite of reservations about their length and structure which he expressed to friends like

---

292 See *ABB*, 387ff. and 392ff. for Zinne's letters to Bruckner, dated Hamburg, 18 April 1892 and 26 March 1893 respectively; the location of the originals is unknown.

293 The original of this letter from Bruckner to Mahler, dated Vienna, 7 April 1893, is in the University of Western Ontario, Canada, Gustav Mahler-Arnold Rosé Collection E5-CM-261. It was first printed in Andrea Harrandt, '"Gustav Mahler. O! mögen Sie nur der Meinige bleiben..." Unbekannte Briefe zu zwei Aufführungen von Bruckners Te Deum in Hamburg', in Erich Wolfgang Partsch, ed., *Gustav Mahler. Werk und Wirken. Vierzig Jahre Internationale Gustav Mahler Gesellschaft* (Vienna, 1996), 57-62. My thanks to Dr. Andrea Harrandt for kindly supplying me with this information.

Natalie Bauer-Lechner who recalled that Mahler was drawn to Bruckner's works by the 'greatness and richness of invention' but was also disturbed and repelled by their lack of continuity.[294] Having been engaged as conductor of the Vienna *Hofoper* in May 1897, Mahler was quickly promoted to the position of deputy director in July and chief conductor in October. The following year, he succeeded Hans Richter as conductor of the Vienna Philharmonic. In 1899, Mahler conducted the first complete performance of Bruckner's Sixth Symphony.[295] In this performance as well as subsequent performances of the Fourth Symphony in January 1900 and the Fifth Symphony in February 1901 he made several cuts and altered Bruckner's orchestration in several places. The critical reaction was understandably mixed. There were those like Robert Hirschfeld who, although no admirer of Bruckner's music, argued that Mahler's alterations were beneficial, and those like Theodor Helm who could not countenance changes which, in their opinion, destroyed the poetic and musical form of the work.[296]

---

294 Natalie Bauer-Lechner, *Erinnerungen an Gustav Mahler* (Vienna: Tal, 1923), 16. In other passages in the *Erinnerungen*, which are not included in the English translation, namely Natalie Bauer-Lechner, *Recollections of Gustav Mahler*, transl. Dika Newlin and edited and annotated by Peter Franklin (London: Faber and Faber, 1980), Mahler is alleged to have expressed exasperation with the uneven quality of a work such as Bruckner's First Symphony and to have stated that Bruckner's cause could only be promoted by substantial abridgement. In a conversation with his brother Otto in 1893, Mahler, in comparing Brahms and Bruckner, remarked that the former's works demonstrated a greater structural coherence, whereas, in the latter's 'you are carried away by the magnificence and wealth of his inventiveness, but at the same time you are repeatedly disturbed by its fragmentary character which breaks the spell' (*Recollections*, 37).

295 Sixteen years after the first performance of the middle two movements only in February 1883, conducted by Wilhelm Jahn.

296 Reviewing Mahler's performance of Bruckner's Fifth Symphony in the *Neue Zeitschrift für Musik* in February 1901, Helm accused Mahler specifically of cutting about 200 bars in the first two movements, inverting certain elements in the first movement and cutting the third theme and the

327

While one cannot condone these 'improvements' today, one has to see them in the context of Bruckner performance practice at the beginning of the 20th century. What cannot be disputed, however, is the generosity of Mahler's gesture on Bruckner's behalf when he agreed to forego royalty payments due from the publication of his own works in order to finance Universal Edition's projected publication of Bruckner's works.[297]

At the end of 1877, exactly a fortnight after the disastrous first performance of Bruckner's Third Symphony, the Vienna Philharmonic under Hans Richter gave the first performance of Brahms's Second Symphony. It was hailed by Hanslick as a 'great, unqualified success' and an extremely convincing reply to the assertion made by Wagner and his disciples that it was no longer possible to write symphonies after Beethoven, the only exceptions being Lisztian 'symphonic poems in one movement and with specific poetic programmes'. Comparing the new symphony with Brahms's First Symphony first performed a year earlier, Hanslick concluded:

> If the thematic elaboration is less astonishing, the themes are more fluent and fresh, their development more natural and transparent and

---

characteristic unison passage that follows it, as well as inserting transitions of his own invention, cutting the re-statement of the great 4/4 melody in the Adagio so that the final *crescendo* of the principal theme had come far too early, and, finally, needlessly accelerating certain tempos. See also the comments on Mahler's working copy of Bruckner's Fifth Symphony by Rudolf Stephan in his *Gustav Mahler. Werk und Wiedergabe* (Cologne: Arno Volk, 1979) and further comments by Stephan in his article 'Zum Thema "Bruckner und Mahler"' in *BJ 1981* (Linz, 1982), 137-43. Concerning Bruckner's influence on Mahler and a comparison between Bruckner's *Te Deum* and the first movement (*Veni Creator Spiritus*) of Mahler's Eighth Symphony, see Constantin Floros, 'Von Mahlers Affinität zu Bruckner' in *BSL 1986* (Linz, 1989), 109-17.

297 See Alma Mahler, *Gustav Mahler: Erinnerungen und Briefe* (Amsterdam: Albert de Lange, 1940); English translation by Basil Creighton as *Gustav Mahler. Memories and Letters* (London: John Murray, 1946), 148.

therefore more effective. I cannot adequately express my pleasure in the fact that Brahms, having given such forceful expression to the emotion of a Faustian struggle in his First Symphony, has turned again to the spring blossoms of earth in his Second.[298]

Bruckner would have been all too conscious of the striking difference in the receptions of the two symphonies. But an altruistic labour of love on the part of Rättig, Mahler and Krzyzanowski helped to bring a year which had begun inauspiciously to a much happier conclusion than the events of 16 December would have suggested.[299]

---

298   Henry Pleasants, transl. and ed., *Eduard Hanslick. Music Criticisms 1846-99* (London: Penguin Books, 2/1963), 159.

299   Rudolf Krzyzanowski (1862-1911) graduated from the Vienna Conservatory in 1878 and later occupied *Kapellmeister* positions in Halle, Eberfeld, Munich, Prague, Hamburg and Weimar.

STUDIES IN THE HISTORY AND INTERPRETATION OF MUSIC